Object Relations Therapy of Physical and Sexual Trauma

Object Relations Therapy of Physical and Sexual Trauma

Jill Savege Scharff, M.D.
David E. Scharff, M.D.

JASON ARONSON INC.
Northvale, New Jersey
London

Production Editor: Judith D. Cohen

This book was set in 10 point Palacio by TechType of Upper Saddle River, New Jersey, and printed and bound by Haddon Craftsmen of Scranton, Pennsylvania.

Library of Congress Cataloging-in-Publication Data

Scharff, Jill Savege.
    Object relations therapy of physical and sexual trauma / Jill Savege Scharff, David E. Scharff.
      p.   cm. − (Library of object relations)
    Includes bibliographical references and index.
    ISBN 1-56821-292-5
    1. Adult child sexual abuse victims−Rehabilitation. 2. Object relations (Psychoanalysis) 3. Post-traumatic stress disorder−Treatment. I. Scharff, David E. II. Title.
III. Series.
    [DNLM: 1. Object Attachment. 2. Psychoanalytic Therapy−methods.
3. Child Abuse, Sexual−therapy. 4. Stress Disorders, Post-Traumatic−therapy. WM 460.5.02 S3110 1994]
RC569.5.A28S32 1994
616.89′17−dc20
DNLM/DLC
for Library of Congress   94-13945

Manufactured in the United States of America. Jason Aronson Inc. offers books and cassettes. For information and catalog write to Jason Aronson Inc., 230 Livingston Street, Northvale, New Jersey 07647.

THE LIBRARY OF OBJECT RELATIONS

A SERIES OF BOOKS EDITED BY
DAVID E. SCHARFF AND JILL SAVEGE SCHARFF

Object relations theories of human interaction and development provide an expanding, increasingly useful body of theory for the understanding of individual development and pathology, for generating theories of human interaction, and for offering new avenues of treatment. They apply across the realms of human experience from the internal world of the individual to the human community, and from the clinical situation to everyday life. They inform clinical technique in every format from individual psychoanalysis and psychotherapy, through group therapy, to couple and family therapy.

The Library of Object Relations aims to introduce works that approach psychodynamic theory and therapy from an object relations point of view. It includes works from established and new writers who employ diverse aspects of British, American, and international object relations theory in helping individuals, families, couples, and groups. It features books that stress integration of psychoanalytic approaches with marital, family, and group therapy, as well as those centered on individual psychotherapy and psychoanalysis.

Refinding the Object and
  Reclaiming the Self
    David E. Scharff

Scharff Notes: A Primer of Object
  Relations Therapy
    *Jill Savege Scharff and David E.
    Scharff*

Object Relations Couple Therapy
    *David E. Scharff and Jill Savege
    Scharff*

Object Relations Family Therapy
    *David E. Scharff and Jill Savege
    Scharff*

Projective and Introjective
  Identification and the Use of the
  Therapist's Self
    Jill Savege Scharff

Foundations of Object Relations
  Family Therapy
    Jill Savege Scharff, Editor

From Inner Sources: New
  Directions in Object Relations
  Psychotherapy
    N. Gregory Hamilton, Editor

Repairing Intimacy: An Object
  Relations Approach to Couples
  Therapy
    Judith Siegel

To our patients and colleagues

who have lived with trauma

and have taught us in the process

Contents

SECTION II

PSYCHOTHERAPY OF THE PSYCHIC REVERBERATIONS
OF PHYSICAL TRAUMA

Section III

TREATING THE EFFECTS OF SEXUAL TRAUMA ON
INDIVIDUALS AND FAMILIES

     Object Relations Technique   299
     In Individual Therapy, Stages in Recalling the Memory
        of Abuse *300*
     Refinding the Voice of the Abused in
        Family Therapy *305*
     Revelation of Childhood Sexual Abuse in a 25-year
        Follow-up Interview *311*
     When One Actual Trauma Reappears as a Fantasy of
        Sexual Abuse and Further Work Does Not Uncover
        a Memory *316*

14. **Trauma in Termination**   323
     Passing the Trauma Back to the Patient *323*
     Trauma at Termination *325*
     Trauma from Colleagues' Responses *327*

15. **Putting It Together: Theory and Technique in Trauma**   329
     Splitting and Repression in Normal Personality
        Development *330*
     Primal Repression and Dissociation: Encapsulation and
        Multiplicity after Cumulative Trauma *330*
     Therapeutic Functions *331*

     References   339

     Credits   357

     Index   359

Preface and

Acknowledgments

It has taken us until now to realize how many of our patients had suffered trauma in the course of their lives, some in childhood and some in the adult phases of development. In the individual case, certainly we had seen the effects of trauma where it was usually at the center of the treatment, but the centrality of the topic across a series of cases was lost in its immersion in developmental issues unique to each case. Contemporary attention in the psychiatric literature drew our attention to the need to review our experience in our current and previously reported clinical work in order to learn from the traumatic continuum represented there—not only in individual patients whose current distress was witness to trauma experienced from the previous generation but also in couples and families where physical and sexual trauma caused strain in the current and the next generation, even when the parents of the present generation were careful to avoid repetition of abuse to their own children.

Therapists naturally want to avoid repetition of abuse too. We do not want to hurt or betray our patients. But that is only one reason for our relative silence on the psychotherapy of abused patients. The other explanation lies in our feeling traumatized by the material without a good holding environment in the psychoanalytic culture until recently. Like Kluft (1990a, b) and Herman (1981), we found ourselves fighting off the impact of treating the survivor of abuse. As writers, we procrastinated, studied anything else, and wrote other books first, because recording our countertransference reawakened the memory of our reception of the patient's trauma. As therapists, and then as writers, we have felt nauseated, anguished, frightened, guilty, and helpless.

In the countertransference the therapist may experience tremendous discomfort when viewed in the transference as an abusive object or when the patient's efforts to avoid such a development lead to a feeling of stalemate, neither of which reflect well upon the competence of the therapist. Even when the situation lends itself to a gratifying case report, the therapist is inhibited in reporting the work because of fear of censure by psychoanalytic colleagues, who might be appalled at the therapist's supposed gullibility for believing as real memories that should have been interpreted as fantastic distortions. In presenting or writing up clinical examples of work with abused patients, the therapist may feel an intensification of worries about exhibitionism, betrayal, breaking of boundaries, exploitation of the patient, and traumatizing the reader.

We have tried to contain these anxieties so that we did not have to split off and dissociate ourselves from this material. We have been encouraged by the positive responses of patients who have been inspired to persist and invest further in their own therapeutic work after reading in one of our books the vignettes of other therapies. Sometimes it eases pain, shame, and guilt to see that, although individual experience is unique, there is a universality to the features of unconscious process and primitive object relationships. As always we have used careful disguise, including combining the characteristics of various family constellations into the presentation of a family or individual history, to protect the identities of those whose vignettes were chosen to illustrate theory and technique, but we have remained true to our best recollection of our own interventions. We hope that our patients will remain safe from trauma while the narratives of their therapies contribute to a more understanding and responsive therapeutic environment and ultimately to a safer society. We are grateful to the individuals, couples, and families who trusted us enough to tell us what we needed to know in order to understand them. We benefited from such teachers as Frank Putnam, Juliet Mitchell, and Joyce McDougall, who address dissociative phenomena and archaic fantasy. Presentations by Joanne Greer, William Larrison, Richard Loewenstein, Charles Olsen, and Joseph Silvio stimulated our interest in multiplicity and childhood sexual abuse. We are grateful for the support of colleagues who encouraged us to talk about our work in its first-draft stage at the Cincinnati Psychiatric and Psychoanalytic Societies, Washington Psychoanalytic Society, and Washington School of Psychiatry. We thank Richard Chefetz for guiding us toward writings on dissociation and hypnotic states and Ralph Gemelli for help in locating the latest memory research. Phyllis Grosskurth graciously validated a reference for us and Sharon Alperowitz located Ferenczi material. We are grateful to Richard Gardner and Creative Therapies for permission to tabulate his ideas on true and false accusations of sexual abuse. We thank Jason Aronson for impressing upon us the need to let the clinical material speak for itself, and we thank Judy Cohen, our responsive editor, and Muriel Jorgensen for shepherding the book to its final destination.

Most of the writings on abuse emphasize trauma theory based on study and behavioral treatment of post-traumatic stress disorder resulting from combat, especially in the Vietnam war, and from studies of survivors of the Holocaust and natural disasters. Findings concerning flashbacks, dissociative phenomena, and panic attacks as stress declarations or desperate attempts to flee from horror are all applicable to understanding symptomatology in children and adults whose bodies were physically assaulted, sexually invaded, or attacked by congenital malformation and corrective surgery. But to comprehend the impact of trauma on mental structure, marital choice, sexual relatedness, and family life, we need a developmental, object relational perspective.

Psychoanalytic knowledge about traumata is not well developed (Hopper 1991, Sandler et al. 1991). With notable exceptions, such as the volumes assembled by Kramer and Akhtar (1991), Levine (1990c) and Davies and Frawley (1994), that develop a psychoanalytic approach to understanding the effects of abuse, psychoanalysis has had more to say about conflict, deficit, loss, and incestuous fantasy than about actual trauma to the self. This book is our attempt to fill this gap.

SECTION I

An Object Relational View of Trauma

1

The Traumatic

Continuum

Trauma and abuse occur on a continuum proceeding from serious failures of care and nurturance early in life to those that happen at later developmental stages, from the severely abusive to the less traumatic, and from the wickedly intentional to the unfortunate. The gravest are attacks on bodily integrity, whereas the least serious are temporary losses and minor accidents. We want to understand the devastation that follows loss of body boundaries due to incest, physical abuse, loss of body parts, and medical interventions. We are equally interested in the similar but less remarkable effects on patients who have been less thoroughly traumatized and in the mechanisms that promote survival. We want to appreciate the strengths that patients in all these categories can mobilize in order to continue their development, despite the odds against them, so that we can maximize these factors in treating both the severely and the less traumatized. We hope that our study of nongenital bodily trauma will amplify our discussion of the effects of incest. In this chapter, we introduce the spectrum of trauma with brief clinical vignettes.

SEVERE PHYSICAL TRAUMA IN CHILDHOOD

The most severe trauma to an infant is either neglect or abuse in the earliest months by the parents. If the failure of care and nurturance is complete, the child fails to develop physically, emotionally, and cognitively and may die (Bowlby 1969, 1980, Spitz 1945, 1946). Although massive early neglect may be found in the histories of many who later suffer physical and sexual abuse, in other cases, the lap-baby stage goes relatively well and abuse does not occur until the child is a more separate person.

Children born with defects or disabilities due to prematurity or birth complications may receive excellent physical care from devoted parents and nursing staff, but the constraints of the incubator box, intravenous feeding and monitoring equipment, and the intrusions of medical procedures violate the child's body and its longing for proximity to its mother's body for food, safety, and comfort. A traumatized sense of self develops at the earliest level and may be ameliorated by future recovery or may be stamped in by repeated invasions of the skin boundary and personal privacy.

Mr. Patrick, described in Chapter 10, was born with a congenital deformity of the urogenital tract. Repeated surgeries and hospitalizations in childhood and adolescence led to an unrecognized cumulative trauma. He developed a false self of being an excellent patient and a compliant teaching case, but he had to encapsulate his trauma in a perverse fantasy that prevented his being in a relationship. John, mentioned in Chapter 4, a loving child who adored his mother, suffered serious illness in his fourth year and dealt with the trauma in a similarly counterphobic way. He did not develop a perverse fantasy, but he expressed his distress by developing another side to him that blamed his mother and retaliated against her, so that she experienced an extreme sense of the loss of what had been a delightful relationship with a healthy, integrated boy.

PHYSICAL AND SEXUAL ABUSE IN INFANCY AND TODDLERHOOD

Physical and sexual abuse begins in the infant or toddler years when parental frustration leads to battering a baby or stimulating the infant. Examples appear in Freud's earliest case histories (Breuer and Freud

1893). His later patient known as "the Wolfman" reported memories of being used sexually by his sister almost as far back as he could remember (1918). It could be that one or both of those children had been abused by a grown-up before their sibling incest pattern began.

Mrs. Feinstein, described in Chapter 11, whose mother penetrated her vagina with her fingers and gave her frequent enemas in childhood and douches in adolescence, recovered a body memory of being pulled up against her mother's naked body as an infant. Freda, whose treatment is detailed in Chapter 12, had as her earliest memory being included in her parents' intercourse. She was invited to sit nude on their bed while they had intercourse, with both of them touching her and she touching their genitals and her mother's breasts. Her parents' neglect and abusive interest in her continued throughout her childhood, and her father had intercourse with her regularly from her menarche at age 8 until she stopped him by threatening suicide at 14.

SEXUAL ABUSE AND NEGLECT IN LATER CHILDHOOD

The cases of sexual abuse that occur in later childhood are traumatic in themselves, but often more so because they occur in the context of family relationships that have been disturbed from the beginning. Sexual abuse develops out of the pervasive atmosphere of neglect that characterizes these families and may constitute a paradoxical attempt to solve loneliness.

Chloe Johnson grew up in such a family. She sought treatment for an aversion to sex with her husband. During a long treatment that included sex therapy and intensive individual psychotherapy, a story of childhood neglect and abuse emerged. She was born when her mother, a sexually promiscuous 19-year-old, became pregnant from a one-night stand with a soldier. Her adolescent mother could not be bothered with her, and she was taken in by her grandmother, who was with Chloe during her infancy. When the mother later married and had children, Chloe begged to join her mother, and at the age of 6 was allowed to do so. She was not much wanted by her mother, who preferred Chloe's half-brothers, but her stepfather took an active interest in her. He was a paranoid, clinging man who was jealous of Chloe's mother, and he sexualized his relationship with Chloe. He walked nude through the house frequently, and asked to comb her long hair while she sat on a stool, paralyzed with fright. Lonely and neglected at home, she wandered without supervision on the dirt streets of her impoverished rural village. She was befriended by a man in a neighboring house, who took her in his bed and asked her to fondle his genitals, eventually proceeding to intercourse. This happened on several occasions, and Chloe remembered feeling that at least someone cared, just as she felt that her stepfather cared more than her mother did. The sex with the neighbor stopped when his wife found out about Chloe's visits and angrily banished her from the house, blaming her for seducing the man. Chloe never told her parents about these incidents. Meanwhile, the relationship with the parents continued to be anxious and traumatic in itself. The stepfather was intermittently psychotic, at times threatening Chloe's mother with a knife. Her mother did everything she could to mollify him directly while carrying on extramarital affairs behind his back. Finally, when she was 12, her stepfather took Chloe into a bathroom, exposed himself, and asked her to touch his penis. Chloe became nauseated, fled the house, and returned to her grandmother permanently, but she never got over the sense of exclusion from her mother and stepfather's family.

In the conjoint individual and family therapy of Judy Green many years ago, David Scharff learned that Judy had experienced severe abuses of sexuality in her young life, but not directly at the hands of her parents. At that time in the first year of his psychiatric residency, he was not sufficiently attuned to the traumatic basis of her difficulties and used a broader focus (see Chapter 13 for an account of a twenty-five-year follow-up interview with Judy).

Judy was 14 when she was admitted to the hospital for ingesting 100 aspirin. Her mother had regretted her marriage before Judy was born and had been ambivalent about her from the first, focusing many of her doubts about herself on the young Judy. Depressed during Judy's infancy, she treated Judy and her older brother with alternating neglect, resentment, and guilty overcompensation. On at least one occasion when Judy was 4, her mother forced her to nurse at the breast, not long after the birth of a younger sister, perhaps because the mother preferred relating to babies and could not stand the more active demands of older children.

Judy's relationship to her father was also marred by a mutual seduction that stemmed from the family's pervasive loneliness. He felt shut out by her mother and usually had little time for Judy, but at times he turned to Judy seductively, calling her "Judy-babe," and encouraged her to play up to him coquettishly. Presumably he wished for gratification that he missed in an unhappy marriage, just as Judy longed for the love and care that neither parent gave her. Judy had one memory of her father picking her up and tossing her joyfully in the air, but her overall sense of her early childhood was of having been achingly alone. Judy's plight was deepened when her father developed cancer when she was 4 and died when she was 5. The distress over this situation may have contributed to her mother's inappropriate encouragement of Judy's nursing at the breast at the age of 4. Judy's mother was especially guilty because she had been having an affair at the time her husband's illness was discovered, and during the illness and decline of her husband, she had been deeply depressed and largely immobilized.

Things improved when mother remarried two years later, but parenting remained generally inadequate. When the family moved because of the stepfather's job, the children were left largely alone. Judy said that she and her older brother engaged in incestuous sexual activity regularly when she was 9 and he was 11. This sibling incest was discovered and stopped after a year, but by age 13 Judy was severely depressed, and she began using sex as a way of acting out. She had intercourse with a variety of boys over a period of a few months. A pregnancy scare became confused with her witnessing of an infant death in a car accident, and she became delusionally convinced that she had caused the death by deliberately failing to warn the driver, who was going in reverse, that an infant was behind the car. Finally, she took an overdose of aspirin and was admitted to the hospital, where she presented as a borderline with a propensity for dramatic exaggeration, an "as-if" quality of claiming to hallucinate, and a sexualized way of relating to staff. Not surprisingly, she quickly developed a sexualized transference to her therapist, claiming to have decided that she wanted to have his baby.

These women had histories of neglect combined with abuse, with which they coped to varying degrees of success. Treatment made an enormous difference to all of them, but they, like other women neglected and abused throughout early childhood, remained concerned with the residue of that abuse.

Girls are not the only children to have been assaulted. Boys are subject to all degrees of abuse from either parent, and not uncommonly from outsiders. The problem of homosexual relations in boys' boarding schools has long been acknowledged. The popular press has been full of cases in which those entrusted with the care of boys, such as teachers or priests, have homosexually seduced or assaulted boys or girls. Years before child abuse was openly discussed in society, W. R. D. Fairbairn (1935) wrote a paper on the problem of child assault, remarkable for its foresight, in which he said that the problem of sexual abuse of boys was in some ways more serious than that of girls. Because abuse of boys was even less accepted by society, boys suffered more profound shame and loneliness.

Lars and Velia were a couple, both of whom had been abused in childhood. (This couple and their family are the subject of an extensive report in Scharff and Scharff 1991.) They came for treatment because both were sexually dysfunctional. Velia had also suffered from severe and recurrent depression, and could remember her father's alcoholic rages and abuse of her mother. From the beginning of her treatment, in a matter-of-fact way, she could report that incestuous play with her brothers in her late childhood and preadolescence had occurred. Although she could not remember for sure, she thought no intercourse had occurred. Later in therapy, a more emotional picture emerged when sex therapy triggered Velia's memories:

> Touching Lars' erection reminded me of the times with my brother when he was 13 and I was 11. We were in his room, and he would unzip his fly and pull out his penis and have me touch it. It didn't feel good. It was hard. The top looked rubbery with ridges on it. I didn't want to touch it. . . . For years, without remembering

this, I've seen an erect penis in everything—not connected to anything, but floating in the air like my brother's penis. Just sticking out from his pants without testicles.

At first she could not recall being interested in it, and then slowly, shamefully, and guiltily she recalled her arousal and interest in her brother's penis. Only after that recollection did she recover the memory of her father's physical abuse of her and her brothers and sister.

Lars' story was different. Not only had he no memory of abuse, but he simply could not remember anything at all about his young childhood. For the first two years of therapy he reported that his childhood had been happy until his father was arrested for approaching a man in a men's bathroom. His father spent some time in prison, and thereafter lived openly in a homosexual relationship. Lars said that he had thought his parents were happily married until this incident, which occurred when he was 17.

Two years later, when the couple had been in psychodynamic sex therapy and family therapy for over a year and Velia had just recalled the additional details and shame surrounding her arousal during her sexual activity with her brother, Lars suddenly recalled the abuse in his childhood.

It happened when I was 12 or 13. My father stopped working because of his double hernia. He couldn't lift anything, so Mom was working to support us. I don't know how we got on to the subject, but one day at home I remember asking my father what it was like to have sex. He said, "Here, I'll show you." He performed anal sex on me. That was the only time that happened. But later on I was talking about it with my brother. I fondled his penis, and then I did it to him twice when he was asleep—or pretending to be asleep.

Later, we were coming back from Boy Scouts with my Dad and three other kids in the car. When two of the kids went into a store I told my father what I had done to my brother. My father didn't say, "That's not right!" He only said, "You've got to be careful when you say things like that!" There was another kid in the back seat of the car, so I got the idea that my father and that boy must have had sex together.

The loss of specific memory and the presentation of a blank history of childhood commonly result from the devastation of mental functioning in the wake of sexual abuse. Although Velia exhibited some loss of painful and haunting memories through repression, Lars' picture was one of a pervasive loss of cognitive function. He had a profound learning disability that had handicapped him all his life, and he was unable to learn complex material or to pass ordinary promotional examinations. When Lars was able to recall the abuse in treatment, his capacity to study and learn improved a good deal immediately, although it did not fully reach the level one might have expected for someone of his intelligence.

This couple's experience makes another point of clinical significance: histories of sexual abuse are found among people seeking help for sexual dysfunction. Although the pairing of their stories of abuse was particularly striking in this couple, it is not uncommon to find two people who marry through a shared interest in undoing damage experienced in their childhood by building a family without sexual destructiveness. (See the case of Tony and Theresa in Chapter 9 for a detailed description of the treatment of such a marriage.)

MILDER FORMS OF NEGLECT

Not all sexual abuse or early trauma is so extensive and easily defined. For many years, psychoanalysts and therapists have heard stories from their patients of receiving enemas, an experience that they felt was clearly traumatizing, but one that was not always thought of technically as child abuse. Sometimes these enemas had actually been medically sanctioned. The frequency of the enemas, the sadism or sexual pleasure of the parent administering it, and the general conditions of life in the family all color the experience. In the following example, alcohol abuse contributed to a sadomasochistic fantasy elaboration of enema abuse and child-beating.

Sandra, a woman who came for treatment in her thirties because of her inability to sustain love relationships, had substituted sexualized acting out for intimacy, had numerous affairs during her marriage, and tended to end up in relationships with men who had no intention of leaving their wives. While Sandra was growing up, her father drank every night and dominated the family with his angry irrationality. Her mother meekly subjected herself to him, and tried to pacify the children while getting her own satisfaction indirectly through them. Her intimacy with Sandra included giving her frequent enemas before the age of 3. In the same period, her father disciplined her frequently by strapping her bare buttocks with a belt. These experiences, we came to understand during her analysis, were the precursors to Sandra's pattern of masturbation beginning in adolescence, when she spent long periods in the bathtub stimulating her anus while running water on her vulva. The trauma inflicted by both parents resulted in compulsive sexualization of her anus, and led to a development of profound unconscious confusion about genital and anal bodily aspects of relating. As she grew, Sandra thrust sexuality to the fore in attempts to get love, but in emotionally sadomasochistic ways that echoed the patterns begun as a toddler with her parents.

Sandra's brother was born when she was 3, and both parents fastened on him with intense interest. She felt cast aside, as many oldest children do with the birth of a sibling. But because this birth came in the context of the subtle and direct abusive behavior from both parents, it acquired additional traumatic impact. In analysis, this was understood when she had a dream of going fishing as a child with this younger brother. He caught a worm while she caught nothing. In her mind, the worm was a hollow tube resembling the foreskin. We came to understand that at age 3 she had fastened on the brother's penis as the thing that was the main object of her parents' interest, and it therefore became hers. She had developed unconscious fantasies of having an internal penis, the worm-like tube that was her rectum, which she could define with her fingers whereas her vagina was a more elusive shape. She developed the conviction, through this confused fantasy, that possession of the worm-like penis was necessary to secure love. It was this that she chased in her driven and promiscuous sexuality, looking for men who could give her the prized possession, then envying them for what they had, which, like her brother, meant that they got what she could not have.

These unconscious dynamics are graphic but not so unusual in psychoanalytic treatment. The point is that the specifics of the dynamics were set in place by early bodily and emotional trauma that

Sandra had experienced at the hands of both parents. The direct trauma to her is what made the birth of her brother traumatic rather than emotionally inconvenient. This constellation meant that the transference and countertransference of the treatment situation were also full of trauma, as Sandra felt rejected by her nonseduceable analyst and was driven to traumatize him in ways that were emotionally the equivalent of her own repeated life traumas and losses in her family of origin and current failed relationships.

Sexual abuse often coexists with physical abuse, but either can occur as the sole type of abuse.

> A law student, Matt, was referred to the school authorities by his wife because of his alcoholism and his angry and unresponsive attitude to his wife and children. The school took the position that he could not continue unless he agreed to treatment, which he did with great resentment. A period in residential treatment stopped the cycle of alcohol abuse, and he was able to resume his role as student and father.
>
> Matt's history made sense of his symptoms. He had grown up as the eldest son in a large family, with an alcoholic father who was in the construction business and a compliant, meek mother. The family was ruled by father's physical threats, and Matt was the only person who stood up to him. In one incident when he was 15, Matt was helping his father build a house. They were standing atop a brick wall, installing the huge triangular trusses that were to support the roof. An angry disagreement erupted between them, and father and son swung the trusses at each other until the son succeeded in knocking the father off the wall. Two years later, the father killed himself at one of his construction sites by arranging several explosive charges next to a gasoline drum to create a massive explosion. A white-hot fire raged for hours, a violent end to a violent man.
>
> When describing these horrifying experiences in treatment, Matt maintained a discordantly matter-of-fact tone and attitude due to the emotional detachment he had found necessary to manage his lifelong experience of violence.

UNSUBSTANTIATED ABUSE

There are some patients who suspect that they have been abused, but who have not been. Such patients fall into two broad categories:

those who falsely claim abuse and those of a more subtle variety for whom accusation of the parent is not the issue, but rather a desperate attempt to make sense of their symptoms and history and to explain the damage to their selves.

False accusations of trauma are unfortunately increasingly prevalent, and such organizations as the False Memory Syndrome Foundation have sprung up to protect the reputation of accused families and child care workers and to warn therapists against being too credulous (Gardner 1992). As popular acceptance of the existence of child abuse grows, more adults come forward with stories suggestive of it. The nature of the repressive and dissociative processes that are induced by early trauma makes memory unreliable, so that patients need time and support to explore their pasts. Some of these suspicions of abuse are correct and in the course of therapy can be validated. Others dissolve after further work on the issues. A therapist who jumps too readily to the conclusion that every patient who suspects trauma has indeed been subjected to it will unwittingly validate false accusations and conclusions and foreclose the healing efforts of taking responsibility for incestuous wishes.

Such was the case with an 18-year-old girl who "remembered" during psychotherapy that her father had molested her. No one else in the family had any memory of it, and the story seemed inconsistent with the family's level of organization and with the girl's overall level of functioning. Ultimately the story shrank to an early childhood memory of taking showers with her father and feeling overwhelmed by her wishes toward his penis, which loomed large. Although we do not recommend that fathers take showers with their children—boys or girls—because it is traumatically stimulating of fantasies, this behavior is not the kind of severe, direct, and often repeated abuse that she had originally implied.

In this case, in addition, the family had always had a policy against parental nudism around the children, so that it seemed unlikely that the event had occurred as remembered. The father, who had been upset by the accusation, was relieved by the evolution of his daughter's reconstruction, which now began to sound more like the oedipal elaboration of early childhood wishes, perhaps stimulated by swimming with the father, by a chance viewing of his genitalia, or by the unconscious transmission of his incestuous wishes toward his daughter. The daughter continued individual psychotherapy to explore further the origins and consequences of her fantasy elaboration. A naive therapist might have supported this girl's accusation and urged her to launch a fruitless and unwarranted crusade against her family for their "cover-up."

On the other hand, therapists can be confused by patients who have indeed survived abuse, but doubt their memories and try to get the therapist to take a position of certainty. Kramer (1985) called this coercion of the therapist *object coercive doubting*, a phenomenon that she found present most often among women who had been abused by their mothers. In our culture, it seems to be particularly unbelievable that a mother could so betray her child's trust. We want to keep an open mind until we have the weight of evidence from the de-repression and reintegration of split-off parts of the self after enough time in therapy.

In more ambiguous cases, patients describe relationships with parents in which a history of sexual abuse would make sense of their difficulties, but they do not recover any definite memory of abuse. In other cases, such as the analysis of Freda (see Chapter 12), recovered memories ultimately support the therapist's suspicion of abuse, years later. The de-repression of associated memories is crucial to treatment and recovery. It is, however, equally important to respect the possibility that there are no associated memories so as not to concoct them and derail the treatment.

The situation in which suspicions of abuse are not confirmed is illustrated by examples from two analyses.

Albert (described more fully in Chapter 5) was a young man who was isolated socially, who had sexual interests in men and women, and whose fantasy life was a rich array of perversions, usually involving violence and death. He had written a short story about a homosexual liaison between two young boys whose sexual interest in each other was heightened when they came upon a dead floating body in a lake. In the long therapeutic and analytic work, therapist and patient alike suspected that there had been early sexual trauma, for as a young boy Albert had begun to seek premature sexual contact with both boys and girls and as an adolescent he had worked in experimental elementary school settings in which sexual expression was encouraged between staff and children. Although this experience could be seen to be independently traumatic both for the young children and for the adolescent Albert, it seemed to confirm him in a role for which he had been marked by earlier trauma. Later, when he was beginning therapy, Albert played in sexually provocative ways with his young nephew and niece until the therapist warned him that further sexual play of this sort would necessitate legal reporting. With considerable relief, Albert was able to stop the sex-play promptly and permanently. Prolonged analytic therapy produced many early memories that made sense of Albert's overall difficulties, but none of them was of direct trauma, and such suspicions faded over the time of the therapy. He reconstructed a narrative of his early life as a bleak and lonely experience with parents who were emotionally impoverished, traumatized people. Albert's trauma was an attenuated one of lifelong exposure to parents who had suffered the direct trauma and whose attempts to encapsulate it left them emotionally remote from their son.

Another patient, Patricia, sought treatment for depression at age 35 as her 17-year marriage was dissolving. In therapy she came to understand the emotionally abusive relationship she had suffered with her husband, but which she had been unable to stop. Staying with him had been an attempt to undo the event that had marked her childhood: her father's leaving her mother and three children when Patricia was 10. The parents had to marry when Patricia's mother was pregnant with her, and that marriage seemed to have been loveless from the beginning. Her father was especially interested in Patricia, and she had fond memories of his creative energy, his reading stories to her at bedtime, and playing sports with her. However, he was a seductive, self-centered man who flirted with women all his life and who, she felt, had a sexualized relationship with her. She idealized him, in contrast to her mother who, left behind with the children and no means of support, had been depressed and bitter during the rest of Patricia's young life.

Early in therapy, Patricia began to see that her father had misused her. For instance, her mother had instigated the parents' divorce after her father had taken Patricia on a beach weekend where he had met his mistress and romanced her in front of Patricia. When they returned home, mother quizzed Patricia, and her admission of witnessing her father's behavior had become the legal centerpiece of the divorce trial. With this realization, Patricia developed a hunch so strong it was almost a conviction that her father had been more than emotionally seductive with her, that he had fondled or abused her more directly in the early years when she had felt so lonely and dominated by the bitterness in the parents' marriage. In the transference, she now felt that the therapist, whom she had previously idealized, would periodically disappoint her traumatically. For instance, on one occasion when he forgot to unlock the waiting room door before she arrived, she was convinced that he wanted to reject her fundamentally. If he began the hour so much as a minute late or stopped the hour a minute early, she interpreted this as a rejection that was the emotional equivalent of her father's leaving after the divorce.

But as therapy progressed, she did not recall any memories that confirmed direct abuse by her father. She and her therapist became convinced that the events that she had felt to be so painful were constituted by the emotional climate of the parents' relationship, their lack of concern for her true self, the father's departure after maintaining an emotionally seductive relationship with Patricia, and the bitter battles between Patricia and her mother, rather than by the trauma of direct sexual abuse. As in the case of Albert, Patricia's search for trauma led to the discovery that she had internalized her parents' trauma, in her case the trauma of their corrupt marriage and its destruction.

The cases of Albert and Patricia are similar to the later cases that Freud understood best, those in which relative neglect forms the seed of traumatic fantasy, about which the conflict gets repressed until it is persuaded back into consciousness by the analytic method of free association and interpretation of resistance.

MEDICAL TRAUMA IN ADULTHOOD

When medical trauma occurs in adulthood, the trauma affects not only the patient but also the spouse and children.

Tony, a brawny electronics worker (whose trauma and its effects on him and his marriage are described in Chapter 9), had to have his right arm and shoulder amputated to prevent the spread of gangrene following a routine injection. Loss of limb to a manual worker was hard enough, but the right arm also carried the association of physical violence and its restraint.

Tony lost the fist that he used to smash into the wall so that he would never hit his wife when he was angry, as his father had done. Without that defense at a time of increasing rage at his predicament and at her for expecting him to become rehabilitated, Tony became immobilized, his wife and one child became depressed, and the family began to unravel.

Arturo, a 16–year-old high-school soccer star from a rural village in Colombia, sustained an injury in one eye when he was helping with the fruit harvest. Infection set in, and failure to remove the eyeball meant that he lost the sight of the other eye as well. Suddenly this fast, well-coordinated fellow could hardly get around, and his athletic girlfriend ended their relationship. Within a year, he successfully realigned his ambition from the athletic to the intellectual realm and found a new sweetheart who had always loved him but whom he had spurned before. With her support, expressed in reading to him and typing up all his dictated papers, Arturo won a scholarship to an American college. It looked as though he had converted trauma to genera. But what the admiring world did not see was the effect of his enslaving dependency on the sweetheart, who went to college with him as his wife. Trauma had provided the opportunity for their coupling. Roxanna had gratefully hitched her wagon to a star performer because she had no confidence in her own ability. Now that the amazing Arturo needed her so desperately, she had no need to face her own dependency and lack of self-esteem. The world was blind to the tempers and the verbally abusive behavior that Arturo heaped on Roxanna in his frustration at home. No one but Arturo knew the viciousness with which his devoted Roxanna fought back. Both of them had lost the ideal self and had substituted for it by locating a new ideal self in him and encapsulating a damaged self in her, instead of together mourning and recovering from the trauma.

ADULT PHYSICAL TRAUMA

Physical abuse is not confined to children. Spouse abuse does not necessarily rest on a developmental history of actual trauma in the family of origin during childhood, as seen in the second example below.

Janet, who came for treatment with her second husband, told of a brief first marriage to a man who became violent during her pregnancy. The jealousy of the coming baby and the pressure of his graduate studies combined to unshackle his aggression, and he beat her severely on several occasions. She began to fantasize using the loaded gun he kept in his bedside drawer to shoot him the next time he tried to hurt her and realized that she might do so if she stayed. She packed her belongings and boarded the bus for her parents' house, and obtained a divorce without seeing him again. When she married again a few years later, she chose an obsessional man who not only never hit her but who could never be roused to anger.

Janet's early history did contain abuse. Her father was a physician, an anxious but strong-willed and intrusive man who insisted on taking physical care of his family, including giving the women annual gynecological exams. He bullied his wife and children emotionally, but never hit them. Janet felt cowed and intruded on by her father. The relationship had been emotionally abusive and physically abusive in the guise of medical care. Although this relationship had set the stage for the choice of her first husband, it did not so condition her that she had to stay with him, nor did she repeat the object choice her second time around.

Hanna, a 30-year-old woman, formed an abusive marriage without any history of childhood trauma. She came for treatment while married to an alcoholic man who had broken her arm two years earlier, and who continued to threaten her physically when she did not feel like having sex or accommodating to many of his notions. She had been unable to break away from him. When she moved out of his bedroom, he would drunkenly throw her bedroom door open in the middle of the night and stare at her threateningly. Her previous therapist had not suggested that she should leave her husband after he had broken her arm, as he had immediately become contrite and begged for forgiveness. It is only fair to remember that the awareness of the professional community has been heightened in the intervening years, so that it is now difficult to imagine a therapist not raising fundamental questions at such a point and recognizing the event as spouse abuse.

In a successful intensive psychotherapy, Hanna was able to reconstruct her history of childhood depression and loneliness in a way that made sense of the tie she had formed and was for so long unable to break with this alcoholic man, but there was never any suggestion that she had been physically or sexually traumatized in childhood. In contrast, her parents had both suffered the trauma of the Holocaust in their own lives. Neither had been in concentration camps, but both had narrow and dangerous escapes from Europe, suffered dislocation in their tortuous paths to the United States in the 1930s, and, once they met, had clung together as each other's salvation. Hanna's case fits with the group of children whose parents have had traumatic histories, and who, despite every best intention, cannot avoid passing on elements of their own trauma to the internal object relations of their children.

THE MITIGATION OF TRAUMA

There are many children exposed to trauma whose families manage to mitigate the trauma so that it becomes a relatively mild stress. Such was the case of a boy forced to perform fellatio by a male babysitter. When he told his parents, they did not blame their son, and worked actively with a therapist to help the boy work through the trauma, including obtaining psychotherapy for him soon after the event. The primary mitigating factor was that the atmosphere in the family permitted the boy to tell his parents what had happened. Dealing with this level of trauma is an extension of the normal holding capacity of parents, who should protect their children and support their recovery when the protection fails or is aggressively invaded.

In another case, a 12-year-old boy asked his father what the word "masturbation" meant. The father said, "Let me show you," and began to rub the boy's penis. When the boy said, "That hurts, Dad," the father stopped and apologized abjectly. The boy then told his mother, who sought treatment for the family. There it emerged that the father had been under enormous stress at work, and had felt for some time unsupported in the marriage. When the moment of abuse was set in context, the boy was able to finish a brief treatment without a residue of profound trauma, and the couple proceeded to work on the marital strain that had provoked the father's vulnerability.

Eight-year-old Junie was in the neighborhood park with another girl when a lone man exposed his genitals to them. Junie reported this incident to her mother with some sense of fright, but also one of curiosity. Despite the fact that Junie's mother, Freda, had been sexually abused by her parents in her own childhood, she was able to calm her, answer her questions, and help her learn to leave the scene immediately should the situation recur. There was no sense that the episode traumatized Junie (see Chapter 12).

The process through which families mitigate trauma in ordinary ways is of further interest because it offers a model for the building of modules of positive functioning in therapeutic approaches to trauma. These psychic genera are described in Chapter 2 (Bollas 1992). In those families who cannot mitigate the trauma, the family's holding and containing functions have been insufficient. In therapy, the holding and containing function is central both to fill in for deficiency in the family immediately and to offer an experience that can be internalized by the family so that their holding and containing of experience and their capacity to detoxify trauma mature.

THE CHILDREN OF ABUSED PARENTS

We have come across many cases of children like Albert, Patricia, and Hanna who have not themselves been traumatized, but whose development of internal object relations is marked by their parents' traumatized development. This phenomenon is now well reported in the case of children of Holocaust victims and others who experienced early traumatic loss, but it is equally true for many children whose parents were sexually or physically abused. Some of these parents become guilty or sometimes self-righteous perpetrators of abuse, but many devote themselves to trying to ensure that their children are protected from the ravages of their own abuse. Projective identification and the transmission of object relations are such, however, that it is almost impossible to protect children from unconscious knowledge of their parents' inner struggles (D. Scharff 1982, Scharff and Scharff 1991).

Chloe Johnson, whom we described earlier in this chapter, brought to therapy her 4-year-old daughter Debbie, whose symptoms of anxiety included frequent, compulsive masturbation even in front of her parents. She was unable to stop by herself, even when her parents asked her, unless they took her on their laps. Although Chloe had a history of neglect and sexual abuse, she had not abused Debbie, her only child, and neither had her husband. Yet, there had been family strains. Because of her own abuse, Chloe had been increasingly unable to respond sexually to her husband Mike, who had become irritable and depressed. In the situation of marital strain, both turned anxiously to Debbie for solace, Chloe when she felt threatened by sex and Mike when he felt unloved. The parents' turning to Debbie made her anxious about their needs. In addition, she was sexually anxious because of her father's intense attention to her, although there was no direct sexual contact. Other factors contributed to the sexualization of Debbie's symptomatology. Debbie was cared for by a loving baby-sitter while both parents worked for the first two and a half years of her life, and she suddenly lost her when the parents moved. The loss, during a period of normally developmentally heightened auto-eroticism, resulted in fixing Debbie's use of masturbation for self-comforting when she was lonely or anxious. Chloe also had a brief affair around this time, in an attempt to split off an enjoyable and exciting aspect of sex when she felt threatened by the demand for full physical and emotional commitment in the unsatisfactory marriage. Despite child analysis, Debbie continued, even into her teen years, to use sexualized attempts to solve problems of loneliness and depression, an echo of Chloe's more dramatic vulnerability to sexual abuse during her own childhood.

The children of Lars and Velia, both of whom were subjected to sexual abuse, exemplify the range of effects of the transmission of adaptation to abuse in the previous generation.

This family, also described in detail in previous publications (D. Scharff 1989, Scharff and Scharff 1991), had three children. The oldest, Eric, developed normally for the most part, but at the beginning of family therapy could be seen to have incorporated an inordinate amount of aggressive object relations. In his play with his brother and sister, at times of stress, he had the Superman figure tear apart their constructions. We came to understand this action as his frustrated reaction to his parents' pressure on him to be the invulnerable and idealized good object for the family, a super hero antidote to Lars' and Velia's abusive fathers. The second son, Alex, was a vulnerable and disorganized boy with hyperactivity and attention deficit disorder. Much like Lars, he had a severe learning disorder. In addition he was encopretic and enuretic, wetting and soiling night and day at any sign of stress. Alex could not experience himself as a competent male. In consort with his constitutional vulnerability, the impact of his parents' traumata sought an outlet in his fecal and urinary soiling and in learning disorder. His body had incorporated their fear of men and boys, and of the father's sodomy by his own father. Finally, Jeanette, the youngest and excitedly adored child, had a sexualization of her personality, as she responded to their overly physicalized, ambivalent way of relating to her. They dressed her in too-short dresses and then warned her to keep her dress down. Jeanette carried the excitement that the parents split off from their relationship to keep themselves safe from their internalization of the effects of sexual abuse, but which they kept alive by finding it in her through projective identification. As their own sexual lives became more satisfactory, they saw the sexualization in Jeanette's development, sorted out the errors of using her to overcompensate for their own vulnerabilities, and helped her more effectively to tame the excitement and provocativeness in her developing personality.

This introduction to the traumatic continuum may suffice until Section II of this book when we describe these and other cases in considerably more detail. For now, we can say that the parents and other adults who do perpetrate abuse have often been traumatized themselves as children. Those survivors of childhood trauma who do not perpetuate abuse nevertheless transmit their pain and their defenses against it in their dealings with their children, who incorporate these into their psychic structure in the form of their internal object relations. In these ways, trauma extends from one generation to another.

2

Post-trauma, Multiplicity, and Childhood Memory Studies

In this book we confine ourselves to the study of personal physical trauma. We do not deal with the horrors of war and its effects on the combatant, the veteran, or military dependents (Fairbairn 1943b, Kardiner 1941, Lifton 1967, Sonnenberg, et al. 1985, Van der Kolk 1987), nor with the study of racial and religious genocide (Laub and Auerhan 1985). Although we recognize that the loss of a parent through illness, suicide, or extreme depression is deeply traumatic (Hopper 1991) and that death (Furman 1974), divorce (Wallerstein and Kelly 1980), kidnapping (Terr 1983), forced separation from family members, and forced loss of country, language, religion, and culture can produce effects of catastrophic proportions (Krystal 1968a, b, Pines 1993), we do not include all kinds of traumatic experience in our study here, although we have learned from our clinical experience with all of them.

Rather, we focus on direct impact to the body in family life. We look at the effects of domestic personal violence on the child, with particular emphasis on the violence of childhood sexual abuse. We also look at impersonal violence to the body of the newborn, the child, the adolescent, and the adult in the form of sudden or massive body part destruction over which the child or adult has no control.

We define physical violence as bodily assault and the coercive use of strength to the degree that physical injury results and threats to life are made or enacted. In choosing examples of physical violence, we do not include families with a preference for physical punishment that stays within cultural norms.

We define sexual abuse as sexual interaction between any adult or bigger, stronger child and an unrelated child. When the adult is in a position of authority, the abuse is particularly exploitative. One form of childhood sexual abuse is stimulation of the child's genitals by an adult or by a bigger, stronger child, for the sexual stimulation of the perpetrator. We also include compulsive, excited enema administration and masturbation without penetration as forms of sexual abuse.

We define incest as sexual interaction between an adult relative or a bigger, stronger child and any child under 18 and see it as abusive, although not always traumatic, since trauma depends on the severity and duration of the abuse, and the reaction depends on the child's constitution. Yet, we would expect that incest would cause serious interference with development. Nonabusive incest between adult relatives may or may not be traumatic. Incest between consenting siblings who are peers tends not to last as long as with adult perpetrators and has been said to cause less damage, a finding that is now being questioned. Courtois (1988) agrees that not all technically abusive relationships are traumatic and not all traumatic relationships are technically abusive, but she cautions that the damage done by both types has been underemphasized because the victims have been unable to acknowledge their full impact. She adds that those daughters experiencing mother–child incest especially underreport their abuse to hide their breaking of two taboos, incest and homosexuality.

Personal and impersonal forms of violence to the body are alike in that the child has no control over what happens. Whether the victim of personal or impersonal violence, the child experiences similar feelings of helplessness. Dissociation and encapsulation are likely defenses in both cases. In both cases of personal or impersonal violence, when there is damage to the body, the child may assume that he or she is to blame for the occurrence and that it is punishment for badness. In either case the child may be angry at the parent who cannot prevent bad things from happening. In both cases the body is involved in processes that are beyond its control, that are part of the person's identity, and whose effects extend over the life-span. However, although the child physically damaged by impersonal violence can feel trapped in an inferior body, this feeling is qualitatively different from the entrapment, guilt, and fear of the abused child. The obvious difference is that the young person who suffers physical trauma experiences a dreadful thing that happens without family collusion and without its being paired with dependency need satisfaction and inappropriate sexual stimulation and sexualization of a caretaking relationship. The trauma of childhood sexual abuse is quite different because of the real family betrayal of trust, the secrecy, the bribes and threats, the sexualization of aggression and affection, and the accompanying level of physical abuse (Kempe and Helfer 1968, Mrazek and Kempe 1981). The child whose physical trauma is sexually abusive and incestuous suffers a repetitive situation of entrapment, assault, concealment, lack of empathy or protection, and hypocrisy by loved ones in the family (Goodwin 1985).

We also study single-shock trauma to the body without intent to exploit, along with the cumulative trauma (Khan 1963, 1964) of sexual abuse of the body, and of medical procedures, and their impact on family life.

We aim to develop a psychoanalytic theory of reaction to bodily trauma that is rooted in the body self and its elaboration through the life cycle in the families of origin and procreation. We were encouraged in our project by two edited volumes that have brought incest to the attention of psychoanalytic readers (Kramer and Akhtar 1991, Levine 1990c). Levine (1990c) presents an eclectic collection that includes Freudian, Kleinian, and Lacanian perspectives. In their edited text (Kramer and Akhtar 1991), Kramer bases her understanding of the impact of childhood sexual abuse on Mahler's developmental stages of childhood and Blos's view of adolescence, whereas Akhtar blends the views of Freud, Jacobson, and Kernberg. Each of them uses aspects of the body of theory comprising the American object relations approach. We, however, rely on a British object relations theory approach based on the conceptual framework of Ronald Fairbairn, whose work has been described by Grotstein (1992) as "the most apt and receptive model to date for our understanding of child abuse and molestation" (p. 66). Within the object relational frame provided by Fairbairn's view of the endopsychic situation, his studies of the effects of trauma, and his concepts of splitting of the object and the self, we integrate concepts from Freud, Klein, Winnicott, Bollas, J. Mitchell, and other psychoanalytic theorists. In addition, we interweave compatible, enriching concepts on human development drawn from clinical family research, infant research, trauma theory, and multiple personality studies; contributions from the child sexual abuse literature; new memory research; and feminism.

TRAUMA THEORY

As early as 1859, Briquet showed that trauma affected the brain's capacity to handle emotions. Freud (1919), Kardiner (1941), and Fairbairn (1943b) studied the impact of war from a psychoanalytic viewpoint. Working with combat veterans, Figley (1985), Van der Kolk (1987), and Horowitz (1986) found that war trauma produced stress that required crisis intervention, abreaction, deconditioning, resocialization, and longer term therapy. Kolb (1987, 1993) studied and treated patients who had been exposed to war trauma. He used the term *massive emotional trauma* to distinguish this type of trauma from the the broad range of traumatic experiences of interpersonal, social, physical, and environmental varieties that are generally subsumed under the term *massive psychic trauma*.

Post-traumatic Stress Disorder in War, Genocide, Natural Disaster, and Childhood Sexual Abuse

In those who have the predisposing factors of genetic vulnerability of the central nervous system or early childhood trauma, the symptoms of post-traumatic stress disorder may become evident and sometimes become chronic. Some researchers after the Vietnam war found that premorbid personality and pathology were less important than the nature of the trauma, the experience of it, and the meaning ascribed to it (Sonnenberg et al. 1985). Quoting from the American Psychiatric Association *Diagnostic and Statistical Manual (DSM-IV* 1994), Kolb (1993) defines the person with post-traumatic stress disorder as one who has experienced, witnessed, or been confronted with a traumatic event or events that involve actual or threatened death or serious injury, or a threat to the physical integrity of oneself or others, and who has responded with intense fear, helplessness, or horror, which in children may take the form of disorganized and agitated behavior. In combat, as opposed to genocide or natural disaster, there is the additional factor of the role stress of failing to protect colleagues who are getting killed while being authorized to produce the same and greater damage to the other side. In Vietnam, there was the added stress of the guerrilla format without zones of established levels of safety from the foe.

Combat veterans' symptoms include repetitive nightmares and daytime thoughts that reenact the trauma, dissociative flashbacks, hypervigilance, startle reactions, and arousal to stimuli that recall the trauma (Figley 1985, Van der Kolk 1987). In general, their symptoms result from traumatic destruction of their ability to screen out and process peripheral stimuli so that the self is constantly under a barrage of stimuli that are misinterpreted as threats to which they respond with primitive fear reactions. Startling auditory, visual, olfactory, and tactile stimuli produce vivid recall of the trauma, because the experience has not been processed in a symbolic/ linguistic form, but has been encoded on a sensorimotor or iconic level (Greenberg and Van der Kolk 1987). Kolb emphasizes that the startle-recall process may just as likely be produced by internal fantasy. The primitive fear reactions of fight, flight, or freezing occasionally lead to feelings of desperation and helplessness. In Kolb's view, this is when dissociation takes place.

We see a similar reaction in the adult who has been physically and sexually abused or physically damaged during development. From their study of 26 female incest victims, Donaldson and Gardner (1982, 1985) reported that all but one fulfilled the criteria for the diagnosis of post-traumatic stress disorder. Although they rarely see death, abused children do see violence and are often threatened with death or the killing of a loved one if they should tell about the abuse. The abused and damaged child experiences a threat to the integrity of the self and responds with fear, helplessness, and varying degrees of dissociation, depending on his or her age, the chronicity of the traumatic events, the degree of pain, the intensity of the fear generated, and the constitutional vulnerability.

Krystal (1968a) reviewed the effects of massive psychic trauma caused by various man-made disasters in the hope of understanding and treating the after-effects of traumatization in the milieu where it is most frequently found: the home. In their study of concentration and extermination camp survivors, Krystal and Neiderland (1968) found that there was little correlation between the severity or length of the persecution and the resulting pathology, because each person interprets the trauma in the light of his or her own psychic reality. They found that the post-trauma symptomatology of depression, masochistic surrender, inhibition of aggression and sexual vigor, and somatization is evidence of traits that were adaptive to the survivor role, which often depended on the person's willingness to adopt the compliance of a defeated slave. They also noted disturbances in cognition and memory. They found that hypermnesia (overly distinct recall) for affectively charged memories of persecution so vivid as to seem real and so persistent as to be virtually indelible occurred alongside total or partial amnesia (forgetting), vagueness of recall, and confusion. They conceptualized the underlying mental mechanism as a failure in repression, an idea that we develop further in Chapter 6.

Krystal (1985) emphasized that trauma was not experienced simply because the massiveness of the stimulus penetrated the "stimulus barrier"—the protective shield against the multitude of stimuli impinging on the ego—but because it was defined as trauma by active affective, perceptive, and cognitive processes. These processes registered the events in terms of the individual's personal subjective reality in the situation of helplessness, to which meaning was ascribed in the light of past experience and attitudes about the self. Because of this finding, he could no longer subscribe to Freud's view of a passive stimulus barrier and instead came to a sophisticated view of the stimulus barrier as an active process for information processing and selective memory storage. Unlike the child's situation in which trauma is heralded by intense affect from which the parent fails to protect the child, in the adult case trauma is apprehended cognitively, and the person's awareness of its inevitability is followed by intense affect, paralysis of intentionality, affect restriction, numbing of pain, and cognitive constriction—a state of surrender that in some cases proceeds to psychogenic death. In those post-traumatic survivors who showed alexithymia, defined as the inability to recognize and make use of emotional reactions, Krystal (1985) described a concomitant cognitive difficulty that hindered attempts at psychoanalytic treatment.

Thinking becomes "superadjusted to reality" at the expense of drive-gratification fantasy. There is an impoverishment of imagination and a preoccupation with the mundane details of everyday events. As de M'Uzan put it: "The patient's language is poor, flat and banal, glued to the present or only producing facts stated chronologically" (p. 462). One way to understand this type of functioning from the point of view of the "stimulus barrier" is that it protects the individual against the return of the previously experienced (adult-type) psychic trauma by blocking drive derivatives (Krystal 1978a,b). Similarly one's capacity for pleasure, joy, and happiness may be sacrificed— resulting in anhedonia. This is the price of simultaneously (but less successfully) blocking off the excessive intensity of pain and distress (Krystal 1978a). An incidental after-effect of the "hypertrophy" of these aspects of the "stimulus barrier" is that these individuals' capacity to utilize and benefit from psychoanalysis becomes impaired to various degrees of severity (Krystal 1978b, 1982b). [pp. 153–154.]

In other words, there is too much reaction to reality and not enough fantasy to interpret. This description applies to phenomena experienced by Bollas (1989) and illustrated in the analytic treatment of the survivor of childhood sexual abuse reported in Chapter 11. Yet, unlike Freudian instinct or structural theory, the object relational perspective, which was not developed by Krystal, offers an analytic way of working with these cases by (1) experiencing the reality of trauma and the failure of the child's holding environment within the analytic relationship and (2) then interpreting the fantasy elaborations and the personal meaning ascribed to the trauma without denying its reality or reconfiguring it unhelpfully in terms of oedipal fantasy.

After becoming aware of a conspicuous silence on the subject of sexual abuse during internment, Krystal and Neiderland renewed their inquiries and found previously unreported cases of rape in women who had already been identified as the sickest women in their cohort. Krystal and Neiderland's (1968) experience informs our study of survivors of physical and sexual abuse. We find the same conspiracy of silence. Adult survivors of childhood sexual abuse show the same features of hypermnesic and vague recall as have been noted in Holocaust survivors. Like Krystal and Neiderland's survivors, they adapt to save their sanity and their lives.

Adult survivors of childhood physical or sexual abuse are humiliated yet special, and they suffer from society's projective identification of them as traitors, harlots, co-habitators of the enemy, and ultimately as the ghosts of the perpetrators. No wonder they have been loathe to speak out. Yet, traumatized people do recover, become able to recall the trauma when they want to or need to, can talk about it when it is helpful to themselves or others, and are capable of thinking about other things as well (Horowitz 1986).

MULTIPLE PERSONALITY STUDIES

Multiple personality is a psychoneurotic condition of the hysterical dissociative type. The condition has been known and vividly described since the turn of the century (Franz 1933, Prince 1906, Thigpen and Cleckley 1957) and has sometimes been treated psychoanalytically (Lasky 1978, Silvio 1993). Thigpen and Cleckley (1957) traced the onset of multiplicity in their famous patient "Eve" to a trauma at the age of 5 when Eve was forced to touch her dead grandmother's face. They reported dream material and drawings that to us are suggestive of sexual trauma or overstimulation of oedipal wishes, but they were so adamant about the folly of dynamic interpretation that no trauma antecedent to the obvious one was uncovered, and oedipal strivings toward the grandparents or parents were not well elaborated.

Recent studies of large samples have related multiplicity to a history of abuse in childhood (Kluft 1985). Not all cases of child abuse lead to multiple personality, but most people with multiple personality disorder have been physically brutalized, psychologically assaulted, sexually violated, and psychologically overwhelmed (Kluft 1985, Wilbur 1984). In sexually abusing families, Kluft and colleagues (1984) reported that the parents' marital relationship is usually one of three types. The parents either preserve a pseudonormal veneer, they are in open conflict of massive extent, or one is overadequate and the other underadequate as a parent. In many cases, the authors found numerous parallels between the inner psychic structure of the multiple personality patient and her family of origin. Growing up in families characterized by secrecy, isolation, and a veneer of pseudonormality, with boundaries too rigid for intimacy and too emmeshed for autonomy, the abused child develops a personality in which parts of the self remain secret from others and are isolated from central integration. The subpersonalities are incomplete, the one without the other, and, again like the families of origin, they resort to internal collusions, coalitions, and exploitations of other alters. Study of multiple personality gives us a unique window into the processes of dissociation in personality formation and a graphic portrayal of dissociation as a defense against trauma.

In the laboratory situation, patients with dissociative disorders are considerably more hypnotizable than the general population, and those with untreated multiplicity also show a greater incidence of the hidden observer phenomenon (Hilgard 1977, 1984) than patients in other diagnostic categories (Kluft 1986). The *hidden observer* phenomenon refers to the experience of subjects who respond in a characteristic way to a particular series of stimuli in a hypnosis experiment. These subjects who show the hidden observer phenomenon feel pain normally in response to a painful stimulus in the first situation. After hypnotic suggestion for analgesia, they feel no pain in response to an identical stimulus in the second situation. Finally, in the third situation, after suggestion that a hidden part of them is still aware of the pain that the hypnotized part cannot feel, they report levels of pain similar to those experienced before hypnosis. From this finding, Hilgard (1977) concluded that information could be processed at different levels of awareness simultaneously. This conclusion supports two clinical findings: (1) that alternate personalities in multiplicity can have separate memory banks with no transfer between them or possibly selective, two-way, and more commonly one-way transfer, and (2) that a person can operate in different levels of ego awareness.

In the real-life situation, by switching into a state of autohypnosis, the child, and later the adult, can remove herself from the trauma (Frischolz 1985, Silber 1979). Relaxation, calm, numbness, and a feeling of disappearance replace the horror of terror, but leave the person in a state of reduced motility and helplessness. The resulting degree of passivity and compliance is apparently adaptive for survival if it does not also lead to psychic death. Study of multiple personality and related dissociative phenomena reveals one of the most extreme reactions to trauma in relation to which we can develop a theory of a continuum of adaptive responses.

Putnam and Cole (1992) have studied dissociative phenomena at various developmental levels and have reported a continuum of dissociative response ranging from the normal and adaptive level to the extremely pathological from which multiple personality results. From his experience with 100 cases of multiple personality disorder, Putnam (Putnam et al. 1986) concluded that, next to physical violence in the family and sexual abuse by nonfamily members, incest is the most common type of childhood trauma reported retrospectively in these cases. Putnam and Cole (1992) describe incest as a disturbance in a primary relationship that has foci of unwarranted sexual contact. It causes a sense of violation to the self, fear, guilt, and, most of all, a loss of the sense of personal safety as a background condition that a child should be able to take for granted. It interferes with self-development, compromises physical and psychological integrity, and disrupts the regulation of affect and impulse control (Putnam 1990, 1993).

Putnam (1994) describes dissociation as a specific, adaptive, dynamic response to trauma. He finds that children are more liable to dissociate than adults, because the ability to dissociate tends to disappear in latency. Access to dissociation as a defense is equally available to boys as to girls, and yet at later stages of life, men with multiple personality are found less often than women, a finding that suggests that women as a group are more likely to experience the extremes of dissociative response with global spatial fragmentation than are men. Global spatial fragmentation as a defensive pattern follows abuse that occurred at an earlier age (D. Spiegel 1984). The tendency to multiple personality (the most developed set of global spatial defenses) forms in a developmental window as a result of childhood sexual abuse that occurred before the age of 8, usually between the ages of 3 and 8 (Putnam 1991), even though multiple personality is not manifest until late adolescence. Kluft (1984a), however, reports that there are more cases of multiplicity in childhood than was previously realized. Herman (1981) emphasizes that most but not all survivors of childhood sexual abuse use dissociative defenses. She has found that whereas most survivors become proficient in the use of trance, "some develop a kind of 'dissociative virtuosity'" (Herman 1992, p. 102). From Putnam's graphic yet scientific report of the extreme outcome of severe incestuous experience, we can learn about the defense of dissociation that is central to developing a psychoanalytic understanding of responses to personal bodily trauma affecting the genitals, other body parts, and inevitably the self.

THE DEFENSIVE PURPOSES AND CONSEQUENCES OF DISSOCIATION

Putnam (1991) describes how dissociation isolates the catastrophic experience and allows the central self to escape from pain and from reality. There is an alteration in the self and a detachment of the self from the painful aspect of the necessary object relationship. Irreconcilable conflicts between love and hate and between need and fear of the important but abusing object are shelved in a place that is sequestered from consciousness and kept away from other repressed parts of the self. Instead of resolution, there is disowning of conflict within the parts of the self in order to go on being as a self. Dissociation as a conditioned defensive reaction has a number of consequences. Putnam particularly notes interference with a sense of unity of the self and disturbances of memory and identity. Regulation of mood and of impulsivity is inconsistent. Perceptions are doubted, memory is discontinuous, and memory for other events may be unreliable too because of the spreading of dissociative responses to the entire process of information storage.

MEMORY RESEARCH FINDINGS

Childhood amnesia for events before 3 or 4 years of age is a normal phenomenon. Schachtel (1947) thought that we cannot recall early childhood, because our thought structures—also called schemata or frames of interpretation of experience—at the time of recall do not match those that were in ascendancy at the time the event was experienced or encoded. The location of involuntary memory is not in consciousness, but is in the soma, giving rise to a "memory of the body" (Schachtel 1947, p. 22). In adulthood the symbolic/linguistic mode of operational thought is dominant and is not up to the task of decoding memories that were stored in the enactive/iconic/sensorimotor mode of the preoperational stage of learning that Piaget (1936) described. In addition, memory is more vulnerable than perception to the effects of socialization, which results in a conventionalizing of the memory. Greenberg and Van der Kolk (1987) agree that memories that do not fit into the expected cultural pattern are usually dissociated.

Based on the work of Piaget and Inhelder (Piaget 1936), amplified by the explosion of research based on an information processing model, in the 1970s memory was described *as a computer* with the tasks of acquisition, encoding, storage, and retrieval by recognition, reconstruction, or recall (Fivush 1993b, Perry 1992). In acquisition the task is to perceive, pay attention, perceive again, interpret what is seen, and order it in relation to earlier perceptions. Then the memory is encoded and stored in the right place for future access. The research of the 1970s used list-learning tasks that were easy to control in the laboratory. Preschool children who do not remember in words but in pictures, and who cannot remember sequences, did poorly at this task of deliberate memory. Yet, the conclusion that their memory is poor resulted from an artifact of the test situation.

Later in the 1980s, research that focused on event recall tasks appropriate to the interests and cognitive style of young children showed that they could give accurate, detailed accounts of their past, but had difficulty distinguishing any one occurrence from others in the series, because the event tended to become generalized according to the script of previous experience. Thus, *autobiographical memory* is learned in social interaction and is best developed when parents talk to their children about the past and develop narratives about their children's history in the family in a dialectical process of co-construction (Fivush 1993a, Nelson 1993b). The child needs the verbal person's representation of the experience in words to develop a memory recounting that serves the purpose of reinstating the original experience (Nelson 1993a). The resulting autobiographical memory is also best remembered in a similar interpersonal context.

Retrieval by recognition is used by younger children, and so they need questions to stimulate memory recall. They cannot provide a coherent, full account on their own (Fivush 1993a). They are not likely to remember as having happened events that did not take place, and their errors mainly reflect a tendency to omit information, not to make it up (Steward 1993). If they took part in the events they are trying to remember, children have better recall for them (Faller 1992). Even in preschoolers, spontaneous recall of the details of daily life is excellent, but they cannot remember the sequences accurately. They cannot put into words memories of events that were experienced in the first year of life. Stress may not affect memory formation unless the child is actually being intimidated. Older children's recall is as good as adults (Perry 1992).

These findings have implications for obtaining testimony from children and evaluating its veracity in courts of law. Children can give excellent testimony that remains accurate over many interviews. Although Loftus (1992) believes that children's memories are readily supplemented and confused by new information, Fivush (1993a) thinks that the research does not show this to be the case. Current research continues to yield more sophisticated models of childhood memory (D. Siegel 1993).

Rummelhart and McLelland's *Parallel Distributed Processing Systems* Model

Researchers now think that human memory does not work like a computer operating on binary digital logic and responding to "save" and "find" commands. Rather, human learning and memory seem to operate like a network of *parallel, distributed processing systems*, allowing for autonomous and sometimes dissociated functioning of different elements (McClelland and Rummelhart 1985, Rummelhart and McClelland 1986, D. Spiegel 1990). Related sets of information are stored independently of each other, and so incompatible memories can be held simultaneously by noncommunicating units after processing. Unlike the computer, the human being's memory is affected by developmental considerations, context, emotion, and the cognitive capacity to reflect upon what is being learned and to collate the stored narrative of memories as a sense of self (D. Siegel 1993).

After trauma, we can imagine that one set of processors in the network, overburdened by the weight, rate, and volume of pain, terror, and humiliation, might fail to register specific painful information while other sets continue the related processing tasks. This theory of memory accounts for dissociation between memories held by different parts of the self and allows for the importance of partial information that is not integrated by an overarching global knowledge (D. Spiegel 1990).

Levine's Levels of Memory

In M. D. Levine's model, there are four levels of memory: registration, active working memory, consolidation, and retrieval (M. D. Levine 1992). Problems in the area of registration show up as symptoms of inattention to events and facts and inconsistent short-term memory for them. When active working memory is disturbed, the child in school has trouble remembering while reading or computing a series of numbers. Difficulties with consolidation result in inconsistent long-term recall and general disorganization. Blocked retrieval processes cause slow recall of information that leads to problems in writing and doing mathematics. One level of memory functioning may work well while another is impaired. For instance, a child may remember verbal information well but have poor recall for visuospatial material, another may not register the material, and still another may record the information but not have access to it, either soon after or later on (Krener 1993).

The child who has been sexually abused may register the situation in the visuospatial form so that it can be recalled in pictures but not words. Sometimes the child prefers not to know of the trauma and actively inhibits the registration process. This inhibition may be selective, sparing the registration process for successful registration of other information important to the child's learning tasks. However, more commonly it spreads to a general inhibition of registration so that the child has trouble learning at school. Some children register the facts of their abuse, but problems in the working memory prevent their having access to the information soon after. Others who record experiences separately each time fail to consolidate the material so that they are not overwhelmed by the cumulative nature of the trauma. Then some others may have accurate registration, working memory, and consolidation, but defensive functions inhibit recall until the ego is strong enough to bear the knowledge that has been out of awareness.

The More Cognitive/Less Cognitive Dichotomy

Krener (in press) summarized the division of memory into more and less cognitive retention processes, as hypothesized by Tulving (1972), Schacter (1989), Cohen and Squire (1980), and Pillemer and White (1989). According to those researchers, the more cognitive processes form semantic/explicit/declarative/language-based memory. This form of memory is conscious, language based, and destroyed by damage to the corticolimbic system and hippocampus. The less cognitive form has been called episodic/implicit/procedural/experience-based memory that is verbalized with difficulty and reveals itself in demonstrated knowledge as skill behaviors.

Multiple Entry Modular Memory

Multiple entry modular memory is a model that views memory as both a processing and a subsystem organization (Johnson and Hirst 1992). The child's perception and reflection about the perception are both influenced by context and emotion, and both are elements of the memory that is encoded. The state of mind at the time of encoding affects the likelihood of later retrieval.

First and Second Memory Systems

Pillemer and White (1989) proposed a theory of *first and second memory systems*. The first memory system operates at birth in response to people, places, and feelings. The memories stored there are iconic and are accessed through images and experiences that recall the earlier time. The second memory system develops after language acquisition and stores experiences in narrative forms, and so they can be reached by words. Overwhelming trauma may be stored in the first memory system, even in the verbally sophisticated older child or adult who normally principally uses the second system (Steward 1992).

Implicit/Explicit Memory

Memories for facts and events are explicit memories that are easily accessible to consciousness. Implicit memories cannot be recognized or recalled consciously, but they are inferred from behavior that proves that the relevant information has been learned and stored. For instance, neurologically impaired amnesics cannot learn and acquire memory for new facts or events, yet they can learn new skills (Squire 1986, 1987, 1992). In other words, they have impaired explicit memory but good implicit memory, sometimes also called procedural knowledge (Cohen and Squire 1980). Although they cannot explicitly remember learning something or remember what they learned, implicit memory functions to improve their performance on processing information. Some aspects of implicit memory are as reliable in preschoolers as they are in adults (Clyman 1993). According to Emde and colleagues (1991), many emotionally engaging infant experiences are stored as procedural knowledge that is not accessible to consciousness under ordinary conditions.

TRAUMA AND RECALL

Now we have a view of the abused child as having an explicit, verbally based narrative self and an implicit, iconic, procedurally competent self. Analysis conducted in the verbal, narrative realm cannot reach memories stored in the implicit system. It cannot recover memories by undoing repression that did not occur. Instinctual conflict that might have been experienced as a result of loyalty to the objects and that might have led to repression is totally overwhelmed by the real danger of annihilation in the unsafety of familial betrayal. The therapist of the traumatized patient is faced with absent explicit memories and cannot rely on the patient's narrative self or psychoanalytic interpretation of repression of instinctual conflict to retrieve them. So the therapist has to infer memory and experience from silence, absence, and gesture—and from observed procedural behavior in the transference and in the countertransference. With the concept of procedural knowledge, we can justify the cultivation of transference as an excellent tool for gathering information from the implicit memory system.

Retrospective studies have shown that childhood sexual abuse was more common than supposed, and yet the likelihood is that its incidence is still underreported and inadequately remembered. Briere (1992b) allowed that, in some cases where the abuse was enjoyed or brought desired privilege, the memory may be repressed to avoid instinctual conflict, guilt, and shame, but that in other cases dissociation is the necessary defense against re-experiencing the anxiety triggered by the memory of the actual abuse. He agreed with Herman and Schatzow (1987) that, when the abuse is experienced as violent and painful, dissociation is most likely. Then memory for the abuse may be incomplete or absent to avoid the reality of experiencing continuing actual distress. In her prospective study of 200 women identified from hospital records as having reported being sexually abused when children in the 1970s, Williams (1992) reported that 38 percent of these women did not remember or chose not to admit to the report of childhood sexual abuse when interviewed years later.

Many therapists have addressed the issue of false memories. Loftus (1992) argued that there is not enough clinical evidence to support the hypotheses that memories have been repressed because they are unpleasant and that if they can be retrieved years later, they will then be credible. Holmes (1990) concludes that 60 years of research have failed to document the mechanism of repression. Dissociation seems to be the more likely explanation for absent memories that are either not formed, are lost, or remain in one ego state to which the rest of the self has no access. Krener (in press) makes the point that, under the force of suggestion and peer pressure in the adult cultural context, dissociation may operate equally well to construct false memories that result from suggestion and cannot be corroborated. She also reminds us that, although later revisions, integrations, and narrativization of memories by the growing and adapting brain usefully enable reconstruction of experience that was perceived but not stored as comprehensible information at the time of the trauma, they also enable a confounding, reworking, and falsifying of recall (Steward 1993).

When in a single dangerous situation, called a Type I trauma

(Terr 1991), children experience a narrowing of the usual perceptual and memory processes, at least until they get used to the danger or have reason to think that their actions can make a difference to what happens to them (Krener in press). There is no psychic numbing, no flashbacks, and no amnesia. On the contrary, children remember the whole event with extraordinary clarity (Terr 1991) and repeat the narrative to themselves and others, but they do have a limited view of the future. In contrast, a recurrent trauma, called a Type II trauma (Terr 1991), is remembered in a spotty way with no clear image of the whole. Self-numbing, self-hypnosis, denial, dissociation, helpless rage, and mute surrender characterize the child's attempts at self-defense. There is no repetition and rehearsal space, no co-construction of a narrative, and no capacity to develop a specific memory. No wonder the survivor of abuse may have vague recall, or memories that surface years later in response to an image that resonates with early, diffuse images and leads to their retrieval in narrative form (Terr 1988, 1994).

In this chapter, we have reviewed the accumulating research information on childhood memory to find a working model for the retrieval of abuse experience in therapy. This information enhances our understanding of the child's vulnerability and need to distort and compartmentalize early experience through exaggerating normal dissociative mechanisms and emphasizing the implicit memory system. Cumulative traumatic events are stored in the implicit memory system where they cannot be accessed by words that are the currency of the adult survivor and the therapist. Access through the transference and countertransference can yield images that connect with others in the iconic format of the first memory system for people and place. As therapist and patient explore images and bodily sensation, the narrative self brings words to the task. A visuospatial reconstruction of what must have happened is then conceptualized in words. As the capacity for symbol formation begins to develop, dreams and fantasies become possible and give further access to unconscious material. This process is illustrated in the case of Wendy Sheldon in Chapter 13 and Mrs. Feinstein in Chapter 11.

3

Freudian and Object Relations Perspectives

EARLY VIEWS ON HYSTERIA: FREUD

Freud found that psychical trauma was the basis of hysterical and neurotic symptoms. He arrived at this conclusion from his investigation of the phenomena of hysteria in which he originally used hypnotic trance induction to de-repress unconscious material locked in physical symptomatology. He then shifted to the technique of forced association. He put his hand on the patient's brow and suggested that the pressure would force a flow of thoughts to conscious speech. He learned that hysterical symptoms were bodily expressions that occurred when feelings of distress had become disconnected from the thoughts that accompanied them during a traumatic moment of a sexual nature. Such a traumatic moment usually occurred during puberty, when sexual desire was maximally stimulated and denied natural expression because of the impropriety of the circumstances. The impropriety most frequently recalled under hypnosis and forced association was that of seduction by a family member or caretaking adult. He claimed that therapeutic catharsis of the repressed affect appropriate to the trauma was enough to eliminate the physical symptomatology.

Later, Freud found that simply requesting the patient to report whatever came to mind produced an equally informative flow, and he then turned exclusively to this new method that he called free association. Now he discovered that the traumatic memory dating from puberty linked not only to other related memories but that the chain of memories also led to memories of sexual abuse from as far back as 2 years of age.

At the same time, Freud was analyzing dreams and discovering a royal road to the unconscious (Freud 1900). From his self-analysis of his own dreams and mild hysterical symptoms, he concluded that his original ideas about a perpetrator in his family were erroneous. Freud's personal prototype of a false memory was not substantiated and so led him to his brilliant deduction of the ubiquity of polymorphous perverse sexual longings and the power of oedipal fantasy as distorting influences on the recall of childhood experience. When Freud turned away from sexual seduction as the inevitable source of trauma, he stopped investigating it as a principal source of pathology, even though he continued to feel that "seduction retains a certain aetiological significance" (footnote 1924 in Freud 1896b). Following his lead, the field of psychoanalysis turned toward the vissicitudes of the sexual instinct in neurotic symptom formation and away from the actuality of sexual abuse at a time in society when it was a taboo subject and might have hampered acceptance of Freud's more universally applicable theories of psychosexual development, the fantasy of the primal scene, and the family romance of the oedipal stage.

Now that those theories are integrated into the culture, we can usefully go back to explore the relevance of what Freud wrote about trauma, infantile sexual experience, and how to defend our belief in the veracity of our patients' recall. Proceeding from the work of the famous French neurologist Charcot on the traumatic paralyses, Freud developed the argument as follows (1893c, d). When a physical trauma affects a person who is constitutionally predisposed by heredity to develop a hysterical reaction, that person may later develop a paralysis that represents a feared injury to the body that is out of proportion to the actual injury that occurred. A hypnotic suggestion may similarly induce the paralysis or remove it in the same subject. From this, Charcot concluded that if the trauma produced physically can also be produced verbally, then the original paralysis was due to an idea that occurred at the time of the trauma, providing the individual is hereditarily inclined to develop a hysterical reaction and enters a hypnotic state of mind in response to the trauma.

From his experience working with Breuer on the hypnotic therapy of hysterical women patients, Freud went on to formulate the thesis that *"there is a complete analogy between traumatic paralysis and common, nontraumatic hysteria"* (1893c, pp. 30–31, italics in original). By nontraumatic hysteria, he meant those cases in which there was no single physical trauma, but there was an emotional trauma or, more commonly, a series of traumatic affective experiences. When no reaction of physical or verbal outrage was possible, the memory retains the original affect that pertained at the time of the trauma. From this he argued that what produces the paralysis after physical trauma is the "affect of fright, the *psychical* trauma" (p. 31). He found that the bodily symptom expressed the mental state as a symbolization of the mental one that obtained at the time of the trauma. In short, hysterical patients were thought to suffer from psychical traumas that had been incompletely abreacted, usually for one of three reasons: they were so severe as to overwhelm the mental apparatus and obliterate more usual defenses; they occurred in circumstances where reaction was impossible for social reasons, as for example in married life; or they occurred in the course of some other intense affect.

With considerable courage, armed with reports of childhood intercourse in the pediatric literature (Stekel 1895) and fortified by receiving confirmation of abuse histories from perpetrator or co-victim, Freud asserted that *"no hysterical symptom can arise from a real experience alone, but that in every case the memory of earlier experiences awakened in association to it plays a part in causing the symptom . . . without exception"* (Freud 1896b, p. 197, italics in original). *"In the end we infallibly come to the field of sexual experience"* (p. 199), and "at the bottom of every case of hysteria there are *one or more occurrences of premature sexual experience"* (p. 203). Freud even challenges Charcot's concept of the hereditary basis for the constitutional vulnerability to hysteria that he had promoted in 1893 as a necessary condition for the development of hysteria. He asks us to consider that there may be only a *"pseudoheredity"* where "in fact what has taken place is a handing-on, an infection of childhood" (p. 209) among the younger generation of a family with poor sexual boundaries. He extends his argument to conclude that "the aetiological role of infantile sexual experience is not confined to hysteria but holds good equally for the remarkable neurosis of obsessions, and perhaps also, indeed, for the various forms of paranoia and other functional psychoses" (p. 219).

One reason for returning to Freud's formulations, now over a hundred years old, is to resurrect the psychoanalytic integration of neurophysiological responses to actual trauma with predisposing factors of constitution, family dynamics and sexual boundary-keeping, previous traumatization, and the use of the hypnoid state as a necessary defense in exceptional circumstances. His juxtaposition of physical and psychical trauma for the purpose of using each to amplify his understanding of the other supports our idea of studying cases of cumulative sexual or physical abuse side-by-side with cases of single-shock physical trauma to the body as we work toward an object relational theory of trauma. Freud's realization that the commitment of married life may impose a restraint on the abreaction of feelings at times of trauma reminds us that he was aware of the trauma-inducing and trauma-maintaining function of current object relationships, an insight that we extend to apply to the even more massive restraint that a dependent child feels because of a life-supporting commitment to parents, however abusive they may be.

How dare the abused child speak out against a caretaker? Who knows what retaliation might follow? Abuse may be the only expression of physical contact that the child receives. It may be argued that some children who have known only an abusive culture may not know that sexual abuse is not right (Gardner 1992). However, at least in the clinical population that we have seen, the child who has not dissociated what has been going on realizes from threats, guilty feelings, and natural revulsion that things are not right. In the case of the child who does dissociate—because of the severity of the trauma, the predisposing affective experiences, and the constitutional tendency to dissociate—it is as if the abuse is not happening at all.

Finkelhor and Browne (1985) outline four traumatogenic factors in childhood sexual abuse: traumatic sexualization of dependent behaviors, betrayal of dependency needs by the significant other, powerlessness to effect his or her own will, and stigmatization experienced indirectly from the atmosphere of secrecy. More traumatic than the element of traumatic physical pain (which may not occur, especially if there is no penetration) and the expectable fear of aggression is the occurrence of premature sexual arousal in the highly affective state of childish love for parents. The ensuing feelings of guilt, shame, lack of control over events, and the child's reactions to them are damaging to the executive functions of the self and to self-esteem. Most hurtful of all, as Anna Freud (1981) points out, is the betrayal of family trust.

THE REALITY OF INCEST: ANNA FREUD

Although trained by her father, and fully in agreement with his views on the Oedipus complex, oedipal fantasy, and the primal scene, Anna Freud did not share his ambivalence about the reality of incest. Probably because she worked with children and supervised child psychotherapists who worked in various clinic and school settings, Anna Freud (1967) gave due attention to the traumatic reality of incest and rated it more damaging than neglect, abandonment, and physical abuse. Simon (1992) has suggested that she was also sensitized to it by her analogous experience of having been analyzed by her father. If Simon's assertion is correct, her comments (A. Freud 1981) regarding the impact of betrayal within the family seem all the more poignant.

THE TRAUMATIC-HYSTERICAL BASIS
OF NEUROSIS: FERENCZI

Ferenczi (1929a,b) challenged Freud's rejection of the seduction hypothesis. He thought that psychoanalysis had gone too far toward an ego-psychological approach and had forgotten the organic-hysterical basis of symptomatology. He maintained that this regrettable state resulted from overestimating the role of fantasy and underestimating the role of traumatic reality in pathogenesis. So far, this sounds like a useful corrective that might have been accepted as such by Freud. Yet, Ferenczi stated categorically that in all cases there was a traumatic-hysterical basis for the neurosis, and his results with former patients who had been recalled for further exploratory work proved it. In addition to restating a position that Freud had abandoned years earlier, Ferenczi was experimenting with introducing touch and mutual discussion between patient and analyst and in general changing the rule of analytic neutrality to correct the power imbalance between patient and analyst, whose silence, by being too similar to the original silence of the perpetrator, may have been inhibiting recall of abuse. Ferenczi's technical innovations, tainted by his boundary problems with such patients as his mistress's daughter, and his certainty about the ubiquity of incest may have been the crucial elements that prevented assimilation of his point of view.

Nevertheless, he was able to allow his patients to express material that others did not evoke at a time in history when the topic was not acceptable. Simon (1992) thinks that Ferenczi's findings are still relevant to contemporary analysts working with the effects of childhood sexual abuse. He sees confirmation of his clinical descriptions in current examples of analyses of incest survivors (Levine 1990c). We are particularly interested in Simon's (1992) observation of Ferenczi:

> His clinical findings include many observations and inferences about split-off parts of the person, altered states of consciousness, repeated highly emotional relivings of the various traumas, and the somatic manifestations of the repressed traumatic memories. He insists on the necessity that the analyst believe in their actuality in order to persist in the attempt to reconstruct and recover these memories. [p. 974]

In his widely quoted paper (1933b) Ferenczi takes the discussion of seduction a step further to include distortions of physical affection between parents and children. Even in cases that do not qualify technically as abuse, the child may express and seek affection from a parent, but if the resulting touch or look is infused with adult sexual passion, a sexualization of the child's experience occurs and sexual fantasy is stimulated. His case reports and discussions (1933a) together with his paper (1933b) go beyond drive theory to develop an interpersonal understanding of how excessive drive behavior results not from an excess of energy but from shaping by parental behavior. Sadly, Ferenczi's work was contaminated by his compulsion to project the abused and unloved child within himself into his patients and to fall into an idealized rescuing countertransference. Yet, his intense need to repair the damage he felt that he had done to his mother led him to extraordinary insights and explorations of countertransference traps with survivors of abuse. We find that Ferenczi was trying to develop a nonhierarchical, interactional, relational field for examination by him and his patients, and in so doing he was moving toward an object relational perspective.

UNRESOLVED RAPPROCHEMENT CRISIS
IN INCEST: MAHLER

Several theorists have applied Mahler's theory of the developmental stage of separation-individuation to understanding the damage caused by incest. Foremost among them, Kramer and Akhtar (1991) applied Mahlerian concepts to the psychotherapy of male and female adult patients abused as children. Fisher (1991) traced the problems faced by sexually abused adults to a specific subphase of the separation-individuation stage of development in Mahler's schema, namely rapprochement. When the abusive or bystanding mother has not been libidinally available to the child for comfort, sustenance, and love, she cannot be internalized as a reassuring figure. The internal image of the mother is not whole, and therefore she is not there to be left. The child's destructive rage turns the mother into a bad mother image from which a good image is kept apart. This preserves a split-off sense of goodness and safety that allows the child to carry on being, but the child remains tied to the internal representation of the bad mother. The crisis of the rapprochement subphase cannot be resolved, and the child cannot individuate. Ambivalence and rage have to be denied to preserve a semblance of a good internal parent. Fisher believed that this is the reason for the need for secrecy, lack of recall, memory that is only somatic, and lack of affect of incest victims. Kramer (1985) noted a lack of self-object differentiation in women sexually abused by their mothers. Unlike obsessional women who simply doubt their experience and halt between two opinions, these women doubted their own perceptions and attempted to coerce the therapist into taking one side of the conflict and stating that as fact. Kramer called this "object-coercive doubting," a phenomenon that she has seen only in women abused by their mothers. We demonstrate the same phenomenon in the case of Mrs. Feinstein presented in Chapter 11.

PSYCHOSOMATIC APPROACHES

Clinical research on the psyche-soma bears upon our understanding of the psychological impact of overwhelming physical sensations on the growing child.

THE SKIN EGO: ANZIEU

Anzieu (1989) described several functions of the skin. It is a sac around the body that has a physical purpose of protecting the body against aggression from outside forces. Its elaborate signaling system warns of the dangers of heat, cold, pressure, vibration, and pain and communicates pleasure, pain, and distress to others by flushing, pallor, pilerection (hairs standing on end, goosebumps) inflammation, and disease. In psychological terms, the sac keeps the inside in and the outside out; it establishes barriers, it contains goodness, and it is a surface through which to experience contact with others and on which to inscribe the resulting relationships. It "underlies the very possibility of thought" (Anzieu 1989, p. 41). Its repair is attended to by the dream function. Following Freud who emphasized that "the ego is first and foremost a body ego" (Freud 1923, p. 26), Anzieu developed the idea of a skin ego serving nine functions for the psyche, eight of them constructive and the ninth destructive to the self. Anzieu's (1989) functions of the skin ego can be paraphrased as follows:

1. Maintaining the psyche as an extension of maternal holding
2. Containing it as an extension of passive and active aspects of maternal handling
3. Protecting it
4. Individuating the self (by color, texture, value, race, etc.)
5. Associating sensory input (when different sensations connect within the general sense of touch)
6. Supporting sexual excitation (after being invested with pleasure by the mother)
7. Recharging the libido (from sensorimotor external stimulation)
8. Registering information about the world (received in sensory traces)
9. Attacking the psyche by burning, itching, and disintegrating

In early life, the infant learns the shape of the self by appreciating sensations impinging on the skin. These sensations enable infants to learn their boundaries before they comprehend fully the otherness of their caretakers (Bick 1968, 1986, Ogden 1989, Tustin 1984). From the repeating patterns of sensory stimulation of the skin, the infant learns to appreciate the rhythm of safety (Tustin 1984, 1986). We extend Anzieu's idea of the skin to include the mucosa, those moist surfaces that line the mouth and the gastrointestinal tract, as well as the nose, the airways, the vagina, and the urethra. The infant may actually be more aware of internal, mucosal sensations of warmth, sweetness, fluidity, and fullness or hunger emanating from the intake of milk than external skin sensation in the first few months when the pain barrier is still operating. Ogden (1989) has called the psychic organization at this stage of life the *autistic-contiguous position*, "a sensory-dominated mode in which the most inchoate sense of self is built upon the rhythm of sensation" (p. 31). Anxiety from this stage of life involves disintegration of the sensory surface, "resulting in fears of leaking, dissolving, disappearing, or falling into boundless space" (Ogden 1989, p. 68). Having a reliable mother transforms this anxiety.

People who have been abused often experience the mother as a void, a boundless and unprotective space, like the terrifying mother of infancy who cannot protect from disintegration anxiety. The child experiences his or her own body as a boundless space whose skin is not intact. The child whose skin is touched or penetrated erotically and aggressively by a parent or family member experiences a violation of the skin and mucosal surfaces. This rupture cannot be repaired by the dream function—or by thought—because dreaming and symbolic thinking have been invaded too. Even if maternal care in infancy has been good, its derivatives in the skin function of maintaining and containing the psyche are now ruined, and there is a retrospective emptying out of good maternal experience. The inappropriately stimulated external and internal surfaces reverberate with pain and sometimes horrible pleasure that obliterate discrimination between types of sensation. The tactile traces that are registered provide a narrow view of the world as the margins of safety shrink. The individuality that the surface lends to the self is limited by the sensory impressions of him- or herself that the child receives from the perpetrator.

No wonder that children whose whole self is not protected by the integrity of their skin and mucosa and who are capable of dissociation choose to protect themselves by creating multiple skins inside themselves to isolate and protect the separate sets of their personality. They may project the psyche outside the skin so that they "aren't there" when the trauma recurs, or may divide inside themselves into a part that is victimized and a part that survives and is able to go on being as if life were safe enough and the skin an effective barrier. Often they foreclose the psyche's experience of disintegration anxiety by locating it in physical experience when words are not available to contain the trauma and modify the affect. Psychosomatic illness is used to effect survival of the psyche, even though the form of the disease may be paradoxically life threatening, because at least a body that suffers is still alive (McDougall 1989).

In the abused patient, fantasies of a damaged skin may both draw attention to and defend against recognizing fundamental damage to the psyche. Compensatory fantasies of a special skin parallel the abused child's gratification from being singled out and defend against feeling totally worthless. Fantasies of a shared skin develop in women abused by their mothers. Guilt after incest may be expressed as a hatred of the skin surface from which impurities are to be purged by excessive washing or squeezing of acne pustules in a relentless, hopeless ritual.

We view the skin as a visible part of the body that signals emotions and on which relationship histories are inscribed. As object relations therapists, we add that the skin, like any other organ, may be used as a projection screen onto which internal object relationships from the self and from the other may be projected.

Therapy may be viewed as providing a second skin to buffer the psyche against disintegration anxiety while trauma is being addressed.

THE CLOSED SYSTEM: FAIRBAIRN

Fairbairn, who eventually formulated an object relations theory of the personality, had worked earlier in his career with children who were subjected to sexual assault. His earlier writings on this topic are less well known because he did not include them in his collected papers (Fairbairn 1952). Review of these papers and of his thesis for the degree of Doctor of Medicine at Edinburgh University, recently published for the first time (Scharff and Birtles 1994b), yields some early psychoanalytic insight into the effects of childhood sexual abuse and the process of dissociation. We now realize that Fairbairn's later development of object relations theory, deriving as it does from awareness of the importance of trusting, good-enough early experiences with the mother and father, owes more than was realized to his clinical experience with childhood sexual abuse.

The theory of dynamic internal object relations that Fairbairn developed is specifically helpful in understanding the effect of trauma on the developing personality. His central idea, that the child's most fundamental need is to be in a relationship with the parents, is clearly relevant to understanding the child's compliance with abuse. His idea that psychic structure forms from the internalization of the child's good-enough experience of that relationship, and the splitting and repression of its frustrating or exciting aspects along with the corresponding parts of his or her ego and the associated affects, is relevant to our understanding of the splits in the self found in the survivor of abuse. The need for relatedness is a far more important organizing factor in human motivation and psychic structure than the force of the drives of sex and aggression that Freud used to explain instinctual tension and the need for its discharge; Freud in turn placed the responsibility for sexual and aggressive fantasy and action firmly with the child and not the corrupt and neglectful parents.

Fairbairn's theory (1994) postulated a six-part structure of the normal personality (Figure 3-1), consisting of sub-units of self and object and the relevant affects organized into three systems by the mechanisms of splitting and repression. We discuss these mechanisms fully in Chapter 6.

The *central ego* has the ideal or good-enough object as the object of its interests and interactions, in relation to which it experiences feelings of satisfaction, confidence, enjoyment, and positive expectations. The better the experience with the parents, the more ideal is the object and the less of it requires repression. This self-object-affect system, the central ego-object relationship, remains largely in consciousness. In this case, a healthy personality results with much of the self available for personal interaction, for loving, and for learning from experience. Extending Fairbairn's terminology, we call this self-object-affect system *the central self*.

The *libidinal ego* has as its object the *exciting object*, an aspect of the parents that creates experiences that excite need and create a state of longing or even craving so painful that it has to be split off from other more gratifying aspects and repressed into the unconscious. Feelings of longing of a tolerable intensity that lend excitement and give color and life to the object are lost from the central self, which is then inhibited, restricted, and unable to generate enjoyment. This libidinal object relationship we call the *libidinal self*, or sometimes the craving self that seeks the tantalizing object (Ogden 1986).

The *antilibidinal ego* (originally with the more evocative name *the internal saboteur*) has as its object the *antilibidinal or rejecting object*,

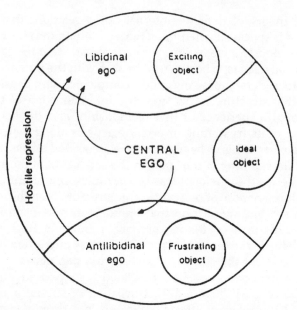

Figure 3-1. The endopsychic situation. Reprinted from *The Sexual Relationship: An Object Relations View of Sex and the Family,* courtesy of Routledge and Kegan Paul. Copyright © David E. Scharff, 1982.

corresponding to the child's experience of the parents as frustrating of needs. Although some frustration and limit-setting are positive elements for the developing personality and strengthen the reality testing of the central self and its capacity for delay, too much frustration leads to a state of rage. The object is perceived in an aggressive way that is unmanageable and has to be repressed along with all the aggression and the part of the ego that is feeling that way. Fairbairn termed this antilibidinal ego-object-affect system "the antilibidinal object relationship," and we tend to call it the *antilibidinal self.* It takes away healthy aggression from the central self and leaves it impoverished. This antilibidinal system joins forces with the central self to repress the libidinal self, because the needy self is even more vulnerable than the angry self and is required to be hidden more thoroughly.

Either of these repressed libidinal or antilibidinal systems can operate independently of the monitoring action of the central self, so that the person may appear to be too rageful to benefit from a current relationship or too sexually exciting to develop sustained committed relationships of trust and affection with peers or spouses.

All children naturally experience their parents as frustrating or rejecting of their needs at some times and may see their parents as ogres, but when the parent or other significant adult is actually abusive, the magnitude and influence of the "bad" internal object are correspondingly greater. Then, the persecuting and rejecting side of object relations dominates personality, represses the good object-seeking tendency, and propels the child toward the adults he or she needs in aggressive ways. When the libidinal self is spurred by sexual stimulation to enlarge as well, the desperate child relates in exciting and provocative ways in an attempt to secure the attention required for positive self-feeling. In this way, the sexually abused child whose needs for love and secure attachment are being frustrated by the fusion of aggression and sexuality in the abusive relationship may develop behaviors that provoke the abuse in order to feed the self and feel loved by the necessary parental objects. The power of the repressed antilibidinal and libidinal object relationships dominates and overshadows the central self. Instead of being the integrative, central part of the self, the central self becomes dissociated from the repressed selves in order to go on being at all.

The physically abusive parent relates to the child in such a way as to to magnify the persecutory rejecting constellation. When the abuse is sexual, there is the added complication that desire is caught up with aggression. This is tremendously confusing for the child, who cannot discriminate between feeling states or between good and bad objects. Errors of perception, memory, and judgment compound the insecure attachment, and hope for a creative resolution is replaced with simple survival as the goal. There can be no hope of resolution of the oedipal complex when the intrusive, body-boundary-breaking parents have in reality obliterated the transitional space in which fantasy and reality should be able to be explored and fantasied possession of a parental object could be given up. In the transitional space that is collapsed, the capacities to symbolize, delay gratification, sublimate erotic fantasy in the form of creative work, and seek objects outside the family are fundamentally compromised.

Personality Formation after Trauma

The tie to the bad object

Fairbairn noted that the child's identification with external objects is such that association with a bad object makes the child feel that he or she *is* bad. In addition, the human being's fundamental need for an object means that the child would rather have a bad object than no object at all. So the child with an abusive parent will do anything to hang on to that parent as an object, including being compliant in receiving abuse. The younger the child, the mightier is the struggle to maintain the tie to the parental object.

Another of Fairbairn's contributions that helps us understand how children treat their abusive objects is his formulation of "conditional and unconditional badness' (1943b, pp. 66–67). He noted that once a child internalized bad objects, the child carried an internal burden of badness with which a bargain has to be struck. Exactly like the boy, the girl has a choice: to define herself as bad or the internal object as bad. If the internal object, derived from the abusive parent, is bad, there is no hope of improving the situation, for the parent is seen as evil or angry. If, on the other hand, the child can convince herself that the parent is only treating her badly because she has been bad herself by doing something wrong, then the child has hope that if she can reform, the object will become good and will begin to treat her well. In Fairbairn's (1943b) words:

> Framed in such terms the answer is that it is better to be a sinner in a world ruled by God than to live in a world ruled by the Devil. A sinner in a world ruled by God may be bad; but there is always a certain sense of security to be derived from the fact that the world around is good— "God's in His heaven—All's right with the world!"; and in any case there is always a hope of redemption. In a world ruled by the Devil the individual may escape the badness of being a sinner; but he is bad because the world around him is bad. Further, he can have no sense of security and no hope of redemption. The only prospect is one of death and destruction. [pp. 66–67]

In addition, Fairbairn's model has the potential to comprehend the difficulties of ego integration that many of the most severely traumatized patients have. The most severe trauma—that is to say, the earliest, most often repeated, most humiliating trauma—handicaps, subverts, or obliterates the central self's role of maintaining personality integration. The result is a dissociative state or multiple personality disorder. In an early paper on the superego, Fairbairn (1929a) showed that he knew that Freud had understood this concept, for he quoted Freud's 1923 paper *The Ego and the Id* in which Freud had written:

> (W)e cannot avoid giving our attention for a moment longer to the ego's object-identifications. If they obtain the upper hand and become too numer-

ous, unduly intense and incompatible with one another, a pathological outcome will not be far off. It may come to a disruption of the ego in consequence of the individual identifications becoming cut off from one another by resistances; perhaps the secret of the cases of so-called multiple personality is that the various identifications seize possession of consciousness in turn. Even when things do not go so far as this, there remains the question of conflicts between the different identifications into which the ego is split up, conflicts which cannot after all be described as purely pathological. [pp. 38–39]

In summary, Fairbairn's model of the personality is a cybernetic one in which separate components of personality are held in check by the central self, the organizing apparatus of the personality. We believe that he did come to see the central self's repression of the too-painful aspects of libidinal and antilibidinal inner object relationships as an integrating function, although he did not specifically state that integration is the purpose of the central self.

The Closed System Personality and the Frozen Tableau

The integrative function of the central self was implied, near the end of Fairbairn's career, in his discussion of the action of the patient's personality to keep his internal world intact against the efforts of the psychotherapist. The patient maintains the inner world as a closed system, not susceptible to the influence of the therapist, not open to change and loss—frozen in an unchanging state (Fairbairn 1958). Fairbairn's idea articulates with Winnicott's (1958) description of the way that a child subjected to trauma attempts to keep the traumatic situation frozen in order to control it. Casement (1985) also addressed the original freezing of the traumatic situation and the organization of personality after trauma to keep things frozen so as to preserve an unencumbered area of self-functioning. He made the clinically useful observation that, if trauma is linked unconsciously to the preceding sense of safety, then when safety is recreated in the therapeutic relationship, paradoxically the patient may fail to recover because of expecting catastrophe to follow safety as it did before.

The child's attempts to control the traumatic fracture of the self and to keep the traumatic relationship static derive from the attempt to preserve parts of the self that can go on being despite the assault. This mechanism can be viewed as a further elaboration of the *closed system* to the point where it becomes the *frozen tableau*. Fairbairn

(1954b) used this expression to refer to the closed system in the hysterical personality that forms when the child is subjected to a confusing combination of excessively exciting and excessively rejecting behaviors that call for excessive repression by the central self, with the result that it is denuded and impoverished. By extension we can say that multiple personality results when the child is subjected to a similar combination, but instead of being "excessively exciting and rejecting" the object is "totally overwhelmingly exciting and rejecting" to a confusing, disorienting, terrifying, and massively destructive degree.

Fairbairn's concept of the frozen tableau also resonates with Davies and Frawley's (1992) observation that the child aspect of the survivor of incest, along with the abusing other and their complex interaction, becomes "frozen in time" (p. 21), isolated from the rest of the personality and unavailable for growth and learning alongside segmental maturation of other aspects of the personality. These ideas also articulate with the colloquial usage of the phrase "frigid" to describe the woman who experiences the sexual arena as the freezer. The bad, traumatic object relationship is in fantasy located in the genitals and then frozen in place to the detriment of the individual's sexual expressiveness and intimate relationship with her partner. This is a type of body memory, a sensorimotor or iconic memory or fantasy based on a memory, creating the behavior of that organ in the interpersonal realm. The fantasy is an expression of the mental mechanism of projective identification that here occurs in the form of bodily splitting to preserve ego integrity. Another outcome that coexists with frigidity—sometimes in the same woman—is compulsive promiscuity as a way of obtaining nurturing from the penis, exerting control over phallic power, exciting and abandoning the erect penis to retaliate against its owner, and proving that a part of the self can have sexual feelings even when the rest of the self cannot feel safely sexual.

ENCAPSULATION

Another response to trauma is encapsulation. Glover (1943) had identified the concept of *nucleation*, a defense mechanism operative when the ego is under acute or chronic stress. He described the pathological expression of ego nuclei that cannot remain in a state of synthesis under stress conditions. Glover then rejected his concept of nucleation and preferred to resuscitate the older term *dissociation*. Yet, there is value in his earlier term because it emphasizes the synthetic function that is belied by the fragmenting connotation of the term *dissociation*.

We have found a useful contemporary approach to this aspect of defense, now called encapsulation. Hopper (1991) views encapsulation as a defense against annihilation anxiety experienced in a state of absolute helplessness and failed dependency needs after catastrophic loss. Hopper describes how the ego cannot bear to retain a comprehensive memory trace of the sensations, affects, and ideas about its self, its objects, and its trauma, and so it makes a summary of them, isolates it from the other encoding that is going on in memory, and puts it inside its own capsule. This summary is rather like a time capsule that, when opened later, will reveal contents of persecutory anxiety and primal depression that are just as they were years ago.

These contents may be vivid fragments that are pointed, sharp, hard, explosive, or encased, or they may comprise more dark space than form, depending on the age at which the trauma took place. Cohen described the existence of dark spaces in the ego as "holes" in the mind that has been subject to unmodified primary repression (Cohen and Kinston 1984). In the absence of structure and symbolic functioning in these holes, there is only unmodified primary process with the dreaded potential of chaos and death, because now the person has become the disorganizing trauma (Cohen 1984). Sometimes the encapsulation is of the goodness of the self, and the object is to keep hope alive in the face of trauma. Both may be present in the same individual. Hopper conceptualizes these examples of encapsulation as the product of the defense against fission and fragmentation of the self and its objects under the impact of the trauma: that defense is the fusion and confusion of self and object. Encapsulation may occur to protect a child from its parents' trauma, as happens in the children of Holocaust victims. From birth, their personalities are formed around the encapsulation of their parents' trauma (see the case of Albert in Chapter 5).

Encapsulation is an attempt to make that which is overwhelmingly large appear tiny and bounded by shrinkwrapping it and putting it in cold storage. This leaves the rest of the personality diminished as well. Untreated patients who use this defense can give interesting material, and yet their sessions feel dull, lifeless, and boring. The therapist's dread of being trapped in a boring hour reflects the self's dread of being as entrapped and controlled by the capsule as the stuff inside it.

Hopper finds encapsulation in response to massive loss. He gives examples of the effects of losing the mother even temporarily for a few months due to illness so early in life that the infant equates loss of mother with loss of self. He describes encapsulation occurring later in life when a person experiences a collective accident, natural disaster, migration, internment, or war. Yet, we find encapsulation most relevant in those situations of loss of safety and relatedness when there has also been physical intrusiveness, stimulation, pain, and interference with body rhythms and self-quieting mechanisms. In these cases, the self's envy of the power and awesome destructiveness of the hated intrusive, depriving object in the capsule threatens to destroy and unleash it and pushes the self back into the state of being in bits (fission and fragmentation) from which it was trying to defend itself by encapsulation. Envy of the therapist properly interpreted is one avenue for breaching the encapsulation.

THE TRAUMATIC CONTINUUM: FROM FREEZING AND ENCAPSULATION TO EGO-SPLITTING

In more minor instances of trauma, or where the child is constitutionally strong and has other good caregiving objects or is older, or has a family where there are some obsessional defenses against fission and fragmentation, the child tries to freeze and encapsulate trauma. In response to more severe and thoroughly awful trauma that occurs early in a family that passively adapts to fission and fragmentation by dissociation, and where the child's ego is constitutionally weak, a shattering effect occurs and multiple personality results—a situation in which sub-units of personality do not respond to the integrative efforts of the massively fractured and depleted central personality. The resulting frozen encapsulation and the diffuse splintering of the personality are at opposite poles of the traumatic response continuum, but both of them result from the process of dissociation.

TRAUMA AND PSYCHIC GENERA: BOLLAS

Bollas describes the individual as a unique being with a sense of self and a personal way of looking at the world: This is his *personal idiom*

(1989). He writes, "This core self is the unique presence of being that each of us is; the idiom of our personality" (1989, p. 9). This idiom is an inherent potential that is brought out in relation to the mother and father who are intuitively aware of the individuality of their child. Bollas agrees with the Kleinian view that the inherent potential personality (what Fairbairn called the pristine self) is subject to the force of the life and death instincts, except that he sees their effect as emanating not solely from the constitutional endowment of instinctual energy but rather occurring in relation to the quality of the object experiences.

The Generative Expression of Idiom

The optimistic and loving coloration of the life instinct is fostered when the parents are good-enough, normally loving people. When the parents are ordinarily thoughtful, empathic, and attuned to their child's moods, anxieties, needs for sleep and stimulation; when they present themselves and their friends and families as worthwhile objects for the child to engage with; and when they maintain a positive view of their child, the child is encouraged to elaborate personal idiom in interaction. This child develops confidence in the benefits of diffusing the self across various relationship possibilities and finds pleasure in experimenting with different views of the world and the self, in the process building a flexible way of being. Bollas (1992) calls this the generative expression of idiom. He writes that a person whose

> engagement with reality is generative will seek to work unconsciously on specific issues that will enable him to re-envision his reality and in turn sponsor new ways of living and thinking. . . . In essence, genera are the inherited proto-nucleations of any child's idiom, so that if he is free to elaborate himself, then life will be punctuated by inspired moments of self-realization, deriving from the instinct to elaborate the self, which I have termed a destiny drive. [p. 70]

In summary, psychic genera are areas of psychic elaboration that reshape the contents of mental life and create a new vision of self and object. They derive partly from constitutional endowment and partly from the child's response to good empathic parenting. Unlike traumatic nuclei that develop in response to abusive parenting, they disseminate goodness, rather than attracting accretions of badness.

Unlike traumatic nuclei, they are received in the unconscious and are not repressed. Clinically we find this concept useful as a reminder to look for and support surviving aspects of the self while we are working on trauma and pathology.

The Traumatized Expression of Idiom

Instead of having nuclei of the self that diffuse through the personality; are free to make object choices, have fun, and face reality; and build into their structure life-affirming sensibility from the good experience that they attract, the abused or traumatized child has an encapsulated nucleus that inevitably enlarges itself by drawing bad experiences to itself, either because that is what is familiar or because it unfortunately results from efforts to oppress that unwanted part of the self as thoroughly as it has been oppressed in interaction with its abusive objects. The encapsulated nucleus paradoxically grows stronger from its oppression. In Bollas's (1992) words,

> Children whose parents are impinging or acutely traumatizing collect such trauma into an internal psychic area which is intended to bind and limit the damage to the self, even though it will nucleate into an increasingly sophisticated internal complex, as resonant trauma are unconsciously referred to such an area for linked containment. [p. 69]

This formulation resonates with Greenberg and Van der Kolk's (1987) observation that, in states of terror, organized cognitive schema encased in rigid boundaries typical of the stage of preoperational thinking are frozen so that dynamic change cannot take place and thinking cannot progress easily toward operational forms. Because of this type of freezing, the traumatized person remains inflexible, not curious, unable to imagine freely, and too frightened to explore. Bollas describes a similar personality profile in patients who are survivors of incest (1989). We illustrate incest survivors' cognitive problems in the following chapters: restricted imaginative thinking in Chapter 11, learning disability resulting in illiteracy in Chapter 13, poor memory for facts in Chapter 1, and inhibited verbalization in Chapter 12.

Bollas sees trauma as allied to the death instinct. In the classical Kleinian view of the death instinct, the infant burdened by its aggressive force is compelled to get rid of the effects of instinctual urgency by projection. In Bollas's concept, the infant is compelled to get rid of the excitation it experiences not directly from the internal force of the death instinct, but from the experience with the external object that excited this feeling state. Under the force of the death instinct, the infant tries to get rid of overwhelming or only uncomfortable states of aggressive, needy, sexual excitation to return to the resting state. Here Bollas is close to the Freudian view of the organism's need for homeostasis as a temporary choice to operate closer to the dead state than to the live one. Following Freud, who held that, under the influence of the death instinct, the person was compelled to repeat, rather than to remember painful and conflictual experiences, Bollas applies his principle of repetition to trauma. Bollas (1992) writes:

> A trauma is just that, traumatic, and the subject who contains such anguishing complexes will usually not seek to symbolically elaborate them, not have them, as it were, spawn newer, more radical perspectives on life; but a trauma is represented, in actings-out, in creative works, in human relations. It is important to make clear here that the effect of trauma is to sponsor symbolic repetition, not symbolic elaboration. [p. 70]

From Bollas's work linking trauma and the death instinct, we are reminded of Freud's (1914a) related concept of narcissism as a result of the need for homeostasis, for return to the nonaroused condition. In an object relational view, we hold that narcissism, like suicidality, is one defense against the trauma of dealing with the traumatizing object. Symington (1993) describes how trauma leaves a person dazed and in shock. To gain distance from what has been happening, the person propels him- or herself into the pattern of the traumatizing agent, pushing away the traumatized infant self and behaving cruelly to others. Anna Freud (1936) named this defensive process *identifying with the aggressor*, an early oedipal-level defense. Symington emphasizes the grandiose aspect of this defense and calls it the *narcissistic option*, although he later acknowledges that there is little conscious choice about this process. Instead, the self is overwhelmed by excessive stress and takes the narcissistic option, rather than submit to the catastrophe of a shattered self. The younger the child when the trauma occurs or begins, the more likely he or she will require a narcissistic defense and will not find ways of diversifying and modifying the experience. The more severe the trauma at the early age, the more likely the narcissistic defense will not work to encapsulate the trauma and a more thoroughly shattered self will result. The constitutionally better endowed, well-regulated, and inventive child in the face of extreme trauma may be able to tolerate feeling the self to have fallen into bits, whereas others may become psychotic or defend against psychosis by dissociative mechanisms that lead to dissociative states, hysterical symptoms, or multiple personality.

Symington (1993) also refers to Winnicott's concept of psychological growth as a series of graded separations from important objects, the tempo of which is disrupted by the shock of trauma. The tempo of detachment is determined by the occurrence of developmental achievements according to an internal timetable modulated by caring and empathic parenting. Trauma makes the child suddenly helpless and more dependent on objects than should be the case. Sexual trauma causes the timetable to go totally awry. For example, the little girl may menstruate while others of her age are still in latency. The good creative space between the self and the external object is obliterated by inappropriate physical proximities and intrusions. Good and bad, love and hate, sex and aggression are hopelessly confused. The most fundamental trauma is that the child cannot count on being held securely and with respect for the body, the mind, the emotions, and the essence of the child.

THE TRANSITIONAL SPACE FOR GOING-ON-BEING: WINNICOTT

The Psychosomatic Partnership

The psychosomatic partnership between mother and baby forms at the moment of birth after the prebirth period of physical symbiosis and psychological speculation about the fetus. As the infant matures, the partnership is composed more and more of psychological elements out of which psychic structure forms. The partnership occurs in *potential space* (Winnicott 1951a), an external space between mother and baby that is taken in as an expanding internal space within the baby in which he or she grows, plays, creates, and thinks as a separate person. We have preferred to call this concept the *transitional space* to reflect the movement between parent and infant, object and self, outside and inside, and experience with the external object and internal object relationships.

Contextual and Centered Holding

Healthy parents provide an unobtrusive, well-managed empathic background for their infants to grow in, as well as a strong presence for holding and handling of their infants and directly relating to them. Against this steady, arms-around background of *contextual holding*, infants find themselves. Within the context, the infant forms a direct relationship with each parent as the object of desire and aggression. We have called this relationship the focused, eye-to eye, I-to-I, or *centered holding* relationship. It supplies the experience of objects out of which the infant's world is built.

The object mother and the environment mother are two aspects of mothering that the infant experiences and holds in mind as images of the mother (Winnicott 1945, 1963a, 1963b). Contextual holding is a function of the environment mother who provides the regulated living space and family life. Centered holding is a function of the object mother who relates intimately in vocal and gaze interactions and in conscious and unconscious fantasies about her child. These two aspects of mothering comprise the holding environment (Figure 3–2, Winnicott 1960a).

At birth the potential space is just that. The unformed self begins to relate through short interactions that are intensely physical. The baby needs to be next to the well-defined edges of its caretaker in order to define the contours and boundaries of the physical and the psychological self (Ogden 1989, after Bick 1968, 1986 and Tustin 1984, 1986). Gradually the potential space opens up, as the now physically and psychologically defined infant becomes more wakeful and aware of the otherness of the mother with whom the infant engages across the variable gap of changing wake-and-sleep cycles. Healthy development requires the gap to be a transitional space between self and other, between the real and the not real.

In physical and sexual abuse the eye-to eye, I-to-I relationship is frighteningly intensified while the holding relationship is alarmingly defective. In this case, the child cannot experience the object of desire and aggression safely in fantasy because the fantasy object is too likely to become real. The capacity for fantasy and for symbolization is severely restricted. Sometimes it is totally distorted by a parent-child role reversal in which, instead of the parent being the oedipal object of the child's longings and frustrations, the child is the object of the parent's desire and aggression. Ultimately the child is unfortunately identified more fully as the parent's object than as its own

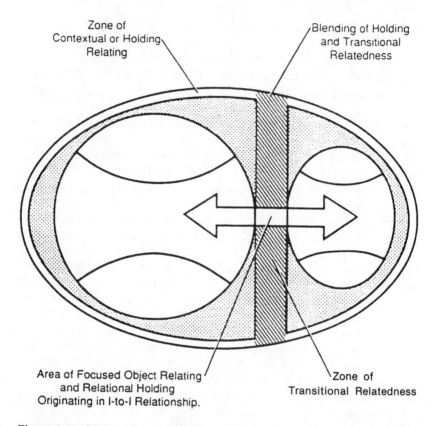

Figure 3-2. Winnicott's organization of the mother–infant relationship. Reproduced from *Refinding the Object and Reclaiming the Self,* courtesy of Jason Aronson Inc. Copyright © David E. Scharff, 1992.

The psychosomatic partnership begins with a physical holding-and-handling relationship between mother and infant. The oval envelope drawn around mother and infant signifies the environmental function provided by the mother's holding—the *arms-around* relationship. Within this envelope, mother and infant have a direct object relationship—the intense I-to-I relationship, communicated in words, gestures, gaze, and physical exchange—out of which the infant constructs its internal objects.

lovable self whose life is more dear than the parent's own. In sexual abuse, a genital-to-genital relationship substitutes for the essential eye-to-eye relationship in which the child usually finds the self. The self that can be found in a state of premature sexual arousal is subject to aggrandizement and denigration.

Grotstein (1992) makes the point that sexual abuse of a child is not necessarily motivated by sexual desire. Sexual abuse may be the expression of the parent's envy of the child's innocence and right to special care and protection that the parent may not have had. Then survivors in treatment may refuse to make progress for fear of losing their sense of entitlement to maintain their innocence and to get a fair hearing and not be abandoned by a bad-object analyst. The drives to object relatedness, secure attachment, and nurturing are frustrated and are then reconfigured by the child as sexual drives that seemed to have originated in the victimized child. Unlike Freudian theory in which the drives seek discharge of sexual and aggressive tensions, object relations theory holds that the person is fundamentally object seeking and that sexual and aggressive impulses take on meaning only in the context of the relationship. We agree with Fairbairn that, when the drives seem to be sexually or aggressively discharging, this is not the normal state, but represents a breakdown of relatedness in the parent-child relationship, one form of which is incest. Even when the father is the perpetrator, the child's rage may be more intense toward the mother who failed in her protective function.

In dysfunctional families where abuse occurs, fantasy and oedipal romance are obliterated by a cruel, physical reality. The transitional space which they should occupy because it is the space for play and imagining, for inventing ideas, for exploring the boundaries between "me" and "not me" is destroyed (Figure 3–3). Its obliteration strains the enveloping contextual holding for the self, because the transitional space and the contextual envelope are in communication inside the self. The transitional space across which the eye-to-eye relationship occurs is collapsed, as the abusive parental object physically and psychologically, sexually and aggressively, enters and usurps the body space of the child as if to claim it as an object for the parent's use. The individual internal transitional space shrinks along with the collapse of the child's bodily integrity and the obliteration of the family transitional space (Winer 1989).

OBJECT RELATIONS THERAPY OF TRAUMA IN PRACTICE

Contextual and Centered Holding

The therapeutic relationship provides the two elements that are crucial for the building of psychic structure and its repair—the

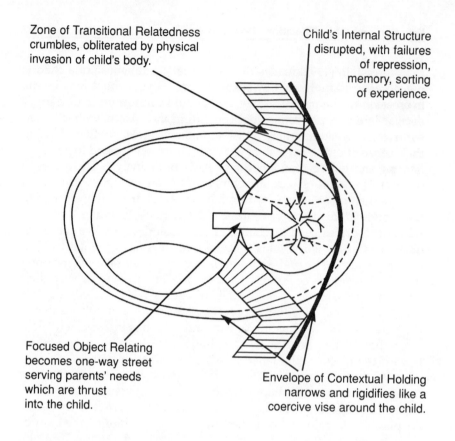

Zone of Transitional Relatedness crumbles, obliterated by physical invasion of child's body.

Child's Internal Structure disrupted, with failures of repression, memory, sorting of experience.

Focused Object Relating becomes one-way street serving parents' needs which are thrust into the child.

Envelope of Contextual Holding narrows and rigidifies like a coercive vise around the child.

Figure 3–3. Distortion of relatedness and psychic structure in physical and sexual abuse.

In physically abusive parent–child relationships, the ordinary envelope of flexible but firm parental holding shrinks to become a coercive iron vise that fixes the frightened child in position to serve parental needs. The transitional space is fractured and obliterated by the brutal immediacy of inappropriate physical contact between child and parent. In consequence, the child's internal organization is invaded and severely disrupted, while the direct object relationship with the parent becomes one of overwhelming arousal, persecution, and rejection. In severe cases and in sexual abuse, invasion of the child's body causes disruption of the child's sense of physical and emotional integrity. The diagram shows the resulting fracturing and distortion of the child's internal structure, which is associated with disturbances in the child's capacity for repression, memory formation, and sorting of complex intrapsychic experience. The child may feel belittled and destroyed in the face of the parent's exercise of power, or may identify with the parent and feel aggrandized and omnipotent.

symbolic equivalents of arms-around holding and eye-to-eye holding; namely, contextual and centered holding. We do not use physical touch to express our intentions, but convey through our attitude of dedication to the therapeutic task that we are holding the patient in the mind. We provide a secure context in which to do the work (the arms-around holding), and we offer ourselves as objects for projective and introjective identification (centered holding) whose experience we make available for analysis.

Going-on-Being in the Potential Space

Winnicott (1956) described how the mother's state of *primary maternal preoccupation* creates a state of mind in relation to which her infant can achieve a state of *going on being* that is a necessary condition for growth and development. He wrote " . . . the basis for ego establishment is the sufficiency of 'going on being,' uncut by reactions to impingement" (p. 303). Similarly, in treating the abuse survivor, we need to create a safe context, free from the impingement of overzealous interpretation of resistance based upon theories found useful in the analyses of patients who have not been physically and sexually abused. We respect the true self (Winnicott 1960b) of the traumatized patient.

In the analysis or therapy of the survivor, we need to support the patient's need for going-on-being in order to have a safe space from which to approach the traumatic material. The area of going-on-being may feel mundane, concrete, and devoid of play and symbols, but it is the potential space in which the collapsed transitional space is refound, expanded, or created from scratch. Within the matrix of going-on-being, we work on specific traumatic material to which we gain access through our own feelings more often than through the patient's dreams and fantasies.

Rebuilding the Transitional Space

As therapists we aim to rebuild the transitional space that Winnicott described. We want to avoid making premature, intrusive suggestions about a suspected abuse history, because we offer a therapy that is quite different from the patient's experience of suffering the imposition of another person's reality. Instead we leave the patient plenty of room to know and not know, to work and play, to re-experience trauma and to go on being. We work together to create a psychological space for self-discovery in the context of a generative relationship. In this kind of space the patient discovers the creative benefits of *negative capability*, the capacity "for being in uncertainties, mysteries and doubts without irritable reaching after fact and reason" (Murray 1955, p. 261). The "paradox of knowing and not knowing, form and formlessness, is at the heart of therapy" (Scharff and Scharff 1992, p. 98), as it should have been in the child's years in the family so that the child could enjoy fantasy and dreams without them becoming actualized, and therefore destructive to and cemented in their development.

Using Countertransference to Reach Trauma

Our countertransference feeling of being abused and our sense of confusion about the way abused patients deal with us are the most important clues to patients' inner states and terror. They communicate to us unconsciously through projective identification and invoke in us feelings of being stuck and helpless, frozen in time, dissociated from reality, bored, indifferent, or dead—countertransference feelings that echo the paralysis of the patient's self-and-object relational system. We may also respond directly to the fear and terror of abuse and may have to work hard to retain our courage to confront the facts. Otherwise we may find ourselves crumbling from fear of doing further violence to the patient. Or we may be coasting as we resonate with the patient's need to go on being in an ordinary way to reassure the traumatized self that a surviving self has the upper hand. We analyze our fear of relating to the abusive object that has had the effect of causing the patient to need to maintain the frozen inner world as a static, closed system in order to defend against the fear of fragmentation and disintegration.

Providing a Generative Analytic Relationship

We offer ourselves as nonabusive, consistent objects who witness the trauma. We do not stand by silently witnessing trauma without confronting it. We provide a trustworthy relationship in which the patient's needs are paramount and the trauma can be reexperienced symbolically and recovered from. We do not provide a corrective emotional experience, but we do create a holding context of acceptance, validation, and respect in which the patient can go on being until he or she can play again. The transitional space is gradually expanded by experience until it supports the growth of an internal world of integrated, differentiated relationship between self and object, achieved through the internalization of the holding and containing function and through the resolution of the transference. Where trauma was, genera shall be.

4

From Traumatic Splits in the

Self to Multiple Personality

The analytic literature has not done justice to the complexity of the splits in the self that occur under the impact of trauma. Berman (1981) noted a lack of psychoanalytic contribution to the multiple personality literature in which role theory, family systems theory, and ego state theory from hypnotism have predominated (Braun 1984, 1985). He found that the literature misused Freud's contributions and ignored those of Fairbairn (Davies and Frawley 1992, Grotstein 1992). This is an omission that we would like to correct, not just to give due attention to the relatively rare syndrome of multiple personality disorder but also to use that extreme example to illuminate less obvious splits in the self that occur under the impact of trauma.

Juliet Mitchell (1984) views multiple personality as a variety of hysteria, a condition that expresses "woman's simultaneous acceptance and refusal of the organization of sexuality under patriarchal capitalism" (pp. 289-290). The hysterical origin of symptoms of hysteria is indicated by the presence of primary identification with a whole object that has not been properly differentiated as "other." Mitchell (1994) uses a striking metaphor to describe the development of the hysterical personality. She sees the child's personality as a piece of tracing paper and the parent's personality as a map onto which the tracing paper is applied. Once the map is removed, the child is always looking for another map to complete the tracing. As an adult, the hysteric operates as if with only a tracing of the self and readily seeks and discards objects to fill in the contours of the self (Mitchell 1994). The person with multiple personality seeks whole objects to identify with and finds them inside the self in the form of alters who seem to be other than the self. Men are not often found in the diagnostic categories of multiple personality. Instead, Mitchell finds that the male hysteric tends to present as a "Don-Juan" character whose excitement and rejection of a string of women represent a search for a temporary object to complete the self by physical approximation.

Fairbairn regarded multiple personality as another example of the differentiation of the personality into independently functioning units, as is found to varying degree in normal, schizoid, and hysterical states. In the normal adaptation to the early relationships, the infant develops a personality that is a system of parts in dynamic equilibrium (Fairbairn 1952). In less favorable circumstances, parts of psychic structure are more thoroughly repressed and are then less in communication with each other in consciousness, but are excessively turbulent in the unconscious (Fairbairn 1954). In trauma, segments of experience and behavior are distributed among various ego states and kept separate by dissociation (Watkins and Watkins 1984). Watkins and Watkins (1984) point out that the human organism adapts, defends, grows, and maintains itself normally by integration, which permits generalizations and concept formation, and by differentiation that permits distinguishing and separating one concept from another to fashion a more precise response to the environment. Processes of projective and introjective identification contribute to integration and differentiation (J. Scharff 1992). The normal result is a growing, modifying central self in more or less communication with less conscious aspects of the self.

    In trauma, where freezing of the situation is not enough, the central self splits off traumatized aspects of the self and tries to maintain access to outside reality. In less severe trauma, they tend to attract each other and to coalesce in one area. As trauma accumulates, there is a splintering of the coalesced self-and-object units, and they act independently of each other outside awareness. They propagate to become an army of subselves too numerous to be destroyed, maintaining their splintered existences at the cost of the whole person.

In the extreme case, these self-object systems serve as alternative personalities that seem to substitute for the central self and become the objects of the intended interaction with others in the real world. These splintered parts of the self (called *alters* in the multiple personality literature) can be predominantly object-organizations shorn of the ego component, or predominantly ego-organizations shorn from the object component, of the normally repressed self-and-object relationships that Fairbairn described. In addition, the normal affect bridge between self and object suborganizations is lost in the splintering process. In severe trauma, these splintered traumatic internal subselves assume an embodied reality as self-organizations through part-object identification, but instead of remaining in unconsciousness as repressed subselves, they become split-off, dissociated units of the self out of contact with other parts. These dissociated units are free to interact as if any one of them is really the central self at the conscious level relating to the ideal object.

The normal dynamic structure of the personality, effected by splitting off and repression of parts of the self that remain in communication with their objects, with each other, and with the central self, is destroyed. In its place, we find a frozen system of poorly articulated, impoverished parts of egos without objects and of objects divorced from their ego relatedness; each of these parts is disconnected from the relevant affects from which the original object relationship derives its meaning and alternates with more flexible, better functioning aspects of the self. However, all of these parts do not add up to a confident, coherent self. In the traumatized person, a part self does not relate at the leading edge of the central self and on its behalf, but instead it substitutes for the whole. Continuing violence to the self persists when this part of the self is experienced more fully as the other person's object than as a part of the self.

The ordinary integrating function of the central ego in normal personality, derived from reliable experience with and internalization of the holding and integrating processes of the mother, is ordinarily an out-of-sight, background function. With the breakdown of the central ego's capacity for repression, integration, and self-care, secret personality subunits arise as if from the ashes of the destroyed personality to supplant the missing integrative function. The central self may then become a subunit of personality on a par with other subselves, instead of an overarching, integrative, truly central self-

and-object relationship that is capable of orchestrating living and learning in social relationships. In its place is an "as if" central self that is not a manager, but a host for the unintegrated alters. Kluft (1984b) uses the term *host personality* to refer to "the one who has executive control of the body the greatest percentage of the time during a given time" (p. 23).

Each subpersonality or alter is a splinter, each an incomplete closed system and living proof of severe damage to integrative capacities of the ego: the normal defensive capacity to split off and repress more integrated rejected self-and-object relationships is overwhelmed. Instead of splitting and repression as the main adequate defenses, we find a predominance of *dissociative splintering* that, because it is expressed concretely through its location in the body in the form of hysterical symptoms, is different from psychotic splintering into bizarre mental objects as described by Bion (1967). The substitution of a rich sequestered inner network of personalities in closed-system relationship to each other cannot compensate for the impoverishment of the central self and ideal object that results from trauma.

In therapy, Berman (1981) advises that each alter needs to be related to without confrontation of the split and denial of other aspects of the self, out of "respect for the experiential reality of the patient, as a step in forming a therapeutic alliance and striving for growth and integration" (p. 297). He recommends that effort should go not into demonstrating all the personalities but into asking the question, "Under what conditions does a person experience himself as cohesive and unified, and when does he experience himself as multiple?" (p. 296).

The patient may develop a lead alter that becomes the interpreter and stands in for the missing central ego. This is a stage on the way to integration. This alter gradually joins forces with the host personality who has authorized the interpretive function. Sometimes the various alters appear to fuse early, but Kluft (1984b) warns that this is usually a flight into health in which integration is being simulated to get free of the therapist whose efforts to correct the multiplicity must be destroyed. We want to minimize hazards for patient and therapist (Watkins and Watkins 1984).

We suggest that during therapy more subselves may be discovered, not simply because they were there waiting to emerge but because they proliferate in response to the threat of intimacy with the therapist that challenges the status quo of the central self. Intimacy with the therapist reinvokes the fear of abuse and stimulates the longing for physical contact that spanned the emotional void in the past. The ego's response to the challenge of the threat of repetition, the hope for safety, and the expectation of change is to divide and multiply. Multiple layers of insulation of one subself from another protect these splinter selves from interaction with rejection and exciting objects who were and are experienced as traumatic and may be rediscovered in the transference. So, as treatment is well into the mid-phase, we see the dissociative splintering in action. We interpret splintering as a defense against the transference fear of the therapist, and eventually we link it to a reconstructive interpretation.

When working with a well-integrated therapist who cares professionally, who is trustworthy and sets limits, who can relate fully and respectfully to each alter without losing sight of the others, who can contain the different bits and feelings and memories, and who can develop a whole picture of the person, the subselves disappear or coexist or come together in due course. No longer simply assembled by their weak as-if manager, the host personality, they can now be actively managed, contained, and, in the best outcome, actively repressed by an integrating central self. The functions of the host and the interpreter infused with the self-affirming, integrative experience with the therapist create a central self capable of maintaining self- cohesiveness through more normal processes of splitting and repression. This new level of integration is achieved through processes of projective and introjective identification. The multiple personality patient projects her host personality into the therapist and experiences more integrative holding there than has been accomplished in her own traumatized mind. The patient introjectively identifies with her own projected parts now that they have been detoxified by the therapist's containing and integrative function, and being less noxious, they can be contained and integrated more easily. She then identifies with the containing, metabolizing, and integrative function of the therapist and internalizes that as well, so that it becomes an autonomous capacity that functions reliably over time.

VICTIMIZED AND SURVIVING SELF-AND-OBJECT RELATIONAL SYSTEMS

In trauma that is not the most severe or that occurs later than the age at which the tendency to dissociate is lost, the personality need not be split into two or more alters. It can be split vertically into separate self experiences that crystalize around the view of the self as victimized or surviving. This is what we have most commonly seen in traumatized patients. The abusive object is split into gratifying and threatening parts to preserve some goodness and to diminish its power to hold the child in its thrall. Sometimes these two aspects of the abusive object are associated with one or another parent to make one bad and the other good, instead of accepting the fact that both parents colluded to perpetrate the abuse by commission and omission.

Mrs. Feinstein (Chapter 11) viewed her father as warm and nurturing while her mother was the one who beat her for her misdeeds, threatened her life, administered humiliating enemas with friends present, and sexually stimulated her. She was terrified of her mother and agreed with her view of herself as an ugly wimp, yet simultaneously maintained a view of her father as wonderful and of herself as Daddy's cute little girl. After years of therapy, Mrs. Feinstein realized that her father used to report her misdeeds to her mother so that she could beat her when she returned home. What she took for warmth was extreme passivity and cowardice. She retained her affection for her father, but she developed a much more realistic view of him and a more integrated view of her own attributes and capabilities.

In the case of body damage due to sudden illness, genetic defect, or accident, the same split occurs in the self and between the parents.

John was an apparently healthy child who had two loving parents and a safe and secure family life. Unsuspected disease suddenly erupted and necessitated a two-week hospitalization for treatment and investigation. He had the help of a specialized children's hospital, excellent preparation for all procedures, developmentally informed nursing, and a parent staying the night with him. He proved to be a stoic patient, remained cheerful, and returned to his usual level of adjustment at school and with his friends. But at home he became so difficult with his mother that it was as if he was a different person at times. Previously always easy to manage, he was still sweet and loving sometimes, but at other times he said that he hated her, threw temper tantrums, refused to take his daily shower, and irritated her with endless questions and accusations about why this had happened to him. He had not seemed at all traumatized by the hospitalization, and so his parents could not understand why he blamed his mother. John preserved his view of himself as a boy identified with his father's mastery and was furious at his mother's failure to ensure the integrity of his body. This was his reaction to trauma even in a situation of excellent previous adjustment and supportive family relationships. A similar level of trauma is more upsetting in situations of less favorable pretrauma adjustment or when the need for therapy is not appreciated by less sensitive parents. With therapy for him and his family, the developing split in this child's personality could be healed.

Splitting the parental couple into good and bad retains one good object to depend on and lets the child deny the awful loss of the reliable parental couple who provide safety and nurture for their child and a model of gratifying appropriate adult sexuality. The corresponding parts of the self that related to those aspects of the object are correspondingly split into fragments, one of which is associated with shame and guilt and the other with feelings of omnipotence. These are the forerunners of the victimized and surviving selves.

5

The False Memory/

Recovered Memory Debate

Recovered memory or false memory syndrome? That is the question therapists are being asked as they face a backlash against the credibility of the abuse survivors. The backlash hurts, but it is to be expected. Supported by feminism, support groups, and psychotherapy, survivors are speaking out (J. C. Reich 1993; Hocking and Company, 1992). They are receiving an empathic response from a society that no longer regards victimization as shameful (Reich 1994). Adults prefer to believe that abuse does not occur because of two simultaneous identifications: identified with the child, they do not want to feel hurt; identified with the perpetrator, they do not want to feel accused, aroused, and guilty (Faller 1992). Herman (1992) reminds us:

> The ordinary response to atrocities is to banish them from consciousness. Certain violations of the social order are too terrible to utter aloud. . . . Atrocities, however, refuse to be buried. . . . The conflict between the will to deny horrible events and the will to proclaim them aloud is the central dialectic of psychological trauma. [p. 1]

Is the backlash aimed at disenfranchising the newly validated, truly aggrieved victims because we cannot bear to see how many of them (or us) there are? Or is it provoked by a rising number of false accusations of abuse based on fraudulently recollected memories produced consciously and maliciously or unconsciously by contagion from massive sex abuse hysteria? As adult therapists, we are involved in this issue when people recover memories of abuse or incest in the course of therapy and face the painful question of whether their memories are real or fantastic, whether they should confront the perpetrator or not, and whether to pursue legal action. Child therapists are involved in the issue when they evaluate suspected child abuse and recommend and provide therapy for abused children privately or in child abuse programs. The value and the basis of psychotherapy are vulnerable to societal attack when therapy is seen both as revealing an immense, unwelcome, horrifying social problem and as irresponsibly fanning fires of false accusations by unsophisticated credulity or, worse, by creating false memories through suggestion used unwittingly by the careless therapist or consciously applied by the naive or self-serving.

As therapists we notice our defensiveness and reach beyond culture-bound attitudes so that we can face the anxiety that our society turns away from. As writers, we are trying to proclaim the effects of sexual abuse on individual and family development, and we are encouraging others to face the problem as well. We face the risk of speaking too forcefully so that our thoughts have to be banished, or of speaking so softly that the full import of what we have seen and heard is not felt by others. We also run the risk of creating a groundswell of sensibility that draws to it the pain of others who have no such obvious or horrendous explanation for equally damaged states of mind and who would rather have someone to blame. Therapists who have acknowledged the facts of sexual abuse need to see it when it is there, but not to look for it purposefully or even create it. We want to know and to tell what is known, but we do not want to create false certainty or universal application of individual premises.

Psychoanalysis developed as we know it today from the discovery that recollections of abuse by neurotic patients were based upon the distortion of memory of early childhood experience under the sway of oedipal wishes and fantasies. This finding led Freud to revise his initial belief in the veracity of his early patients' accounts of incestuous abuse recovered under hypnotic suggestive conditions. In this respect Freud was the first to point out the possibility of false memory. Yet, Freud's later analytic technique of free association — also variously described as bullying, coaching, breaking down resistance, and insisting on recall of primal scene material by Crews (1993) — is seen as equally likely to produce false memory as was the earlier technique of hypnotic suggestion so disparaged by Freud himself. Crews (1993) holds that irresponsible therapists who suggest to their patients the presence of memories, manipulate their recall, naively believe in those memories as facts or even use them as evidence, and whose methods are deplored by classically trained Freudians are actually following the Freudian tendency to discount the influence of the patient's suggestibility under stress. For all these reasons, he asserts that "Freud is the true historical sponsor of 'false memory syndrome'" (Crews 1993, p. 66). We refute Crews' conclusion. Freud chose to explore the avenue of the patients' conflicts rather than trauma as the basis for their symptomatology precisely because he doubted the factual validity of memories.

For all his rhetorical elegance and powers of persuasion, Freud seems to us to have been genuinely interested in responding to his patients' language and dreams, making sense of things, and revising theory to fit the facts as they emerged, rather than in selfishly prodding for memories to "shore up his dubious premises" as Crews suggests (1993, p. 63). Freud chose to explore the avenue of the patients' conflicts as the basis for their symptomatology, after he realized that trauma was not the *universal* basis for neurosis. His choice was based in his skepticism about false memories, rather than arising from any wish to create them.

WHEN A MEMORY IS LONGED FOR

Albert was a perpetrator of sexual abuse against boys aged 10 to 12. After he stopped this behavior, he continued to have fantasies of molesting boys. One of his fantasies was that sexual molestation would be acceptable to his culture and to his therapist (D.E.S.), as he had heard it was in antiquity. Because he could not imagine anyone desiring him, molestation seemed to be his only hope for sexual relatedness. He had never been molested, so far as he could remember, but he wished he had been. He had the feeling that his behavior and fantasy life resulted from a sexual trauma, and he looked for it in his dreams and memories. I did not suggest or confirm the wisdom of his course of action in therapy. I followed his material closely for a history of abuse, but I kept looking for other factors too, especially hoping to find the clue in the transference.

Albert found it difficult to relate to me except through stories of the past. At times there were long silences, absences, and interruptions in the therapy process, which were features of Albert's need to keep me out of his intimate space. Did the therapist represent an intrusive, abusive object? Albert did not think so and maintained his commitment to me over several years. He worked on his internal parent figures and tried to cope with his responses to his actual parents in the present, including reporting their dreams to me. Albert presented his mother and father as decent people who worked hard, provided a safe environment, and treated their children well, and so it remained a puzzle as to why he was so schizoid and sexually nonfunctional. Frustrated by his lack of change, he scanned his material even more actively for an explanatory trauma.

At last, he despaired of changing. He told me that he had just realized that his attempt at using therapy to change himself was a waste of time, because all these years he had really been wanting me to change his actual parents. Unless they could be changed, he could not change. I said that Albert had felt let down because I had not appreciated this underlying fantasy while going along with the search for an abusive parent who would then require treatment. Albert responded by talking about his parents' traumatic losses.

Albert's father had lost his own father when his wife divorced him and moved back to Canada. The first winter that Albert's divorced grandmother and her children were there, she could afford only a small apartment, and Albert's father as a young boy had to sleep on the outside porch. However, more significant than the loss, dislocation, and poverty caused by the divorce, were the neglect and isolation suffered by Albert's father before the divorce when his mother locked him in his bedroom while she had parties downstairs in the big house. He told Albert that on one occasion he had been so angry that he threw his toys out the window into a construction site next door where they sank into some hardening concrete and were gone forever. The image of the loved toys being petrified fit with my impression of Albert being encased in a schizoid shell. The age of his lonely and furious father had to have been about 10 or 12, the age at which Albert found boys to be sexually stimulating.

Albert's mother lost her mother when she was 4. In rage that her house had been reclaimed by the bank, Albert's grandmother took an axe to destroy it. She was taken away to a mental hospital where she spent the rest of her life.

Unlike his grandparents, Albert's parents remained married and devoted to their children. But theirs was an anxious kind of parental devotion in which they were constantly on guard against threats to the family. They had also taught Albert to be on the lookout for bad things. He kept expecting trauma that never happened. Its absence left him feeling empty and in a state of longing to have had something bad happen to him, such as being molested.

To find the missing calamity to give meaning to his parents' world view, Albert had visited trauma upon other children of the age his father was at the time of his life trauma. I thought that he was longing for something to happen to him that would be traumatic so that he would feel alive, unlike the lost toys. Failing that, I thought that he wanted to give to a young boy, in whom he could see both himself now and his father as a young boy, an experience of trauma. By creating an attentive older man/younger boy dyad joined by the trauma of sexual molestation, he hoped to feel close to his remote father. By using the enactment of a trauma fantasy with a boy, he created a sexual couple drawn together in trauma in imitation of his own parents, who as a couple shared early traumatic loss, so that he could feel closer to them and make them better.

In Albert's case, no memory was recovered and the issue of its being real or false receded. His case shows that some perpetrators are reacting to the intergenerational transmission of trauma even though they have not been sexually abused themselves. It also makes the point that a false memory could easily have been created if Albert's therapist had not been rigorous in tolerating the state of not knowing.

THE NEED TO AVOID SUGGESTION

Yapko (1993, 1994) is extremely concerned about memories of abuse that are discovered or remembered through the directions provided by a therapist. Yapko (1993) therefore advises against the use of guided imagery and hypnosis for removing repression. He warns against the less obvious injunctive effect of advertising our interest in abuse, because, in his experience, under these conditions, memories of abuse surface that fit suspiciously well with the therapist's expectations and the client comes to believe in their validity. This phenomenon has come to be known as the *"false memory syndrome,"*

> a condition in which a person's identity and interpersonal relationships are centered around a memory of traumatic experience which is objectively false but in which the person falsely believes. . . . False memory syndrome is especially destructive because the person assiduously avoids confrontation with any evidence that might challenge the memory. Thus, it takes on a life of its own, encapsulated and resistant to correction (Kihlstrom 1994, p. 6).

Assuring the reader of his deep and genuine concern for survivors of incest and sexual abuse, Yapko (1993), who has had the profoundly moving experience of sharing in survivors' anguish and the slow rebuilding of their lives, warns of the hurtfulness of refuting a survivor's recovered memory of having been abused and cautions against skeptical dismissal of such claims. Yet, he also points out that, with the tide of public opinion turning toward sympathy for the abused, we therapists may be too credulous. Our credulity could then be abused, and we could collude with our patients' abuse of their falsely accused abusers. The recovered memory is not to be believed readily when it has arisen after the therapist has introduced abuse as a likely explanation for the symptoms or has made a hypnotic intervention, because memories recovered in these ways cannot be retrieved without being altered by the memory-enhancing effects of suggestion (Spiegel 1980). This approach to memory recall is not purely de-repressive, he claims: it is injunctive and suggestive. Therefore, the memories cannot be relied upon. Loftus (1992) introduces more doubt into the veracity of memories. During or prior to the official retrieval process, new information can be incorporated into the original memory where it operates as a supplement— "an alteration, transformation, contamination, or distortion in the memory" (Loftus 1992, p. 8). Finally, Yapko (1993) warns of the damage done by suggesting sexual abuse to the patient who then accepts the idea and believes that it happened. The consequence is that the therapist's act redefines the identity of the patient and governs the patient's future.

Kline (1958) found another reason that memories could not be relied upon—countertransference. Some hypnotists were much more capable than others of producing a hypnotic relationship and a deep hypnotic state in which behavioral experience approached a meaningful level of validity. Hypnotists using the same procedures but less able to participate at the unconscious level in the hypnotic relationship were unable to achieve the same results, and instead "elicited *simulated* rather than *genuine* behavioral response," including such areas as hypnotic age regression, memory recollections and evocation of fantasy material (p. 66).

PSEUDOMEMORIES

Yapko, psychologist and hypnosis expert, offers therapists some practical precautions against creating pseudomemories when there are no memories to start with. The following list of precautions against pseudomemories is excerpted from one of his tables (1993, p. 229), and is reprinted here with permission.

- Don't ask leading questions.
- Don't assume molestation simply because it could be.
- Don't suggest that molestation has occurred directly or indirectly.
- Don't use hypnotic intervention to establish veracity.
- Don't assume the presence of repression rather than dissociation, or vice versa.
- Do listen, follow, experience, and explore.

All these suggestions are quite compatible with an analytic approach. We think that the analytic method, being nondirective and nonsuggestive, is less likely to create false memories. We follow Yapko's advice to be aware of injunctive elements that might intrude into our preferred analytic neutrality. We agree with Yapko that the premise of sexual abuse can be considered only after knowing the patient well and carefully evaluating our impulses toward validating and invalidating what we are told. And we are encouraged by Herman and Schatzow's (1987) finding that adult survivors' reports of childhood sexual abuse—even if not remembered until after some time in therapy—could be fully corroborated in 75 percent of cases and substantially verified in another 9 percent.

THE PUBLIC DEBATE

In the present climate of opinion in which abuse survivors are speaking out, there can be found curiosity, interest, and sympathy, all of which can be tremendously validating and empowering to the survivor. Yet, Courtois (1988) notes that

> the pervasive media coverage extended to child sexual abuse in recent years is highly disruptive for some survivors. . . . Acknowledgment can lift the protection of repression and dissociation. A flooding of memories, emotions, and symptoms can ensue. . . . Finally some media stories on false allegations and inadequate response by child protective services evoke reactions of rage and helplessness and reinforce feelings of guilt and the survivor's questioning of the reality of her own experience and that of other children. [p. 139]

Some critics of recovered memory therapy would say that the flooding is not due to de-repression, but rather to contagion among the highly suggestible. We recognize that there may be an element of "jumping on the bandwagon," but the main phenomenon is one of greater societal awareness and capacity to admit to and tolerate the pain of childhood sexual abuse.

Yet it would not be long before society generated a massive protest against the protest through media blitzes, talk show exposés, and court cases. Patients came forward to document the pressure exerted on them by poorly trained, zealous therapists who helped them retrieve memories of abuse and encouraged them to accuse their parents of being perpetrators. Later concluding that they had not been abused after all, these patients turned in anger against the therapists whose suggestions had abused them in a different way. In prompt response, the False Memory Syndrome Foundation (FMSF) was formed (Summit 1992). FMSF, a coalition of accused families and prominent mental health professionals, claims to have "documented a horrendous problem and made strides in bringing that problem to the attention of the mental health community" (Freyd 1993, p. 1). Like many therapists who understand their own patients' points of view, Prager (1993) responds with frank disturbance at what she feels to be a reactionary attack on her integrity and her patients' credulity. Certainly, there may be reactionary elements, families who willfully deny their wrongdoing, and others who are too dysfunctional and dissociated from reality to remember, but there are other families who are puzzled and hurt by accusations that do not fit their shared picture of their child-rearing years. We need to keep in mind the total picture of family memory, family members' differing levels of responsibility, and the nature of family memory as a consensual view or as a series of views that are segmentally valid and invalid, and held by one or another family member. This tremendously complex issue leaves therapists in the awkward position of taking sides, sometimes in court, and facing the same charges that have been leveled against the patient and the family. Now the therapist faces the charge of lying or trying to break up the family that confronts the accusatory survivor. The therapist is accused of being in denial like family members who attempt to prove their innocence.

No one is surprised when court cases in which a grown child sues an abusive parent grab pages in local and national newspapers or capture prime-time spots on talk shows that stimulate curiosity, evoke sympathy, or assuage guilt (Bikel 1993, Crews 1993, Gardner 1993, Ofshe and Watters 1993, Yapko 1993). In addition to the lure of scandal, discussion of the acceptability of recovered memory as testimony makes for interesting reportage. But now the debate about the credibility of recovered memory has extended to questioning the validity of repression as a concept and the value of psychotherapy itself (Gray 1993). The debate among professionals is so intense—and the resulting schism so threatening to the future of psychotherapy—that it has been the subject of media attention (Crews 1993, Jaroff 1993).

Jaroff (1993) lines up both sides of the debate, quoting Loftus, Ofshe, and Singer against, and Alpert and Courtois for, the validity of recovered memory. As examples of the unreliability of recovered memory, he cites court cases of accusations based on recovered memory that were later recanted and Singer's (1990) series of later disavowed satanic abuse cases. Then he extends the argument to the validity of what has now been called recovered-memory therapy. Here Jaroff quotes critics of recovered memory, Ganaway and McHugh: Ganaway deplores hospitals that have become "memory mills" and worries that stories about false recovered memory will ruin the hard-earned credibility of the abuse-survivor movement. McHugh thinks that therapists have used recovered memory to make therapy easy. Jaroff also quotes Courtois who refutes the criticism as a backlash of rage at therapists for confronting society with the appalling facts of childhood sexual abuse.

AN UNSUBSTANTIATED ACCUSATION

Mrs. B. had been in psychotherapy for 3 years to help her become less compulsive. Her husband supported her decision to have therapy, and in general sounded like a gentle, respectful, and loving man who encouraged her growth and development as a woman and as a professional. Mrs. B. was quite dedicated to his two adolescent children from a former marriage and enjoyed cooking and arranging things for their every-other-weekend visits. In therapy, Mrs. B. succeeded in placing a lower priority on her work so that she and Mr. B. could start a family of their own. With their two children, a boy and a girl, Mr B. was a warm and caring father. Mrs. B. found that she enjoyed combining the roles of wife and mother, and content with her progress, she terminated therapy. Some years later, Mrs. B. called me quite upset, and asked for a meeting with her and her husband, so that they could discuss a terrible accusation that her youngest stepdaughter had made.

Vania, now 22 years old and working as a research assistant in California, had called Mrs. B. to tell her that she had been attending a co-dependency peer group two or three times a week and wanted to see a therapist twice a month. She asked Mrs. B. not to tell her father about this. Mrs. B. was pleased that her stepdaughter was trying to work on her problems related to substance abuse, offered to help pay for it, and respected her wish. The next time Vania called, Mrs. B. asked how her therapy was going. Vania replied that they were working on problems of physical, sexual, and mental abuse and that Mrs. B. should not leave their children alone with their father. Mrs. B. was too upset by this assertion to keep it from Mr B., and she told him immediately. He was shocked, hurt, and puzzled. He said that there may have been mental abuse from the divorce, but there was no physical abuse and no sexual abuse. He and Mrs. B. called the other child from his first marriage and asked if she had thought that he was in any way abusive or inappropriate as a father. She said that the charge was nonsense and guessed that Vania must be wanting attention. Mrs. B. was sure that she could believe her husband and felt supported by her other stepchild.

Two months previously, Mr. B. had had a letter from Vania asking for money and saying that she was in a week-long program that included meetings on the 12-step model eight times a week and a massage therapist once a week. He showed me her letter and noted that "massage" had been spelled "message." He said that he thought her message was that the parents had done something to her and should pay for it. He was quite willing to contribute to her therapy and had sent her over $1,000. When he heard about her follow-up care, he was alarmed. He was still willing to help pay for therapy, provided the therapy was with a qualified therapist and provided that Vania also paid something according to her means, now that she was working. He was thinking of flying out to the West Coast to see her therapist to talk over what had happened. He found himself torn apart by this turn of events, and his mind kept going back over the past.

He went on to tell me that at the time of the divorce, Vania's mother could not raise her and Mr. B.'s job required traveling, and so she was sent off to boarding school. Vania was 14 when Mr. and Mrs. B. married, and they had kept in close contact with her, especially after her mother's co-dependency support group helped her decide that she should not interact with her children any more. The older girl was in college, Vania was in boarding school, and both girls spent their vacations with their father and stepmother. Vania was the baby, and the divorce hurt her the most. The older child was more confident, but Vania always had a strong need for love and attention. She wanted to be treated like a little girl. She wanted her feet and her back rubbed. She liked to be babied and she was.

When Mr. B. called to talk directly to Vania, he found that she had only a vague sense of being abused by him. The group had been encouraging her to confirm what they thought must have happened, but she had not actually remembered anything specific. Mr. B. said that no reputable therapist would accept that as an explanation for her difficulties or a way of dealing with them, but he thought that a peer group might. He knew the truth about himself, and he wanted her to know it too. He thought that Vania must not be in a good therapy situation, and he was wondering what he could do about it. He knew that the therapeutic relationship was important, and he did not want to break it up or interrupt Vania's efforts. He told me that he was proud of her for trying to solve her problems before she got married, unlike her mother whom he had finally left because of

her continued use of substances. He repeated that his conclusion was that Vania seemed to be saying that he was responsible
and should pay.

Mr. B.'s response was one of hurt, puzzlement, and anger.
There was no sense of narcissistic entitlement and no moral
outrage. He remained deeply concerned about his daughter.
There was no patriarchal family dynamic in his current family,
and his little children seemed secure and outgoing. There was
no power imbalance in his present marriage. He did not use
threats, and he was not seductive. He did not have and had not
had a problem with substance abuse. He denied the charge, but
he did not seem to be in denial. I concluded that he did not fit
the profile of a perpetrator and advised that he request a
consultation with Vania's therapist and assess her competence
to work through the issues.

Gardner (1992) deplores the current rash of accusations that he
describes as sex-abuse hysteria (p. 189). He welcomes the backlash
against false accusations, which he thinks are encouraged by the
present legal system. Under the provisions of the Child Abuse
Prevention and Treatment Act of 1974, professionals to whom sexual
abuse is mentioned can be prosecuted if they fail to report the case to
Child Protective Services, even though it may be their considered
professional opinion that no abuse has taken place. Any individual
reporting child sex abuse is granted immunity, so anyone is free to
make an accusation whether it is genuine or malicious. Obviously this
has the excellent effect of bringing needy cases to attention and, since
the program is funded, offering the victim free treatment, but it
encourages a rash of irresponsible reporting by people with a
grievance against a parent or a spouse. After reviewing 3,000 hours of
examiners' interviewing techniques and reporting, Gardner concluded that the investigators are not usually well trained, and some of
them are not credentialed at all. To get the child to tell them what they
expect and wish to hear, Gardner claims, they ask "sledgehammer"
leading questions, use leading gestures, deliver reinforcing hugs, fail
to understand a child's comprehension of what a lie is, make the
mistake of interviewing the child only in the presence of the parent
who is supporting the accusation, coerce the child who recants an
accusation to "tell the truth," contaminate the neutrality of the
process by the use of "anatomically correct" pictures and dolls that
stimulate sexual ideation, overlook the total lack of medical evidence
to rationalize their belief in incredible and preposterous claims,

pathologize normal behavior including masturbation as signs of sexual abuse, and generally tend to err on the side of validating accusations to be on the safe side and also to ensure a flow of referrals to the treatment service so that funding is not cut. In contrast, there is no funding to help the children who have been used to make false accusations or to help the falsely accused who also are deprived of due process.

Gardner's words carry emotion and urgency, along with clarity and confrontation of the crisis of false sex abuse accusations. He offers a valuable and articulate statement of the false memory position in the debate. However, his disparaging of credulous therapists and his ready dismissal as preposterous some experiences that patients report lead one to question the one-sidedness of his view, even though he accepts the reality of childhood sexual abuse. He is incredulous of the possibility of belated flashbacks, body memories, and recovered memory in adults who had remembered no childhood sexual abuse until it emerges in therapy. His view that many adult-child sexual encounters are not to be regarded as detrimental to well-being is intended as an antidote to the malicious accusation hysteria that he sees in the courts, but unfortunately it raises the possibility that he may not be sufficiently alarmed about the prevalence of sexual abuse of children.

Nevertheless, Gardner's attempt to remain free of bias in the way that he gathers testimony is an important model. He takes great care to set up his own testimony to the court as if he were an impartial evaluator, not an advocate, and he outlines the open-ended techniques for child evaluation that he thinks a responsible well-trained sex abuse investigator ought to use—encouraging the child to talk for a while; moving on to verbal projective tests and then free drawing and story telling; and providing ordinary doll sets or families of animals that the child may or may not gravitate to for traumatic re-enactment play in displacement. We must avoid leading questions (Loftus 1975). In a neutral setting, the child therapist or evaluator has the best chance of differentiating between true and false memories (White and Quinn 1988).

INDICATORS FOR IDENTIFYING CASES IN WHICH ABUSE HAS OCCURRED

When Incest Is Suspected or Claimed by a Child

Schetky provides a list of factors to look out for when assessing a child's memory of childhood sexual abuse in the legal context (1993).

She advises moving from the general to the specific, praising the child's effort but not the content of the memory, avoiding leading questions, and encouraging free recall. But memory research shows that younger children cannot manage free recall and need to be asked questions to stimulate their retrieval. Gardner (1992) describes in detail the criteria that tend to indicate that abuse has occurred. No single one is pathognomonic of sexual abuse, but the more of these criteria that are satisfied, the more likely is the child to have been abused. We agree with his conclusion that the quality of the findings and the language in which they are expressed may be more revealing than the sheer quantity of criteria that are satisfied. Weighing the clinical material calls for good judgment, freedom from bias, and thorough training.

We have created Tables 5–1 through 5–4 from Gardner's chapters (1992), not only for the child therapist who is evaluating or treating abused children but also for the adult therapist. These findings throw light on evaluating the validity of recovered memories and trying to understand the experience of the incest survivor in adult psychotherapy.

Any of these characteristics could apply to the individual case in either group, and so it is the overall picture that gives the best estimate of what has really happened. The reliability of the evaluator is much improved when he or she is the first to see the child and hear the story.

Equally important is an evaluation of the accusing parent. Usually, the accuser is the mother and the accused the father. Gardner (1992) gives an equally long list of her characteristics and emphasizes the importance of tracking the evolution of the accusation by obtaining her early history, family patterns, attitudes to men, reasons for seeking vengeance, and current circumstances (Tables 5–3 and 5–4). He finds most cases of false accusation occur in the context of custody disputes.

Gardner (1992) finds that the falsely accusing parent–who is usually the mother–is motivated by rage at being scorned by her divorcing husband. She punishes her husband by excluding him from his children. The stress of divorce and worries about economic support provoke a regression. In women who project, divorce aggravates paranoid anxieties that are then expressed in plotting, keeping notes, and devising paranoid strategies, such as alleging child sexual abuse. The borderline woman may decompensate and become delusional and present bizarre evidence. The sexually inhibited woman projects her sexual longings and then distorts and

Table 5-1. Child Characteristics Positive for Incest

Hesitancy to reveal the abuse and tendency to avoid the subject
Fear of the investigator
Fear of the accused finding out and hurting him or her
Guilt in the older child who knows the consequences to the accused
Guilt for feeling responsible for the abuse occurring
Rich details that demonstrate an internal visual image of the surroundings
    of the abuse
Ordinarily credible story without fantasy elaboration
Internal consistency of the story
Affect appropriate to the content
Spontaneous feel to the story
A story that does not change over at least two interviews
Unself-conscious use of colloquial sexual terminology
Signs of sexual excitation, such as rubbing genitals, talking about sex inap-
    propriately, or obsession with sexual body parts
Medical evidence of trauma to the genitals
Worries about genital damage that is not there
Excessive hesitation about undressing in front of peers
Playing at traumatic re-enactments with doll or animal families provided
    previous therapy has not encouraged this
Depression and suicidality
Flinching and discomfort in the presence of the accused
Looking listless, tired, sad, wan, pathetic, withdrawn, or timid
Keeping up a cheerful facade, being compliant and uncomplaining
Presence of psychosomatic symptoms, such as stomachaches, nausea, and
    headaches
Regressive symptoms, such as enuresis and encopresis
Feelings of betrayal by the bystander parent
Fearing going to sleep and nightmares (a less reliable indicator unless the
    content is specific)
Gradual progression and escalation of the abuse
Pseudomaturity in girls
Seductive behavior by girls with the accused father
Using school as a refuge unless there are learning problems
Antisocial acting-out of anger
Tension and hypervigilance
Runaway behavior
Accusation that does not extend to other perpetrators

Table 5–2.   Child Characteristics Positive for False Accusation of
                 Incest

Willing and eager to tell the story
No fear of the investigator, repeats story to anyone
Anger at, but no fear of, the accused
No guilt about the consequences to the accused
No guilt about causing the abuse, because none occurred
No surrounding details, just a description of an abusive event
No internal visual memory because nothing happened
Incredible story with fantasy elaboration
No internal consistency to the story
Angry affect, rather than sadness or listlessness
Rehearsed, speech-like litany
Story that changes over two interviews
Use of proper adult sexual language
No signs of sexual excitation, no obsession
No medical evidence
No anxiety about damaged genitals
No problems in the locker room
No re-enactment play unless coached to do so
No depression or suicidality
Anger perhaps, but no flinching and discomfort with the accused
Acting aggressive and complaining
No psychosomatic symptoms, because a false accuser is likely to
     externalize conflict
No regressive symptoms because there is no trauma
Positive feelings for the accusing parent
No specific nightmares
Only one or two suddenly occurring full-scale abuse episodes described
No pseudomaturity in girls
No seductive behavior
No excessive use of school as a refuge
Could be antisocial acting out, but less likely
No need for extreme tension and hypervigilance
No running away
Accusation may extend wildly in psychotic, psychopathic children

---

disowns them in the hated husband. Her sexual abuse charge may be
an extension of other feelings or delusions of jealousy about other
women. The hysterical woman becomes more histrionic, erratic,
liable to exaggerate, and likely to misinterpret the significance of signs
that she takes as evidence. She is also most vulnerable to being swept
along in a mass hysteria.

Table 5-3. Mother's Characteristics Positive for Validating
Incest

Sexually abused herself, unless she is projecting and vengeful
Not especially impulsive
Passive or inadequate, subjugated to domineering husband
Socially isolated
Not moralistic
Not paranoid
Not seeking divorce or custody
Feels pain over the possible need to remove the father from home
Does not exhort the child to tell the truth
Reluctant to report
Welcomes the impartial examiner
Worries about economic losses
Does not exaggerate the medical findings
Tries to limit the number of interrogations the child must go through
Does not involve a crowd of supporters
Does not have blind faith in experts and the legal system
Receptive to the lie detector test (more useful than actual result)
Inhibited socially and sexually
Leaves it to the child to tell the story
Does not prompt or lead the child
May accept sympathy and help from the accused father's parents
Straightforward in dealing with the evaluator and paying the fee

Lastly Gardner reminds us that we must make every effort to
see the abused child, the accusing parent, and the accused separately
and in combinations so as to obtain as broad a picture as possible.
Schetky (1993) advises minimizing the number of interviews to
minimize the trauma to the child. Forensic evaluations should be
avoided unless we have the time, the training, and the supervision to
do a thorough evaluation. White and Quinn (1988) advocate assessing
the investigatory independence of previous evaluators and ensuring
our own. They refer to external independence—not being allied with
any individual in the investigation—and internal independence,
being personally unbiased as to the outcome, introducing no assumed facts, and having no personal agenda. Even if we are not
involved in the legal assessment of allegations, we can learn much
from forensic experience that illuminates the clinical situation. Independence from a personal agenda is always a tenet of therapeutic
neutrality.

Table 5–4. Mother's Characteristics Positive for Detecting False
Accusation of Incest

Has no history of sexual abuse (especially valid if woman projects)
Reports impulsively to experts
Assertive, aggressive, pressuring, acts independently from husband
Outgoing, unconstrained, argumentative, marshals support
Teaches sex abuse materials to children
Excessively moralistic against sexuality, may show religiosity
Used escalating exclusionary tactics against husband before allegation
Involved in a child custody dispute
Produces audiotapes of child telling her about the abuse
Prompts and reminds the child to tell the truth
Wants to deprecate and humiliate the father
Relishes the thought of destroying and incarcerating the accused
Exaggerates abuse vociferously
Fails to ask the father about the possibility of abuse, prefers experts
Shuns impartial evaluators
Seeks an aggressive lawyer as her advocate
Blind to the economic cost
Marshals support in the community
Indiscriminately values any expert who agrees with her
No shame over the revelation of abuse in the family
Does not want to take a lie detector test
Wants to sever the child's relationship with the accused forever, especially
when this is a repetition of a family pattern
Uses the term "the truth"
Is theatrical and exhibitionistic
Exaggerates and attributes sexual significance to nonsexual activities
Paranoid, vague, circumstantial, and evasive
Obsessively devoted to collecting proof
Believes in the preposterous
Extends sex abuse danger to the family of the accused and excludes them
from therapy
Duplicitous in dealing with the evaluator over fees and meeting times

When Childhood Incest Is Later Remembered by an Adult

In nondirective, nonsuggestive psychotherapy, a man or woman may
recover deeply buried memories of events that were dissociated to
avoid distress during the time when they were current in childhood

or have been repressed because of conflict. These patients tend to doubt the validity of the memories and may wish that they were fantasies. Knowledge of how to deal with children who allege abuse helps us work with adult patients who may be survivors of abuse. Understanding the different types of memory and retrieval strategies appropriate to different developmental stages helps us make sense of the spotty memories that start to surface. Just as children need some questions to act as stimuli to their recall, adult patients need some, but not leading questions. Just as children remember forgotten events best when they return to the scene of the trauma in imagination, the adult patient gradually summons up the courage to do the same. Just as children remember best in an interpersonal context, adult patients use the therapeutic alliance for co-construction of the narrative of the abuse.

With time to explore the memories in the context of an insight-oriented therapy that deals with all aspects of the patient's inner and external life, past and present, patient and therapist gradually come to a shared view of what the memories indicate about the patient's life experience. Psychoanalytic therapists who are willing to keep an open mind do not bring the issue to closure by premature validation or dismissal. By the time that there is a degree of internal consistency about the reported family life growing up, the corroboration of siblings, the echoes found in the present family relationships, and manifestations in the transference, the therapist feels that the patient is indeed dealing with actual abuse history. Therapists who rapidly resort to hypnotic interventions and short-term methods, or who have a mindset of looking for abuse, may accelerate mere impressions to states of false certainty in place of confidence in the emerging reality of the patient's view of the past. This level of confidence is established thoughtfully over time in a broad-based psychoanalytic therapy that deals with repression as well as dissociation and that works through resistance. We are open to the possibility that this confidence level could be achieved in cases where the therapist who is qualified to do so uses hypnotic techniques judiciously, but we do not use hypnosis ourselves (Olsen 1993). In Chapter 13 we describe and illustrate various ways that memories resurface in individual psychoanalysis and in individual, family, sex, and marital psycho-therapy. In some cases, abuse memories were recovered and validated, and in others suspicion of abuse faded as the patient's internal experience became clear.

When Childhood Sexual Abuse is Later Falsely Remembered

The patients in this category welcome the discovery of an abuse history because now they have a simple answer and someone to blame for their problems. They project into the accused their own disavowed sexual impulses and attack them there as viciously as they do in themselves, which provides their internally assaulted ego some relief, but also lowers their self-esteem. They can believe that all of their psychological problems stem from their abuse and not from their own actions, murderous oedipal rage, frustrated longing, or from the neglect of parents whose deficiencies are nebulous. These patients do not feel the shame and uncertainty that the adult survivor has to surmount, and they are glad to tell everyone about the abuse and make a showcase of themselves on the media to hurt and expose their parents in particular and the opposite sex in general. Hysterical and paranoid tendencies are commonly found, and the accusation may be more delusionary than willful. The single accusation can be followed by a paranoid spread to the extermination of all contact with relatives who support the accused or attempt to remonstrate, and beyond into the adversarial legal process (Gardner 1992). Some of these patients who later realized that they had created false memories of abuse in response to suggestions from their therapists got together with supportive mental health professionals to found the False Memory Syndrome Foundation.

Our impression is that these patients who discover mistaken memories have been especially easily influenced by therapist, media, and cultural suggestions because they have a level of personality diffusion that is directly related not to abuse but to difficult early experience in a family whose disorganization and vulnerability derived from the parents' unresolved traumas and early losses. The children experience an internal void that echoes with hurt and doubt and cries out to be filled. A therapist or therapeutic program full of certainty may offer a simple, initially satisfying way to fill that inner void and offer an identity.

As we illustrate in Chapters 1 and 4, some adult patients have formed an erroneous conviction of having been traumatized that derives from encapsulating their parents' actual experience of trauma. Whether traumatized or not, these patients' parents also hurt. Even though there has been no abuse in these families, there has often been a family-wide degree of suffering or disorganization. The imposition of a simple solution provided by the therapist's certainty of abuse temporarily "solves" the patients' hurt at the cost of increased splitting and projection of shared hurt onto the parents. The parents are then blamed for villainy, rather than being understood to have been unable to manage loss, hurt, and emotional deficiency. Rather than participate with adult patients in blaming the parents who share their adult children's vulnerabilities, we should be encouraging such patients to open a dialogue with their parents, supported by adjunctive family therapy when necessary, in order to decrease the splitting and increase the areas of shared understanding and compassion, whenever possible.

THE CHALLENGE TO THE ANALYTIC PSYCHOTHERAPIST

The debate over true and false recovered memories continues in professional meetings, in the media, and in the responsible therapist's mind. In the clinical situation, each recovered memory is scrutinized and its validity debated. The therapist eventually arrives at an opinion in any one case or accepts a state of not knowing. In terms of public debate, most therapists would not want to be lined up either for or against the validity of recovered memories as the media tend to portray them doing, because each case is different and conclusions are arrived at in different therapeutic situations.

For the analytically oriented psychotherapist, the crucial questions are these. First, do the problems with validity result from the use of suggestion and hypnosis applied by naive, undertrained therapists or unscrupulous memory mills? If so, are we justified in distancing ourselves from the accusations and in concluding that the criticism does not apply to our way of working on repression and dissociation analytically? We think that the criticism rightly applies to irresponsibly suggestive therapies, and we do not accept the idea that these therapists are applying psychoanalytic principles. We believe that training, ongoing supervision, consultation, and personal therapy allow us to tolerate ambiguity and prepare us to work with patients over the long time that it takes to recover deeply repressed memories, explore them thoroughly, and evaluate their significance for the patient. Nevertheless, we take heed of Yapko's (1993) warning to be on the lookout for suggestive questioning and injunctive statements.

Second, faced with the shame of finding our therapeutic aims and methods discredited by societal backlash against the findings of the occurrence of childhood sexual abuse, will we maintain the integrity of our nondirective, nonjudgmental approach in which we follow where the patient leads? Will we continue as child advocates to speak out against abuse that compromises, and in some cases devastates, development? At the same time, can we retain our compassion for the perpetrator who was often abused in childhood too? Will we support the falsely accused abuser without feeling that we have undermined the position of the adult survivor? Can we maintain our sense of balance when psychotherapy is under this level of public scrutiny while also being under the threat of health care reorganization that is poised to discriminate against emotional illness by restricting reimbursement?

Last, can we defend the concept of repression—a fundamental tenet of psychoanalysis—against the assault upon it generated by the false memory syndrome proponents? Some critics argue that there is no such thing as repression. Perhaps they would also say that there is no such thing as the unconscious either. Other critics contend that there is repression of single incidents but not of cumulative trauma, which they believe leads instead to a failure of repression. We agree that trauma produces a failure of repression. The unprotected self cannot repress—push down into the unconscious what is unpleasant—because this usual defense mechanism is overwhelmed and so the self resorts to dissociation (Fairbairn 1954, Janet 1889, Pickle 1994). There are critics who accept the definition of repression as the avoidance in consciousness of unpleasant experiences that could otherwise return to haunt us, but who scoff at the probability of repression accounting for our having no awareness of our repeated traumas for years until something triggers a memory. What they do not accept is the related concept of dissociation. Dissociation and repression are both implicated, separately or together, in various types and degrees of trauma. To argue for one or the other is to ignore the complex interaction of reality, fantasy, and the defensive process. In Chapter 6, we proceed to examine and compare the two concepts of repression and dissociation.

6

Repression and Dissociation

Revisited

We are convinced of the difference between repression and dissociation and of the self's need for both these defenses in normal and abnormal development. Human behavior, motivation, thinking, and feeling are affected by unconscious processes of dissociation and repression that derive from and influence early experience in important relationships with significant others in a mutual process, the results of which are taken in and provide the stuff of personality.

The terms *repression* and *dissociation* are used loosely and sometimes interchangeably in the professional literature. Erdelyi (1992), who documented Freud's use of dissociation and repression, prefers to find no distinction between them, but he does distinguish amnesia (the effect) from repression (the cause). Vaillant (1990), in contrast, thinks, as we do, that the terms dissociation and repression do have specific meanings and that distinctions between them should be drawn. Rather than relying on Freud, Vaillant uses Anna Freud's 1937 definition of the aim of repression: "to forget the idea but to retain the affect in consciousness" (Vaillant 1990, p. 260). He develops the following definitions of repression and dissociation:

Repression serves to alter ideational content while preserving affective state, to forget ideational content, to prevent the identification of conflictual material and to forgo cherished goals.

Dissociation serves to alter affective state and avoid emotional distress by altering one's sense of identity and refusing to perceive personal responsibility for one's situation. [p. 260]

REPRESSION

Repression was the term that Freud gave to the mental mechanism through which the conscious ego turned away undesirable thoughts and memories and kept them in the realm of the unconscious along with the id impulses emanating from the unconscious where they gave rise to the unacceptable material (1915a,b). Because he equated the unconscious with the id, and because in his theory the id operated independently of the ego, Freud thought that repression of these impulses in the id was quite compatible with the maintenance of an intact ego, and therefore splitting was not of concern. Freud used the term repression both loosely (1906) to mean any ego defense and specifically (1894) to refer to the defense in which the idea is pushed into unconsciousness and so forgotten, but the associated affect remains in consciousness and the idea often returns in disguised, symbolic form (Vaillant 1990). Later Freud (1923) invoked the superego as an additional agent to secure the repression of id material by the ego and to exert an inhibiting force against one part of the self (the id) by another (the superego).

So far we have been describing *repression proper,* a mental response to *internal conflict.* In his paper on repression (1915a), Freud also described a precursor of repression proper; namely, *primal repression,* a mental response to a *deficiency.* Primal repression occurred because of a developmental delay in achieving repression proper or because of an inability to cope in secondary process ways with an overwhelming assault on the stimulus barrier, so that the primary process became the organism's primary method of dealing with, and communicating about, experience (Frank 1969).

Freud had invented the term repression to account for the patient's resistance to improvement (1917b). He rightly perceived the tremendous force of the hysterical patient's resistance to being helped by him, and conceived of it as resulting from an equally forceful and active mechanism in consciousness for keeping the unacceptable ideas hidden. Direct leaks could occur when the repressed material pressed for re-emergence to gratify the sexual or aggressive drives, but was kept in a state of tension by the opposing ego and the dammed-up energy finally broke through as a discharge. Indirect leaks could also occur in the form of hysterical symptoms in which an afflicted body part substituted for the recognition of a painfully denied wish, or in neurotic symptoms that represented a compromise between the direct sexual or aggressive expression of the drives and the ego's demand for acquiescence to the necessities of reality and social control.

A few years later, Freud again referred to trauma as the cause of the mental organization that he called *the repetition compulsion* (1920). He noted the need to repeat and re-enact trauma in dream sequences, a finding that called into question his earlier theory of the wish fulfillment basis of dreaming and therefore of the pleasure principle itself as the basis for human motivation (Cohen 1984). Aggressive and self-destructive forces could not be accounted for except by invoking another instinct countervailing to the libido, namely, the death instinct. Cohen and Kinston (1984) remarked upon the inadequacy of the intensely intrapsychic Freudian theory of conflict-based and deficiency-based repression. Cohen (1985) pointed to the need to integrate Kardiner's (1941) view of the traumatic neurosis as a psychophysiological response that is both an adaptation to the trauma of the real world and a failure of the normal adaptive capacity that utilizes symbol formation and psychic representation. Cohen also invoked Klein's (1946) object relational amplification of the vagaries of the death instinct in order to explain the drastic alteration or destruction of previously formed psychic structure that follows massive trauma. Trauma cannot be understood without the premise that psychic structure depends on environmental support for its formation and maintenance.

Klein's (1946) theory gives us the concept of a trauma-induced and retraumatizing psychic organization called the *paranoid-schizoid position* in which anxiety due to the traumatizing effect of the death instinct has to be deflected and projected into the mother for detoxification. However, this anxiety then returns to haunt the infant who identifies the mother with the aggression emanating from the self and projected into her so that she becomes a persecuting object, unless, as Bion (1967) described, she functions as a good "container," a metabolizer of these anxious bits and pieces. When the infant identifies with her containing function, he can move gradually away from the inevitability of the paranoid schizoid position to a more integrated position. In this more mature state, which Klein (1946) called *the depressive position*, the infant becomes capable of experi-

encing his mother as a whole object about whom he has both
ambivalent feelings and concern. Despite the relational context in
which Klein arrived at her theory, she gave surprisingly little attention to the effect of actual environmental trauma and followed Freud
in emphasizing the internal death instinct as the source of the
trauma-based psychic organization. Nevertheless Cohen (1985) holds
that Klein's theory is an advance because it specifies mental mechanisms of splitting, projection, and projective identification in conditions of traumatic disruption of organized functioning. Cohen and
Kinston (1984) suggest that repression proper occurs in order to
internalize interpersonal terror and gain mastery over it through its
transformation into symbols of unacceptable wishes and fantasies
that existed during the trauma and that come to represent the
otherwise unknowable trauma. In this way the trauma-based self-
protective behaviors due to primal repression—behaviors such as
denial, splitting, and projective identification—can be modified. Yet,
primal repression itself cannot be modified because, being devoid of
representation, it cannot be defended against internally, but can only
be defended against in relation to an object that mediates its need.

Cohen and Kinston's review of the effects of trauma in terms of
drive and structural psychoanalytic theories takes us only part of the
way and leaves us in search of ways to augment our understanding.
Trauma confronts psychoanalysis with the need for an object relational theory in addition to classical models.

REPRESSION AND DISSOCIATION COMPARED

Fairbairn was fascinated by the differences and similarities between
repression and dissociation. Like Freud, Fairbairn had treated patients suffering from hysteria (1927). He had also had experience with
cases of childhood sexual abuse (1935) and war neuroses (1943b).
These cases brought him in touch clinically with the phenomena of
dissociative states that would lead him eventually to the concept of
splits in the ego from the severe, as in these cases, to the normal
during the process of the creation of the human personality as a
dynamic system of parts under ego control.

Early in his career, Fairbairn (1929b) reviewed the literature on
dissociation and repression and first described dissociation as the
more general category of which repression is a special case. He added
to the existing literature an original categorization that we summarize
in Table 6-1.

Table 6–1. Types of Dissociation

Dissociation of mental content that is *irrelevant* to the attention of the subject

Dissociation of mental content that is *incompatible* with other content

Dissociation of that which is perceived as *unpleasant*

   Either (1) unpleasant mental contents or (2) unpleasant tendencies in the self toward unpleasant mental contents

---

Repression, he wrote at that time, is a special form of dissociation to be grouped in this last category, the unpleasant. It is to be differentiated from other forms of dissociation of the unpleasant in that repression of the dissociated elements consists essentially in repressing tendencies that derive from the mental structure itself, whereas in the less striking forms of dissociation of the unpleasant, the dissociated elements consist of the mental content alone.

In simple dissociation of the unpleasant, what is dissociated is part of the mental content which is felt to be unpleasant because of its relation to a prevailing tendency. In repression, what is dissociated is part of the mental structure which is felt to be unpleasant because of its relation to the organised self. [Fairbairn 1929b, p. 74]

REPRESSION AND DISSOCIATION DISTINGUISHED: REPRESSION OF MENTAL STRUCTURE VERSUS DISSOCIATION OF MENTAL CONTENT

Fairbairn argued (1929b) that repression is an active force exerted by the main part of the personality—which he had the foresight to call "the organized self" —against another part of the self. Most dissociation occurs to make mental *contents* unconscious. Repression is aimed not at the contents but at their *effect on the self*. Repression occurs to keep a part of the *self* unconscious to avoid the pain of conflict it would bring if allowed to become or remain conscious. A nice distinction, and one that we move beyond, but to which we return later.

By the 1940s Fairbairn had abandoned his discussion of the difference between repression and dissociation. His thinking about dissociation had been transformed beyond easy recognition to the processes contained in the universal "splitting of the ego." In his later formulations, splitting was inevitably paired with repression to reject painful content and to build unconscious structure compartmentalized away from consciousness. These internal structures, he said, are themselves in dynamic relationship and are simultaneously able to initiate or potentiate repression of other internal self-and-object structures. The formulation posits the interaction of repressed content with the evolving structure of the mind that must contain it. He saw this sort of interaction as equally relevant for the pathological organizations both of neurotic personality and of multiple personality disorder.

Near the end of his career, Fairbairn (1954) noted that the concept of dissociation had been largely overtaken by the concept of repression, which had come to form the cornerstone of psychoanalytic theory. However, he thought that this shift incurred a loss of direct understanding of the more severely split ego-states, such as those found in multiple personality. His understanding of repression had changed over the years until he reached the position that *repression was always paired with splitting* of the personality, a phenomenon that we regard as a modified form of dissociation in a more pervasive, comprehensive, and normative form. By then, Fairbairn had also moved away from the problems of trauma in early life and in war that had been part of his earlier experience. These severe situations are ones in which the central ego's capacity to repress is overwhelmed, and the splits in the ego therefore become so severe that subpersonalities or states of being evade the integrating capacities of a central organized self. It seems likely that the early work with abused children and war trauma neuroses—perhaps along with his own experience as a combat officer in the First World War—deeply influenced him and is part of the reason that his final theoretical formulations remain so useful in studying the forms of severe psychopathology seen in multiple personality, dissociative, and hysterical syndromes.

FAIRBAIRN'S MATURE CONCEPTS OF DISSOCIATION AND SPLITTING OF THE EGO

The term *dissociation* was introduced by Janet (1889) to explain the concept of hysteria. Fairbairn (1954) paraphrases Janet's view of the hysterical state as follows:

In terms of this concept the hysterical state is essentially due to inability on the part of the ego to hold all the functions of the personality together, with the result that certain of these functions become dissociated from, and lost to, the rest of the personality and, having passed out of the awareness and control of the ego, operate independently. The extent of the dissociated elements was described by Janet as varying within wide limits, so that sometimes what was dissociated was an isolated function such as the use of a limb, and sometimes a large area or large areas of the psyche (as in cases of dual or multiple personality); and the occurrence of such dissociations was attributed to the presence of a certain weakness of the ego — a weakness partly inherent, and partly induced by circumstances such as illness, trauma or situations imposing a strain upon the individual's capacity for adaptation.

Dissociation as described by Janet is, of course, essentially a passive process — a process of disintegration due to a failure on the part of the cohesive function normally exercised by the ego. [p. 8]

Prince (1919) disagreed with Janet's depiction of the dissociating ego as feeble. He pointed out that dissociation is accompanied by the intelligent synthesis of certain ideas, feelings, and perceptions to create separate personality systems. We agree with this point of view, but we also see dissociation as the result of genetically endowed, transgenerationally transmitted, and environmentally conditioned ego weakness and failure of integration of the self (Braun and Sachs 1985).

Modern views follow Fairbairn's later thinking that dissociation involves a discontinuity of parts of the mind and of mental functioning — rather than a split of contents alone. Repression might today be seen as the less pathologized mechanism, whereas dissociation has come to be associated more closely with severe splits in the personality and with such concepts as hypnogogic states and multiple personality. Nevertheless, modern theorists (Putnam 1989) view dissociation of parts of the personality, as did Fairbairn, as a normal process throughout life, but one whose prominence at certain periods in early childhood predisposes to severe pathology and severe splits in the functioning self or ego, if traumatic conditions overwhelm ego capacity. Thus, repression could still be viewed as a subcategory of dissociation, but now as a more normal one having to do both with ordinary splitting and with covering up of conflictual parts of the personality at war with the central organized self. Dissociation implies splits of consciousness and of self-states of the personality — with loss of the self's integrative capacity.

We conclude that repression occurs in order to maintain cohesion of the self. Dissociation occurs so as to fragment parts of the self and sacrifice some in order to save others and to keep the overall sense of the self from annihilation.

Both dissociation and repression can now be seen to exist on a continuum from normal, nonpathological examples to pathological extremes: repression ranges from the normal sorting of material into unconscious internal object relations to the severe depletion of personality in schizoid states. Dissociation ranges from giving us the capacity to daydream, have a hypnogogic hallucination as we fall asleep, isolate ourselves from pain and substitute a physical pain for an emotional relational conflict, or subject ourselves to severe nonintegration, as is found in multiple personality disorder.

REPRESSION AND ITS CONNECTION TO SPLITTING

Fairbairn's (1954) conclusion suggests that Janet thought that dissociation is not meant to happen. It happens unintentionally, as an error of omission by a weakened ego, in contrast to repression, which is an intentional act of commission on the part of a strong ego. From this, we have concluded that *dissociation is a default position, an inbuilt adaptation to a failed response situation.* How is the cohesive function of the ego normally exercised? Fairbairn spells out various forms of repression (see below) that secure the dynamic balance of the healthy ego and the compromised one. We suggest now that *dissociative phenomena result from a failure of repression, rather than from a special type of repression.*

Fairbairn also used repression to refer to the activity of pushing material from consciousness to unconsciousness and keeping it there. Like Freud he thought of it as an active process. Yet, the drive that he thought fundamental was the drive for attachment, not the sexual and aggressive instincts. He did not think in terms of repressing the drive for attachment, however. In his object relations theory, Fairbairn dispensed with Freud's idea of an id separate from the ego. Instead, he conceived of the personality as comprising a unitary ego at birth, ready and needing to relate. When experience with the object is intolerably frustrating, the ego represses its experience of the object into unconsciousness. However, it saves the good part by splitting off the bad through a dissociative process that is accompanied by repression. He borrowed the term *splitting* from Bleuler (1950), who introduced it to describe the ego fragmentation seen in schizophrenia. Fairbairn thought that there was no fundamental difference between that kind of splitting and the kind seen in hysteria where, as did Janet (1889), he found that dissociation was accompanied by a split in the ego. Splitting the object necessarily involved splitting the ego, because ego and object are in an intrapsychic relationship within a dynamic structure of personality.

In Fairbairn's view, splitting and repression always occur together. The point of splitting is to shear off the bad and get rid of it responsibly inside the self so as to maintain a conscious relationship with a good object. However, the relationship with the bad object is also maintained in unconsciousness because a part of the ego that relates to the bad part of the object is split off and repressed with it, along with the affects that connect them. Like Freud's, his model depends on a horizontal split between consciousness and unconsciousness. However, unlike Freud, who thought of the unconscious as a seething cauldron of impulses, Fairbairn conceived of it as an organized system of relationships of parts of ego and object in intimate connection under varying degrees of splitting and repression, all of them in dynamic relation. Where the quality of the bad object is excessively exciting or rejecting, the extent of splitting from the good object is extreme and leaves an impoverished object in consciousness connected to a deprived ego from which excessively libidinal and antilibidinal egos have also been split off. This circumstance requires that the repression be maintained more rigidly, to keep the pain of the excessive excitement and rejection away from the ideal object of the central ego and to protect the diminished ego from assault. This explains the intensity of the hysteric's repressed sexuality and the compulsive sacrifice of it (Fairbairn 1954).

Fairbairn's combination of the processes of repression and splitting has been regarded as confusing to those who wish to separate them (Rinsley 1979). Fairbairn's ideas have been appreciated and integrated into his psychoanalytic thinking by Kernberg (1975), but on the topic of splitting and repression the two differ. According to Fairbairn's theory, splitting and repression occur simultaneously, whereas Kernberg regards repression as a higher-level defense than splitting. Kernberg defines splitting as primitive dissociation, which he finds in psychotic, borderline, and some highly neurotic forms of pathology. In contrast, he holds that repression predominates in normal and neurotic conditions.

Fairbairn would have agreed that repression is an active process requiring ego strength, whereas dissociation is a passive process that emanates from ego weakness (Janet 1889). He guessed that that difference accounts for the supremacy of repression in psychoanalytic thinking. He regretted that, although Freud at one time had written that dissociation and splitting of consciousness were fundamental manifestations of hysteria, he had lost interest in the concept as he became more interested in repression encountered in analyzing resistant cases of obsessional neuroses and character pathology. Grotstein (1992) comments on this development as Freud's movement away from the vertical to the horizontal splitting of consciousness and unconsciousness in the personality. To us, Fairbairn's explanation of the concepts of splitting and repression reflects the complexity of horizontal and vertical defense schemata, and yields a complex, dynamic, three-dimensional view of personality.

For Fairbairn, repression was a multifaceted process occurring at different levels in the dynamic ego. The original ego introjects the inevitably somewhat unsatisfying object as a first line of defense. Fairbairn did not spell this process out, but we presume that he meant that introjection was a defense against the catastrophe of non-attachment. The second line of defense is to split the unsatisfying object into its rejecting aspect and its exciting aspect, leaving behind an ideal object. Fairbairn called this *direct and primary repression* by the ego. Now follows a splitting of the ego into corresponding exciting and rejecting parts that cathect the exciting and rejecting object elements, leaving behind the rest of the ego, now called the central ego. Fairbairn called this process *direct and secondary repression* by the remaining central ego. The endopsychic structure of the personality now consists of a central ego cathecting an acceptable object called the ideal object, and two split-off and repressed ego structures each cathecting a repressed internal object. One, called the libidinal ego, cathects the exciting object. The other, called the antilibidinal ego, cathects the rejecting object. The antilibidinal ego is further hostile to the aims of the libidinal ego and supports its repression by the central ego by sustained persecutory attack. Fairbairn called this *indirect repression*. This completes Fairbairn's picture of the role of repression in the formation of personality as a dynamic structure in the normal situation. At the same time Fairbairn found in this dynamic endopsychic situation the potential for all psychopathological developments in later life, their exact form being determined by whether the libidinal and antilibidinal objects were internalized inside the self or externalized in relationships (Fairbairn 1954).

DICKES

Dickes (1965) reported the occurrence of hypnoid states during analytic sessions when patients were unable to deal with sexually and aggressively intense affects and memories that derived from actual incestuous abuse. He described a variety of hypnoid phenomena from mild chronic nonalertness and fatigue, through dopeyness, boredom, tuning out, and nodding off, to a deep state of apparent sleep. Dickes went to great lengths to make the case that the hypnoid state is not a state of drowsiness or sleep. Rather, it is a state of altered consciousness, but unlike the hypnotic state, it is spontaneously induced. The child learns to experience a hypnoid state while experiencing the hypnotic overtones of crooning, lullabies, and rhythmic sucking at the breast and at a later age invokes a similar state as a defense. In Dickes' view, the hypnoid state is instigated by the internalized parents who are present in the ego and superego to counter the unacceptable impulses and to maintain the ego's level of repression of the unacceptable material. He wrote, "The ego, subservient to the superego and executive organ of the psyche, then institutes the hypnotic defense in the service of repression" (Dickes 1965, pp. 396–397). He described the hypnoid state as a defense that is necessary to defend against the emergence of overwhelming sexual and aggressive affects elicited by childhood sexual trauma, showed that it operates as a resistance in therapy, and held that its function is to maintain repression. He did not use or refer to the concept of dissociation.

DAVIES AND FRAWLEY, GROTSTEIN, AND GABBARD

Davies and Frawley (1992) reviewed the origins of the concept of dissociation and attempted to update its definition in accordance with contemporary research on traumatic and post-traumatic disorders. Their formulation differs from the classical idea of dissociation as a regressive defense against overwhelming sexual and aggressive drive discharges stimulated by assault, as they take an object relational perspective. They write (Davies and Frawley 1992):

> We use the concept of dissociation to refer to an organization of mind, not unlike splitting, wherein traumatic memories are split off from associative accessibility to the remainder of conscious thought, but rather than being repressed and forgotten, as would be the case in a topographical/structural

model, they alternate in a mutually exclusive pattern with conscious ego states. . . . Unlike splitting, in which the goal is to protect the good object from the murderous impulses of an angry frustrated self, dissociation aims to protect the person from the overwhelming memory of traumatic events and the regressive fantasies that these memories trigger. . . . We view dissociation not merely as a defense against drive, but, rather, as a process that preserves and protects, in split-off form, the entire internal object world of the abused child. [p. 8]

They point out that, before Freud developed his concept of the repression of memories and impulses that were unacceptable to consciousness along a continuum of layers progressively farther out of reach of consciousness, like the layers of an onion, he was writing about the alternation of differing experiences of consciousness in the hysterical patient. Breuer and Freud (1893–1895) had already described something quite different from Freud's later theory of layers of repression of memories or impulses. They had postulated coexisting, mutually exclusive ego states that cannot be connected in time. Intolerable feelings of overstimulation can be warded off and controlled by dissociation, which promotes an autohypnoid state (Fleiss 1953, Shengold 1989) that also permits drive discharge in the form of traumatic re-enactments both naturally in childhood and in the transference when it occurs in therapy. So Davies and Frawley do not regard dissociation as a defense and a resistance to the emergence of abuse material, but rather as a process that contributes dissociative experience between patient and analyst in the transference-countertransference. It is through this process that analysts can understand from inside their own experience what was the child's experience of self and object, and the survivor can rework her adjustment to her traumatic reality in a safe holding environment. In treatment, analysts do not interpret dissociative states so much as simply enter them to reach the unavailable memories. In our view, we need to do both—interpret the defensive function of dissociation and welcome it as an avenue for work. We join with Davies and Frawley in recommending that the analyst contain, comprehend, and only then interpret the introjective and projective processes occurring in the transference-countertransference.

We view dissociation as an umbrella term that applies to a variety of resulting coexistent ego states that alternate rapidly or slowly with greater or lesser degrees of fragmentation. We see these ego states as partially developed internal object relationships that are inadequately repressed and therefore need to be split off from one another to give the others a chance. Davies and Frawley find that these ego states carry an adult or a child identity, quite out of touch with the other, and that the inner child is further divided into good, bad, sad, naughty, angry children, and so on. Although we regret that many Americans who do not need therapy are now walking around communing with their inner children as a result of the popularization of this concept, and although we are uncomfortable with reifying these fragments as if they actually were people (Yapko 1993), we agree with Grotstein (1992) that a substantial proportion of adult survivors of incest do experience themselves in this way. Some have learned to conceptualize themselves like other survivors they read of in the popular literature or meet in their support groups, but only those with multiple personality disorder require their alters to be related to as separate selves. The clinical example in Chapter 11 illustrates the appearance and disappearance of inner children.

Grotstein (1992), commenting on Davies and Frawley (1992), noted that the authors distinguish between dissociation as resulting in a dissociated ego state, and splitting, which refers to the division of the bad object from the good object. Grotstein himself (1981) suggests that dissociation and splitting are not so discontinuous and that dissociation is an extreme form of the splitting of ego and object that Fairbairn described.

Fairbairn also conceived of splitting as a ubiquitous and protean function, ranging from healthy emotional sorting of experience to pathological dissociation of ego and object. He thought that splitting operates not only to tame the ravages of aggression but also to exclude intolerably painful internal object relationships from con-sciousness even in the normal personality. So, splitting arises not just to keep the good object and the central self from being contaminated or destroyed by the bad, as Fairbairn said, but also from the need to separate out and sort differing aspects of objects into categories that correspond to how the ego perceived the experience, as Bion thought. When these aspects of objects are totally incompatible, or when bad and good are hopelessly confused in inappropriate but pleasurable sexual stimulation, the split self-and-object relationships cannot be well categorized and repressed. Instead they form in parallel, divided by vertical splits in the ego, and coexist as mutually exclusive entities. We find that in more severe dissociative states, the ego and its object do not remain connected by their relevant affects, but split apart and operate like loose cannons up and down the vertical lines. This splitting pushes the person to act out confusing, alternating identifi-cation with self-and-object fragments, leading to an intrapsychic

nonrelatedness that is expressed in personal interaction as a fundamental sense of nonbeing, even though there may be massive
amounts of sadomasochistic activity on the part of the part-objects
and part-egos mainly stemming from the paternal transference. What
appears as the profusion of multiple personality is really the absence
of a single, integrating self.

This sense of nonbeing has also been referred to by Gabbard
(1992), who notes that the therapist can reach this level after interpreting to the patient the sadomasochistic enactments as a defense
against the maternal deprivation. A clue to detecting the nonbeing
comes to therapists when they find themselves being experienced as
indifferent. The patient can also be precipitated into this state after
revealing her closely held secret, because holding her secret has
functioned for her as a substitute internal holding for the absent
maternal holding (Goodwin 1990). Bigras and Biggs (1990) described
a melancholic emptiness or deadness that derives from experiencing
the bystanding, nonintervening mother as an absent object. Gabbard
finds that the ineffectual, remote mother may be reactivated in the
transference-countertransference; for instance, when the patient remains aloof or the analyst feels disbelieving, lacking in interpretive
energy, or downright dead (Lisman-Pieczanski 1990). Sometimes the
analyst will want to get rid of the patient, in echo of the mother's
avoidance of the problem. Gabbard reminds us of Bernstein's (1990)
belief that a satisfactory introjective identification with the analyst,
male or female, as a caring maternal figure facilitates the recovery of
traumatic memories.

The maternal deprivation can be understood by a therapist who
can be experienced in the transference in various negative ways and
yet can contain these projective identifications and modify them
gradually. Then the patient introjects a frustrating object that is,
however, a reliable, empathic containing object, and so can achieve
the internalization of a whole object. This internalized whole object
can then hold together the split parts of the self and eventually may
be strong enough to repress them properly and allow their integration.

CONCEPTS OF MEMORY

Encoding: Processing Perception and Registering the Memory

Psychoanalytic clinical research has shown that memory is an associative process. Memory is not a matter of stamping in an image that

is filed away by topic and date. Memory is not like a computer with its rigid internal logic (Christianson 1992, Gardner 1992, Palombo 1978, Yapko 1993). In the human brain, it is not the case that all data carry equal weight, are organized entirely according to the logic of the directory system, and are equally accessible to the "find" command, because, unlike the computer, the human being possesses emotion, will, and intelligence to alter the field of perception, and is changed by the learning process. The human brain is perhaps like a network of parallel distributed processing systems that are not fully under central control, but that operate autonomously and sometimes at cross purposes (Spiegel 1990). However, there the analogy ends, because encoding of memory in the living human being is influenced by the affective condition of the ego at the time of the experience, the level of arousal, the motivation, the similarity of the experience to earlier experience, and the relationship among the people involved in the experience that generates the perception, idea, or fantasy to be remembered. New memory accrues in association to already established memories laid down at earlier stages of development. As these new memories deriving from a maturing perceptual ability are encoded, they refashion the original memory to which they become attached, and yet they carry within them earlier versions of similar memories. In other words, memory is contextual. Memories fill in for each other to create a sense of continuity of past experience. They are subject to influence from outside sources as well when parents contest and reshape the child's perceptions both helpfully and unhelpfully.

Once a number of memories form a reliable constellation, a sense of self is established with a belief in what future experience will be like. Other subsequent experiences that are not similar to those that have gone before generate perceptions that do not fit with the cluster. Either they can be filtered out by selective inattention early in the encoding process, they may be encoded but not rehearsed sufficiently to stamp them in, or they may be stored in a compartment connected to the state in which the experience was perceived but not connected to other storage compartments. Or they can be filtered out by cognitive dissonance (Aronson 1969) so that they do not challenge the prevailing memory constellation. All of these possibilities seem to be aspects of a dissociative process (Terr 1993). All of these processes affect the capacity to learn from experience and to accept and integrate new ideas in the intellectual, emotional, intrapsychic, interpersonal, and social realms.

An internal object relationship is the memory trace of a relationship (Bollas 1987). It is subject to the same principles as other examples of memory. There is a tendency to relate to future experiences in ways that confirm perceptions that are already in memory. The infant's learning environment is provided by the mother whose capacity to metabolize her own and her child's anxiety so as to secure a comfortable level of arousal, a state of need satisfaction, and confidence in her containing function sets the scene into which she introduces new experience and, in interaction with the infant's endowment, determines how the infant perceives and remembers. The mother-child relationship is the original matrix in which the infant learns to modify perception and memory in the light of experience and to develop a learning style.

Recall and Recognition

The retrieval of memory is governed by the same psychological factors that affect perception and storage. Like encoding, retrieval is an associative process. It occurs normally in one of two ways: by spontaneous conscious effort to recall the information starting with nothing, and by recognition in which a clue—usually a word—presents itself and attracts to it the ideas that are associated with it in memory. Memory of emotionally tinged, interpersonal events, rather than of cognitive information, is reached associatively from words and also from sights, sounds, touches, smells, and sensations of vibration and proprioception (the sense of the position of the joints and muscles). These last two senses refer to the body's experience of itself and its position moving through space. In therapy all these avenues of stimulating memory recall apply. In addition we encourage access to the clues provided by dream material in which associations are already at hand, and where image and word stimuli are connected without regard to the conscious, logical progression of waking life, but use the primary process logic of dream memory instead. The technique of free association proceeds from the natural base offered by the dream to give access to the earlier versions of remembered experience.

In the usual case, memories of early life are repressed, refashioned, and reconstructed almost seamlessly except where there are unresolved conflicts that interfere with normal repression. The controlled regression of analytic therapy permits gradual access to the lower reaches of the storage banks through a painstakingly slow process of making associative links. Yapko (1993) holds that it is not possible to delve into the recovery of a deep, repressed memory by the sudden application of a hypnotic technique without altering the memory in the process (Spiegel 1980). The suggestion required to induce the trance also affects the retrieval process so that it is less accurate than when the memory is recalled naturally. Paradoxically the hypnotized person feels more certain of the accuracy of a memory recalled after suggestion (Loftus et al. 1989). Hypnosis is a remarkably effective technique for gaining access to various ego states, giving them a voice, and changing the perceptions and their affective impact in those alternating states of consciousness (Watkins and Watkins 1982) in those patients who can be hypnotized. However, it is not valid as a retrieval mechanism, lie detector, or gauge of the level of accuracy of recovered early memories.

In some situations of trauma and constitutional predisposition to dissociate, memories are inadequately repressed. Instead they are encapsulated or dissociated. Access to these memories may be gained quite suddenly in the form of belated flashbacks that are stimulated associatively by new trauma, intense interpersonal experience that calls for states of arousal such as sexual interaction, life-threatening illness or death of oneself or of a family member, and the removal of defenses in psychotherapy. We also gain access to them through our understanding of the use of body parts to contain memories of early object relational experience. Gardner (1992) objects to the concept of body memory on the grounds that there are no memory cells except in the brain. Indeed, there are no memory cells in the end organ, but the end organ responds reflexively to signals from the brain that are changed or intensified based on responses to memory encoded in the brain's map of the end organs. The ensuing reflex stimulation of those organs that are more vulnerable at the current developmental stage may lead to repeating patterns for dealing with stress in physical routes. In addition, unconscious fantasy influenced by the memory of the past experience of self and other can be projected not only into the other but also into one's own body. One organ can become the container for an internal object relationship that is a threat to the integrity of the self. In hysterical, nontraumatized women there may be projection of oral longing into the vagina where wishes to suck, bite, and masticate have to be viciously bitten off in fantasy before they damage the penis, which is viewed unconsciously as the organ of nourishment when the breast has been frustrating in excessively exciting and rejecting ways. Sexual panic or frigidity then becomes the body's sign of the conflict.

In the traumatized patient a similar mechanism can be found. It does not mean that the body has actually remembered events, just that the body, through its response to stimulation corresponding to the brain map, is the vehicle for expressing the accretion of memories of a particular object relationship. The traumatized patient may also report a classical *body memory*. Mrs. Feinstein (in Chapter 11) reported a bizarre incident while driving during which she had a vivid sensation of being a naked toddler pulled up along her mother's naked body. The automatic activity of driving produces a state of autohypnosis in nontraumatized, nondissociating people who describe occasional episodes of "highway hypnosis." In Mrs. Feinstein, an adult survivor of incest, the autohypnotic state yielded a specific image that was so distressing to her that she had to pull off the road and collect herself. Mrs. Feinstein finds it hard to believe that she could possibly remember anything that happened at such an early age, and yet it seems to her to be consistent with her later remembered experience of childhood and adolescence. Even though at the end of her treatment she remained unconvinced of the validity of this memory alone, she acted upon the information contained within it and warned her brother not to let her mother babysit for his 1-year-old child. In addition to the autohypnotic condition during motoring, Mrs. Feinstein arrived at her body memory experience in the context of recovering other vivid, sensorily elaborated memories in her analysis and to some extent in the transference.

The physically traumatized person is likely to need physical routes of expression. She gains access to her internal object relationships through physical sensations, flashbacks, body memories, and recovered memories reconstructed in the course of therapy, especially within the transference, until she has a sense of what might have, and what must have, taken place. We gain access to the intrapsychic and interpersonal conflict expressed in body language through our capacity to put this into words while simultaneously relating to the person in a preverbal way; that is, by silently holding images in the mind, experiencing and being experienced, processing, and finally commenting upon the patient's use of the mother within the transference as a recreation of the mother-infant relationship.

In *dissociation* a vertical amnesic barrier between coexisting states of consciousness prevents the interchange of memories, not all of which have affective significance, whereas in *repression* a horizontal repression barrier between consciousness and unconsciousness operates against unacceptable impulses that remain buried deep in the unconscious (Hilgard 1976, 1986). Hilgard (1986) identified two types of repression. The first kind of repression is a form of dissociation. When repressed material is subject to recovery as a memory, it then qualifies as a type of dissociated memory now available to consciousness. In the second kind of repression, the repressed material is recovered only indirectly in highly symbolic forms and its meaning inferred and interpreted without recovery of actual memories. Access to dissociated consciousness is direct, whereas access to the unconscious is by inference.

W. McDougall (1938) thought that dissociation is a result of conflict that leads to repression of some degree before association occurs, among separate sets of dispositions that normally enjoy healthy differentiation, synthetic fusion, and association, leading to a logical structure and sense of personal history in the developing personality. There is normally reciprocal influence among the parts, with subordination and dominance of some in relation to others. This promotes a logical, hierarchical structure of communicating, integrated parts. In dissociation in response to conflict, there is a failure of the associative mechanism so that the parts stop communicating in order to lessen the sense of internal conflict and the strain of continued repression. When repression fails, there is a loss of hierarchy among the separate sets of the personality, which therefore cannot be in a reciprocal relationship, according to McDougall, as is demonstrated in multiple personality. McDougall offered a more complex view of the process of dissociation than the mere falling away of atoms from consciousness that he read in Janet. Since he emphasized the reciprocity of parts of the self, McDougall's views could be regarded as precursors to the object relations view of the endopsychic situation, but he did not go beyond a unidirectional view of dissociation of parts from logical structure to arrive at a fully dynamic desription of personality function and structure.

This point of view of dissociation as a unidirectional process is false, according to H. Spiegel (1963), who thought that the error happened because of the absorption of dissociation into the concept of repression in contemporary psychoanalytic writing. In contrast to McDougall, H. Spiegel (1963) held that in dissociation "fragmentation can occur *from* central awareness to the unconscious, or it can surge from the unconscious *toward* central awareness" (p. 152). He also emphasized that along with fragmentation there was coalescence, and so dissociation could lead either to pathology or to the creative restructuring of personality. He conceptualized dissociation as a dynamic, multidirectional, nonlinear, three-dimensional concept; he thought of consciousness as a dynamic state of ever-changing levels and dimensions of action and change in which maximum awareness was a transitory experience. This concept fits well with Fairbairn's (1954) view of the endopsychic situation as consisting of internal object relationships in dynamic relation. Like Fairbairn, Spiegel unshackled dissociation from the repression umbrella and instead subsumed repression as one category of dissociation. Spiegel's dissociation-association continuum allows for dissociation as both a pathological mechanism and a healthy one that fosters selective inattention to facilitate concentration and reintegration.

We can observe the dissociation-association continuum in the case of the survivor of incest who, in a state of terror and ego weakness, needs dissociation for analgesia from pain, humiliation, and terror and thereby facilitates the healthy functioning of self, object, and affect in the part of the personality that has been kept apart from the trauma.

7

The Fate of Freud's
Seduction Hypothesis

Freud's theory of the origin of psychopathology in repressed sexuality (1893c) permeated our culture and led to a revolution in sexual attitudes. As a result, the normal sexual behavior of children could then be acknowledged and discussed. Further changes produced by the women's rights movement and enlightened sex education over the last 20 years have created an environment in which society can also tolerate and respond to the revelation of the sexual abuse of children, which until recently was less often reported and attracted less concern than cruelty to animals or other forms of maltreatment of children, with both of which it often coexists especially in the earlier years of a child's life (Steele 1980). Briere and Runtz (1990) find that the coexistence of physical abuse aggravates the effects of sexual abuse. Gabbard (1989) reports estimates of the prevalence rate of incest in the histories of outpatients at 30 to 33 percent (Rosenfeld 1979, Spencer 1978). Briere (1992a) integrates other studies to come up with a figure for the sexual victimization rate of 20 to 30 percent for women and 10 to 15 percent for men. Gelinas (1983) documents the persisting negative effects of incest.

For years there was little psychoanalytic interest in incest

(Simon 1992), perhaps because the reality of trauma threatened the viability of the concept of the Oedipus complex (Greenacre 1971). Reviewing the state of the art in the 1950s and 1960s, Simon cites only a few scattered analytic articles, such as Rascovsky and Rascovsky (1950) on consummated incest, one widely read study of adolescent girls (Kaufman et al. 1954), and an important study of incest and family dynamics within a larger examination of parental trauma (Johnson 1953). One book (Furst 1967) minimized the confusion and distress of incest survivors and suggested that it was the psychic reaction that was traumatic, not the event itself. A textbook chapter (Lorand and Schneer 1967) emphasized the rarity of incest and attributed its occurrence to the breakthrough of the victim's incestuous drive and oedipal strivings. Society was not ready to listen to survivors, and their personality structures meant that they did not qualify as suitable for psychoanalysis.

Then Margolis (1977, 1984), Shengold (1963, 1967, 1974, 1980), and Steele (1970, 1981) started a trend in which analysts faced the facts of incest. However, even now that Apprey (1991), Dewald (1989), Kluft (1990a), Margolis (1991), Steele (1990), and others (Kramer and Akhtar 1991, Levine 1990c) have treated survivors and have contributed to the literature, there is, in Kramer's (1991) view, "an overall lack of psychoanalytic data about incest" (p. 173). The data are increasing rapidly (Gabbard and Temlow 1994) and are undergoing scrutiny (Good 1994, Raphling 1994). Now that analysts are more willing to discuss such cases in workshops at meetings such as those of the American Psychoanalytic Association (Greer 1992), we see that the emerging data need to be pulled together. In this book, we integrate findings from individual psychoanalysis with those from the individual, couple, family, and sex therapies to develop a broadly analytic theory of the causes and effects of sexual abuse as influenced by the theories of traumatic stress, feminism, and family systems. Object relations theory gives us an analytic approach that applies both to interpersonal and intrapsychic issues and takes us from the individual to the societal level (Davies and Frawley 1994, Scharff and Scharff 1987, 1992, J. Scharff 1992).

At the societal level, sexual abuse, which affects more female than male children, is a symptom of the prevalence of the patriarchal family in which there is a power imbalance between the man who is in charge, is physically stronger, and usually earns more money and the woman who is there to nurture but not take charge (Herman 1981). Less often reported, but occurring more frequently than we used to think, boys have been sexually abused as well (Lew 1990), and women may perpetrate abuse on boys or girls. At the individual level, sexual abuse, frequently stimulated by alcohol or drug abuse, is a symptom of the perpetrator's narcissistic, borderline, or psychotic pathology. At the family level, sexual abuse signifies a serious dysfunction often transmitted to the next generation by parents who had been physically or sexually abused themselves (Goodwin 1989). This aggressive identification gives a sense of justification and even moral approval for acts that do not seem deviant in that family subculture: sexualization of the power imbalance is sanctioned. Sexually abusing parents, like those who are physically abusive, "suffer from the same severe lack of self-esteem, have a poorly integrated sense of identity, tend to be somewhat emotionally isolated, and have a history of emotional deprivation, physical abuse, and often very chaotic family lives in their early years" (Steele 1980, p. 73). The nonabusing parent tends to overlook or actively condone the spouse's behavior, and this negligence on the part of the bystander can hurt as much as the cruelty of the perpetrator. In our view, damage is done separately by each parent, both as abuser and as bystander, and also by them together as an impoverished parental couple who put their needs for stimulation, satisfaction, denial, and control of their child before the child's developmental needs.

Because of the enactment of incest, the usual oedipal romance that stems from the normal erotic longings of childhood cannot occur in fantasy and be resolved after renunciation. The transitional space for relating, in which the parent can fondly respond to the child's wishes with fantasies about the child as a potentially sexually desirable person, is destroyed (Winer 1989). As the family generational boundary is broken, so is the child's ego boundary threatened. The child who is exploited and uncared for by those who should be providing security and bodily comfort without erotization cannot enjoy normal development and suffers long-term effects (Herman et al. 1986).

The symptoms and character structures of adults who were sexually abused as children form a heterogeneous group (Schetky 1990). Some survivors fail to thrive, some cannot learn, some develop phobias or seizures (Breuer and Freud 1893, Goodwin et al. 1979). Somatoform symptoms are commonly reported (Loewenstein 1990). Some suffer from dissociated states including multiple personality (Kluft 1990a, Putnam 1989), and many develop a defensive splitting of the ego originating in the need to preserve the tie to the good object while disavowing the hated object (Burland and Raskin 1990). Unfortunately the good object may be a pimp or an abusive male who rescues the woman from incest only to revictimize her (Kluft 1990b). Incest may lead some women toward a homosexual orientation (Meiselman 1978). Confusion between sex and affection, and confusion over the role of incest on choice of object cause some women to have doubts about their sexual preferences (Westerlund 1992). Some incest survivors have sexual dysfunctions—vaginismus (a reflex vaginal muscle spasm that prevents penetration) and frigidity (a frozen state of aversion to penetration and all sexual touching)—to avoid sexuality. On the other hand, compulsive promiscuity may occur as a search for nurturance and mastery over sexual trauma. In general, periods of promiscuity may alternate with celibacy in young adulthood when the impact of incestuous experience is greatest (Finkelhor 1980), but in later adulthood the more common picture is one of sexual inhibition, rather than aversion or compulsion (Westerlund 1992).

If the abuse occurs before the age of 3 years, character pathology is likely to be severe with undifferentiated self–other boundaries and sexual perversion (Burland and Raskin 1990). With massive deficits in the development of their drives, ego, superego, and object relationships, incest survivors are severely impaired in the capacity to establish intimacy, regulate self-esteem, and modulate affect (Etezady 1991). Many are actively suicidal under the compulsion to repeat the abuse and to kill the hated parent, now in the form of an internal object with which the self is identified. All have problems with trust and ambivalence in current and future intimate and family relationships. These must be addressed in every stage of a transference relationship (Huizinga 1990, Levine 1990a,b, Raphling 1990).

THE SEDUCTION HYPOTHESIS

Freud contributed both to the possibility of the revelation of childhood sexual abuse and later to its suppression by therapists and ultimately by society. Freud (1892–1899) reported sexual abuse of children in vignettes contained in his early correspondence with Fliess. Freud told Fliess in letter 60 (1897) about a woman whose insomnia began the day her brother was driven to the asylum. Later she revealed that the real reason for her sleeplessness was the childhood trauma of having her father ejaculate on her without penetration from the ages of 8 to 12. Another woman became paranoid about her neighbor's gossip and disapproval of her imagined longing for a former lodger (1895). She had been traumatized by her memory of his putting his penis into her hand, and so she developed a paranoid defense to keep judgment away from her own ego. Freud (1896b) tended to think that the trauma was contained in the memory, rather than in the actual event. He remarked that premature sexual experimentation could lead to perversion or neurosis and he noted that patients who have had something sexual done to them at night often fall asleep (1896a). He believed that psychosis and not neurosis resulted from sexual abuse that occurred earlier than the age of 15 to 18 months and that these abuses were concealed behind later memories of abuse. He found this constellation in cases presenting with epilepsy. He also discovered that premature sexual activity diminishes a child's educability (1905b).

Further examples of sexual abuse of young people appear in the case histories of hysteria. Fraulein Elisabeth's uncle exposed himself to her (Freud 1893a). Katharina, whose hysterical symptom was a vision of an angry man's face, described repeatedly defending herself from her uncle's advances without recognizing them as sexual until the time of her consultation when she remembered the traumatic sight of her uncle having intercourse with the maid and re-experienced her guilt at having knowledge relevant to her parents' divorce (Freud 1893b). Twenty years later Freud (1893d) admitted that this so-called uncle was in fact Katharina's father and regretted his falsification (p. 134, n2). Crews (1993), influenced by Esterson's (1993) allegations of Freud's tendencies toward fakery in concocting the evidence for his theoretical conclusions and of his equivocation about his principles and practice, offers the explanation that Freud tampered with the identity of the seducers and "retroactively changed most of them to *fathers* so that a properly oedipal spin could be placed on the recycled material" (p. 62). To us, a more likely explanation is that Freud might have felt the need for discretion and that he, like his patients, must have felt burdened by the possibility of a father being a seducer and decided to hide it. Despite any discomfort with the facts of these cases, Freud (1896b) built a theory of hysteria and sexual dysfunction on his acceptance of the reality of reported or reconstructed childhood seduction of his patients.

THE REJECTION OF THE SEDUCTION HYPOTHESIS

Doubt set in as soon as Freud applied the seduction theory to his own material in his self-analysis. Alternative theories suggested themselves, and he lost confidence in the seduction theory (1906). It is informative to trace the development of his doubts from what we know of his correspondence (1897) with his confidant and mentor, Fliess. Freud mentioned his own "mild hysteria" (letter 67 p. 259). Soon after, Freud wrote that in every case of hysteria, the father, "not excluding my own," had to be blamed as a pervert (letter 69 p. 259). He immediately doubted the validity of his theory ostensibly because "such a widespread extent of perversity towards children is, after all, not very probable" (p. 259), and he began to think in terms of seduction fantasy, rather than fact. In the next letter Freud stated "*der Alte* [my father] played no active part in my case" (letter 70 p. 261). He went on to confide that in his case "the 'prime originator' [of my troubles] was a woman, ugly, elderly, but clever" who put the fear of God in him and gave him an overblown idea of his capacities. From analyzing his dreams, Freud discovered that he thought of her as a critical, scolding instructor in sexual matters for which he had to give her his money and in which he was found unsatisfactory. He hit a period of resistance in his self-analysis and turned to external versions of reality. From questioning his mother, he discovered that this nurse was dismissed for stealing, and Freud concluded that he had arranged a sexual seduction and abuse fantasy to explain her disappearance (letter 71).

Did Freud arrive at his brilliant conception of infantile sexuality and the powerful organizing force of the Oedipus complex from his successful analysis of childhood distortions, including his own (1906), or from his inability to tolerate the depression and guilt of sullying his father or experiencing his ambivalence about his exciting and rejecting, and finally abandoning, nurse? He finally abandoned the seduction theory when he realized that (1) his early patient population had included a disproportionate number of cases in which seduction played a part, (2) he had been unable to discriminate between fantasy and memory, and (3) normal people also reported seduction histories (Freud 1906). He explained fantasies of seduction as defenses against remembering the subject's own sexual activity in masturbation as a child. Freud did not entirely repudiate the seduction hypothesis, but he did eschew its universality and importance. When he let go of the universality of the seduction hypothesis and usefully discovered oedipal fantasy and childhood masturbation, he extended psychoanalysis toward the neurotic population. In so doing, he moved away from the hysterically afflicted, and he unhelpfully fostered therapists' defenses against recognizing the facts of sexual victimization, except in the most obvious cases.

Returning to the subject in his summary of psychoanalysis in the 1917 Clark lectures, Freud (1917a) agreed that fantasies of sexual abuse were often based on real memories, but not as often as he had originally supposed. If a girl states that the father is the abuser, he said, "there can be no doubt either of the imaginary nature of the accusation or of the motive that led to it" (Freud 1917a, p. 370). He admitted the occurrence of real abuse by male relatives, with the qualifier that these episodes related to later childhood and were falsely transposed to earlier times. The degree of doing and undoing in his summary is striking to us.

Freud later claimed that the scenes of seduction had not happened, or if they had, the seducers had been older children, not parents (Freud 1925). Seduction memories and neurotic symptoms were based not on actual events but on wishful fantasies. Freud regarded his earlier credulity in the seduction theory with some amusement and noted that his confidence in his theories and results was now shaken. He wrote, "I was at last obliged to recognize that these scenes of seduction had never taken place, and that they were only phantasies which my patients had made up or which I myself had perhaps forced on them" (Freud 1925, p. 34). Yet, later in the same paragraph he wrote, "I do not believe even now that I forced the seduction-phantasies on my patients, that I suggested them" (1925, p. 34). He did not address the possibility of his having suggested to his patients that seduction material was to be conveyed as fantasy, rather than as a memory of actual events.

Simon (1992), after extensive study of original documents, contends that Freud did not reject the seduction hypothesis out of fear of rejection by Viennese society. He admits, however, that Freud, like many creative geniuses, ignored certain facts in order to see a coherent theme from which to construct a good theory. Simon adds that Freud did not stop believing in the actuality of reported incest. What he rejected as implausible were his own reconstructions of fragments of memory as true memories of seduction. This led him to substitute for actual incest the trauma of witnessing the primal scene or invoking the image of it during masturbation. "'Primal scene' thus served as a distraction from, and defense against, the fuller awareness of the trauma of actual sexual abuse of children by parents" (Simon 1992, p. 971).

THE INFLUENCE OF THE ANALYST'S CODE OF ETHICS

In her account of the ambitious efforts of Freud and his secret ring, an international committee of specially chosen colleagues who pledged to secure the international spread of psychoanalysis, Grosskurth (1991) documented Freud's awareness of and discomfort with the sexual victimization of patients by his most prominent colleagues.

According to Grosskurth, in 1909 Jung denied the extent of his involvement with his patient Sabrina Spielrein. He finally admitted to sexual playing about [sexuelle Speilerei] with her. Jung apologized for drawing Freud into the imbroglio, and Freud responded by assuring Jung that "it was not your doing but hers" (McGuire 1974, p. 238). Kerr (1993) also documents the conflict between Freud and Jung over Jung's involvement with Spielrein and shows how sexual politics led to theoretical divisions in psychoanalysis. According to Rutter (1989), this was not Jung's only indiscretion. He claims that there is evidence that Jung had sexual relationships with two of his patients, a pattern of repetition that is commonly found among therapists who have sex with one patient. It is also found that therapists who abuse their patients have been abused themselves. It is therefore not a surprise to read that Jung (Jaffe 1965) suffered sexual abuse in childhood (Grosskurth 1991), which made it difficult for him to deal with his transference to Freud (McGuire 1974).

"My veneration for you has something of the character of a 'religious' crush," Jung wrote to Freud. "Though it does not really bother me, I still feel it is disgusting and ridiculous because of its undeniable erotic undertone. This abominable feeling comes from the fact that as a boy I was the victim of a sexual assault by a man that I once worshipped." [p. 95]

According to Grosskurth, "Freud could not afford to recognize Jung's perfidy or his unprofessional conduct. . . . The analyst was always right, the patient inevitably wrong" (1991, p. 40). By his silence, Freud failed to confront Jung and therefore did not give him the opportunity to interrupt the abuse cycle, in which he suffered from the compulsion to repeat sexual abuse with patients. On a dark note, Kerr regards as unsubstantiated but not disproved Masson's (1984) assertion that Freud was, as Jung had suggested to some of his confidants, involved in an extramarital affair with his sister-in-law. He wonders if Freud was silenced by his own complicity in this compromising relationship that Jung may indeed have known about and held over him. On the other hand, it is equally plausible that Jung was reading into Freud's life his own boundary-breaking behavior.

Freud's other close colleague and member of the ring, Ferenczi, had been sexually involved for years with an older married woman named Gisella Palos, who may have been in analysis with him for a time. In 1911 Ferenczi began to analyze her daughter, Elma, and he became infatuated with the young Elma. Ferenczi referred her to Freud for consultation. Freud took over Elma's analysis and advised Ferenczi to marry her mother. Ferenczi took Freud's advice to return to his unendingly faithful, forgiving, and accommodating Gisella— but not until 8 years later. Ferenczi's seduction and betrayal of both women are striking examples of a traumatizing, collusive enactment of oedipal fears and fantasies. Ferenczi's personal situation and relationship to the supportive but disapproving Freud vividly represent for us the philosophical debate over real or fantasied sexual involvement with family members in the oedipal romance. This debate later polarized Freud and Ferenczi.

The other prominent member of the committee was Ernest Jones, whose reputation was already tarnished by sexual scandals. When a former patient accused him in 1912 of making sexual advances to her, Jones paid her blackmail money to keep quiet. In the same year, Freud, who was analyzing Jones's mistress Loe Kahn, discovered that Jones had had a sexual adventure with Loe's companion Lila. Freud advised Jones that he should not let anyone else know of his indiscretion. Later Freud learned when analyzing Joan Riviere that she too may have had an affair with Jones when he was analyzing her, a claim that Jones disputed. Jones held that Riviere was impelled by fantasy, but Freud was inclined to believe her account. Despite his knowledge of Jones' sexual victimization of women patients, Freud did not break with him. Yet, Freud found Ferenczi's habit of kissing his patients disgraceful because it was likely to *lead* to sexual victimization. He lost confidence in Ferenczi as a successor, but maintained his belief in Jones' effectiveness, despite his misdemeanors.

Because Ferenczi did believe his patients' stories of their experiences of early sexual abuse, he was widely regarded by his colleagues as paranoid (Grosskurth 1991). In embarrassment, Freud dreaded Ferenczi's proposed presentation to the Weisbaden psychoanalytic congress in which Ferenczi intended to affirm publicly his belief in the veracity of his patients' early childhood sexual abuse. In his paper (1933a), Ferenczi criticized the analyst's superior attitude to the patient and his failure to listen to what the patient really wanted to say, particularly in cases of reporting actual abuse. He encouraged analysts to allow their patients to loosen their tongues. Freud criticized the paper on the grounds that Ferenczi was rejecting the unconscious, and Jones, who had agreed to its publication, took the opportunity of Ferenczi's death to suppress the undesirable paper for years.

Freud himself has never been accused of sexual victimization of patients. As far as we can tell, Freud himself did not break the trust of his female patients by engaging in illicit sexual activity with them. Whether or not he was guilty of duplicity in his marital life, as Masson has suggested (1984), Freud treated women patients with respect, and he tried to rescue those who were in danger from their erotic transferences to his colleagues. Yet, he did not dissociate himself from colleagues who did sexually victimize their patients nor from parents who permitted their own children to be abused. As we show in Chapter 8, he did not speak out against the parental bullying of Dora as a potential sexual victim of her father's mistress's husband. Freud seemed to put the cause of the promulgation of psychoanalysis, even by his unethical colleagues, ahead of his concern about the abuse of women in psychoanalysis or in childhood.

We are left with the impression of Freud as a man of intellectual honesty and integrity confronting the facts of seduction and brilliantly deducing underlying fantasies of wished-for seduction. He held both fantasy and reality possibilities in mind. Yet, because of his own experience of abuse in childhood, whether real or imagined, whether from his father or from his nurse on whom he depended as a child, and from his confrontation with therapist abuse of patients, whether received directly as requests for help from analysts or secondhand in reports from patients about analytic colleagues upon whom he depended as an adult, Freud tended to deny the actuality of seduction by displacing it from the father to an uncle, another male relative, an older child, or a nurse, and from the analytic colleague to his female patient. The possibility of actual sexual abuse by the analyst, the mother—or by the female analyst—he did not address at all. He was uncomfortable about the seductiveness and coercive zeal of analysts who wished to impress their theories upon their patients, and yet he was blind to the incestuous aspect of analyzing his own daughter (Simon 1992). Like any other theoretician, his psychoanalytic theory was hampered by his cultural orientation, his history, his narcissism, and his personal stake in theory building. Educated in the

19th century, Freud tended toward a dualistic, homeostatic approach. He had both a dualistic drive theory and a trauma model, and, despite continued attempts, could not integrate them in his hypotheses about etiology (Grubrich-Simitis 1988). We think that object relations theory provides the linkage that he would have needed to complete the task.

This history of psychoanalytic thought and practice brings out two major points. First, if we are to develop a useful analytic understanding of those patients for whom incest has been a reality, we must recognize that there are analytically oriented therapists who have been sexually abused themselves and who have been traumatized in classical analyses by interpretive insistence on the fantasy basis for their symptoms. Some of them will become perpetrators of sexual abuse of patients. In one study (De Young 1983) 30 percent of adult survivors of incest had been sexually abused by a therapist. Many of us, from Freud until the present, have been too uncomfortable to deal effectively with the sexual abuse of patients by our colleagues. Waiting for professional licensing bodies or professional associations to police their members is like offering therapy to survivors without educating children and their families about appropriate family behavior. We need more informative articles and books like those by Barnhouse (1978), Gabbard (1989), Pope (1989), Peterson (1992), and Rutter (1989). We need curricula on ethics permeating all professional courses, such as the one implemented at the Washington Psychoanalytic Institute (Winer 1993), and we must expect therapists to complete their personal therapy before working without supervision. Supervision and peer supervision give important support for the therapist with weak boundaries.

Our second point is that childhood incest can be a reality, and when it is, it should be faced and the trauma of it validated, not interpreted as a distortion or avoided because it is uncomfortable. We do not intend to dispute the validity of Freud's discovery of incestuous fantasy normally found in the oedipal phase and leading to neurotic symptomatology. We do, however, hold that in relegating his former seduction theory to an occasional explanatory role, he underserved the needs of a population from whom he had learned so much. Generations of patients who had suffered childhood sexual abuse were encouraged to accept their oedipal wishes and traumatic memories as fantasies and distortions, without confronting the reality of the abuse. Doing so compounded their unconscious shame and feelings of being blamed for what happened or for imagining things that should not have happened. Generations of analysts overvalued fantasy and neglected to develop the technical methodology for dealing analytically with the actual events of trauma and their effects on development in the child, the adult, and the next generation.

Analysts have now progressed to the point of open discussion of problems encountered in the analyses of patients who were sexually abused as children. Now we discover that all of us have more cases in which abuse is a factor than we had realized.

As soon as therapists become willing to keep an open mind as to what may be discovered, they face a backlash of accusations against them for eliciting "false memories." Parents who have indeed been accused wrongfully, and others who so claim, have united against their accusers in stories that make newspaper headlines, in a Philadelphia-based association called the False Memory Syndrome Foundation (Freyd 1993), and in a frenzy that Crews (1993) describes as a delusion of the criminal justice system. Certainly there are children who have been led to believe they were abused by their allegiance to a delusional or consciously fraudulent parent who wishes to discredit the other or whose tale of abuse is confirmed in evaluation by unsophisticated validators using anatomical dolls and leading questions (Gardner 1992). No doubt there is now abuse of the concept of abuse by those children who were not abused at all, but who felt badly treated to a degree that left them wanting to hurt—or gain financially from—their parents.

We need much more work on the problems of discrimination between recovered memories and fantasies (Gardner 1992), so that we are swayed neither by the current emphasis on actual abuse nor by strict adherence to classical interpretation of memories as deriving from oedipal longings. We do not want to collude with the patient's need for object-coercive doubting of the validity of memories (Kramer 1985), nor do we want to move prematurely to a concrete explanation for complex psychological phenomena. Here, our training in tolerating ambiguity and not knowing helps us wait until the patient's material settles into its final reconstruction of early experience as one of actual trauma or one of relatively frustrating or overstimulating object relationship. Mature use of *not knowing*, of being in a state of *mystery and doubt* (Keats in Murray 1955), and of being free from the confounding influence of *memory or desire* (Bion 1970) enables the therapist to arrive at the point of clarity—only when it is not prolonged and perpetuated to avoid recognizing those instances in which actual trauma is the basis for the neurosis.

8

An Object Relations

Re-analysis of Dora

Freud wrote *Fragment of an Analysis of a Case of Hysteria* in 1901 to illustrate the use of dreams in a psychoanalytic treatment (Freud 1905a). In his previously published case histories in *Studies on Hysteria* (Breuer and Freud 1893–1895) Freud had established that painful ideas and memories cause illness. He had illustrated the theory of a dynamic unconscious with the principles of repression, symptom formation, conversion, and resistance. He had described the synthetic function of the ego and the way treatment worked by eliciting the original traumatic situation and offering the ego a chance to restore function. He had replaced hypnosis with free association and built a therapy based on abreaction and catharsis. He had described transference as a false connection with prior situations, imposed on the persona of the doctor in the current treatment. In *The Interpretation of Dreams* (1900), he described the method of working with dreams, posited the topographic theory of conscious and unconscious mind, developed the outlines of the pleasure principle, and along the way outlined the Oedipus complex.

Although not published until 1905, the same year as Freud's *Three Essays on the Theory of Sexuality* (1905b), the Dora case, written in

1901, is the earliest masterpiece of psychoanalytic discovery. Not only was it the first case to illustrate the analysis of dreams but it was also the first one in which Freud put sexuality at the center of his explanations and interpretations of neurosis. He discussed the theory of bisexuality and its role in Dora's early development and in her later conflicted feelings for men and women. He described the role of infantile sexuality and incestuous wishes in the development of her neurotic condition, and he coined his famous aphorism that neurosis is an outcome that is the negative of perversion. By this he meant that in neurosis, the person maintains conflict as a mental phenomenon, whereas in perverse development conflict would not be experienced but would be lived out as perverse symptomatology and character. Finally, and perhaps of the greatest significance, this was the first case in which Freud described transference not only as an inevitable pitfall of analytic work but also as a therapeutic tool.

Other discoveries were reported in "Dora." Freud described Dora's symptoms as her way of living out events from her earlier life through symptomatic acts in lieu of remembering them, something Freud later described in detail in his famous paper on technique, "Remembering, repeating, and working through" (1914b). He described the concepts of primary and secondary gain: he held that symptoms or self-defeating behaviors are maintained because they enable a person to obtain attention, protection, or pleasure that is not the primary, conscious aim of the behavior or symptom. He also averred that symptoms and neurotic constellations are nearly always determined not by a single source, but by multiple patterns that converge on one point or pattern—the principle of multiple determination. He described the action of regression as a defense against internal conflict and elaborated on the concepts of repression and resistance announced in *Studies on Hysteria* more than 5 years earlier (Breuer and Freud 1893–1895). He was a more sophisticated therapist in 1900 when he saw Dora than he had been in the early 1890s when he and Breuer saw their patients, and he had developed his technique even further by the time he published the Dora case study nearly at the same time as his *Three Essays on the Theory of Sexuality*, in 1905.

A TRAUMA CLASSIC

The Dora case has become a standard text in the training of psychoanalysts. Beautifully written, logically and persuasively argued, it has been appreciated as a work of genius, "the classical analysis of the structure and genesis of hysteria" (Erikson 1962, p. 455). Yet revisionist texts since then have led Crews (1993) to conclude that "today the Dora case is more often regarded as one long indiscretion on Freud's part" (p. 59) . . . "one of the worst instances on record of sexist hectoring by a reputed healer" (p. 60). Like others writing from a feminist perspective, Lakoff and Coyne (1993) deplore Freud's view of women as inferior beings who are incapable of morality and accurate perception, and they portray his analytic method as one that furthers male domination of women through the power imbalance of the treatment setting in which, like father, the analyst knows best. Our point here is not so much to dispute Freud's attitude to men and women, which we view as culture-bound, but to build on his analytic insights about Dora from a modern perspective that includes an understanding of adolescence, family dynamics, object relations theory, and trauma theory. A classic paper on psychoanalytic theory and technique, the Dora case is also a trauma classic.

THE FAMILY, DORA'S SYMPTOMS, AND HER DEVELOPMENT

Dora was 18 years old when Freud saw her for a 3-month analysis. The information about her situation and her family offers us the opportunity to go beyond Freud's conclusions to construct an object relations view of Dora's development, symptomatology, and character as we look at her situation, which we argue was one of prolonged physical and emotional abuse. Freud was more sympathetic to women and to Dora than the climate might generally have fostered in his time. He was nonjudgmental about her childhood eroticism, an aspect of development that he had discovered. He knew that Dora's father and her suitor were corrupt, but he did not show any sympathy for her victimization and insisted on her taking responsibility for her own trauma. He did not understand the role of Dora's mother, whom he saw as depressed and mean-spirited, rather than abusive, when she unconsciously sacrificed Dora in the midst of her own marital discord and depression.

Dora was born in 1882. When she was 6, her father was ill with tuberculosis, and the family moved to a town Freud calls B _____ in a rural setting in the mountains. She developed neurotic symptoms from an early age. At 7, she was enuretic, and at 8 became dyspneic (chronically short of breath) following a brief mountain expedition, after which she required a 6-month rest. She later referred to this condition as her "asthma." She had the ordinary childhood illnesses, which she described as always originating with her brother, and then at 12 developed unilateral migraine and a nervous cough after a "common catarrh" — a chronic runny nose. She was, in short, a girl with many symptoms that recurred frequently. When Dora was 10, her father suffered from a detached retina, and when she was 12, her father had the confusional attack for which he first consulted Freud. Freud saw her at the age of 16 for a cough with hoarseness. He recommended psychological treatment, but the attack, like the others, passed and nothing was done.

There were two traumatic incidents with a family friend, Herr K., in Dora's adolescence: a kiss when she was 14 and a proposition at the side of a lake when she was 16. Dora was by then already suffering from neurotic symptoms: migraine and a nervous cough and hoarseness. Nine months after the scene by the lake, when Dora was 17, she had an attack of appendicitis — which Freud later construed as an hysterical pregnancy. Finally, in 1900, when Dora was 18, the family moved to Vienna. By this time, she tended to lose her voice completely from the nervous cough once in a while. She was on unfriendly terms with her father and mother and was isolated, tired, and depressed. "Low spirits and an alteration in her character had now become the main features of her illness" (p. 23). When she left a suicide note saying she could no longer endure her life, and subsequently had a first attack of loss of consciousness after an argument with her father, he brought her for treatment. She underwent analytic treatment with Freud from October to December 1900. Freud wrote up the case history in January 1901, the month after she left treatment, but saw her again for a single visit in 1902. He held up publication of the case for almost 5 years until November 1905.

Dora's father dominated the family. Freud saw him as imaginative, energetic, and constructive, although capable of falsifying his judgment and deceiving himself into thinking he was a man of integrity. The father cared for Dora, although he unconsciously exploited her, and he denigrated his wife. At a time in medical history when the father's symptoms of mental confusion and detached retina were not clearly known to be late effects of syphilis, Freud had made the correct diagnosis and had cured the father with treatment for neurosyphilis. Freud had also known the father's sister who died of marasmus, which we would now diagnose as anorexia, and an elder brother whom Freud considered to be a hypochondriacal bachelor.

Freud never met Dora's mother. Despite his negative judgment of the father's integrity, Freud seemed to believe his picture of Dora and accepted at face value their shared derogatory view of Dora's mother. He was led to see her as an uncultivated, foolish woman who gave all her efforts to domestic affairs, especially after her husband's illness and their ensuing marital estrangement. She did not understand the children and cleaned so obsessively that no one could enjoy the house. Dora, who had gotten along badly with her mother for years, distanced herself from her mother's influence and criticized her mercilessly. Freud gave Dora's mother the colloquial diagnosis of "housewives' psychosis." Without seeing her, he had no independent assessment of her personality and its role in Dora's development. His view of the mother is actually a composite picture of the internal object mothers of Dora and her father, not of the mother herself.

Freud began the analysis by looking for psychic trauma, which he confidently predicted would involve Dora's sexuality. Information came quickly, as Dora told him that 2 years earlier she had been propositioned by "Herr K.," the husband of a "Frau K." who had nursed her father through his long illness. Herr K. had propositioned Dora during a private walk by a lake, and when she told her parents about the incident 2 weeks later, he denied Dora's accusation, and told her parents that she had a vivid imagination, confirmed by his wife's telling him that Dora read books on sex. Her father told Freud that he did not doubt that Dora's view of this incident was responsible for her depression and suicidal ideas, but he and his family believed her story to be a fantasy. Dora's father told Freud,

> I myself believe that Dora's tale of the man's immoral suggestions is phantasy that has forced its way into her mind; and besides, I am bound to Frau K. by ties of honourable friendship and I do not wish to cause her pain. The poor woman is most unhappy with her husband, of whom, by the by, I have no very high opinion. She herself has suffered a great deal with her nerves, and I am her only support. With my state of health I need scarcely assure you that there is nothing wrong in our relations. We are just two poor wretches who give one another what comfort we can by an exchange of friendly sympathy. You know already that I get nothing out of my own wife. But Dora, who inherits my obstinacy, cannot be moved from hatred of the K.'s. She had her last attack after a conversation in which she had again pressed me to break with them. Please try and bring her to reason. [p. 26]

Freud was not persuaded by Dora's father's account. He believed Dora that the proposition by the lake had indeed happened.
He thought that it constituted a psychic trauma, central to understanding Dora's symptoms. Dora also told him of an earlier and
predisposing trauma when she was only 14. Herr K. had arranged to
meet Dora alone at his place of business where he surprised her by
clasping her to him and kissing her on the lips. Freud thought that a
young girl would have been sexually excited by such an approach,
but Dora reported that she had a moment of violent nausea, tore
herself free, and fled, avoiding the K.s thereafter.

Freud thought this story indicative of hysteria. "I should
without question consider a person hysterical in whom an occasion
for sexual excitement elicited feelings that were preponderantly or
exclusively unpleasurable" (p. 28). He thought she had turned genital
arousal into disgust by reversal of affect and by displacement to her
mouth, expressed as nausea where the symptom joined with her
other oral problem of being a poor eater. Furthermore, Freud thought
that Dora's vivid recollection of the feeling in her chest when Herr K.
embraced her represented the upward displacement of her memory
of his erection. Her avoidance of men and her social avoidance
generally could also be traced to this episode.

Dora was merciless when it came to the story of Frau K. and her
father. She was convinced that they were having "a common love
affair." Frau K. had nursed him during his severe illness when Dora
was 12, and thereafter they had arranged to have adjoining bedrooms
in the hotel where they went after his recovery. There was a story that
Frau K. had saved her father's life by following him into the woods
when he would have killed himself out of despair, but despite her
mother's credulity, Dora thought it was a cover-up for the two of
them being seen alone in the woods. After his convalescence, Dora's
father visited Frau K. regularly when her husband was out and gave
her handsome presents. He also met her in other cities to which she
could now travel because in the course of their relationship Frau K.
herself recovered from her own neurotic inability to walk and became
healthy and lively.

Freud did not dispute Dora's version. He felt that one of her
reproaches was particularly justified; namely, that she was used as
"hush money." Despite her affection for her father, she was furious at
him for handing her over to Herr K. as the price of Herr K.'s tolerating
the arrangements between her father and his wife. Although there
was no formal agreement on this score, Freud described her father as

one of those men who know how to evade a dilemma by falsifying their judgment upon one of the conflicting alternatives. If it had been pointed out to him that there might be danger for a growing girl in the constant and unsupervised companionship of a man who had no satisfaction from his own wife, he would have been certain to answer that he could rely upon his daughter, that a man like K. could never be dangerous to her, and that his friend was himself incapable of such intentions, or that Dora was still a child and was treated as a child by K. . . . [E]ach of the two men avoided drawing any conclusions from the other's behaviour which would have been awkward for his own plans. It was possible for Herr K. to send Dora flowers every day for a whole year while he was in the neighbourhood, to take every opportunity of giving her valuable presents, and to spend all his spare time in her company, without her parents noticing anything in his behaviour that was characteristic of love-making. [pp. 34–35]

Behind Dora's reproaches of her father was an equally strong current of self-reproach. Dora had, for many years, supported her father's affair with Frau K. She had taken care of the K.s' children and done so out of a secret love of Herr K., just as Dora's own governess had taken care of Dora out of a love for Dora's father without caring at all for Dora herself. When Freud told Dora that she was, after all, in love with Herr K., "she admitted that she might have been in love with Herr K. at B _____ , but declared that since the scene by the lake it had all been over." Freud then declared that the accusations aimed at her father were all true of Dora herself, many of whose symptoms could be explained as symbolic declarations of love for Herr K. He added a footnote:

The question then arises: If Dora loved Herr K., what was the reason for her refusing him in the scene by the lake? Or at any rate, why did her refusal take such a brutal form as though she were embittered against him? And how could a girl who was in love feel insulted by a proposal which was made in a manner neither tactless nor offensive? [p. 38]

This question, we will see, is a crucial one for Freud's conceptualization of the case—and represents a crucial misunderstanding of the trauma and of Dora's object relations.

Dora's illness and symptomatology, Freud went on to argue, were aimed at persuading her father to pay attention to her and to let go of Frau K. She was deeply hurt at his disbelief in her story of the scene by the lake, which Freud was convinced was true. He then went on to interpret her nervous cough in terms of the sexual situation. Using her accusation of Frau K. for only being interested in

her father as a "man of means," Freud pointed out that Dora knew
her father was "a man without means," — that is to say, impotent — yet
she accused the pair of a sexual affair. Dora said she knew there were
other ways of obtaining sexual gratification and confirmed that she
was referring to the throat and oral cavity for sex. Freud then told her
that her spasmodic cough was an embodiment of a fantasy of herself
in a scene of oral sexual gratification with Herr K., and her cough
soon disappeared.

Freud then explained that Dora's love for Herr K. has been
transferred from her ardent oedipal love for her father, that she was
jealous of Frau K., and that she longed for revenge against her as a
rival. Before Herr K. pressed his attentions on her and drew her
oedipal feelings toward him, Dora had identified with Frau K. as the
successful rival to her mother — which even earlier Dora herself had
been. Dora continued to deny loving Herr K., although even her
friends suspected it from how thunderstruck she had been on seeing
Herr K. unexpectedly. After this denial, Dora associated to events
pertaining to Herr K. in such a way as to convince Freud that her
recurrent depression stemmed from missing his affection.

Finally, Freud described a countervailing feeling in which it was
Frau K. who was the object of Dora's intense affection. For many
years, she had been close to Frau K. and had even shared a bedroom
with her while Herr K. slept elsewhere. Dora had been Frau K.'s
confidante and advisor, and they had discussed everything, including sex. Dora discussed Frau K. intimately and lovingly, describing "her adorable white body" as a lover might. Yet, Frau K. had
been part of the calumny of betrayal, joining with Herr K. to shower
doubt on the story of the kiss by the lake, and had lent evidence, only
available from her intimate knowledge about Dora's reading of sexual
materials, to enable Herr K. to discredit her to everyone. Frau K.
seemed to care for Dora only as an extension of her father and had
sacrificed her immediately and coldly. Both her father and Frau K.,
each of whom Dora loved individually, had betrayed her to secure
their couple relationship. The betrayal by Frau K. was even more
devastating because Dora's love for her, Freud thought, was more
deeply unconscious. It was not only that Dora was jealous of Frau K.
for receiving her father's love. According to the principles of bisexuality, Dora's current of love also embraced Frau K., and she was even
more jealous of her father for receiving Frau K.'s love. Dora's Oedipus
complex involved incestuous longings for her father (the positive

Oedipus) and for her mother which were displaced onto Frau K. (the negative Oedipus).

So far, Freud tells the story of a young, hypochondriacal, hysterical, love-starved girl. He sees her as hurt by having been spurned by the objects of her desire: her father, father's girlfriend, and, in a circuitous way, by a potential lover. This potential lover is an older man who has propositioned her in a direct way not only on at least two dramatic occasions but also apparently in many more ways, such as by sending her flowers every day for a year, a demonstration of continued interest that most normal girls would return with affection. This preliminary reconstruction emerged in the analysis before Dora told Freud the first of two dreams that would be central to the further unraveling of the story and would set the cornerstone of Freud's report.

DORA'S DREAMS

The first dream was a recurrent one that contains a great deal of information about the trauma.

> A house was on fire. My father was standing beside my bed and woke me up. I dressed quickly. Mother wanted to stop and save her jewel-case; but Father said: "I refuse to let myself and my two children be burnt for the sake of your jewel-case." We hurried downstairs, and as soon as I was outside I woke up. [p. 64]

Freud determined that the original exciting cause of the dream was the scene by the lake with Herr K. The dream first occurred 3 nights after the incident, before Dora had told her parents about it. In the analysis, Dora's first association to the dream was to recall a recent dispute between her parents. Her mother wanted to lock the dining room door, thereby also locking her brother into his bedroom, which could only be reached through the dining room. Her father protested that something might make it necessary for her brother to leave the room. The fear of fire that Dora thought of in this connection led her again to think of the town of L ____ where her father had said he was afraid of fire.

She next said that during the four days after the scene by the lake, she was on guard against Herr K. When she lay down for a nap the afternoon after the scene by the lake, she awoke to find him standing beside her. He said he refused to be prevented from entering his own bedroom. Fearing his return, she obtained a key from Frau K. and locked the bedroom door while she dressed the next morning, but when she went to lock the door again later, the key was gone. Since she could not lock the door, Freud thought, she conceived the idea of dressing quickly in the morning to minimize the risk of Herr K.'s importuning her and rehearsed that intention in the recurrent dream. This memory of these events is connected to the theme of locking and not locking the door expressed in her first association to the dream. Dora's determination to get away from the K.s as soon as possible was represented in the dream by her report, "As soon as I was outside I woke up."

We find that Dora's trauma is also represented in the dream. Dora is threatened in a situation by more than fire, and for more than 4 days. The danger is a recurrent one in which she is chronically unprotected by her parents and is in danger of being burnt, and this general danger has crystalized into an acutely threatening situation because of Herr K.'s proposition. As Dora and Freud continued to work, the intensity of the threat became clearer. A year before these events, Dora's father had given her mother some expensive jewelry that she did not like. In her anger, she had told him to give it to someone else. Just before the lake incident, Herr K. had given Dora a present of a jewel-case. When Freud asked Dora if she knew that a jewel-case represented the female genitals, she said, "I knew you would say that," a response that Freud regarded as the equivalent of acknowledging unconscious knowledge. She did not protest when he continued that she must have felt under pressure to return Herr K.'s favors. Freud then said,

The meaning of the dream is now becoming even clearer. You said to yourself: "This man is persecuting me; he wants to force his way into my room. My 'jewel-case' is in danger, and if anything happens it will be Father's fault." For that reason in the dream you chose a situation which expresses the opposite—a danger from which your father is *saving* you. [p. 69]

Continuing with the theme of oedipal threat and Dora's longing to express incestuous impulses, Freud noted that the dream expressed everything in opposites. Turning the escape theme of the dream on its head, therefore, he said, "Then it means that you were ready to give your father what your mother withheld from him; and the thing in question was connected to jewellery" (p. 70).

We can note that once again, in this dream, Dora's father chose her safety over love for her mother. Then in this line of unconscious thoughts, said Freud, Herr K. had replaced her father, and Frau K. her mother.

So you are ready to give Herr K. what his wife withholds from him. . . . This dream confirms once more what I had already told you before you dreamt it—that you are summoning up your old love for your father in order to protect yourself against your love for Herr K. . . . These efforts show . . . that you are still more afraid of yourself, and of the temptation you feel to yield to him. In short, these efforts prove once more how deeply you loved him. [p. 70]

Freud does not recount Dora's reaction to this extensive interpretation. From her breaking off the analysis a few weeks later after another dream, we can imagine that she felt assaulted by it. What Freud said has the ring of truth to the modern therapist—but only of a part of the truth. For he put libidinal wishes above everything, above defense, and certainly above the sense of threat and fear in the dream. Preoccupied with Dora's erotic arousal, Freud ignored the continuing theme of her wish for safe holding and rescue by her father. When Freud insisted on his interpretation of the events, something else happened in the therapeutic relationship: the assault on safety was repeated symbolically. As Freud proceeded relentlessly to track down the material of Dora's unconscious wishes, he overrode her resistance and her fears, with the effect of retraumatizing her in the analytic space.

This is easy for us to say in hindsight, for it is at the end of this case report that Freud himself discovered the place of transference in analysis. As her father stood beside her bed instead of Herr K., so Freud sits behind her couch, an ambiguous figure of help and threat at the same time. At the point when she has this dream, Dora is ambivalent about Freud as a combined figure of threat and help. Furthermore, as he works, he throws more light on the corruption in the family. From Dora's perspective, he is inflaming her as he accuses her of wanting a sexual relationship with Herr K. It must have threatened her with becoming just like the aspect of her parents and the K.s she both longed for and feared. When Freud offered his version of her reality, his treatment itself had come to be a threat both to her safety and to her integrity.

Freud did not immediately finish pursuing all aspects of the dream that held his interest the first day, particularly the ambiguous words *"something might happen in the night so that it might be necessary to leave the room"* (p. 65), which he repeated to her accurately at first and interpreted as her intention to escape the attentions of Herr K. When Dora returned the next day, Freud showed Dora that while in the dream her mother feared that her jewel-case would be burnt, Dora feared the opposite – that her jewel-case/genitals would become wet with sex. He said that Dora was summoning up the intensity of her oedipal longings for her father to defend her against the strength of her feelings of temptation to respond sexually to Herr K. Later, Freud returned to the ambiguous phrase, now remembered as *"that it might be necessary to leave the room; that an accident might happen in the night"* (p. 71). He had, he said, reached the conclusion that the words, "an accident might happen," referred to a time when her father stood beside her bed: she must have been a bed-wetter as a child. She agreed, she said, that she had wet her bed, but not until her seventh or eighth year, and that stopped a short time before her nervous asthma. Perhaps Dora had indeed used the word "accident" and Freud forgot to write it in the report, but it seems possible that Freud misremembered her words to tie the dream to a definite urethral event that happened in childhood, rather than retaining the more frightening sexual possibility of a nebulous "something" that might happen.

In the case report, it is only after reporting the dream work that Freud reported a reconstruction he had made *before* Dora told him the dream. He had surmised that she had engaged in infantile masturbation based on his observation of her putting her finger in and out of a locket at her waist, and had interpreted to her that guilt over it had led to her childhood illnesses and that these also represented an identification with her father's sexual activities and sexually transmitted illness. He thought that her shortness of breath was an identification with her parents' intercourse, which she would have overheard from her adjoining bedroom, and that she blamed her father's illness with making her ill just as he would have made her mother ill. Freud paraphrased her thoughts that it was from her father that she got her evil passions, which were punished by illness. And it was by him that she had been essentially handed over to Herr K. The dream, coming shortly after these interpretations, seems to be a response to feeling affronted by these speculations in a way similar to the combined arousal and confusion she felt in response to Herr K. by the lake.

The dream, then, tied together the elements of Dora's perception of being in danger from Herr K. and from her father who had handed her over to him with the wish for rescue from her father who had saved her from bed-wetting, as well as being the object of the fantasies that accompanied the childhood masturbation. It is worth noting that we now understand an overuse of childhood masturbation to be an attempt by the child to give solace and refuge to herself at times of abandonment and anxiety. In an object relational view, Dora's childhood masturbation and bed-wetting are not only instinctual derivatives of repressed oedipal longing but are also in part symptomatic expressions of anguish about the loveless parental couple. The image of the fire, which represented the danger of being burnt in a family situation that was too hot to handle, also opened the way to associations to wetness—bed-wetting accidents of childhood, sexual stimulation resulting in wet drops in the vagina, Dora's "catarrh" or chronic postnasal drip that she associated with her mother's vaginal discharge, and her mother's compulsive use of cleaning fluids, a compulsion Freud thought Dora understood as a reaction against the dirty sexuality and the syphilis that she thought Dora's father had given her mother. This current focused on her jealousy of her mother, her longing for the gratifying intercourse with father that mother might have, and at the same time a fear of her mother's possible gonorrhea and resulting need for obsessional cleanliness. All of this played into her ambivalence about the relationship with Herr K., who seemed to hold out the promise that she could have what Mother had from Father but who threatened her with the consequences of denigration, depression, triviality, obsessionalism and disease, all of which she saw in Mother.

THE DANGER IN THE TRANSFERENCE

After Freud interpreted Dora's infantile masturbation and its relation to bed-wetting, Dora brought an addendum to the dream: each time after waking up she had smelt smoke. Freud surmised that the fear of being burnt referred to the smoke on Herr K.'s breath and clothes during the kiss, and stimulated Dora's fantasy of oral intercourse.

Freud recognized the dream's reference to him as one who had often confronted her resistance to his interpretations with the aphorism, "There can be no smoke without fire." He detected her wish for a kiss from him. Dora insisted that the smoke referred to Herr K. and her father, because they were both heavy smokers—as if Freud was not! Freud recognized the transference, but he did not see himself as the smoker or the one who burned her, even though he tells us that he was also a passionate smoker like Herr K. and Dora's father.

In his final comment on the dream, Freud noted that Dora's recurrent dream referred to her feelings about the treatment. "The dream-thoughts behind it included a reference to my treatment, and it corresponded to a renewal of the old intention of withdrawing from a danger" (p. 93). Freud's sensitivity to Dora's repressed erotic longing, combined with his overvaluation of the appeal of wealthy older men, blinded him to her negative feelings about him. Although he recognized the transference, he did not explore this aspect of the dream directly in relation to him with the tenacity and perspicacity he brought to bear on the many other determinants of the dream provided by her family relationships and developmental course.

THE SECOND DREAM

A few weeks after the first dream and three days before stopping treatment, Dora brought a second dream. In the dream Dora was walking in a town she did not know. In the house where she lived, she found a letter from her mother saying that, as Dora had left home without her parents' knowledge, she had not wished to write to say that her father was ill. "Now he is dead, and if you like, you can come." Dora went toward the station, but could not find it, despite asking repeatedly where it was. She saw a thick wood, went into it, and asked a man who said to her, "Two and a half hours more." She eventually got home and was told that her mother and the others were already at the cemetery.

The complex analysis of the dream took up the last 3 days of the treatment. On the last day, Dora, who 2 weeks earlier had made her decision to terminate, informed Freud for the first time that this was indeed her last day. Freud and Dora agreed that the suddenness of this announcement of imminent departure repeated a hurtful experience that Dora suffered with a former governess of the K.s. This young woman had taken Dora aside a few days before the scene by the lake and told Dora that Herr K. had seduced and betrayed her. The governess had written to her parents about it, and they had told her to come home immediately. She had intended to give 2 weeks notice—which Dora was imitating in her behavior with Freud—but she stayed to see if Herr K. might change his mind about her. He had not. When she told Dora about his courting her, the governess said that he had said to her that "he got nothing from his wife" —the same words Herr K. used in propositioning Dora by the lake. From this and other work on the dream, Freud drew the conclusion that Dora slapped Herr K. *not* because she was affronted by his offer, but because he used the same language with her that she knew he had recently used in seducing the governess. Even so, Dora did not tell her parents (a reference to the governess' writing her own parents) for 2 weeks because she hoped Herr K. would persist and come up with a proposal, instead of a proposition. When she did finally tell her parents about the episode, it was with the hope that Herr K. would come forward and admit his love for her. Freud pressed on. He said that Dora had said the K.s had often discussed divorce and Dora actually hoped Herr K. would leave Frau K. and marry her, a thought not out of the question in view of her identification with her own mother's young age at marriage. This made unexpected sense of another piece of Dora's story, namely her attack of appendicitis, which occurred 9 months after the scene by the lake and which Freud and Dora now agreed symbolized the delivery of an hysterical pregnancy that was the fantasy result of the intercourse for which Dora longed.

The first major current of this dream traced Dora's longing for and identification with Frau K. and illustrated Dora's negative oedipal longings. Associations led Dora to remember a trip to Dresden where she stared for 2 hours (a reference to the 2½ hours in the dream, reported at other times as 2 hours) at the Sistine Madonna. She could only offer in explanation of her fascination the words, "the Madonna." Freud thought that this image referred to herself, the motherly caretaker of the K.s' children, the girl who herself longed to be a mother, the girl who identified with the purity of the Madonna unsullied by sex, the girl who identified with Frau K. as her beloved caretaker. Freud speculates that, at the deepest level, it was Dora's love for and identification with Frau K. that fueled the dream and drove Dora's longings.

The second current of the dream referred to the strength of

Dora's aggression as revealed in the sadistic revenge spelled out in the dream: Dora's leaving home, and her determination to leave Freud, enabled her to take revenge on father, mother, and Freud — and on herself when she cut herself off from a complete analytic result.

> Her breaking off so unexpectedly, just when my hopes of a successful termination of the treatment were at their highest, and her thus bringing those hopes to nothing — this was an unmistakable act of vengeance on her part. Her purpose of self-injury also profited by this action. No one who, like me, conjures up the most evil of those half-tamed demons that inhabit the human breast, and seeks to wrestle with them, can expect to come through the struggle unscathed. [p. 109]

So Dora fled the older man, as she did at home, on vacation, and in her dreams. Such a traumatic, foreclosing termination is an enactment of the trauma.

In his work with Dora, Freud found out more about dreams in the clinical situation than he had known when he wrote *The Interpretation of Dreams* (Freud 1900) the previous year. In the Dora paper, Freud is not trying to present his body of theory. Instead, he demonstrates the technique of dream analysis, to which we now add our object relations perspective. The first dream reflects the patient's current situation, her internal object relations situation, and the meaning to her of her relationship to the therapist. Her exciting and rejecting objects, her self in danger, and the transference to the analysis are all represented in the first dream, whereas the second dream explains the deadness of her internal objects and the role of aggression in her internal reality. In the transference expressed in this dream, Dora kills off Freud as a defense against her sense of danger. At the same time, the second dream holds out the hope for a sense of the future, as it links Dora to a suitor — a nonincestuous, untainted object about whom she has age-appropriate fantasies related to the escape from her dangerously closed inner world.

In a postscript written before publication of the case, Freud recognized the transference re-enactment of the termination and described another new feature of analysis: repeating instead of remembering. Dora had acted out part of her recollections and fantasies instead of remembering them in words. He came to understand that he might have safeguarded the treatment if he could have linked her feelings for him in the analysis to the earlier versions pertaining to Herr K. and her father.

We do not want to criticize Freud unfairly for his lack of understanding of Dora's feelings about him, for it was only in writing up this case that he came to understand the potential of transference and drew it to our attention. Yet, with the benefit of his further work on transference as the main tool of analysis and with further modern elaboration, we can now see with hindsight that the two dreams signaled Dora's fear of being traumatized in the relationship with Freud. The current episode to which the first dream referred was the transference danger of Freud as a father-substitute who stood threateningly and seductively by her analytic couch smelling of smoke as Herr K. did at the time of the kiss and the scene by the lake. The treatment stirred her longings, on the one hand, and offered to save her from them, on the other. This combination felt traumatic to her once again, and she determined to flee from it. Freud's inability to understand that his treatment felt to Dora like a re-enactment of the traumatic situation undoubtedly contributed to her breaking off her analysis.

Although Freud recognized the transference as erotically stimulating *during* the treatment, and before publication saw the transference warnings contained in the dreams' message, he did not reach an understanding of his unconscious re-enactment of trauma. In tying together Dora's anger at threats from her father, Herr K., and Freud, we can add that her father had handed Dora over to Freud just as he had to Herr K. The treatment arrangement recapitulated the traumatic situation itself. The trauma was continued when treatment was begun as a means of getting Dora to leave her father in peace about his marital triangle. The evidence in the case strongly suggests that she unconsciously felt that her father and Freud had teamed up to betray her just as Father and Herr K. had done previously. In this light, nothing could have been more painful to Dora than when Freud missed the point with his announcement that she wanted a sexual relationship with Herr K. and was angry at its failure. So, of course, she left him abruptly with a slap in the face, not unlike the physical slap that she delivered to Herr K. by the lake. Dora's way of terminating left her therapist feeling short-changed and traumatized. Hers is the first reported case of reversal and repetition of the trauma in the termination phase. Because we experience this phenomenon as the rule, rather than the exception in work with survivors of trauma, for comparison we provide other examples similar to Dora in the epilogue to this book.

Even with the knowledge gained in the years since Dora's treatment, there is no guarantee that we could now achieve a better result than Freud did in treating Dora. Such difficult adolescents challenge any therapist's staying power, and they often quit, rather than face incestuous danger. Sudden termination is still a risk when the treatment threatens the patient with a sense of recapitulation of the trauma, or when the trauma has to be inflicted on the therapist if its true impact is to be appreciated.

In a similar vein, Freud asked whether things might have worked out better for Dora if Herr K. had understood that, despite her slap of rejection, she was actually in love with him and waiting for him. Probably not. Even if Herr K. had loved, respected, and married Dora, it is unlikely that she could have stopped repressing and displacing her sexual response to him because he was such a contaminated, incestuous object. Freud asserted, "Incapacity for meeting a *real* erotic demand is one of the most essential features of a neurosis" (p. 110). In seeing Dora as neurotically inhibited in responding sexually to her loved object, Freud failed to see her as a girl who had been traumatized when her incestuous fantasy was actualized inappropriately.

THE DEVELOPMENTAL CONTEXT OF DORA'S TRAUMA

Dora's case gives the first view of adolescence in the psychoanalytic literature. Even though Freud treated Dora essentially as though she were an adult, he described many developmental issues without understanding their normative patterns. To put the traumatic events in developmental perspective, we should review Dora's childhood and adolescence.

We have only sparse information about Dora's early childhood. Presumably Dora had a difficult relationship with her depressed mother. Freud surmised that the mother was resentful of her husband's sexual proclivities and infection, and that she was sexually unavailable as a result. We might speculate that the young Dora was pushed at her father to take her mother's place emotionally, to relieve her mother from sexual duties, and to preserve her mother's attachment to her husband vicariously.

Freud uncovered Dora's early childhood masturbation and interpreted that her guilt over it was expressed in bed-wetting that also brought her concerned father to her bedside. It brought a symbolic sexual intimacy in which he took care of her genitourinary functions. A bodily problem was substituted for an emotional problem and led to a pattern that continued throughout Dora's development and expressed itself in several symptoms. This was the first analytic conjecture of a neurotic constellation of the hysterical type in which an organ expresses a conflict of the internal object relationships, an idea that was elaborated by Fairbairn (1954). During some of this period of childhood, Dora was exposed to parental intercourse, which both excited and frightened her and which may have contributed to compulsive masturbation. Between the ages of 7 and 8, she suddenly gave up masturbation and substituted shortness of breath—which she called asthma—a symptom that echoed the sounds of the parents having intercourse and perhaps also those of the father's earlier pulmonary tuberculosis. Through Dora's identification with mother's hypochondriasis and father's illness of sexual origin, her feminine development was essentially a conversion illness, where character was intertwined with bodily expression of emotional issues.

Freud also thought that Dora had a masculine identity modeled on identification with her older brother. By bed-wetting, she was trying to keep abreast of his enuresis as though she were a little boy, a wild creature. Yet, her "asthma" formed a boundary between phases of her development. At the age of 8, she became girlish—and ill—for the first time. This developmental switch formed a background for her intense identification with Frau K. as an exciting but ill woman.

During the preadolescent years between 10 and 13, children regress and usually act as though driven backward by the approaching storm of sexuality. Earlier conflicts are refueled as the child substitutes aggression for sexuality. Girls experience a renewed concern about their gender identity. Dora handled this conflict by fusing her loving identification with Frau K. and a passionate, sexualized idealization of her. At the same time, she reacted violently against her parents, as children of this age often do, hating them both for their depression and betrayal. This is a common developmental attitude for preadolescents. The betrayal fundamentally consists of failing to contain the growing child and failing to live up to the idealization of earlier childhood. The preadolescent also practices a ruthless denigration in the service of the move away from the primary objects and the primary couple, away from the dependency that binds the child too tightly, so as to form attachments outside the family. As much as the young child has idealized each parent and the parents-as-a-couple, so now each parent and the couple are scorned. It is as if the child can only move beyond the family over their dead bodies. It was during this developmental phase of his adolescent daughter that Dora's father suffered the detached retina and the confused state, both probably signs of late-stage syphilis. In the course of his second illness Frau K. moved in and nursed him, displacing Dora from the role of nurse that she had filled earlier.

We have reviewed these developmental matters because it is important to understand that the meaning of a traumatic situation is determined by its exploitation of the specific developmental phase in which events occur. Preadolescent and early adolescent girls tend to denigrate their mothers and rid themselves of the idealized oedipal father by developing crushes on safely unapproachable figures, such as pop stars or teachers. This pattern is safe if the new figures of interest and attachment do not sexualize the transferred idealizing relationships, but children are vulnerable during this phase to sexual exploitation in the same way that their earlier idealization of the parents makes them vulnerable to incest. When such figures of displacement become vastly overly exciting, there is an assault on ego development.

In the period of adolescence itself, heterosexual development proceeds as young people broaden their interests and work on establishing their identities. They continue the movement from their original families to peers, often by first establishing intimacies with peers of the same sex and later moving to mixed-sex groups. It is only then that they move to heterosexual pairs in which dyadic intimacy is found. The movement from the family of origin to the intimacy of a heterosexual pair that presages the family of the future may be a slow one as it was for Freud himself or a rapid one, such as when a young woman marries an older man and need not wait to achieve financial security, as was the case for Freud's mother and father.

Through this journey of several years, between the ages of approximately 13 to 18, adolescent girls work on their identity. They are eminently suggestible and open to influence, often trying on many identities modeled on their attachment figures, idealizing now one adult or peer, now another, casting off yesterday's identity like yesterday's clothes, denigrating old enthusiasms with the scorn for old fashions. We observe their changeability, their idiosyncratic use of language, and their absolute certainty alternating with an obvious insecurity about themselves, their bodies, and their choices. During these circuitous travels in search of a sense of self, adolescents are also searching for a sexual identity and for the person or people who will help to stabilize such an identity. When two adolescents form a relationship, they each contribute shared insecurity and identities in formation. The benefits of mutual influence are uncertain, but at least there is no power imbalance. When an idealized adult imposes his or her own needs and identity on a teenager through conscious manipulation, or even through the more subtle process of projective identification, there is great danger of traumatic influence on the suggestible adolescent.

In Dora's case we see some ordinary adolescent features of the reworking of the reawakened Oedipus complex. Yet, there are many aspects of Dora's case that are pathological. Dora alternatively embraced and fought off a number of identifications with disturbed women: her depressed mother; her aunt who died of anorexia; her governess who was excited and spurned; Frau K., her father's companion and probable mistress; and the K.s' governess who told Dora about her affair and betrayal by Herr K. The K.s talked of divorce in Dora's presence and made her their children's governess, and then Herr K. began to court and proposition Dora. The danger and ambiguity in the arena of nonincestuous objects were so great that, instead of being able to move away safely from her family of origin toward a nonincestuous family of displacement, Dora fled from Herr K. back to her father. One of the traumatic effects of this excitement was to bind Dora too tightly to the family when, from a developmental point of view, she should have been given room and helped to move beyond the narrow family circle to peers. Instead, there was an assault on her movement away from the family, and she became isolated and overly interested in the small circle of adults around her family.

What Freud did not understand was that both Dora and her father split ideal and denigrated qualities so as to convince themselves and Freud of their picture of the mother as a foolish, depressed, and obsessional woman. The mother did seem to stand by passively and watch Dora idolize her father and later Herr K. The family style combined sexualization of relationships with unacknowledged vengeance, ambivalence, self-serving rationalization, and deceit. Freud also did not address the way that the mother's attitude may have provoked the father's excited attachment to Dora, his affair with Frau K. later, and perhaps other affairs.

Between the ages of 12 and 14, Dora's adolescent oedipal crisis was displaced onto a nearby family instead of peers. This pattern seemed to continue in her later adolescent years. Not only Dora, but the whole family was unable to reach outside itself, or at least outside a marginally widened family circle, to have their needs met. Not until the second dream do we see a spark of interest in a suitor of her own age, a young man who is appropriately outside the family circle.

THE OBJECT RELATIONS AND FAMILY PERSPECTIVE

As much as Freud already taught us through the Dora case, we can go beyond his original conceptualizations, using the richness of his description to generate a contemporary view. Standing on his shoulders, we can now see further than was possible almost a century ago.

Let us begin with an object relations view of Dora and her family. From this point of view, we can see Dora's internal reality developing within her family, a family in which depression, blame, and deceit are prominent features in relationships. Dora's father and mother have a loveless, despairing marriage. Dora is closer to her father, and her brother is closer to her mother, than the parents are to each other. The mutual blame and denigration that presumably exist between the parents color Dora's internal objects with the same angry and depressed qualities. Her insistence on Freud's acknowledging the truth of her version of history can be understood as her trying to validate her experience of compromise—as an adolescent cry for integrity, for setting things right (Erikson 1962).

In an object relations version of Dora's story, we can understand her sexualized casting about for objects of identification and care in a new way. In her mother and father's loveless and sexless marriage, the mother uses illness and obsession to distance herself from her husband, and the father uses his illness with its multiple symptoms to hold off his wife, to excuse many trips away from her, and to cement a sexual liaison with another woman. Yet, it must also be true that Dora's mother has unconsciously countenanced this situation, beginning with her early sanction of the adoring relationship between Dora and her father in which Dora is given to her father in exchange for his staying away from her mother, and her later acquiescence in the sexual affair between her husband and Frau K.

In a similar vein, the family has set up a liaison with the K.s, in which Dora's father and Frau K. have the sexual relationship that is lacking in both married couples while Herr K. is allowed and even encouraged to carry on a courtship of Dora from the time she is 14. Actually, this courtship is one that involves both Frau K. and Herr K. with Dora, for in their relationship, Dora holds the position of a mutually loved and idealized object, a stand-in child for their own loveless marriage.

In this traumatic situation, Dora's relationship to the K.s is heavily sexualized. With Frau K. she is subject to the intimacies of sexual interest and failure, to sexual arousal as they read sexual books together, and to the homosexual stimulation of sleeping with a beautiful, sexually arousing young woman during Dora's own period of adolescent sexual awakening.

At the same time, Herr K., frustrated in his own marriage and tantalized as he stands by to see his wife and Dora's father in a passionate and flagrant affair, turns to Dora, the sexually budding daughter of his friends, who is also his wife's surrogate daughter. He woos and propositions her at least from the time she is 14, sends her flowers every day for a year, and acts as a friend and advisor to her father at the same time. (It was Herr K. who brought Dora's father to see Freud at the time of his confusional episode when Dora was 12.)

As we have seen, this incestuously traumatic situation occurred throughout the adolescent phase of sexualization of development. In those families in which there is sexual assault on children, the family's development is almost always sexualized long before the actual trauma begins, as it was here. The climate of a sexless, loveless marriage between Dora's parents set the stage for her father to turn to Dora as he sought an exciting object, if not an actually sexual incestuous one. Dora's mother's depression should be understood as stemming in part from her exclusion from the love of the marriage— even if she had a hand in arranging her own exclusion out of her own unconscious object relations constellation. Dora's legacy from this situation is an exaggerated idealization of her father and a denigration of her mother. She was already predisposed to set up and echo such a split between her objects because of a profound identification with her depressed and unloved mother who also desperately sought love. Dora could not have done otherwise than have an unconscious identification with her mother, and live out both her own early longing and neglect and those communicated from her depressed mother by turning to her father and to the K.s for compensation.

Disappointment follows when Dora feels excluded and betrayed by the couple that has become her substitute for the failed parental couple. We suggest that, even more than a sexual relationship with her father, Dora would have wanted a relationship to a loving couple who could care for and value her (D. Scharff and J. Scharff 1991). The need for a good internal couple exerts a powerful pull in normal families and an irresistible seduction in incestuous ones where the child is compelled to form the loving couple herself with a parental partner. It is the wish for a loving parental couple that draws Dora to Herr K., not, as Freud supposed, simply her sexual wish for an older man. Herr K. would be appealing to Dora because of his connection to Frau K., because of her adolescent need to displace her love objects from her immediate circle, and because he still represents the hope that she will find the loving couple to care for her.

THE OBJECT RELATIONS OF DORA'S CUMULATIVE TRAUMA

Dora's difficulty can be seen to begin with her parents' marital difficulty, one in which their emotional and marital failure is handled by splitting and projective identification. Father splits his object and projects the denigrated image into mother and idealizes both Dora and Frau K. Mother's depression is handled by projecting both her sexuality and appealing qualities, on the one hand, and her depression and hopelessness about objects, on the other, into Dora. At the same time, she forms an emotional pair with Dora's older brother. In this way, the couple participates in a complex plan of dividing good and bad, sexual and nonsexual objects. The K.s must also be recipients of the parents' projective identifications: father's sexual idealization into Frau K. and both denigrated self-image and parental-lover into Herr K. Dora's mother, whom we know little about, must have participated in this too, perhaps projecting a lost internal sexual self into Frau K. and encouraging a sexualized exciting object in Herr K. in order for them to form a couple with Dora of the kind the mother could not have herself.

Dora's illnesses signaled difficulties in object relations that she could not manage or resolve and that she unconsciously handled by locating them in bodily dysfunction. Many of these involved identifications that Freud already noted in his study of her neurotic and hysterical conversion symptoms. They involved fundamentally the substitution of a bodily problem not just for an emotional but for a relational problem as well (Fairbairn 1954). Her shortness of breath, hysterical loss of speech, a limp that she developed after the appendicitis, the "appendicitis" itself—all had specific symbolic significance. The propensity of her body to express emotional matters was presumably determined not only by constitutionally given psychophysiological responsivity but also by the early holding and handling of her by her parents and caregivers.

Dora's family had a propensity to sexualize emotional matters, to overemphasize the sexual aspects—as father sexualizes the relationship with Frau K. and possibly with Dora. Conversely, it failed to recognize sexuality where it was obvious, as in the case of the family's failure to intervene when Herr K. sent flowers to Dora or to confront the father and Frau K.'s sleeping in obvious proximity and disappearing into the woods together. The overall impact is that sexual issues are pervasively although unconsciously emphasized by family members, even while they also looked the other way.

Dora's oedipal development, which is openly idealizing and excited toward her father and denigrating of her mother, is actually built on the splitting and introjection of early experience of the caretaker parent as conscious ideal and unconscious repressed exciting and rejecting parts, which are then allocated to father and mother, respectively, at the oedipal stage. With her mother, there is a negative identification and a hostile distance that speak of early failure, for which Dora presumably sought compensation in the excitedly idealized relationship with father. Yet, there is also an idealization of Frau K. as an exciting object and part of herself, an expression of the *negative Oedipus complex*, first described by Freud (1905b) in his *Three Essays on the Theory of Sexuality*. There is little to report about Dora's relationships with peers, both boys and girls, because her adolescent need to extend her relationships to peers is severely hampered by the incestuous collusive circle in and around her family.

The transference–countertransference interplay reflected and embodied the sexual danger Dora felt. Freud described, and therefore we know he felt, the seduction to exciting material she had to offer him—veritable jewels of discovery. He felt the sting of her slap as she rejected his ideas, his efforts to understand, and his therapeutic situation to which she would not return. He knew, dimly at first and more specifically upon reflection, that he had been treated as Dora treated Herr K.—first as a potential analytic suitor and then as an offender. As in the family and this intimate social circle, sex and danger were interwoven. The excitement was exaggerated and the danger overlooked until too late in the day. Dora's parents—and in the transference, Freud—failed to provide safety and sponsored, or seemed to sponsor, danger instead.

It is through an object relations view that we can see the extent of Dora's traumatic situation. The harm here is not carried out with the swiftness of a single trauma, as in an unexpected sexual assault. Neither is it the absolute corruption of physically incestuous families. This situation is more subtle. The substitution of Dora for mother is symbolic and emotional in the beginning and is brought into focus when she is given in offering to the husband of her father's mistress as an unconscious substitute for mother, on the one hand, and in trade for Frau K.'s availability, on the other. Yet, the situation is chronically traumatic nevertheless. It produces a distortion in Dora's personality, in her health, and in her sexual life that she did not outgrow or resolve. She did not suffer from extreme states of dissociation or alterations in states of consciousness, but she did retain a propensity for depression and sadistic acting out that dominated her life and her relationships. Her vulnerability localized itself in psychosomatic and sexual areas, whereas her more generalized symptoms included panic, with severe depression, suicidality, and perhaps manifestations of borderline personality organization. The results of multiple, cumulative trauma (Khan 1963) are devastating for growth, development, and future relationships and are difficult to deal with in treatment.

WHERE FREUD MISJUDGED THE TRAUMA

In this family, sex was an organizer of relationships and provided the route through which the parents attempted to solve relational problems. They did this in several ways. Mother avoided sex to avoid damaging relationships, while father hunted for it to obtain caring. They both unconsciously stimulated premature sexualization in Dora and did not give her a secure base for her sexuality.

Mother felt unsafe sexually, and father's attempts to obtain love involved successive compromises to safety. The result fundamentally compromised their ability to be a solid parental couple for providing safe holding to Dora. Her sense of safety was fundamentally compromised most acutely in the crisis with Herr K. Sexual arousal, aggressive assault, and betrayal of safety form a combination that gets inside the child as a pervasive lack of confidence in the self or the object world. It brings a wish for revenge toward fundamentally needed objects and contributes to the sadism that hysterical patients bring to their relationships. Freud did not understand this issue in child and adolescent development, focusing as he did on the individual's sexual drive. He wrote, "I looked upon her having told her parents of the episode as an action which she had taken when she was already under the influence of a morbid craving for revenge. *A normal girl, I am inclined to think, will deal with a situation of this kind by herself'* (p. 95).

On the contrary, a normal girl, with a normal family she trusts, will go to her parents, confident of receiving a protective response from them. Freud thought that her telling them was motivated by revenge and that she delayed telling them because of her hope that Herr K. would persist. Yet, surely the family's reaction proves that telling was in itself unsafe and brought its own version of assault on her credibility and integrity.

Freud seriously misjudged Dora in the assessment of her central self. He must have been correct that she was drawn to Herr K. and even that she felt betrayed when he addressed her in terms that she knew he had used in propositioning another woman. Yet, he overlooked her panic when her central self was endangered and repulsed. Her nausea at being kissed by Herr K. and at feeling his erection when she was 14, her confusion at seeing him in the street, her slap, and her running away occurred because she hated the idea of his sexual affection, all the more for her own attraction to it, because it made her feel bad. Her sexual excitement turned to rage and panic as her sexual fantasy object was violated when Herr K. threatened to become a real sexual object confused with an incestuous one. The natural reaction of a normal girl was not, as Freud supposed, that of ordinary sexual arousal and reciprocation. A normal girl would feel disgust and fright, mingled alarmingly with arousal. The combination would leave her confused, revulsed, often nauseated, and terrorized. A normal girl, in such circumstances, wants compassion and rescue. If she feels free to tell her parents, she gets their protection. What girls receive instead in families with a climate of sexualized, incest-promoting failure is a deaf ear and a blind eye and, in the worst situations, an attitude that sanctions and promotes incestuous involvement.

That is what Dora got in this family. It is in reaction to this set of events that her depression deepened, that her penchant toward an eating disorder progressed, and that she became suicidal. Dora was offered to Herr K. by the family as a sexual sacrifice and similarly offered to Freud for treatment. Perhaps she quit to avoid her feelings for Freud becoming overtly sexual or to protect the family from the things she might say if she stayed.

Fairbairn noted years ago that the reason children feel bad when they are abused is that association with a bad object makes the self feel bad (1943a). It was Freud's assumption that a normal girl would consider an older married parental suitor, such as Herr K., to be a good sexual object. In fantasy, maybe. Yet, the transgression of adults who press their sexual suit is that the child is not allowed the fantasy in safety from actual transgression. Not only did Herr K. press his suit but father and mother also invalidated Dora's correct and heartfelt perception of its inappropriate perversity.

It must be said that Freud completed the picture in one way. He did not sanction the corruption of the adults, but he did accuse Dora of secretly wanting sex and of falling ill only at her inability to reciprocate and at Herr K.'s failure to overcome her reluctance by offering her commitment. Yet, her story admits another, more plausible explanation: despite her longing—about which Freud was probably right—she was primarily repulsed, immediately, thoroughly, and repeatedly. From the first proposition, she was nauseated. Fleeing from Herr K. at the lake, she wanted safety from the passions that threatened to consume not only herself but also her entire family. The first dream and its story make it clear that she was not waiting for Herr K., but fearing him from that day on. Finally, she reported her situation to her family, who denied the gravity of it despite what they all knew. When she told Freud, he told her that she had wanted Herr K.'s sexual advance and had been disappointed in its failure only because she knew Herr K. had propositioned others, not her alone.

In former times, therapists who treated child victims of sexual assault, abuse, and incest erred, partly as a legacy of the Dora case, in inferring that abuse happened as a result of the victims' sexual longing. They are right that as children their patients had a sexual interest in adults. They all do, and we all did. Yet, it should remain a fantasy interest, reciprocated only in fantasy. The interest of the central self is for safety from the realization of these fantasies. That responsibility lies with the adult.

We have not understood Fairbairn's lesson. The central ego of the child knows full well that it is not good to be involved sexually with parents and parent-surrogates. Children normally carry a deep aversion to incest, which, in traumatic situations, is accompanied by nausea, dissociation, and profound splits in the ego. Dora was deeply aversive to Herr K.'s propositions that excited and repelled her. This pairing of excitement and persecution by objects is the hardest thing for a child or adolescent to handle and often results in the development of hysterical symptoms, ranging from conversion phenomena and somatization to hypnogogic and dissociative states that seriously erode the ego's integration and the self's integrity. An actual erotic assault breaks through ego boundaries.

In object relations terms, Dora's family located the antilibidinal rejecting object relationship system in the mother and the exciting object relationship system in Dora, and they then cooperated to make the most of Dora's role. In this way they hoped to compensate for the frustration in mother's development and in the parental couple by not only contributing to and supporting the sexualization of Dora's development and relationships but also by building relationships that were close enough to the family for them all to derive excitement by association.

Dora was seduced and abandoned in many ways by at least three of the actors: her father, Herr K., and Frau K. We might speculate that longer analysis or more information would confirm a similar but earlier role for her mother, who must have been the original model for the internal object who alternately excited and rejected her and whom Dora now so violently and thoroughly rejected. Her trauma is not due to the disappointment she suffered at the hands of Herr K., Frau K., or her father. Her chronic trauma results from the repeated alternation of seduction and excitement with rejection, denigration, and invalidation. The trauma was fundamentally one of a failure in the parental relationship and its consequences, as played out by the parents themselves with Dora and later by the K.s as their proxies. This is the story of most sexual abuse by parents: the trauma is essentially one of a series of failures of the parent-child relationship, the final and most brutal one staged in the sexual arena.

In follow-up, Dora saw Freud for a single visit 15 months after she stopped treatment. He learned that she had been to see the K.s, confronted them with the facts of the affair and the scene by the lake, and obtained validation from them that she carried home and told her parents. She married some years after that, in her early twenties. Freud had no further follow-up on her development to give us, and we are left with the impression of a surprisingly good outcome—until Felix Deutsch (1957) revealed the findings of his chance professional encounter with Dora as an older woman. Deutsch reviewed the lifelong effects of Dora's trauma on her object choice, sexual symptomatology, and personality formation. Deutsch tells us that, for the rest of her years, Dora remained a hypochondriacal shrew, making life miserable for her husband and children. Her personality functioning—presumably including her sexual behavior—recorded the persisting effects of her aggression and depression and of her rejection of her family's version of relationships in response to erotic trauma.

PSYCHOTHERAPY OF THE PSYCHIC REVERBERATIONS OF PHYSICAL TRAUMA

9

Focal Trauma

in an Adult Couple

In this chapter we demonstrate the unfolding process of object relations therapy of physical trauma. In the initial interview, a couple presented with what appeared at first to be a simple but severe single-shock trauma that was inflicted unexpectedly on an apparently normally functioning family at a single point in time. The effect on them was dramatic and severe, disrupting family and individual functioning. As evaluation interviews and treatment sessions progressed, a traumatic background was unveiled. The previous "normalcy" of the couple's version of their life could now be understood as a firmly held defensive fiction that helped them cope with the encapsulation of trauma they struggled with individually and that determined the constellation of their couple and family relationships. In later treatment sessions, we begin to see that ordinary losses encountered in the course of their life together had become traumatic to them, ironically because of their defensive style.

Married for 12 years, Tony and Theresa have three children, an 18-year-old daughter from Theresa's first marriage, and two boys, aged 8 and 10. Husband and wife both worked shifts on an electronics assembly line. Eight months before calling the clinic, Tony developed gas-gangrene after a routine shot for asthma, for which he had just visited the doctor for the first time. Within days, his right arm and shoulder had to be amputated to save him from overwhelming infection. A month before this interview, Tony called the clinic for individual help and help for the couple, reeling under the stress of the trauma. The couple was in their mid-thirties, American born of immigrant South American Indian families. Tony was an only son who was adored and dominated by his sisters and mother, while his alcoholic father spent no time with him. Theresa was dominated by her four older brothers and the oldest child, her sister. Her parents divorced when she was young, her father left, and she was cared for by the extended family during a time when her mother was hospitalized for rheumatic fever. Hers was a close family who fought constantly.

Trauma was cumulative for Tony and Theresa, culminating in the medical trauma that finally brought them in for help. Their defenses against trauma had determined the form of their presentation of that medical trauma as a sudden and isolated event, a picture that could not be maintained once therapy was underway.

Finally, in a family session and in a detailed evaluation of the most symptomatic child, we see the effect of these events on the various children and how trauma in the family is introjected by a vulnerable family member. The progression of the sessions reveals the therapist's recovery from his initial need to defend himself from the impact of the trauma, and shows the improvement in his holding capacity as he and the family get to know each other.

THE FIRST SESSION

Dr. David Scharff: Tell me, please, what brought you in here and why you asked for an interview together.

Tony: Well, the main reason why we are in here is because of the accident that happened to me in February, the amputation of my arm and shoulder.

Dr. Scharff: (Realizing how fit Tony seemed after so recent a trauma and defending himself by focusing on when it happened, rather than what.) February of this year?

Tony: Right. And I rebounded quite quickly, but in time I've gone into a state of depression.

Dr. Scharff: (Reflecting his hopeful start only.) So at first you bounced back?

Tony: At first, yes, I bounced back quite rapidly, because I saw how it affected everybody, everybody was very broken up about it. And now that everybody's seen that I've gone on my way pretty well, I've gone into a slump of depression. It's affecting me, both of us.

Dr. Scharff: Who's everybody that thought you were doing so well?

Tony: Everybody that was there during the time I was in the hospital—my parents, my sister, all of my family, my wife, and kids.

Dr. Scharff: So, you'd had all of them in mind.

Tony: Yes.

Dr. Scharff: You think you were bouncing back in order to help them feel better?

Tony: Yes, I know I was doing it that way.

Sitting with this couple, I felt the impact of Tony's bodily trauma. They were both obese, had the rosy brown skin of their Indian origins and short, thick hair, and wore smart tops and pants. Next to each other facing me stolidly, they used so few movements that their bodies could have been made of stone, in contrast to their faces that were full of life and movement. Their bodily stillness was so profound that I felt they could have been paraplegic twins. Tony was missing his right arm and shoulder, an amputation so thorough as to be riveting. I felt like touching my own shoulder to make sure it was still there. His amputation was so much more than I am used to seeing nowadays that being with him was almost traumatic in itself. I knew it was going to take me a long time to get used to the enormity of his loss. So, I was relieved when the couple took a long time going over the details of the medical disaster that had resulted in the amputation.

Tony: I've always been the type of individual, I like to be on my own, don't like to have anybody worry about me. I like to be on my feet. But briefly, what happened was, I suffer from asthma, and I was having frequent asthma attacks, on and off, within the year. But I'd always refused to see a doctor. Then in January of this year, I had one where I had to go to the hospital and get treated for it. The doctors would see me very frequently, and they had suggested I go see a specialist to find out exactly what it was that was flaring up my asthma. So that's what I did, I went to see a specialist, and something went wrong when I went to see him.

Dr. Scharff: You weren't having an asthma attack at that time?

Tony: During that day, I was having problems breathing, but I wasn't actually having a full-blown asthma attack.

Dr. Scharff: So the reason for seeing him was just for the trouble that day, or just because you had agreed to go see him?

Tony: Constant problems of my asthma. It wasn't just trouble that day. It was a continuous thing, and I wanted to find out what it was.

Dr. Scharff: What went wrong?

Tony: Well, I had gone there, the first day, and he had given me a shot, two of them as a matter of fact. When I got there, he saw I was having problems breathing, so he gave me one shot to help me breathe a lot better while we continued with the examination he was giving me. Then before I left him, he suggested I have another shot to make me feel comfortable for the next time when he wanted to start the treatments. Something went wrong with that second shot. I went to work that evening and was having big, bad pains in my arm. Next morning after work I went home, I told my wife, and she took me to the hospital. And I woke up 3 weeks later like this.

Dr. Scharff: I see. What happened in the meanwhile, Theresa?

Theresa: His arm was swollen out of proportion. When I saw it that morning, it was like a balloon. I put an ice pack on it.

Tony: Things went so quickly . . .

Theresa: They went too fast. . . . They were happening too rapidly.

Tony: Everything went so fast, because from the time I was admitted until they told me exactly what had to happen, it was only a couple of hours. Everything went so fast they had to amputate my arm within the next day.

Dr. Scharff: Why within the next day?

Tony: Well, a day or so.

Dr. Scharff: That was to save your life?

Tony: Exactly. It was a life-threatening situation and they had no choice, they had tried the hyperbaric chamber and that didn't work.

Dr. Scharff: And that didn't work?

Tony: It was an overwhelming infection—galloping gas-gangrene they said. But my whole body was becoming infected, and my condition was getting worse. My kidneys had stopped working.

Okay, so what I've heard about it afterward is that the only choice they had was to do it, and there still was no guarantee that it was going to be successful.

Dr. Scharff: But you said that you were in a coma through the next 3 weeks. Why was that?

Tony: It was a medically induced coma . . .

Theresa: Yes, they kept him on a slow continuous drip of morphine, where they had to keep him sedated. With all the family coming in, I felt it would be best to keep him under sedation most of the time, because I didn't want it to go through his mind that, "Here's family he hasn't seen in years—more than 10 years—and they're coming to see him." I didn't want him to think he was dying, which is what he would have thought if he'd seen them all.

It was hard to believe that she had decided, or that the doctors had recommended, that he be given a medically induced coma for so long — beyond what would seem to be necessary for pain relief. The pain to be relieved must have been the emotional pain of loss. I was shocked at this description of medical induction of dissociation. It fit with my own dissociated state in the interview, in which the shock of seeing Tony's maimed body was so great that I maintained emotional distance from him without intending to do so because it served to keep me from feeling nauseated. It was a distance I was only slowly becoming aware of as we talked.

The description of the hospitalization, the operations, and the period of physical recovery took a long time, during which I recovered my capacity to be more in touch with the couple. It was as if they had to tell every detail of the traumatic story, or else they would not feel that I could understand them. I felt like the listener in Coleridge's, "The Rime of the Ancient Mariner," transfixed by the dreadful story that the sailor has to tell.

At first after he got out of the hospital, Tony was cheerful but distant. Both of them had been working as skilled technicians, but now he stayed home with the younger children while Theresa began working double shifts. He could not look at his body for a long time, but he could manage to take care of their two boys before and after school. The company they both worked for had offered all the resources for retraining and re-employment for Tony while he underwent rehabilitation, but he had been unable to get himself to take advantage of these offers and had sat at home staring at the TV for the more than 6 months since he had left the hospital.

After I had listened for a long time, I felt that I could turn the focus back to their relationship.

Dr. Scharff: Well, what's happened since then between the two of you?

Before they could answer I jumped in, drawn like a magnet to focus again on Tony.

Dr. Scharff: Tony, you say that you've gotten more depressed, but that for some time you've managed to look okay and cheer everybody else up.

Theresa: I think he was very frantic about his family.

Tony: You have to first think of the family, the family and the children.

Dr. Scharff: While you were keeping cheerful, did you manage to do it well enough that it didn't hit you how awful you felt about your arm?

Tony: Yes. I mean I kind of wanted to be that way because it was still like a dream to me. I didn't want to wake up and face reality. I couldn't look at myself in a mirror for a long time. Everytime I needed to wash the area, she would do it for me. I just didn't want to face it.

Theresa: He wouldn't touch the area or anything.

Dr. Scharff: It looks like your arm is really entirely amputated. Is that right?

After watching the videotape of the interview, this question seems absurd. It is clear how thorough the amputation is and I had plenty of time to look at it and get used to it. I asked because of my shocked disbelief at the magnitude of the loss. I was responding to the impact of visual shock with the classical compulsion to look described by Horowitz (1986). He thought that our eyes need more information to resolve the incongruity between our ordinary schema of how a body should look—namely intact—and the actual sight of the body before us—namely with a part missing—and so the eyes are automatically glued to the damaged body. Staring also serves to redirect attention to the actual injury and away from castration fears that are kindled by association.

Tony: Yes, it is, and the shoulder.

Theresa: The shoulder, half of his collarbone . . . the shoulder and everything!

Dr. Scharff: So you couldn't look at all at first. How long before you could look?

Tony: Must have been a couple of months.

Theresa: About July!

Dr. Scharff: July? More than a couple of months. That's nearly 6 months!

Tony: Yeah. A couple of months. I just couldn't do it.

Dr. Scharff: What would happen if you tried?

Tony: Well, I do now. I have no problems with it now.

Dr. Scharff: But when you first started looking?

Although I had intended to move us toward understanding the effect of the loss on the couple, the power of the bodily loss took me back to the physical loss. This is the place the couple's trauma is riveted too. Each time they try to deal with its impact, they are brought back to the facts of the irremediable physical loss.

Tony: It's like, reality right there, you know. It's a feeling that I can't explain, I mean I have lost something I can't replace. And I have feelings inside of me that I need to let out, but I still have to contain myself for now. A lot of anger! A lot of anger! I have a lot of questions that need to be answered. And nobody wants to answer them for me.

Dr. Scharff: Do you think you can talk about them here? Have you talked about them together? Or have you kept your questions and your anger from Theresa as well?

Tony: No, I've kept a lot of it from her. She doesn't need to be hurt anymore.

Dr. Scharff: Are you mad at her too?

Tony: Oh, no! I'm not mad at her. She did more than what I expected, because she was there day and night, every day from the time I was in the hospital 'til the time I was on my feet, day and night! She's a lot stronger than what I thought. And she saw a lot more than I did, 'cause she saw me there, all strapped up, the tubes running all around me. And she had them coming to her for her to make that decision! And the strain for her to make that decision knowing how much it would affect me, but to make the right one: "For him to live we have to do this. And you have to sign the papers to give us the permission." I think that hurt her a lot more.

Dr. Scharff: You think it hurt her? Is he right, Theresa?

Theresa: At the time, in the hospital, I think it didn't hurt. Because I think my medical background—I used to work in a hospital—came out a lot. I was sheltered by that, knowing that I was in the profession and thinking, "I can deal with his situation." I tried not to look at him personally, as my husband, but as a patient who needed the attention. When I signed the papers I said that this was going to save him, so this was what had to be done, regardless of how I felt right then. But later, when I went to an office where the physician had a skeleton, that's when it hit me, 'cause I was looking at the skeleton and realized what part of his body was gone. That's when it hit me.

Dr. Scharff: When was that?

Theresa: A couple of days after they had amputated. And then I saw it in his face and sometimes in the way he acted. He told them what he thought they wanted to hear, but I knew he was doing it too fast, and that he was going to come down crashing.

Dr. Scharff: You could tell he was really out ahead of himself?

Theresa: Yeah, that he was going too fast.

Dr. Scharff: So then what's happened since then?

Theresa: Now he's crashing, and there are a lot of confrontations and crashing, not just with myself but with the family as a whole.

Dr. Scharff: Is he giving you a hard time?

Theresa: We're fighting constantly.

Dr. Scharff: Are you? What are you fighting about?

Theresa: Everything and anything.

Dr. Scharff: Let's hear an example.

Tony: She thinks I've changed, that I'm not as passive as I used to be. I'm more aggressive now.

Theresa: He was very passive before.

Tony: I wouldn't argue about anything. . . .

Theresa: Nothing!

Tony: As long as I could watch my football games.

Dr. Scharff: And you liked it that way, Theresa?

Theresa: Oh, I like an argument, but not all the time, and not always when I come home from work.

Dr. Scharff: You like an argument?

Theresa: Yeah, sure.

Dr. Scharff: Was he not giving you enough arguments for a while?

Theresa: No, he gave me my share before. But now he's giving them all the time every time. It's like I work for twelve hours because I'm working double shifts to make up for his not working. And then I come home, and get an argument about a lot of things. If I come home five minutes late, he's arguing about that.

It was only at the end of this evaluation session that the anger that was dividing them came into our discussion. Earlier in the interview, they enacted their shared defense of complimenting each other, downplaying the resentment that had led to uncontrollable and unending arguments that had ensued as Tony moved beyond his numbed immobility and paralyzed depression. The long narrative that they were compelled to give me, complete with reassurances that neither had any resentment toward the other, recreated the splitting of anger from their traumatic loss. This had made it impossible for them to understand the origins of their anger, which was leveled by each of them at the other every day, fracturing a marriage that they both firmly said had been loving and trusting until the amputation.

At the end of the interview, we agreed to meet again for a three-month course of time-limited weekly couple psychotherapy, which seemed likely to be sufficient, given their apparently good pretrauma marital adjustment. We agreed to start in four weeks time. In addition, Tony would begin the individual therapy already offered to him by the clinic.

SECOND COUPLE SESSION

Dr. Scharff: It's been four weeks since we met. Where are things?

Tony: A lot has happened since the last time we met. Her and I have had a lot of sit-down discussions. There was one real bad one where a decision had been made where it was probably best that we give each other some space, in other words a slight separation. Then after more discussion, after more re-evaluation of what we really wanted, we decided that's not really what we wanted. We were just too angry at what had happened. And we hadn't communicated with each other exactly how we felt.

Dr. Scharff: So the two of you were pretty mad at each other?

Theresa: (Nods vigorously.) Yes. At everything!

Tony: (Nods, too.) At everything. We thought we were mad at each other, but we weren't. We were mad at the situation. We were very angry at everything that happened.

Dr. Scharff: When was this fallout?

Theresa: Two weeks ago

Tony: About two weeks ago.

I noticed that their bodies were far more mobile than during the first session when I had felt them both to be great, twin, stone statues. Today they were moving in their chairs, nodding vigorously, and speaking in echo of each other. Something had stirred that seemed previously to have been frozen.

Dr. Scharff: Is that the most dramatic thing that's happened between the two of you?

Theresa: That's the icing on the cake.

Dr. Scharff: "The icing on the cake?" That's an interesting way of putting it.

I was struck by her use of this cliche. I wondered if Theresa meant to say the tip of the iceberg, but that did not seem to be it. I thought that the phrase "the icing on the cake" usually refers to the best part of a good thing, an odd way for an argument to be described by people who had so vigorously opposed angry confrontations with each other, unless she derived some pleasure from the new developments. Perhaps she meant that the argument topped off their new way of relating. Theresa got more specific.

Theresa: I think a lot of the arguments were just spouting off. Spouting off, until that major explosion.

Dr. Scharff: When you say it's "the icing on the cake," what do you mean?

Theresa: I felt a lot of relief afterward, after we reached that peak. Then we both exploded. And we both were screaming at each other. It was like: "I don't want to talk to you anymore!" And we'd just go upstairs. But up until now we'd go upstairs and continue the argument. As I said, it was the icing on the cake. Because it wasn't something that he just got frustrated and went downstairs and locked himself in the basement and just moped about it. It was like he continued and followed me wherever I went in the house.

Dr. Scharff: He followed you around the house. Screaming at you?

Theresa: No, he's not the yeller. I am.

Dr. Scharff: He followed you around the house while *you* were yelling. Why'd you follow her, Tony?

Tony: Well, 'cause I just thought it had finally hit where we had to make a decision one way or another. It was months and months and months that we've been arguing about little things. But I felt that this was finally going to come to a head at that particular day. She said she didn't want to discuss it, but I felt that she really did. So I just pursued it and kept after her, saying, "Well, this is not what's bothering you. What's really bothering you?"

Dr. Scharff: So, you were looking for space to be mad at each other?

Theresa: Yes.

Dr. Scharff: We discussed last time that you've been so frightened of being mad at each other that you thought you had to go far away to avoid it. Do you feel better now that you actually did blow off a lot of steam, a volcano of pent-up anger?

Theresa: I feel like we don't want to get into a confrontation or we will break up 'cause. . . .

Dr. Scharff: You're afraid that if you get mad at each other, then you'll break up?

Theresa: Right!

I didn't get it. They seemed to be doing much better together. I started trying to persuade them to my view, but fortunately Tony took us directly to the object relations history that explained their reasoning.

Dr. Scharff: But the evidence from these episodes is that if you don't let yourselves get mad at each other, you'd have to break up to avoid being mad at each other. So, because you're so afraid of the damage that you might do, you could break up to avoid that damage.

Theresa: I think that's right.

Tony: So either way it's damaging.

Dr. Scharff: I don't think so. *Not* talking about it is what's damaging.

Tony: So what you're saying is we need to explode every once in a while?

Dr. Scharff: Well, I don't know about "explode." The explosion comes when you both sit on it. Then every time it comes out, it gets more and more explosive. You both try to smooth things over for a long time and then they blow. As opposed to letting off some steam when the pressure's going up. Both of you are scared enough that you don't let off the steam, and then suddenly you find you've got a real mess on your hands.

Theresa: I think we also try to watch when we are around the kids. We don't like to argue in front of them or anything, because of the time in the hospital.

Dr. Scharff: Did you argue in front of them before?

Theresa: No. Not like this. No, none. We talked, right enough.

Dr. Scharff: I don't know about the arguing in front of the kids. I imagine it doesn't make them any more anxious. Usually kids know when their parents are hiding stuff, and that scares them more than saying it. I don't mean that you should be awful to each other in their presence, but not acknowledging something that's there scares kids too.

Tony: My parents used to bicker a lot around us.

Dr. Scharff: Tell me about that.

Tony: Whenever we were there, they were very bitter. And they used to do it in front of us.

Dr. Scharff: What would they do?

Tony: Argue and throw things at each other while we were sitting there trying to eat some dinner.

Dr. Scharff: Did they hit each other?

Tony: Not quite. My father used to hit my mother. Not frequently, but not very rarely. And I used to have to intervene to stop it.

Dr. Scharff: What would happen?

Tony: Well, I'd just have to pull them away and throw him outside for a little while.

Dr. Scharff: Would he be drunk?

Tony: Mmm-hmm!

Dr. Scharff: And would she be drunk too?

Tony: No.

Dr. Scharff: He was the drinker. Did he drink a lot?

Tony: Yes, he did.

Dr. Scharff: So he was drunk a fair number of times?

Tony: A fair amount of time, when he was home! He wasn't home very much.

Dr. Scharff: Then he'd be home and be drunk. And they'd argue a lot. Did the drinking have a lot to do with it?

Tony: Now I believe it did.

Dr. Scharff: So then every once in a while, he'd hit her?

Tony: Every once in a while. He wouldn't always hit her, but they'd wake us up. And they'd be so loud. I would hear a lot of noise, so I'd get up and have to separate them. 'Cause he would grab her and throw her against the wall and try to hit her 'cause they got into an argument. I'd have to come in between. Grab them and try to stop them while my sisters were trying to calm my mother down.

Dr. Scharff: How old were you?

Tony: Twelve to 13 years old.

Dr. Scharff: You think it happened maybe when you were younger too?

Tony: I know it did!

Dr. Scharff: And would you still be trying to separate them? Or before that you didn't?

Tony: Before that I don't have any recollection. Well, maybe I didn't want to see it. But as the years went on, I tried to do something about it. I used to get in between them. I did get myself hurt, but I'd see him hit my mother, and. . . .

Dr. Scharff: So he'd hit you too, just because you were standing there?

Tony: Just 'cause I was the son, and I had no business in between mother and father conversations. So when it came the time when he was hitting my mother, that's when I'd think it was my responsibility to do something about that. During the times when they argued—that is, when he started to be abusive—that's when I would step in and say something about it.

Dr. Scharff: So you wouldn't get abused directly. But you would get hit trying to intervene.

Tony: That was my life's story! I used to get the same thing with my sisters. I used to intervene with them, and then *I* used to get the brunt of the punishment just 'cause I was intervening in their punishment. It was also because I had to be responsible for my sisters' actions.

Dr. Scharff: So what would happen to you for being responsible for them?

Tony: I used to be punished 'cause they did things that they weren't supposed to.

Dr. Scharff: Like what?

Tony: They would stay out a little bit late. Or go places they weren't supposed to. Or meet people they weren't supposed to be meeting. My parents used to come and ask me, "Why are your sisters doing that?" I used to say, "How do I know? I wasn't there!" But they'd say, "You're responsible for them and you have to know exactly what they're doing at all times."

Dr. Scharff: How much younger were your sisters?

Tony: I have a sister that's a year older and the other one that is two years younger.

Dr. Scharff: But you were responsible for both of them even though one was older?

Tony: Yes, I was.

Dr. Scharff: The story about your anger, the anger in your family growing up, was that it was very threatening. You would be active trying to stop it from being physically threatening to your mother, and in the process you'd take a few hits.

Tony: It wouldn't bother me, 'cause like I said, I'd rather have taken the punishment, 'cause I could take more punishment than they could.

Dr. Scharff: This explains why you're dedicated now to not having the anger surface between the two of you: 'cause it was so destructive then.

Tony and Theresa (Both at once.): Yes!

Tony: I saw it destroy my family.

I was impressed with the readiness of the explanation of the early history of physical abusiveness in Tony's family, which made such clear sense of his part in avoidance of it now, even at the cost of never having things out between him and Theresa. And I realized that the trauma to his arm was not the first trauma he had experienced. It was already beginning to sound as though his childhood was one of a considerable amount of physical abuse. I wondered if Theresa had been through a similar experience.

Dr. Scharff: How about in your family, Theresa? Why are you so committed to avoiding anger even though you're the yeller?

Theresa: I was the youngest of six. I had four older brothers, and my sister was the oldest. She left, and I was left to tend to my brothers, even though they were older.

Dr. Scharff: You were left tending your brothers?

Theresa: Yeah. I had a tough time. I would go to school, come home, cook and clean, and then go to work. I had to watch after them and tend to their every whim. So I had to deal with my brothers, and fighting with them all the time.

Dr. Scharff: You were fighting and telling them what to do?

Theresa: No. My mother would tell me, "Clean your brothers' rooms." They wouldn't let me into their room to clean it, and so I would be punished by my mother. I was, you know, always fighting with them. My Mom would tell me what to do, and I would have to fight with them to do it. It was just the point that I had to follow my mother's instructions even though she wasn't there.

Dr. Scharff: So you weren't supposed to be responsible for their behavior but you were supposed to be the maid.

Theresa: Exactly. And I had to cook.

Dr. Scharff: But you would get mad at them?

Theresa: Yeah, I'd go after them with the broom. And I've never acted that way with Tony. I never threw a broom or anything at him.

Dr. Scharff: Do you want to sometimes?

Theresa: Mmm-hmm. Sure. Sometimes I want to punch him. But I still would never do that.

Dr. Scharff: You mean like punching your brothers? Why won't you punch Tony?

Theresa: 'Cause when we first started dating, and we were talking to each other and all that, we promised each other we would never raise our hands to each other, no matter what!

Tony: If it ever got to that point, we would just walk away. 'Cause then there would be no saving the marriage!

Theresa: We'd just walk away. There would be no respect.

Tony: . . . There'd be no respect after that.

Theresa: So, we refuse. . . .

Dr. Scharff: But there's a part of you that must feel like it some of the time. I'm not asking you to hit him, Theresa, but I'm wondering about this part of you.

Theresa: No, I will hit the wall before I hit him.

Dr. Scharff: Do you do that?

Theresa: Yes. I've done that.

Dr. Scharff: A lot? Hurt your hands?

Theresa: Tony's broken his knuckles a few times, but I haven't.

Dr. Scharff: On the wall?

Theresa: Yeah. Concrete, brick, whatever.

Dr. Scharff: When you were mad at him?

Tony and Theresa: Yeah.

Tony: I would walk out and come back in, and she would say, "Where are you going?" And she would look at my hands and they'd be bleeding. . . .

Theresa: Or I would hear rumbling outside the house. And that's when I'd know he was hitting the wall.

Dr. Scharff: The two of you share this business of redirecting your anger so it doesn't land on each other, not just so you won't hit each other—which you agree about—but to show your respect in the marriage. . . .

Tony and Theresa: Or our children either.

Dr. Scharff: You don't hit your children?

Theresa: No. We punish them. . . .

Tony: Every child needs a spanking and a little bit of discipline every once and a while. But out of anger, no! If I'm angry at them, I'll leave them alone until I calm down and then I'll discipline them.

Theresa: I tell them to find their wall for me. "Hold the wall," is the expression. They know exactly that they are supposed to find their wall and go stand at it.

Tony: It's like standing in the corner. . . .

Theresa: So they know when we go out or whatever, or if they misbehave in a store, they go find the wall.

Dr. Scharff: The walls absorb a lot in your family!

Theresa: Oh, yeah, they sure do!

Dr. Scharff: The trouble is, using the walls that way has been part of building a wall between you, a wall of anger that you have rules about. And so far, there's no door through the wall. It's not just that you don't hit each other. You don't direct the anger at each other either. Neither of you wants to know that you're mad at each other until things build up so much that it might blow. Then you're afraid it's going to blow, so you have to sit on it all the more. Finally, you feel you have to get away from each other to avoid the explosion. So the marriage could break up in order to save you from being mad. Theresa, your family had a lot of similarity to Tony's. This pattern had something to do with your mother saying you had to take care of your brothers whether they would let you or not. You were furious at that, but you thought that if you treated a husband the way you did your brothers, there'd be no respect and the marriage would break up. Now, did your parents fight?

I notice in retrospect that I minimized the report that Theresa did scream a good deal at Tony and that he was the one who built the wall by turning away from her and leaving the room. I think there was an effort by them too to discount the cumulative effect of her anger, which was more alive than I gave it credit for. This turned out to be an important factor in their emerging discord. But for now, we were busy with discovering the striking aspects of congruity between their histories.

Theresa: My father left before I was born, so it was just that my mother fought with my brothers and my sister and I used to see that. I would see terrible anger. At one point when I was 5, she left my older sister babysitting us. My sister took us to my grandmother's house and went to the beach with her friends. When she came home that night, my mother was waiting for her.

Dr. Scharff: Your sister went to the beach?

Theresa: Yeah, and my mother beat her severely. I opened the door, and all I could see was my mother dropping the belt and grabbing my sister by the head, ready to bang her head on the radiator. That's when I intervened. Ever after that, I was always telling my mother, "Hit me, don't hit my brothers and sister!" And so I was always the one getting beat. I used to beat anybody that used to touch my brothers.

Dr. Scharff: How much older was your sister?

Theresa: She's 14 years older.

Dr. Scharff: So she was 14 years older than you, but your mother was beating her, ready to punch her head against the radiator and you came in and started yelling at your mother?

Theresa: Yeah, I was only about 5.

Dr. Scharff: And you said to your mother, "Beat on me. Don't beat on my sister?" And what happened? Did she beat on you?

Theresa: She took the strap to me for jumping in when I wasn't supposed to.

Dr. Scharff: But she let go of your sister? And then after that, you'd do the same thing if she tried to beat on your brothers?

Theresa: Every time I saw her come to hit them – she didn't hit them with her hands, she hit them with whatever she had in her hands. . . .

Dr. Scharff: Meaning?

Theresa: Whatever! A cast-iron pot, a frying pan, whatever. She would throw it or she'd hit you with it.

Dr. Scharff: Would she break any bones?

Theresa: No, she would crack my head.

Dr. Scharff: Literally, would you have a broken skull?

Theresa: I had about ten stitches.

Dr. Scharff: What did she hit you with?

Theresa: A cast-iron pot.

Dr. Scharff: How old were you?

Theresa: Around 10.

Dr. Scharff: When I listen to this story, it makes quite a lot of sense to me that you have handled things the way you do together, by handling your anger, by avoiding and neutralizing it.

Theresa: We've always been angry at our parents.

Dr. Scharff: *Both* of you have always been angry at your parents. Tony, you've been angry at your dad, and Theresa, you've been really furious at your mom. But, you both had a clear role in your family of being the caretakers. You took care of everybody in sight. You, Tony, as the only boy; and you, Theresa, as a kind of mighty baby who was going to keep all the other kids from being beaten. As a result, you took a lot of beatings yourself.

Theresa: I had a brother 2 years older than me and very passive. There's so much that he wouldn't do even if they would punch him or whatever, he would never fight. He would look to discuss things calmly and quietly.

Dr. Scharff: Did his voice get lower and lower the more they would yell, the way you say Tony's does if you yell?

Theresa: Yeah, and he would never yell. My older sister was very loud.

Dr. Scharff: I think you're telling me that this sister and brother are a kind of model of your marriage with Tony. He becomes like your passive and withdrawing brother, and then you become like your screaming sister combined with Tony's quarreling and demanding mother whom he keeps trying to please but is also resenting. So the way the two of you act is a pattern made up of the two families you grew up in, each trying to manage as best you could. And this pattern becomes unmanageable when you each fear you've run into your violent parents, that the two of you might become a violent couple. Then, just as your brother and sister had different reactions to your mother's hitting and yelling, Theresa becomes the screamer and Tony becomes the passive, withdrawn one—and the result is that you're more like brother and sister than husband and wife.

In this second session, the exploration of the couple's defensive avoidance of anger led them to tell me about their early histories of physical abuse in both families. They had organized themselves to avoid the histories with which they grew up. As with many couples, their valencies seem to match in this area, a kind of twinning of internal objects that echoed their twinned physical presences. Each of them had taken the role of hyper-responsible "parentified child" (Boszormenyi-Nagy and Spark 1973). Together they had made a conscious contract to avoid all physical displays of rage and to counteract the violence with which they grew up. Over the years, Theresa raged louder and stronger, while Tony pulled into himself more stubbornly. However, in the bargain, they found that they could not reach across the growing gap between them. What should be a transitional zone for the nurturance of object relations and the everyday resolution of conflict had become instead an emotional wall built over the years of their marriage. And in graphic illustration of this emotional metaphor, they both turned the rage on physical walls even when, in Tony's case, the damage was to himself.

Painstaking work in the early phase of therapy shows the dynamics that determine the shared defensive style of the couple, whose cautiousness embodies a shared lifetime of guarding against resentment and retaliation, and the therapeutic encounter with it. In the process, the object relations history of the defense reveals the shared history of trauma and lets the therapist know of the anxieties that have shaped their shared holding as a vulnerable organization ill equipped to weather the current trauma, and primed to distrust the therapist as if he were a doctor who might make the right diagnosis but give a lethal treatment—someone who would expose them to just what they feared the most in the name of parental care. It became clear that they were extremely wary about where we were heading.

In the sessions that followed, the couple became increasingly able to focus on their anger, yet continued to fear that doing so would become unmanageable. The sessions seemed to me to be going well, to be creating an enlarging transitional space in which they could feel safe while telling each other of their accumulated resentments, finding new ways to take back projective identifications, and gently trying to understand more about each other. Not until Theresa failed to show up for an appointment did I suspect a disturbing undercurrent. It remained silent and split off until near the end of my work with them when their view that sharing more could be dangerous was enacted.

THE EFFECTS OF TRAUMA ON THE FAMILY

First, let us consider the ramifications of trauma for the larger family. In an early couple session, I reviewed the effect of the hospitalization, the amputation, and the subsequent family strain on the children. Tony and Theresa spelled out in detail how each had handled the situation. Their 18-year-old daughter Doreen, previously an A-B student, was not doing as well in school as she had before and was spending as much time away from the house as she could. Although staying out at friends' houses might be viewed as an appropriate defense for an adolescent, Theresa noted that Doreen was in flight, like Theresa herself who was working double shifts and feeling grateful to be out of the house to avoid Tony's depression.

The youngest child, Miguel, the first who had asked to see Tony's chest and scar, seemed to be adjusting best. He was curious, outspoken, and moved actively toward the trouble; brought problems up at dinner; and after a brief period of difficulty in school was doing well again.

However, the middle child, Tony Jr., was having real trouble. He still could not look at Tony's body, and his grades had slipped. At first they described him as a good student who now was failing, doing nothing in school, and sitting deep in depression watching TV whenever he was home. Later it became clear that he had been severely learning disabled even before the trauma, although he had indeed functioned acceptably well within the special educational setting the school had provided. However, now he was able to do almost nothing. It sounded as though he had become profoundly depressed at school and at home and that his learning disability had become markedly worse in the wake of his father's amputation and depression.

Theresa now said that in the initial stages of the emergency she had been so preoccupied with Tony that she had not even thought about the children and had not gone home for several days. First Doreen and then grandparents had taken care of the children, and Theresa had the impression that the boys had thought at first that their father had died and perhaps that both parents were dead.

I asked them if they would like to evaluate the overall family situation to see if any of the children, but especially Tony Jr., needed help. They agreed, and we arranged a family session shortly after Christmas.

THE FAMILY SESSION

The family session graphically confirmed what Tony and Theresa had told me. Doreen, a thin attractive girl, spoke easily in a friendly way, but she confirmed that she would rather not talk about these things, that she was on the run from the family, and that she had trouble concentrating on schoolwork these days although she was an ambitious girl.

Both boys, Miguel, aged 8, and Tony Jr., aged 10, were rotund like their parents. However, Miguel was a ball of friendly energy, investigating my toys and chatting openly. He played with the ambulance with a man on a stretcher that fitted into it, confirmed that he had been scared when his father went to the hospital, and that indeed, when he had not seen either of his parents for several days, he thought they might both be dead. He drew a picture with two sparse Christmas trees, one black and one orange with nothing else around. I asked if their Christmas had been sad this year, as though the trees couldn't even manage to be green, and he agreed. The family was not back together yet, he said.

Tony Jr. gave a different picture. He sat like a lump on a couch by himself, wide eyes taking everything in, saying nothing. In response to my request, he could not draw anything, and he could not even comment on what his brother said or drew. For a long part of the family session, he held a "transformer," a small toy space shuttle that could become a robot. He mechanically moved the nose and wings of the shuttle to expose the head or arms of the robot, but he could not say anything about his concern. I could see that his absent-minded play might express his concern with his father's arm and bodily intactness, but I did not think it would be fruitful to try to discuss it directly with him, since he could not respond to anything I said. Each time I said or asked something, he would shake his head silently and sadly, or say only, "I don't know."

In the session we discussed the impact of the trauma with the family, and afterward I indicated to Tony and Theresa my concern about Tony Jr.'s depression and the fall in his overall functioning. They readily agreed to an individual evaluation for him. I saw him a week later.

THE EFFECT OF PARENTAL TRAUMA ON A CHILD

In the individual session with Tony Jr., he was as silent as he had been in the family session. It was not that he was sullen, but that he seemed unable to find anything to say. The toys, paper, and magic markers lay uselessly before him. He barely moved, and in response to my saying the toys were there for him to use, he picked up a toy, fiddled with it aimlessly, and soon dropped it. He answered questions monosyllabically, and then the two of us lapsed into silence until I tried another question. It was like pulling teeth.

Late in the interview, when I had for a while stopped trying to inject energy into the interview, I felt that his depressed paralysis had gotten inside me. *I felt I could understand what it was like to be Tony, unable to move or interact with what and who was around me. I let myself feel this for some time, sinking into it, and bearing the depressed immobility that had gotten inside me.*

Then, rousing myself, I asked Tony Jr. to draw a picture of his family. He picked up a pencil and stared at a piece of paper for several agonized minutes. Again, he could not proceed, and we sat there for some minutes while he stared at the paper, a marker stuck in his lifeless hand.

It was late in the interview. I felt that I had absorbed quite a lot of Tony's experience, and it was time to see if a shift in attitude from inquiry to play would ease his paralysis. I said, "Here, let's try something else. I'll draw you a squiggle. Let's see if you can make it into something for me to guess." Together we would play the "squiggle game" invented by Winnicott (1971). This time, Tony Jr. was able to join me in drawing a series of pictures that emerged when we took turns drawing random lines for each other to complete as a picture. We would then guess at what each other had drawn. Tony Jr. entered into this game with mounting engagement and enthusiasm. At first, he timidly followed my line closely to make a snake, showing his dependence on me (Figure 9–1). The sense of threat here is denied in his next drawing of a stereotypically happy face (Figure 9–2). More boldly, then, he enjoyed challenging me to draw (Figure 9–3), and finished with three particularly revealing pictures. The first of these (Figure 9–4) he said was a dinosaur. I noted its open mouth, but did not say anything about the eagerness and aggression lurking there. The next one (Figure 9–5) he said was a ghost. When I asked if it was scared, he said, "No, it's doing the scaring. It's a scary ghost."

He seemed to be opening up, and I dared to ask if he was ever frightened of anything. He demurred. I pressed on to inquire if he ever had dreams.

"Only one," he responded. "It was in Mexico, during a vacation my family took there. I dreamed we were all in our car together, my brother and Mom and Dad. We were going somewhere. That's all."

"What about your sister?" I asked.

"Ah, she's not there because she has to work," he said. He could not say more about the dream. The vacation, he said, had been fun.

I could see we weren't going to get far talking about the fears, so we returned to the game. I took my turn and drew a rather primitive but intact face. He completed the final squiggle and made a face (Figure 9–6) that conveyed to me the full force of fragmentation and

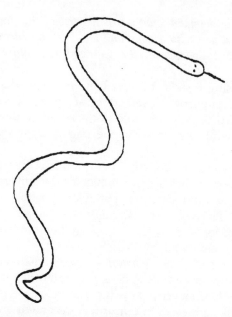

Figure 9-1. Tony Jr.'s snake. Tony's line followed Dr. Scharff's squiggle closely. The snake image is a product of Tony's dependency on Dr. Scharff and his need for defense.

disintegration that I felt might well underlie the paralyzed depression that he had shown both in the family session and during most of this individual session. I speculated that his immobility covered a fear of disintegration that was expressed in the eloquence of this face. "He's scared!" Tony said. "He's seen the scary ghost, and he's the one who is scared."

My experience with Tony, sketchy as it was, convinced me that he had taken in the full impact of his father's trauma as a fear for his emotional and bodily integrity, and the family trauma as a fear of its disintegration. The dream spoke for the hope of integration, for a closed boundary around a neatly encapsulated family, self-contained in the car, an outcome that might require the sacrifice of his sister, who might welcome extrusion at her age since she had to work anyway. I was soon to see that family disintegration was an issue shared by his parents. I referred Tony Jr. for detailed evaluation of his learning disability, which I thought might require specific interven-

Figure 9-2. Tony Jr.'s balloon happy face. The stereotypically happy face reflects constriction of affect and denial of the snake's attack.

tion, in addition to individual psychotherapy that he also needed. Intensive psychological and educational testing confirmed my clinical impression of a boy with a moderate lifelong specific learning disability, which had been rendered far more severe during the past year by his depression and suppression of aggression. The psychologist and I recommended intensive individual psychotherapy for Tony Jr.

IN THE WAKE OF TRAUMA, THE FAMILY UNRAVELS

As the marital therapy unfolded, Tony Sr. and Theresa's story changed radically. What looked initially like a focal trauma imposed on a well-adjusted marriage gradually was replaced by a story of cumulative trauma, beginning in the physically assaultive situation in each of Tony and Theresa's young lives and continuing thereafter. Tony had

Figure 9–3. Dr. Scharff's girl's face. Dr. Scharff kept his girl's face at the same affect level as Tony's face. Tony enjoyed Dr. Scharff's struggle to make something of Tony's challenging squiggle.

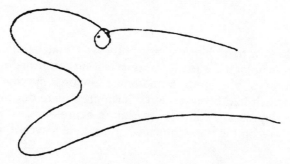

Figure 9–4. Tony Jr.'s dinosaur. Tony now dares to express eagerness, curiosity, and aggression.

felt imposed on during his entire childhood by having to assume the responsibility that should have been his father's, and periodically he had to fend off his father's drunken approaches to his mother. Theresa's premature parental role resulted in an overgrowth of responsibility and a bitterness that she covered successfully most of the time. She left home at 15 to get away from her mother and brothers, married,

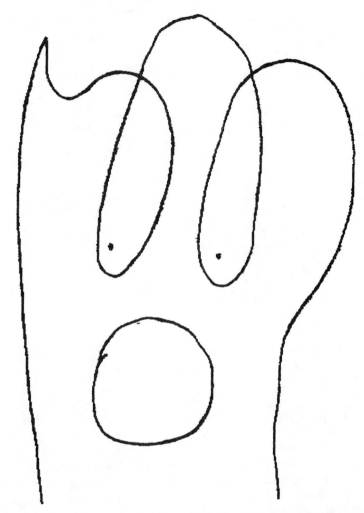

Figure 9–5. Tony Jr.'s scary ghost. Tony Jr. is now able to address horror and fright.

and became pregnant with Doreen. That marriage ended soon after, and although I never discovered much about it, I wondered if it had been abusive. Theresa's daughter, Doreen, was 5 when she met Tony, who was extremely fond of Doreen and adopted her when he and Theresa married the next year.

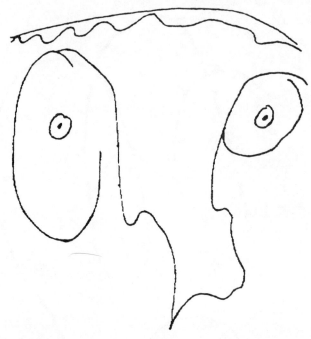

Figure 9-6. Tony Jr.'s face, scared by ghost. At last, Tony reveals his fragmentation in response to the scary ghosts of trauma.

During the course of therapy, after I confronted the meaning of Theresa's missing appointments, other traumata surfaced. The most significant had occurred five years before I met them, when Miguel was about 3. Theresa had had profuse, unexplained pelvic bleeding and, after a diagnosis of fibroids, had required a vaginal hysterectomy. Afterward, she began to have pain on intercourse, but she did not tell Tony about it. She returned to the doctor many times, but he could give her no satisfactory explanation for the pain. She had a procedure to loosen her vagina on the theory that the pain was due to an episiotomy scar, but got no relief. In these years, she began to be irritable and depressed. Tony found her attitude increasingly hard to take and could not understand her loss of interest in sex when they previously had an active and mutually enjoyable sexual life.

I grew to see Tony and Theresa as a couple with a lifelong history of trauma, with only some periods of relative freedom from it. Their marriage had been organized by mutual agreement to guard against hurting each other and had apparently been successful in doing so for the first few years. Yet, the loss of her uterus had thrown Theresa into a depression with psychosomatic components. As far as I could tell, it was largely her failure to mourn her bodily injury and the loss of her procreational self that had precipitated Theresa's depression, chronic anger, and the loss of sexual well-being. Yet, the couple had never discussed this, so Tony never understood the reasons for her changes of mood and loss of sexual interest. When she told me about them in a session, I asked Tony if he had known about her vaginal pain. "I do now," he answered. In response to rejection he had withdrawn emotionally, while she experienced his withdrawal and reinforced passivity as an additional loss at a time when she felt in need of more support.

So the traumatic amputation had followed the loss of Theresa's uterus and vaginal sexual competence. It had occurred in a context of depression and anger and had fueled the already existing distance and mutual resentment between them. I could no longer see their situation as one of focal trauma likely to resolve with support for their mourning and rehabilitation, but as a situation of chronic and multiple trauma that would require longer-term therapy. They agreed to an extended course of couple therapy.

Therapy did not go well. Tony and Theresa had great difficulty coping with the revelation of anger, which seemed to accumulate in the therapy as it had in their life, and both of them dug in their heels in fear that they would be run over by the other's resentment. They described themselves as stuck in a doorway in which neither one would go first or follow. Tony Jr. had not gotten the therapy he desperately needed because Tony and Theresa, who had been reliable about appointments in the early phase of therapy, stopped following through. Soon after this, Theresa discovered that Tony had begun an affair with a woman he had known before their marriage. Theresa made a suicide attempt and then began individual therapy herself. The suicide attempt was particularly distressing, because neither of them attempted to contact Tony's individual therapist, me, or any caregiver. I did not hear of the incident until our regularly scheduled appointment almost a week later. Tony became even more unavailable and moved out of the house without notice soon after, at which point Theresa became considerably less anxious: the worst had already happened.

A second family meeting as the couple's relationship unraveled showed me that the children were suffering from the same lack of communication and contact that had characterized the adults' relationship. Their father had not told them that he was moving, and their mother's mute distress frightened them. Neither parent offered an avenue for discussion or processing the family-wide fragmentation. The splintering of the family carried the sense of trauma on into the next generation.

Soon after, Tony stopped showing up for our meetings, and both he and Theresa dropped out of their individual therapies. Tony's last communication with me was that he might be interested in working on the marriage at some point, "But for now," he said, "I just need some distance and time to think about what I want to do."

Eventually, he moved away from the area to stay with relatives, lost contact with the children, and failed to pursue his own rehabilitation.

The effects of this trauma and the failure of therapy confronts us with our helplessness. It feels like a trauma to our integrity as therapists. Despite considerable understanding of why the traumatic amputation was so debilitating to Tony and to the whole family, a clear and consistent therapy frame, and supportive concurrent individual therapies, all of which should have been helpful, intervention seemed to do just what the family feared transferentially from the beginning. Designed to treat both acute and chronic dysfunction in order to make things go better, it nevertheless only served to rub salt in the wound and could not prevent the disintegration of the family. Three therapists had to live with the disappointment that no one in the family seemed to get an adequate amount of help.

But if we are not always successful, we can at least learn from our failures. A sturdier family might have been able to absorb the shock and horror of the amputation, to stand the mourning required for the acute loss, and to regain its equilibrium. The events that made this situation so destructive to Tony and Theresa's family went far beyond the focal trauma. Long before then, the accumulation of the trauma of childhood physical abuse and complications of reconstructive surgery in adulthood—and the family's style of trying to survive trauma by displacing anger—led to a defensive marital projective identificatory system that made the couple vulnerable to the effects of the loss of Tony's limb, earning potential, and self-esteem as a well-controlled man. The focal trauma then became one more in the series of cumulative traumas, the last straw that broke the couple and passed the trauma on to the next generation.

10

Repetition of Trauma

in the Transference

In this chapter, we explore the life circumstances in middle age of a man whose physical trauma was present from birth. We examine his adjustment to the original trauma and to the subsequent trauma of surgeries, hospitalizations, invasive medical procedures, and teaching rounds. We expect that therapy will carry with it the threat of further exposure, investigation, and invasion about which he must feel great ambivalence. We find that he has been able to lead a productive, independent life, but without the pleasure of long-term relationships with women or the challenge of taking greater authority at work. In his case, trauma has not led to multiple splits in the personality. His response to trauma was to capture it in a perverse fantasy through the process of *encapsulation*, a concept that we elaborated in Chapter 3. We examine how his trauma colors his transference to his previous therapist and to Dr. David Scharff in a consultation interview. We use Dr. David Scharff's countertransference experience to understand the patient's trauma.

Mr. Patrick, a 47-year-old man, asked the intake worker at the clinic for a new therapist. He needed some more individual therapy, but he did not want to return to his former therapist at the clinic, a psychologist whom he had liked well enough but with whom he had parted on bad terms. She referred him to me (DES) for consultation before assigning him to a therapist. It would be my task to see what had gone wrong and whether it could be repaired. I saw from the case notes that he had had about a year of psychotherapy with Dr. Michaels less than a year ago, and that before that he had seen various medical social workers in connection with problems adjusting to the trauma of his physical condition.

Born with congenital malformation of the genito-urinary tract, Mr. Patrick had required surgeries at birth, and at ages 8, 15, and 26. He had seen many physicians and therapists, and now he would be seeing me. He agreed to meet me in my office with the videocamera running, but he protected himself from exposure by choosing to sit with his back to the camera. What the viewer sees is the immobile, high back of his chair; above it his mobile, extremely expressive, gesticulating hand; and, in the distance, me, looking rather on the spot.

With the goal of finding out enough from him about his history and his experience of therapy to determine my recommendation, I began by trying to get a sense of why he had returned for therapy at this point. Mr. Patrick spoke openly and generously, except in response to certain themes. He did not show feeling about his medical interventions, but as he spoke about them, shifts in his word flow pointed to encapsulated areas of trauma. From one-word answers I got to his feelings of being hurt by me. It was from their elaboration in the transference that his trauma could be realized.

Mr. Patrick began quite easily. "Okay, well, as you know, my life story has been one of physical problems since the day I was born and acknowledgment of those problems with psychological ramifications since, well, on and off for years starting in undergraduate school. I'm 47 now. Then two years ago I was seen by Dr. Michaels, and that was for a very particular problem relating to sexuality issues, and progress was made. We started out at once a week, we ended up twice a week, I was uncomfortable and stopped it."

With almost no input from me, he continued at breakneck speed.

"Now right now," he said, "what's happening is I changed jobs in July, and it's the most responsible job I've had in my entire life. I've realized my discomfort with that responsibility, and so I've sort of been going over my lifestyle of avoiding adult responsibility issues and how that relates to the sexuality issues I worked on with Dr. Michaels a year or so ago. I'm really thinking that I've intellectualized and led my life in many ways that I don't like very much at this point. I don't like the term 'mid-life crisis' at all, but what I have is like that. It's a case of looking back at my life and not liking what I see.

"Then there's a lot of physical aspects to this, I mean as you may know, and I have to mention, I wear this ostomy bag for collection of urine—ostomy surgery when I was 26. And in the middle of today, I have to have a leakage problem and I apologize if there's any smell or anything like that, because it occasionally happens. So there's those kinds of issues that get in my way and certainly prove my reason for being late. I had to stop in the bathroom and so on, and that's problematic. But anyway, in May (I'm coming back now) I was working on my previous job, and I was holding this pocketwatch in my hand and I dropped it as I was closing the van door and I smashed it on my thumb. Well, I've been having difficulty with my thumb. It's not broken, but I should have had it x-rayed. I was feeling this discomfort in it that I don't think—I think, was psychosomatic—I don't think it was rational."

I was already struck by Mr. Patrick's doing and undoing of his experience of physical pain and inconvenience, and also of his capacity to think about it and trust his judgment.

He continued, "It hurts a little, and then it doesn't hurt, and so on. Once I had made the appointment to get this therapy process going again, I started to feel better. I have this very, very years-long process of chomping on my fingernails when I'm nervous and after I called Dr. Michaels to get a referral to the clinic, it actually stopped for a few days. So it's this whole pattern with my body that's the problem. At my last job someone called me self-defeating—I hate that term and I hate the term masochistic—but the fact is I've been self-punitive and self-punishing for decades in the way I live my life and I want to do something about that.

"But anyway, so, I've decided I don't like the way I've been living my life and I do need therapy. It's been hard. A friend told me that it's impressive that I'm coming to these insights and so on. Someone else thinks it's good. Well, it doesn't feel good! Believe me, it doesn't feel good, and this goes back to my previous therapy. I don't like admitting to myself—and with my physical history, I've had a tumor removed, I've had the ostomy surgery, I've had brain surgery—that I think of myself as sort of a burden to the medical profession, and now I'd also be a burden to the psychiatric or psychological profession and use more health care resources than are necessary. Though I've finally come to admit that I need them. I've tried to think that, though it is depressing, it is not failing. It's just that I have a defective body, and now I have a defective psyche or whatever you want to call it as well, and I'm just admitting that to myself. I even thought that maybe I need medication, 'cause that's what I'm used to in the medical sense. Like, I get these periodic kidney infections, so I have a doctor who's very helpful. He's Dr. Benson at Howard University Hospital. When I start to get sick, you know, I call him and I go in and I drop off a specimen, and it's literally true, I feel better. This is worth mentioning: In January, I was in Richmond and I started to feel sick, I called him up, he called me back long distance, and I literally started to feel better while talking to him, even though the infection obviously didn't go away. And then in February I think I got a stomach virus and was really sick—I was even having trouble walking the steps—and he called me on a Saturday and I started to feel better. So there's a whole mind-body issue in my life. . . . I don't respond like that with doctors of psychology like Dr. Michaels, but with medical doctors, physical symptoms that are clearly there become less, as I think I said before."

As he slowed down, I cut in to suggest, "The care of your body calls forth a special kind of relationship with Dr. Benson that really gets inside you in a different way from one with Dr. Michaels who just talks to you."

"Well, that's an important point," he replied. "Because now I'm starting to think of both of them that way, 'cause, like I said, when I started to talk to him more and started the ball rolling on this, I started to feel better."

My interest was piqued. He felt that he needed a new therapist, but he had had a positive transference reaction talking to the rejected therapist.

"You did?" I asked incredulously.

"Yeah, that's what I meant, the chomping at my fingernails stopped, and this funny business with adult responsibility became much less of a problem, it became hardly any problem, and there was a noticeable difference. But until recently I felt—all my life—I have a defective body and need doctors to help me, and, once they show they're willing to help me, I feel better. But I didn't want to admit there was a psychological problem that deep—until now."

I was thinking that this would be a good time to ask about his therapy and elicit the history of the transference.

"So you had the experience with Dr. Michaels over a period of about a year, is that right?" I asked.

"Almost a year," he allowed. "Nine months, to be exact."

In contrast to his easy, associative style, his sudden precision startled me. Perhaps the length of the nine-month period was significant as a gestation period that had to be interrupted before the birth of discovery and work on defect. Yet, I was glad later that I didn't speculate. I stayed with the facts.

"You were seeing him first once and then twice a week," I continued, "but during that time you didn't really like admitting that you might have a need."

"Well, what if I say why I went to see him last time?" he offered.

"Yes, I want to hear about that," I accepted. "But first could you orient me about your medical situation and then we'll go into why you came into therapy last time—and why you quit."

Mr. Patrick complied. "I was born with a condition called extrophy of the bladder. It's meant that I've never had a normal penis. It was completely open."

"The penis was open," I repeated, as if to be sure that I heard correctly and could take this in, but really I think I was beginning to react to the trauma, and needed a break, a chance to exert some control over the interview. I was remembering my days on the pediatric ward and the awful sight of a little child born with such a deformity.

"It was splayed," he affirmed. "The bladder was outside or something, so when I was an infant, they operated so that I would urinate rectally, and that went on for years and years until ostomy surgery. Then I had an open penis with these little cherry-like things, small cherries at the base of my penis, and they got removed, when I was . . . "

"The cherries were?" I repeated, cringing at the thought of the removal of round things that reminded me of testicles, and completely obliterating the age at which this had occurred. When he completed my sentence, he showed how he had misunderstood me.

" . . . were right at the base of my penis where it was open, around my stomach."

"What were those?" I asked, still preoccupied with testicles, even though the man's voice was quite male in register and he had secondary sexual characteristics.

"I don't even know," he replied. "I had those removed and by the time I hit puberty and I would masturbate a lot, ejaculation would come right out of the opening."

"So the opening was at the base of your penis?"

"Yeah. Where those objects were until they were removed. Then when I was 15 the penis was closed, and it's very short, and when I have an erection it actually goes up against my stomach."

"Were the surgeons waiting until you were 15 so you could get the maximum growth out of it, or you don't know why they waited?" I asked.

"I don't know," he answered. "No, but I do know the doctors said I needed a special position for intercourse, and I've never had intercourse even though I'm heterosexual. I don't want to live in a special position."

I wanted to follow up on the viablity of his potency. I continued saying, "So, when you were 15 you had surgery on your penis for reconstruction." I noticed I started to get short replies.

"Closing it up."

"Closing it up. And did that work out?"

"Well, physically, yeah."

"Does it look small, but normal, is that the way it is?

"Yeah."

Then he added to his short answer, "But actually the erection goes all the way against my stomach."

I couldn't imagine the kind of erection he was describing. Would his description be equally unclear to everyone, or was the story having a traumatizing impact on my imaginative capacities? I was seeing his penis disappearing into his stomach like a vagina.

"I'm not sure quite what you mean by that," I admitted.

"Instead of just going out, it goes tight all the way back, and uh, so there've been all kinds of issues in sexuality for too many years, way too many years. . . . You know, this is the hard part."

"I'm not clear what you mean by going against your stomach," I persisted. "Do you mean that there's a swelling in the base of the penis that pulls the penis inward, or are you telling me that the angle of the erection is pulled back against your stomach?"

"All the way," he nodded.

"You mean that the penis collapses against the stomach," I said, still not getting it.

"There's still an erection," he explained, quite patiently.

"There's a noticeable erection?" I said, sounding hopeful and relieved.

"Right," he said and summarized it clearly. "In other words, instead of just going out, it goes up, because of the surgery."

"And you can't make it bend forward?" I queried.

"Oh, no," he said. "I can pull it forward with my hand."

"So it can be an erection that extends out in front of you," I clarified.

He qualified my perception. "Only if I have my hand there."

"Okay," I said. "So it could be sufficient for penetration."

"Presumably," he said, unconvinced and unenthusiastic.

"But you don't know because you've had no experience," I said. "Right."

Had we been discussing his deepest concerns and experiencing his puzzlements? Or had he been dealing with my castration anxiety? At least I had shown that I was interested in the details of his physical condition, and now he took the initiative to move into the psychological area that he had said he did not like to face. As the subject of intercourse could fortunately be set aside now, he spoke much more spontaneously of his concerns.

"See," he continued. "The part that's hardest to tackle even now, for way too many years, is my sexual fantasy. Well, it's visual. Even now in some ways, it's still visual. It was with both women I've known, but 9- and 10-year-old girls were the chief objects of my fantasy."

"What is the image you remember of that age and level of development?" I wanted to know, feeling on familiar ground again.

"When I was about 12½, there was this friend of the family's, a 9-year-old daughter who showed me her vagina and all that, so I'd fantasize and remember that."

"What happened in that episode?" I asked.

"Well, just that I stayed over at her house, because my parents were out of town or something. We were going to put our pajamas on. Then she got her underpants off sitting on the bed in front of me. We had a race to see who was done first. Then I went in the other room and put my pajamas on and went back into her room. She wasn't paying any attention. Then she propped her legs all the way back to take her underpants off, and so I found that very exciting."

"Is that the only time you've seen a female or girl's vagina?" I wondered.

"Oh, no," he said. "I mean, I go to topless-bottomless bars. I buy magazines . . . "

"Were there incidents during the rest of your adolescence?" I asked this question to see if he had totally missed out on adolescent exploration that could have been more exciting than this memory from childhood.

"Maybe not," he admitted. "Well, at some point, I saw my

mother naked. Not a lot. Maybe once or twice, when I was 12. That wasn't so pleasant, I mean pubic hair, and so on."

"Not so pleasant means . . . ?"

"Yeah, maybe I wasn't supposed to see it, and all that kind of stuff."

"So, seeing the girl was exciting at the time, when you were about 12," I said. "But seeing your mother was not so pleasant. Did it gross you out? Did it frighten you, what?"

"As we talk about it now,' he considered, "I thought she looked strange." Associating to one of the adult women he had been with, he continued, "'Cause then I remember, when I was 21, I got involved with a woman in Greece, and she had a lot of pubic hair. This is the closest to my true love of my whole life. Although we were just together that one summer, I got involved with her. And I didn't like that she had all that pubic hair, actually. Then when I was 26, I got involved in social nudism in Europe. I was willing to take everything off, and I enjoyed it very much. Part of the enjoyment was seeing girls naked, no question about it. Girls and women, too. But to this day, I don't like pubic hair on women. Even in these magazines I started getting around '68, '69, '70, porn about women, social nudism, whatever, I prefer the less hair the better, without question."

"Okay," I said. "How about pictures of men?"

"I don't like them."

"Pictures of men and women together?"

"Those I really don't like. No."

"What you like is looking at women . . ." I began to say.

"Yeah," he said emphatically.

"But the less pubic hair they've got, the better you like it," I concluded.

But he was not quite done. "*No* pubic hair, preferably, because there's magazines like that now."

"Where there is no pubic hair," I repeated. One last question. "Breasts?"

"Not really interested."

"Okay," I said. Now I had understood. "So it's female pubic areas, without hair. And of those, you're interested in looking at grown women's genitals, only if they don't have pubic hair. But was there something else you wanted to tell me about your interest in young girls?"

"Yes," he said. "That's what's changed since 1990, in the therapy with Dr. Michaels. That's the good news."

I began to feel that we were getting close to the therapy assignment problem that he had come about.

"So tell me about that," I said. "Does that take us back to what brought you for treatment originally?"

But I would not get to "see" that, yet. He diverted the discussion to tell me of more details about his wishes to see the female genitals.

"Well, there were two incidents," he told me. "First, there was a woman who I used to work with when I lived in Palm Beach, and around New Year's, 1990, I went back to visit the area and I gave her a call. Just talked to her on the phone and talked about old times. She told me she and her husband used to hang out in the nude in their back yard and I found that whole thing very exciting. This was a woman, you know, who I knew when she was married, but I would compliment her physically, and so on. She's since gotten divorced and remarried, but we had nothing physically. Anyway, so I wrote her this letter saying I found that whole conversation very exciting and asking her this series of questions about her nudism. Then I started asking about her masturbation and all that. Anyway, it was a really inappropriate letter. She wrote back a kind letter, but saying, 'I don't want you to write me again.'

"Well, I wrote a letter apologizing before she even got my first letter. But I got that second letter back a few days later unopened, marked 'Return to sender.' So it was that first one that made her stop writing to me.

"But something else happened later that month, the other thing I wanted to tell you about. I went to visit my cousin Sue who has a daughter around 12. Oh, I forgot about this 'til this minute: Sue is a few years younger than I am, and she is the other person I saw naked when she was a child. She's a cousin I'm still close to. And she was just very unself-conscious when she let me go into the bathroom with her, at least once anyway.

"She raised her daughter to be like her, so it was literally true that from the time Sue's child was born in 1980, I was looking forward to seeing the daughter around age 9 or 10—not younger but not necessarily older. The summer of 1989 I was with the two of them at Sue's mother's swimming pool, and the little daughter was somewhat immodestly changing out of her bathing suit, but just as I was about to see her vagina, my aunt moved in between us. Like I almost got to see the vagina but I didn't. That was frustrating after all these years of looking forward to it. So the following January, I was visiting them. My bedroom was next door to the girl's bedroom, and we both got up early on Sunday morning, we were talking. I said something about, 'You're getting to be a young woman,' and she said something about developing breasts. So I asked her if she had pubic hair, and she said no.

"Well, that whole situation made me uncomfortable, because I thought she'd probably go and tell her mother. So I confessed it to Sue. Because for years and years and years, I thought, well, I have these fantasies about girls, but nobody gets hurt. I can really get away with it. But between the letter to that woman and this situation with Sue's little girl, I thought this is becoming a threat to society. I ought to do something about it. And that's crucial, because I felt that the therapy the first time was a punishment I deserved for being a threat to females. I told Sue that I needed therapy, because I had done something wrong and I needed to serve my time. Sue was very open about it."

"She did not end your relationship with her?" I said.

"No, she was very understanding. As I've said to her just this past weekend, the fact that I was able to tell her of that whole problem with girls was in itself very helpful."

"So you didn't *see* your young cousin," I said. "You only asked about her development. But you could feel yourself intruding—and wanting more, I assume—but you also felt that this was not going to be good for this child, or for you."

"Yes, and it's literally true that my feelings toward girls have changed with therapy."

"Okay," I said, and seized upon his reference to change in therapy in order to pursue the central issue of his referral. "What happened in your therapy? You've said already it was a self-imposed punishment for your misbehavior, the price to pay for your danger-ousness to society."

"Well, also hopefully to do something about the threat I posed," he replied rather positively.

"You did have the idea about change as well," I agreed. "But was the price you had to pay and the change you had to make only for that piece of behavior, or for some destructiveness in your character?"

"Because the behavior was a product of my psyche," he agreed.

"So, you're also saying you saw yourself as a potentially dangerous person, to certain kinds of people," I said.

"Becoming dangerous, at least," he qualified my understanding. "I'd had these fantasies for decades, but I'd never actually had one when a child was around, until that day with my little cousin. Except I did go to these nudist places, and there, of course, I got a good look!"

"You say this as though it was different," I sensed. "Did you feel that the nudist situation was in better control so you could just look?"

"Yes," he agreed. "They didn't even know I was looking."

"Did you ever fondle or touch a child?" I asked to be sure how far the danger of the perversion was enacted.

"Oh, no! Certainly not! I wouldn't do that."

"Was anything ever done to you?" I asked. "Did anyone ever touch you?"

"Well," he began. "This was something extremely helpful that I learned in therapy, something I hadn't thought about before. To this day, I feel uncomfortable about intimate touching. I give Dr. Michaels credit for realizing the cause of this."

Here was another positive report of the work with Dr. Michaels. I kept wondering, what on earth had gone wrong? My interview wasn't perfect, but he seemed quite patient with me. As I sat there thinking about it, he continued.

"When I was a child, in the hospital, whenever I would go for check-ups, they would have rounds or grand rounds. The doctors would bring tons of students, and then would examine my penis in front of a bunch of strangers in order to show the great surgical healing and all that stuff. I didn't give it much thought, but it would happen repeatedly. It was like, 'Oh, well, this is his medical history, so let's look and see how he's doing.'"

"This happened in front of the whole team, with people trooping through? Were you the subject of grand rounds in an open amphitheatre—that kind of thing?" I was remembering my days as a medical student. Earlier in the interview, I was glad that my medical background prepared me to talk about extrophy of the bladder. Now I felt uncomfortable and exploitative.

"Well, it wasn't in a private room," he agreed. "It was in an open ward. It was a great hospital. I mean I'm glad to have helped the teaching process, but I . . . "

"You think it was traumatic for you, do you?"

"No, I wouldn't say traumatic," he disagreed. "But the idea of being touched in public, and so on, wasn't easy."

"Oh, so that's a situation where *you* would be touched!" I exclaimed. "You must have been examined privately as well, but to be touched and displayed in the public setting of hospital rounds seems to be a special situation that was important to you and, in retrospect, even traumatizing, I would guess."

"When I talk to you, I think that," he said. "But I don't think I felt it at the time. I just felt I was an object of examination."

Now I was no longer made uncomfortable by my countertransference. I realized that I was contributing to a repetition of the trauma of hospital rounds by meeting him on camera. I guessed that there might also have been this element in his transference to Dr. Michaels. I might be able to get to that by speaking about his transference to the context of the interview.

"Now, what do you think about being here?" I asked. "In a private room, but on camera at this moment? It seems to me to have the potential for making you feel the same way. We're certainly grateful to you for agreeing to be interviewed in this setting, but what about the downside of this situation?"

"Well, you're right," he said. "It's sort of the same, especially since the whole issue of discussing my interest in children is quite uncomfortable, but as I say, —and this interview included—I think doctors clearly saved my life, so I owe them a debt of gratitude. Just recently I was at the hospital and I asked a doctor what would have happened if they hadn't operated on me. He said I probably wouldn't be alive now. I believe it: they saved my life! I mean, if I hadn't had the surgery as an infant, I may have died under age 2, because urination wasn't really ever possible normally, and I would have died of a kidney infection."

"You are convinced the risks would have been great without medical intervention," I said.

"Oh, yeah!" he said emphatically. "That's why I feel I owe a debt of gratitude. What's interesting about this is that I started to see myself not just as a physical specimen of interest to the medical profession, but also as a psychological specimen. Especially now discussing the child thing!"

"That's what you would be most uncomfortable discussing in any setting," I acknowledged. "Here, being on camera offers the same kind of heightening of the situation, and stands for being touched intimately as you were with the gang of observers there. It may feel like a violation too."

He wanted to let me off the hook. "The difference though, is that I was a child then," he said. "I didn't consent to it then, which I have here."

"Okay," I said, able to let it go and move on. "Let me see if I can get a sense of your medical experience. You had a number of other surgeries too, right? These original ones were all about closing your bladder to provide for urination. Was it always through a bag?"

"No, I did it rectally," he reminded me.

"Until when?" I had to ask.

"'Til the bag," he said. An obtuse answer.

"Which was installed when?" I asked, now more precisely.

"1971," he replied. After a pause, he added, "At 26."

He was giving me the short answers I had received earlier when we had discussed his penis and the removal of the 'cherries.'

"Why did they change it?" I asked, getting a longer answer this time. I seemed to be getting the facts, but stripped of any sense of loss of the body that I would have expected.

"Because urinating rectally causes kidney infections," he explained. "In 1970, they said they could do a bag or take out a kidney. I said I don't want to wear a bag, there's enough things wrong with my body already, so take out the kidney. But it didn't solve the problem. If I knew then what I know now, I would still have two kidneys. But the doctor did say my kidney looked like it had gone through the lawnmower, so . . ."

"You mean, it probably wasn't much of a loss?"

"Apparently not."

"Your other kidney, how is it?" I asked.

"Normal," he said proudly. "I drink tons of water. I'm a great patient. Even though I get periodic infections, they are controlled absolutely. I normally get them in the summer. I didn't get one this summer. For a while I would take medication every day, but I decided the germs can't be removed permanently, so I stopped treatment and now I just treat it when I get something."

The sense of medical trauma was building in me. It was a relief to hear him display his coping strength and pride in his one good kidney.

I started to draw up a list. "So as a kid you had surgery on your penis, then you had the kidney out for infection, and then the surgery for the bag. And since then?"

"Brain surgery," he said.

I couldn't believe it. What next, I thought. I asked, "What for?"

"I won't tell you the whole story," he said as if to spare me. "But in 1986 I would be masturbating, and after I would ejaculate I would feel dizzy. It was clear something was happening. I was really dizzy and having trouble walking when I'd get up in the morning. This went on for days. Something had burst in my head."

"A blood vessel?" I suggested.

"I guess," he said as if it was irrelevant. "I went for surgery and they took care of it."

This was extraordinary. He knew so much more about his genito-urinary system than about his brain.

"There's no damage," he said almost carelessly. "I'm fine. I feel that my mind is the strongest part of me, and I don't want that affected."

I realized that the brain, now recovered, had not been admitted as a threat equal to the other bodily damage that could be repaired but never really corrected. He regarded the brain problem as purely incidental to the masturbation experience, whatever it was.

Returning to the subject, I said, "You mentioned that it was after masturbation that you experienced the dizziness that led to your brain surgery. Do you think you connect the brain difficulty to your masturbation?"

"That might be," he said. "But I didn't stop masturbating. Well, I did for a long time right after the surgery 'cause I was a little worried that the exertion had caused the brain thing, but really, that's just when it happened – after masturbating. I'm not going to stop doing it, but the broader issue is I never know when my body is going to get me again."

"It's not a reliable part of you," I agreed.

"It's not just that. It's that I really think I'm being punished for something."

I thought about the likely cause of his guilt. Perhaps the unfamiliar thrill of masturbating to orgasm with an ejaculation coming from the tip of his intact penis was felt to be undeserved in a boy who had thought of himself as exposed and defective.

I tried it head on. "What do you need to be punished for?"

"That's the strange part," he said. "I don't know the causes of guilt. I learned in psychology class that there's three consequences to guilt, which aren't rational, but I don't recall them. If I try to remember them, three questions, not answers, come up in my mind. 'Why is this done to me?' 'How do I know what to do?' and 'Why did nature ever do this to me?'"

Perhaps this was a bit much for me. The three responses speak poetically of his sense of castration. If I had stayed with him here, I might have heard more of his feeling like a hurt, imperfect boy, who felt castrated. Perhaps to deal with it, he imagined himself as one of the girls whose genitals he so wanted to see. Perhaps he missed his pristine old non-phallic self before he got the penis of which the surgeon was so proud. Yet, there was other territory to cover in this single interview, and I decided to move on to the object relations history.

"I want to shift a bit now to ask how you got along with your parents," I said.

"Good with my father," he said. "Lousy with my mother. My Dad died of a stroke at 62. We were close. But it was silent, we didn't talk that much. Starting in childhood we would play catch after supper, and that helped us to bond until he died in 1966.

"On the other hand, my Mom was always very good when I was dependent, but she didn't like giving me up. We started to not get along when I went to college. I don't remember much earlier that being a problem, but it really got very bad after that. I wasn't talking to her at the time she died in 1989. I didn't even visit her in the hospital. We hadn't talked for a long time. It would go for spells like that. Then I would relent and start talking, and then something else would happen. I mean it was the type of situation where she had said there was a right way and a wrong way to do things. She'd say you're doing them the wrong way. This is the kind of issue that makes me want to be in therapy, because I realize that corrections are inevitable. I'm talking about having a defective psyche. But I wonder if I had to take her words as strongly and as angrily as I did, 'cause she was obviously someone who wasn't in the best shape herself. I realize it's my individual personality that made me overreact to certain situations. I let it affect my whole life. Even the self-punitive thing. I mean I have a good friend who's paralyzed from the neck down, who wasn't born that way. But he's having a wonderful, very successful life, even though it's been a struggle for him. He *could* make excuses out of his physical situation. Compared to him, mine is quite minor. I spent decades worrying about how women would look at me with my clothes off, and I go to this nudist place and no one seems to much care. Not that I got a relationship out of that situation."

If I had stayed with his train of thought, I might have heard something about his sightings at the nudist camp that would have related to his experience of his mother, but the interview was more than half over and I hadn't yet heard about the therapy with Dr. Michaels that was the subject of the consultation.

"All right. Now," I said, coming to the point. "Let me ask you to shift a bit again. Can you tell me what happened in the therapy with Dr. Michaels? You began therapy with him because you felt that you'd done something bad, and you should pay the price—as well as feeling that you'd like to change. What happened?"

"Well, this is sort of important," he said, ready to tackle the subject, I thought. "I went to see a social worker—sort of comparison shopping. The social worker said it was too much for him to handle this kind of thing, and he recommended me to someone else. So, even though my original focus was that I wanted to work on just this one problem of the two recent situations of wanting to see the female body nude—the woman in Greece who stopped writing to me and my little cousin whose vagina I wanted to see—Dr. Michaels made the point that the situation with the woman was punitive, that I was angry with her, and that I was expressing hostility toward her that came from somewhere else. I gave that some thought, so by the time I saw Dr. Michaels, I was ready to focus on that woman in Greece and my cousin's daughter, and I was thinking about my years of interest in children." He seemed to be about to go off onto the topic of his fascination with girls again, but he didn't. "It got problematic, way beyond that." He fell silent.

"So what happened," I prompted, "in the therapy with Dr. Michaels?"

"Well, we made progress on that issue about the woman in Greece and especially with children," he said.

"What did you learn?" I encouraged him to reflect.

"Well, my theory toward children is that I like looking at them because even if I'm going to be only sexually masturbatory, I like the innocence and purity of the 9- or 10-year-old girl—not a 3-year-old, but also not an adult with menstruation and pubic hair. I didn't have any trouble when we would talk about these things. But he also talked at one point in a way that I had mixed feelings about. Dr. Michaels used the word "pervert" or "perversion" or something like that, which made me very uncomfortable. We talked later about the whole question of how society views me and my behavior. To this day I don't know if therapy changed me because I just sort of integrated from him the idea that it's wrong so I don't do it any more. Or did something else go on? Because the feelings just absolutely changed after we talked."

I wondered if he had suffered a relapse. Could that be why he was seeking therapy again? So I asked, "What are your feelings now?"

He took me back into the subject of his sexual interests. "Well, the good proof came when summer rolled around, and I went to nudist places and wasn't interested in children after decades of that interest. I still prefer women without pubic hair. Absolutely! And I still prefer mostly looking. And I'm still not interested in intercourse. But I have orally stimulated women now, and I want to do that again. There was one woman that I met through nudism. We were both horny so she tried to perform oral sex on me but it wasn't at all enjoyable. She was more interested than I was. Nothing much happened. It was very brief. That was while I was seeing Dr. Michaels, so we discussed it."

Back to business, I tried again, "Now, I have a picture of your therapist as someone that you could talk with about your interest in hairless girls and women too. You could discuss with him your anger at this woman you wrote the letter to, the one who stimulated you to hope for more but who rebuffed you after the letter you wrote to her. It sounds like the relationship with her might have been the closest relationship you'd had with a woman, perhaps with anyone." Here I was doing it now—backing off the issue with Dr. Michaels and getting lost in Mr. P.'s wishes to be close to a woman.

"No," he asserted. "The one from Greece was the closest. This one was more a case of getting to look at her. There's another one which I haven't mentioned yet, this very young Scandinavian woman, very pretty, that I worked with. She flirted with me and we ended up getting together a couple of times. She had pubic hair, and it was still very sexy. But I didn't take my clothes off in front of her. I mean, I stimulated her orally and so on. Yeah, she was very flirty. She was really young—18 or 19. I was in my early thirties. It didn't work when we tried it at my place, but then she got her own place, and I went over. She came to the door wearing only a robe, and then you know, we talked about me performing orally on her, and I did. It was a bad job and she didn't enjoy it. But then I asked her to turn over. I love women's asses and I really just wanted to get a good look, so she did just turn over. I ended up kissing her ass, but she bent all the way over so I could see her anus, but I think she wanted me to perform orally. I've thought a lot about that experience to this day. And then I wasn't with anyone other than myself 'til this woman in the nudist place in 1980 or whatever. It was over ten years."

"You haven't had many real relationships," I said, feeling the bleakness of it. "Lots of looking at pictures and at people in the nudist colonies without being able to be in relationships to them." I felt affectively in tune now, and I took the plunge. "Okay, now what was it that seemed not right about the relationship with Dr. Michaels?"

"Well, very simply, I wanted it *just* on the sexual issues," he said. "And then he wanted to keep going beyond that. I ended up going twice a week, and that felt pretty good. Initially, I had only wanted once a week and I didn't want to go for long. Then it was sort of like he tricked me into twice a week, so there was that issue."

I could well imagine their struggle. I had experienced a version of it in this interview when I intended to stay with my central task, but kept getting diverted. I had noticed how he tended to revert to his sexual preoccupation and specifics in this interview, while I was trying to hone in on the relationship aspects. He tried to narrow it to genitals and asses, and flirtacious specifics, while I tried to take it back to the more general relationship of intimacy. He was recreating the transference difficulty with me that he had felt with Dr. Michaels. He had been balking at my pushing in the direction to which he had objected when Dr. Michaels took a similar course.

"So Dr. Michaels becomes like the doctors in the ward, not so much putting you on display as they did, but intruding without permission," I suggested, well aware that the same could be said of me.

"Sort of," he said, sounding guarded.

"Did you feel manipulated and tricked a bit?" I asked.

"Well," he said, trying to be reasonable, "Whether he tricked me or not, it felt something like that."

"Then he used the word 'perversion,' which upset you," I said.

"Probably."

"Did you get past that with him?" I said, wondering if I would get past this repeat round of question-and-short-answer.

"We talked about it, yeah," he said unconvincingly, waiting for me to prod.

Just to be sure, I asked, "You told him you were upset about it?"

"Yeah."

"And how did he take it?" I prompted.

"Well, I think he sort of, sort of corrected himself—this was sort of manipulative—well, he said 'I said *perversion* and not *pervert*, sort of . . .' "

"Like you weaseled it out of him?" I suggested.

"Yeah, a little bit. We did have some valuable discussion in relation to it. But then the other point was, he would want me to keep going and going, and . . . 'We have a lot of work to do,' he'd say. That wasn't good enough for me, like I'm going to go twice a week for the rest of my life! 'Cause my brother, who's doing fine and doesn't have these physical problems, he sees a shrink, he's been going for fifteen years, once or twice a week, but he's married now, and he's doing fine, and his life is, you know, great. I see that as an indulgence, and I'm not going to go to therapy as an indulgence."

"Okay," I said. "But what is it that's bringing you back to therapy now? What's changed since you stopped? I understand that you stopped partly because the idea about girls no longer threatened to break through, but also because there was this thing about Dr. Michaels prying into your . . . ["intimate life," I was going to say]."

" . . . Keeping going," he filled in. "The way it finally ended up was this: I had decided I'm not comfortable with this. He had been on vacation and we had missed appointments, and he said, 'We really need to get on schedule with this,' and I said, 'Well, I don't want to go anymore at all.' We had one or two appontments to finish up, and that was it."

"So that was it," I said, feeling sorry for them both. "You left with some resentment of him for wanting to keep going and get inside you."

"Well, now, if I admit the experience, if I go back to him, I'm going to have to say, 'Well, you told me so. And yeah, I admit you were right, I needed more help.'"

I wondered if the resentment came up only around this issue of readiness to terminate, or if it preceded that. I asked, "Other than your disappointment with him when he was pressing for more and you were pressed to get away because you had got what you came for, how do you feel you got along with him?"

"Fairly good," he said.

"I mean, do you feel that he was someone who was concerned about you?" I said.

"Well," he went on, "There was one other issue of the way it went, 'cause I'd talk about something, and he'd throw in an interpretation, and he'd say, 'How does this sound?' I thought he was playing speculative games here, so I was uncomfortable with that approach. 'How does this sound to you?' he'd say."

"So you felt it was a little bit too speculative, too trivial, too haphazard?" I was beginning to get somewhere. I was glad that I hadn't erred in the analytic direction too much. In fact, I'd been aware of asking a lot of questions, like a concerned and interested physician. It had seemed defensive to me, but when I heard what he had to say next, it may have been just what the doctor ordered.

"Yeah, maybe the medical model spoiled me," he said. "While you have this infection, then you use this drug. And if it's not right, then you change it. So you get the right medicine, and you're better."

I was struck not so much by the contrast between Dr. Michaels and the medical model, but with its similarity to Dr. Michaels' speculative, trial-and-error approach. But I stayed with his perception.

I said, "There's a comforting, definite, quality of finding whatever works."

"Yes, but here's what I'm getting at," he said. "The therapy was manipulating me to need another level of care. And I could benefit from that. What I'm getting at is I'm admitting to myself that, for decades, I was using very good money to sort of relieve myself." He looked ashamed of himself.

"What is it that enables you to come this fall, and admit that you need more?" I asked.

"The business with my job where I've had more responsibility than I've ever had," he said.

"So you actually face added responsibility, although you also describe yourself as an underachiever," I remarked.

"Yeah, well, I didn't say that, but you say that," he retorted, sounding stung.

"Well, I'm using it as a summary word," I said. "If it's not the way you feel, let's change it."

"I mean, I agree," he said. "But I don't think I said it." He showed me that autonomy in the area of naming the defect was clearly worth fighting over. "But yeah, I've spent a lifetime avoiding these kinds of adult situations."

"So you're left acting like a child who looks but must not touch. In other words, you don't get into relationships with grown-ups."

"The only part that's not like a child is my mind," he said. "You know, I get involved in political stuff, I read the papers."

"Intellectually, you've grown up," I said. "Emotionally, you're a child."

"That hurts to hear," he told me.

I responded, "I know I'm moving you a little bit toward the pain. Perhaps this is what was hard for you with Dr. Michaels."

"Yeah," he went on to confirm my idea. He seemed to be

referring to both Dr. Michaels and me. "It's like this is an expert telling me that I'm defective."

"Logically," I began, defending my autonomy, "you just told me what you're worried about, and the ways in which you feel you're defective, but if I then use your word to show you that I have heard you—and especially if I understood you well enough to find my own word to express your experience, you feel criticized and maybe humiliated."

"What you're saying is just like what I say, I know that. Like friends will say it's good that I'm admitting this stuff to myself. But what I don't like is why I have to go through life like this. I've had enough physical problems, I mean, that's a given, and I'd rather be psychically okay."

"So when I say something to you like 'underachiever' or 'defective,' you feel upset . . . " I said.

"And uncomfortable."

"Hurt?"

"Yeah."

"Hurt in some way that echoes the hurt you felt with Dr. Michaels?"

"In that one issue where he used the word 'perverted,' yeah."

"Perversion," I reminded him of Dr. Michaels' amendment. "There's also a threat that maybe defect would be used against you, and then you'd then have to pay the price of being in therapy longer than you want to."

"Yeah, but more the central issue at this point is whether or not I'll admit that there is a serious problem."

It was so obvious that he had a serious problem. Anyone in his situation would face huge challenges at every stage of life. The main problem for him as I saw it concerned his inability to be in—and maybe even to conceive of—a relationship of intimacy and sexual pleasure. Yet, he was not psychotic, he was not disabled, he had an excellent job, he had socially acceptable ways to indulge his scoto-philic impulses, and he had the ego strength to stop himself when his problem was about to harm or offend others. I was not sure if he defined the problem the way I did at all. I began to sound like the devil's advocate, not with any intention to provoke or effect a maneuver. I think I was responding unconsciously to his need for opposition to me.

"I really think in some ways, there isn't a serious problem," I began.

"Well, that I don't agree with at this point," he said sharply, opposing me immediately.

I clarified my point. "The outside world is not demanding change of you: your boss is pleased with your work, women are not demanding more of you in relationships, you are not hurting children. It's only a problem if it's a problem for you. It only matters if you have come to want more, to expect more of yourself."

"But it's not to be simply that it would be nice. In other words, if I break my arm, I gotta go to the doctor. With this issue I am wrestling with—I mean, I've been in and out of therapy for years, you know, social workers and somebody on and off for years—it's a case of saying, you know, it's not just this problem or that problem, it's. . . ."

I didn't wait for him to finish his sentence. I think he was about to say, "The problem is me," a direction toward which I had been heading him after I succeeded in freeing myself from the sexual specifics, but when the moment came, I couldn't bear it. I finished the sentence for him, like a good, protective doctor who knows what's what.

"It's a general problem," I said. "Your growth did not really move past childhood in a number of areas that leave you missing ordinary life experience in some important ways . . ."

"Again it's uncomfortable to hear you say that I'm still a child," he told me.

I didn't deal with his transference to me as therapist, but continued in the medical vein. "I was going to ask you at what age you locate yourself?"

"I'm a case of arrested sexual development," he replied, sounding like a doctor himself. "At the age when relationships formed, 9, 10, 12, something like that."

I was needing to wind up the interview. I said, "I'd like to say a couple of things about therapy. First, it's not worth doing unless you face the truth. Second, the real worth will be in the relationship with the therapist. You want it to be with somebody you trust, who has your interest in mind, who cares about the work and your well-being. Once you have all that, it's going to be painful for you. I can't even mention these words without you feeling pain. How much more are you going to feel when you really start to get into it?"

"Well, it's the medical image: when I talk to medical doctors there's not pain, then when I get a shot there is pain. Is that the realization, that using these words is like having the pain? It's part of the treatment."

"Well, I mean that it's only in the areas of pain that you need the treatment. When you're in those areas you're going to feel it. That's how you know you're there. You talk to me about your job, about your mother, you talk about feeling safe about the children, in many of those areas you're not in any pain. Then you talk about some of the things with Dr. Michaels, you talk about my calling you 'defective' or 'immature,' you're upset already. If we really got into those areas, you'd be more upset. Therapy would have to do with working on your hurt."

Returning to his medical model, he said, "But again, I think the real issue is the question of trust that this is going to hurt but if you take that shot, the infection will go away. Still, if I don't admit that it was traumatic, then I won't benefit as much I guess. But if it just hurts for the sake of hurting. . . ."

"Then explore it," I said. "I think there must have been some earlier traumas that you can't remember. Early surgeries. Being in the hospital without your family."

"They would come down from upstate New York and stay with my aunt."

Now we were getting to the earlier trauma. As before, entry to this hurtful material took the form of rapid question-and-answer in a medical case history–taking model.

"Where were you?" I asked, wanting to set the scene.

"New York City, at the Presbyterian," he said, not getting too close.

"Pediatric ward, from what age?" I asked.

"Well, starting in infancy I'd go back for checkups, and I guess I had surgery when I was 8 and when I was 15."

"You were there by yourself," I emphasized. "How long?"

"A week or two, I don't know," he said, shrugging.

"How'd you feel?" I asked. "Were you lonely, in pain? On display?"

He gave a measured response. "I felt that uh, self-discipline was very important. I remember, I was very thirsty, you couldn't fast the night before a kidney x-ray, and you had to stay very still when they took the picture."

"Couldn't fast or couldn't drink?" I asked for clarification of what must be a significant slip.

"I mean, you had to fast, you couldn't drink," he corrected himself. "I'm sorry. Yeah, you couldn't drink."

"You'd be in very tight control," I said. That was obvious, even now.

"Yeah, I'd be thirsty," he remembered.

I was glad that he could get beyond control to remember his physical thirst. I was struck at how he had undone the totality of the oral deprivation at this frightening time, by focusing only on not having fluid. He didn't mention any wish to be fed.

"You'd be really good, a good little boy," I said, realizing that this had been crucial to his adaptation.

"Yeah, it was for my benefit, ultimately, or my family's, or whatever."

"And you thought that then?" I asked, quite impressed at his fortitude and capacity for creating a coping strategy.

"Yeah, this is what you gotta do to feel better," he told me, just like he had told himself back then.

"And so, you'd be like a statue of a brave little boy, not even knowing how frightened or lonely you were," I said.

"Scared, yeah, 'cause you couldn't move during the pictures either, so that was more self-control," he said. "I prided myself, I think, on being a good kid."

"So there would be x-rays to reveal your kidneys," I said. "And in those hospitalizations, I suppose they'd be handling your unreconstructed penis."

He blocked thinking about that and moved on to recalling the later demonstrations when the penis had been reconstructed.

"No, it was more the grand rounds thing," he said. "Normally, when I'd see a doctor in rounds after surgery, they would say, 'It's really a very good job,' and they would examine my penis as a practical achievement."

Using this last detour to support my recommendation, I said, "What I'm emphasizing is that if you go into therapy, there will be some pain, not because pain is good punishment for you but because that's the area where you want to grow. Where it comes into the relationship with the therapist will be the place to work. The loneliness, the good little boy, the fear of being looked at, are frozen inside you. All of these are ways of not being able to be in a relationship. You had nobody to turn to, and when you couldn't turn to anybody, you handled it yourself. You don't have to be that way any more."

"It was rational at the time," he said.

"Sure. What else could you do?" I agreed. "That would cost you. We don't treat children like that anymore, families are encouraged to be there. I think that your fear and loneliness may have been a major part of the trauma, even more than the physical trauma."

"Well, but there's something else," he said. "I mean, this gets into all sorts of things with my mother. She wouldn't send me to overnight camp because she said that the children would make fun of me, so the message was that she clearly thought I was defective. That's the other part that is going to be painful. In admitting these problems I'm inflicting pain on myself. 'You have to do it also,' that's what I think you're saying."

In facing his trauma and working on the hurt, he would be agreeing with his mother's perception of him as defective. He did not want to identify with her as that type of dependency-inducing object.

I said, "You don't want the therapist to do as your mother did and try to protect you from yourself. If a therapist does that, you'll never deal with other people."

To emphasize his mother's protectiveness, he said, "Well, and the other point was when I had brain surgery at age 41, she was right there. As long as I was dependent she was great, but then I'd get independent and she was not so great."

"Okay, now, we have to get to a decision," I reminded him. "Do you want to see Dr. Michaels or not? Do you want to see if knowing this little bit more about why it's not so surprising that you got resentful of him will enable therapy to proceed?"

He spoke first from the negative: "Well, in some ways I feel I'm at a new plateau in terms of insight about myself, so I like the idea of starting new with someone else. Right now I'd feel guilty seeing him because it's like we'd probably spend sessions talking about how I badmouthed him in front of you and the camera."

"On the other hand he does know all about you," I said, reminding him of the positive.

"Right, and I thought of that," he said.

So, if he thought of it but couldn't act upon it, a transference feeling must still be needing interpretation.

"It seems to me that some of the bad feeling is like that feeling about your mother . . ." I began.

"He didn't protect me in that sense," he protested, not wanting to portray Dr. Michaels like his mother.

"No, he exposed you," I agreed. "But my main point is that like her, he tried to cling to you."

"He didn't let me go," he said, thoughtfully, not angrily.

"Right, like your mother," I said again. "I think that your resentment may be about that."

"Yeah!" He nodded, and went on, "And it happened in other relationships too."

"If you can manage it," I said, "the best situation for you is to see him, and work on what went wrong."

"If I can't, it's because I feel he's going to be mad at me for what I've said about him now, although it's been more about other business."

"He's not going to be mad," I tried to reassure him. "I mean, I don't think so. This is ordinary stuff for therapists."

I was not addressing his guilt at doing to Dr. Michaels what had been done to him, exposing his defect.

He alerted me to that right away. "To be criticized in front of other therapists? I'm saying that I didn't like that he called me a pervert, I didn't like that he wanted me to keep going, I didn't like that he . . . "

"How are you going to be in a relationship if every time someone makes a mistake or does something that's hurtful, you gotta end the relationship?" I asked.

"Sounds good to me," he laughed.

"Yeah, that's how you've been living your life," I said. "Even if you decide you're not going to work with him, I think there's some advantage to going and just talking that through with him. He's going to survive it. This is his job, he does the best he can and makes mistakes sometimes. Maybe it wasn't a mistake. We'll see."

"But what if he starts bugging me about going twice a week instead of once a week?" He wanted to know what to do.

"How often do you want to go?" I asked.

He started fudging, "Well, I mean, there's issues like with my job, I never know when I'm going to be paged, and my schedule is uncertain, and all that."

I came straight out and said, "You should go twice a week."

Surprised and pleased, he laughed and asked, "Why?"

"The work will go a whole lot better, faster, and deeper," I replied. "You're now asking depth questions."

"And it won't be for twenty years?" he asked, scared of a lifelong problem.

"No, but you're talking about at least a couple of years of work.

You've worked nine months with him on one problem, now you're talking about changing your character, the way you live your life."

"That's the whole problem," he said. "That's the point."

"Okay, it's going to take you longer, if that's what you want," I said. "Twice a week will work better if major change is what you have in mind. You don't have to do it the way I suggest. It's just a recommendation based on what I think you want."

"Well, what I can see myself doing is seeing him once and seeing how it goes."

"That would be fine. And if you say, look, I'm just too uncomfortable, fine, then we'll give you somebody else."

"And there's a whole bunch of people?" he asked.

He just wanted to know his options, but into my mind came the image of all the medical students and physicians interested in his case.

I answered simply, "Yes, there are a lot of people who'd be very glad to see you, no problem."

"Yeah, it has to be a man," he said. "No question about it, it has to be a man. I will see Dr. Michaels once."

"Say you really don't feel comfortable seeing him again, we'll set you up with somebody else, and you'll do the work with him," I assured him.

His final comment surprised me and gave me hope. He said, "Well, I have thought of this point, of the pain of going over everything again if it's a new person."

Mr. Patrick returned to see Dr. Michaels for a single interview and chose to work with him in twice-a-week therapy. He did so for almost a year, with gains in a number of areas. Then, he wrote to tell me that he had stopped. I was disappointed to read that, although the work had been helpful, he had developed some of the same feelings again in treatment.

In therapy of trauma, the trauma is repeated in the transference. It is not uncommon for this repetition to cause the patient to quit the therapy in fear or to create a false readiness to terminate by constricting the goals. When the patient manages to remain in one therapeutic relationship, there will often be an intermittent quality to the work. The down times are not usefully regarded as periods of resistance against the emergence of conflict over fantasy material. It is more helpful to accept them as necessary periods of respite for ego strengthening and rebuilding the therapeutic alliance before facing trauma again, either through direct recall or in the transference. Mr. Patrick had dealt with this need for respite and return to the issues by engaging in multiple therapies over the years.

But at 47 years old, he had to confront the rest of his life. When I saw him, he seemed to be at a point where he could tolerate more anxiety in his therapeutic quest. He needed a therapist who could deal with his congenital malformation with empathy but not pity, with discretion but not protectiveness. He needed a therapist devoted to him like his mother, but able to let him go to face his peers, so that he could have a chance of exploring the world of sexuality in a relational context. He needed a therapist who could deal not just with the usual transferences to father, mother, and sibling objects, but one who could accept the fear, rage, and gratitude of his transference to the doctor as a healing authority who inevitably is identified with his original and repeated medical trauma.

All of this was reflected in condensed form in the transference and countertransference of the consultation interview. I could feel his testiness develop as I tried to steer him away from the concreteness of the physical defects and fetishes he had developed to help him cope with his sense of isolation and inadequacy. I could feel his resistance against my questions as I tried to make links between these areas and the issues of his difficulty in relating. In short, we could together experience an episode that was a shortened version of the difficulty he had in all relationships and in therapy as well. He had recovered enough resilience and enough tolerance for the pain of renewed investigation to enable him to reconnect to Dr. Michaels and to find again a valued relationship with him. Since he carried the conviction that his capacity to damage others meant that he would, inevitably, spoil all relationships he valued, this was salutary in itself. It was one of the few times in his life he had been able to undo the damage. While that recovery held, he could push on to new territory. Yet, the ground did not hold under the impact of trauma repetition in the transference. We can hope that there will be another "next time" for Mr. Patrick and his therapist.

Treating the Effects of Sexual Trauma on Individuals and Families

11

Mother–Daughter Incest

SINGLE-SHOCK AND CUMULATIVE TRAUMA

A single-shock trauma is a massive, sudden event of catastrophic proportions that leaves the victim in a terrified, helpless situation and results in a state of hypervigilance in case of repetition. It is the kind of trauma experienced during a rape, a single episode of childhood sexual abuse, a kidnapping, a raid, a murder, a suicide, a traffic accident, a natural disaster, an invasive medical procedure, or sudden loss of a body part or function. The single trauma is experienced in the light of any previous trauma, and its meaning to the individual depends on his or her previous life experience and sense of self. In contrast, cumulative trauma refers to the serial repetition of traumatic events, each of which is singly traumatic, but the accumulation of which produces a living state of terror and helplessness so severe that it requires characteristically pronounced defenses and survival techniques. It is the kind of trauma experienced in a prisoner-of-war camp, in a war zone, in a concentration camp, in a violent community, in repeated medical procedures, in humiliating abusive relationships, and in incest.

The following clinical situation illustrates the impact of the cumulative trauma of prolonged childhood mother–daughter incest and violent physical abuse on a woman who later suffered a sudden, massive injury to which she had a classical single-shock trauma response and yet who also experienced it as a further accumulation of earlier trauma. The example also shows the avoidance and transmission of trauma in the family and in the transference, the survival skill of going-on-being alongside traumatic repetition, the thawing of the frozen capacity for symbolization, dreaming of the transference, and the obligatory imposition of trauma in the countertransference in the termination phase.

PSYCHOANALYSIS FOR CUMULATIVE TRAUMA

Mrs. Feinstein, a 36-year-old married woman with two children, Liz and Sam, had discovered in previous supportive psychotherapy that she had been sexually abused by her mother for years as a child and adolescent, a fact that had not come to light before—even when she was interviewed by a psychiatrist after a suicide attempt when she was 17 years old or during a work-up for epilepsy when the abuse was still occurring. The recovery of memories of sexual abuse had helped her recover from a tendency to panic during intercourse with her husband, Ron. Yet, she still suffered from suicidal ideation, poor self-esteem, rages at her children and fears of hurting them, immobilizing depression, and irritable bowel syndrome. In family therapy, the family worked on the impact of their mother's history on their lives, and family life improved. However, Mrs. Feinstein requested more intensive individual treatment from me (JSS) because she still felt suicidal at times, slept a lot during the day, felt guilty whenever she was furious at her children, suffered bowel eruptions whenever she was upset, and felt bad about herself despite all her good works for the Jewish community.

Mrs. Feinstein had enjoyed and benefited from her work with her previous therapist, an emotionally expressive woman who cried with her and gave her a hug when she felt in need. However, Mrs. Feinstein thought that at this stage when she needed to explore the past in greater depth my more rigorous approach would be better for her, because of my firm, professional boundaries. I was impressed that she, who had had no doors inside her house growing up, appreciated the value of boundaries. Although she was often suicidal, she had not made a serious attempt for many years, and I thought that her treatment could be managed on an outpatient basis. She was not an educated woman, but she was highly intelligent, psychologically minded, and deeply committed to resolving the burden of the past. Although many advise that psychoanalysis is not the treatment of choice for patients who have had the trauma of childhood sexual abuse, I felt that this patient had sufficient ego strength to warrant psychoanalysis. She also had good family and community support for her everyday functioning and for her treatment.

In psychoanalysis, Mrs. Feinstein moved between her present experience and her past life. Like many other abused patients, Mrs. Feinstein focused on actual events, rather than on fantasies or dreams, which were rarely experienced. Sometimes I would find myself feeling bored at the mundaneness of the material. I now think that my countertransference stemmed from my disappointment that there were no symbols or dreams to play with or interpret correctly to gratify my sense of myself as an analyst. I think that it also represents my identification with a mild dissociative tendency that kept the patient away from a repetition of the trauma in the transference. At first, I felt guilty and tried to shake myself to attention and sometimes stretched my imagination to come up with something that magically reached the unconscious theme behind the manifest content. However, gradually I came to appreciate that these times were necessary to the process of the analysis. They represented the sense of going-on-being that the abused child works so hard to preserve as a defense against trauma and chaos (Siegel 1992). I had to let these psychologically uneventful times simply be and not try to unravel them or find more in them than was there. These times actively maintained me in a neutral attitude and prepared the therapeutic alliance to bear the next exploration of the encapsulated trauma and its impact on the transference.

PSYCHOSOMATIC ENCAPSULATION OF TRAUMA: THE ENEMA

The first encapsulation to be explored was the recovery of memories of frequent enemas. When upset, ashamed, and humiliated by slights from acquaintances and neglectful behavior by her workaholic husband, Mrs. Feinstein had abdominal cramps and diarrhea. I asked for details of her gastrointestinal symptoms and looked for their connection to dissociated affective experience. Mrs. Feinstein appreciated being able to talk about the unmentionable, but felt that I was too interested in smells and bowel movements. She felt disgust for my perverted interest in her material and hated me when I expected her to tolerate the investigatory barium enema requested by her physician. She felt that I wanted to poke into her, smell her, and talk about her outpourings, just as her mother did. Here was a negative transference toward me as a re-edition of Mrs. Feinstein's enema-giving mother who held her down for a daily enema and sat by chitchatting until the exposed and humiliated child produced.

In Mrs. Feinstein's case, this was not the only indignity that she suffered in childhood, but even if it were, we would still call this childhood sexual abuse, although others might disagree. For instance, when I presented this material at a psychotherapy teaching meeting, a senior analyst disputed that frequent enemas could qualify as sexual abuse. Certainly the practice may have been more commonly medically sanctioned in the 1950s than in the 1980s, but we believe that two factors qualify this as sexual abuse: (1) the experience of being penetrated against her will and (2) the level of sexual excitement that the patient could see in her mother's face as she watched her child in pain. In adolescence, her mother switched to subjecting Mrs. Feinstein to vaginal douches with a similar attitude of excitement and determination. Incidentally, a former surgical nurse who is now a nurse therapist reported to us that, in her experience of giving hundreds of enemas, she has encountered many adults who are terrified of the enema and are subsequently amazed to find that it does not hurt. Children often remember the enema as a painful and humiliating experience.

Mrs. Feinstein was able to analyze her fear of the recommended medical diagnostic procedures. She was amazed to find that the experience of the barium enema was not a sexually intimidating event, but a matter-of-fact procedure administered by an empathic, nonintrusive nurse. After a diagnosis of irritable bowel syndrome was made, fiber supplements prescribed by her physician gave Mrs. Feinstein considerable relief from her abdominal symptoms, except for occasional remarkable regressions that responded well to analytic interpretation.

The patient moved on to recall physical abuse. Her mother had beaten her for provoking her. From her experience of being provoked by her own children, Mrs. Feinstein could tell that she had been sassy and stubborn about doing things that were forbidden, such as going to dances and dating boys as a teenager, but she was not out of control, did not drink, smoke, or use drugs, and performed well at school. She cleaned the house compulsively to give her mother no room for complaint, and she fed the other children when her mother left home on a drinking binge. Yet, her mother was quick to hit out nevertheless and on one occasion left marks on Mrs. Feinstein's neck from trying to strangle her.

In this phase, Mrs. Feinstein did not experience a negative transference toward me. However, she did hate some of her colleagues and neighbors because they abused her. When I interpreted this displacement, she said that she had no such feelings toward me, because I simply was not inconsistent or aggressive toward her as her mother had been and as others were now. Comparing this analysis to others in which I had felt hated or abused, I felt that I was not being a necessarily bad-enough object to effect a thorough working through. As a matter of fact, I felt that I was being actively prevented from being viewed that way and was instead kept as a good object—not ideal, but acceptably trustworthy. I often wondered if I had been seduced into providing a corrective emotional experience, rather than an analysis. I did not relish presenting this material to colleagues, because I had the fantasy that my work would be judged inferior. I have come to see this worry as a countertransference response, an introjective identification with the patient's self as being inferior and ungratifying to her mother. I think that similar problems of the analyst's narcissism account for our failure as analysts to present more of our work with these cases for review either informally or in the literature.

RECALLING CHILDHOOD SEXUAL ABUSE

Mrs. Feinstein went on to recall the sexual abuse. As a child, she had been visited in her bunk bed by her mother who, in a state of sexual excitement, snuggled behind her in a revealing negligee and, holding her daughter's pubic area, pulled her toward her, manipulated her daughter's genitals, and rubbed her vulva against the patient's buttocks. Mrs. Feinstein remembered as a child then doing the same to her teddy bear as her way of masturbating. Her mother told her that they had to be together this way, alternately because her child was so ugly that no man would ever want her or because she was irresistibly beautiful to her mother. Mrs. Feinstein was thoroughly confused by her mother's inconsistencies of feeling, expressions of physical affection and aggression, and incompatible views of her child. When her mother approached her sexually, Mrs. Feinstein feigned sleep. In analysis, she did not go to sleep on the couch, and she did not experience me as a likely perpetrator. At this stage of the analysis, however, she used to sleep away parts of the day after her sessions. I saw this as a way of recalling her abuse and her defense against it and as a way of keeping its enactment safely out of the transference.

Male analysts report the inevitable difficulty of being viewed as a likely perpetrator. Perhaps I was influenced by that into thinking that this analysis should follow the same lines, but I have not been experienced as frightening. Why not? Some might argue that the abuse itself was not frightening because there was no pain and no penetration. Her mother was giving her attention and a kind of love at these times of sexual activity, and so interest and attention on my part in the analysis might be viewed as a repetition of the abuse that was ego syntonic and free of the illicit physical excitement that led to shame. The only time that Mrs. Feinstein got really upset with me and wished to never see me again because I had such a perverted mind and was so cruel occurred after a session when we explored the pleasurable aspects of the genital stimulation by her mother. When I recognized that she might have partly enjoyed it, Mrs. Feinstein thought that I was saying that she had therefore caused the abuse and had sought it out. She felt furious at being accused by me and only gradually came to see her cooperation with the abuse as different from being responsible for it. Sorrowfully, Mrs. Feinstein admitted that she had enjoyed it to some extent because at least at these times she felt loved and needed by her mother. Then she was precipitated into another shameful memory of intense jealousy when she heard noises that led her to think that her mother was also sexually involved with her brother. Her negative transference at this time of painful remembering soon gave way to a reinstatement of the positive transference.

THE MITIGATING INFLUENCE OF
GOOD OBJECT EXPERIENCE

Mrs. Feinstein had a good object in her mother's mother, a calm, kind, religiously observant woman who adored her grandaughter and did not approve of her own daughter (Mrs. Feinstein's mother), the black sheep of the sibship. Mrs. Feinstein knew that she had identified with her grandmother, and she agreed that she had identified me with her grandmother. My age and my strict adherence to analytic neutrality and clear boundaries struck me as unlikely to invoke that grandmother transference. However, the calm, nonintrusive atmosphere and my belief in a way of looking at things probably provided the valency for receiving this projective identification.

I think that it was the availability of this good object that mitigated the bad object mother. Mrs. Feinstein used to say that she was very lucky that she was not crazy, but I said that there were factors other than luck that determined this. Her father was nurturing, and as a child she was fond of him, which may have helped her development until he died when she was 10. In analysis she recognized that he was too passive to stop her mother from hurting her and had even set her up for beatings from her mother. She discovered her rage at him for being a bystander to her abuse and realized that she had introjected an ineffectual object from her experience of him. As a little mother to her siblings and her dolls, she was able to mother herself somewhat. Her intelligence and practical abilities enabled her to leave eventually and make a secure and orderly life for herself. She must have been constitutionally not so vulnerable to the use of dissociation as a defense as to lead to a splintering of her personality, but only used dissociation to the extent that it encapsulated the trauma or led to cries for help in the form of epileptic seizures and a splitting of herself into a victimized part, a surviving part, and a suicidal part. Yet, the most crucial factors in assuring her sanity were the presence of her loving grandmother and the comfort and inspiration of Judaism that offered atonement and reconciliation, motivational ideals, and structure. These religious ideals are now part of Mrs. Feinstein's identity.

THE GOOD AND THE ABUSIVE OBJECTS
IN THE TRANSFERENCE

As analysis continued, Mrs. Feinstein held me mainly in the grandmother transference. Instead of tending to draw me away from the neutral position by the force of projections that demanded introjective identification, Mrs. Feinstein seemed to insist on fixing me in my neutral position—*on neutralizing me*—for her own safety. Her transference was analyzed mainly in its displacement onto her children, husband, neighbors, and colleagues in whom she found abusive objects whose mistreatment she became able to confront and survive. After a period of good health during which Mrs. Feinstein even considered termination, the abused transference crystalized in relation to a malicious neighbor. Everyone else in the Jewish community recognized this woman as a nuisance to dismiss, but Mrs. Feinstein was particularly vulnerable to her critical attacks. After an especially virulent dose of abuse from this woman, Mrs. Feinstein became seriously suicidal, but stopped herself in time and realized her need to continue the analytic process.

I conceptualized Mrs. Feinstein's transference neurosis as taking the form of an avoidance of a repetition of being victimized by an abusing object and of refashioning her abusive object in me as a fantasy version of a good-enough mother based on her experience with her mother's mother. Therapeutic action in analysis took the form not so much of the analysis of and taking back of projections, but rather the analysis of introjective identifications with her objects and with her analyst as a good object (see J. Scharff 1992, pp. 59–65). Mrs. Feinstein used introjective identification with the good object projected into the analyst so that I would be familiar, safe, and real, rather than an object of nebulous potential in an ambiguous analytic space. That creative space was not welcomed as a breath of freedom as it is by patients who are neurotically defended against conflictual fantasies. What Mrs. Feinstein valued was the consistency and ordinary devotion to the patient's needs offered by a reasonably healthy analyst. This left me feeling nailed down and not used fully. Her gain was my loss. I lost the transitional space I value. I think that similar dynamics in other analyses of adult survivors of incest lead analysts to conclude that such patients are not analyzable, a conclusion that we challenge. We cannot expect all analyses to look alike. Our task is to be available for self-and-object exploration, however that may need to occur.

No longer suicidal, Mrs. Feinstein was again committed to continuing treatment, about which she could now experience ambivalence. The belief system of psychoanalysis caused her some conflict, and she began to question both her grandmother's religious beliefs in the power of faith and mine in what she called science. I saw this as her search for autonomy. She became puzzled by the meaning of her life, her inability to find the right goal for herself or to understand how best to express her love of God in service to the community. She was doing well with this exploration and making considerable gains in her relationships at home, at her volunteer job, and in college courses.

ADDITIONAL SINGLE-SHOCK TRAUMA

One Sunday I received a call from Mr. Feinstein. He explained that Mrs. Feinstein had been hit by a drunk driver who sped into her compact station wagon as she was leaving the mall with her children on Thursday evening, and that she had been given a 10 percent chance of survival from surgery for abdominal and spinal injury. He wished that she had been driving their Volvo and he was upset that he had taken the bigger, stronger car on his business trip that day. He ended by saying that Mrs. Feinstein's analysis was canceled indefinitely. Mrs. Feinstein was on a respirator and in intensive care for a month. For ten days she was unconscious. When she woke up, she was disoriented, obnoxious, stubborn, and outrageously demanding of the nurses, who, however, enjoyed this behavior as a sign of her aggressive grasp on life and were surprised to discover how sweet and thoughtful Mrs. Feinstein was once she was better. With her religious faith and a tremendous outpouring of love and support from her community, Mrs. Feinstein made a spectacularly rapid recovery and was discharged from the hospital three months later.

The worst element of her hospital stay was that she kept thinking that her children were dead, even though she saw them daily. Later when they came to see her, she worried that *they* would think that *she* was going to die. She took comfort from a vision of light in which she saw her dead father at the foot of her hospital bed, saying to her, "It's not your time yet." It had been wonderful to see him in this way, but she wished that she could also have seen her dead grandmother. "She would have known to tell me that my children were all right," she joked.

At home, the reality of her limitations were more obvious. She could not resume analysis, but, after another two months of physiotherapy and rest, she could be brought to see me in her wheelchair for once-a-week psychotherapy to help her with her rage about the accident. She realized that she was furious at the drunk person who had crashed into her and caused her so much trauma. New symptoms since the accident included the following: flashbacks, night-mares, panics when driving, fears for her children's safety, increased irritability at her children's behavior, and depression. She was depressed about many new things: the constancy of her back pain, limitations of mobility and energy, and interference with life goals, especially educational and occupational goals.

All these symptoms were typical post-traumatic stress reactions to a single-shock trauma. Although they were specific to the accident trauma, in general Mrs. Feinstein experienced them as a repetition of the abuse that she suffered at the hands of her mother in childhood and adolescence. A single-shock traumata was experienced as one more in the chain of the cumulative trauma of her childhood. This time, however, many people knew about the trauma, strangers rushed to help her, and witnesses and police were in unanimous agreement that she had in no way contributed to the accident. After the accident, Mrs. Feinstein's mother called to commiserate, and Mrs. Feinstein was quite ambivalent about accepting her mother's concern.

Some months later when Mrs. Feinstein was able to resume her analysis, the main thrust of her therapeutic efforts focused on the meaning of her life. She became acutely aware of the paradox of the simultaneous existence of a suicidal self and a miraculous survivor self. She explored the antagonism between her spiritual side and her psychological side, and the contrast between her old loyalty to her grandmother's view of the power of faith and her reliance on my way of working, experienced as a potential conflict between her and me.

The following extract from an analytic session illustrates her need to find meaning and her conflict between the old object found through religion and the new object found in the transference.

AMBIVALENCE AND EMERGING AUTONOMY

Mrs. Feinstein began the session by talking about all that she had suffered and would continue to suffer, possibly without adequate compensation. She felt quite overwhelmed and unsure that psycho-analysis could help with the facts of her life. As usual what got her through this moment of helplessness and despair was a Hebrew quotation, and she wondered if her reliance on that would upset me.

I said, "You've been much more aware of a sense of conflict between the world of feelings and the world of the spirit, and worried that it may be a problem between you and me."

"Yes, I am," she agreed. "I think about it inside me as well as between us. I've got to the point in the "Y" where psychiatry goes this way and religion goes this way and it's no longer a circle. When I leave here, I go on down the religion path. Here I can go only on this path.

"It feels so odd to have survived a situation that nine out of ten people would have died from. I don't know why I am lucky, but I am. Daddy came to me in the hospital and said, 'It's not your time yet.' Here's the medical community thinking Science saved me and I'm thinking God wasn't ready for me! He wasn't ready for me the times I tried to kill myself either. My friend says a person who tries to commit suicide is selfish. But, my God, look what that person is going through. That person feels so isolated, so withdrawn, so pushed away by society that you can't bear the loneliness."

I noted that she had displaced thoughts about herself onto "that person" and then had suddenly changed to "you." I thought that she meant me—that I could not bear her hurt. Or did she mean that I could not bear my hurt, my loneliness? I certainly felt a bit shut out. All the talk of God made me feel a bit irrelevant. Perhaps I was hurting and was upset by her reliance on something other than analysis, even though I knew that she needed the religion that had saved her life as a child. Working on this freed me to put her conflict into words, and perhaps it gave her back her own experience of pain that she had displaced into "that person" and "you."

I said, "Saved as you've been from near death a few times now, you seem to have more faith in God than in me or your own efforts in psychoanalysis. You seem torn between the two paths."

I first thought of saying "loves" rather than "paths," but I think I felt inhibited, either because it might seem incestuously seductive or because of the threat to me that religion was her real love, not psychoanalytic understanding and self-healing.

"Yes," she replied. "My grandmother said that it was all written down that God was all-knowing. God always gets His way. It can't be true or the world wouldn't be in such a mess. I don't know. Could it really be His will that I should be sexually assaulted, that my mother should try to kill me, that my father should die and leave me with that moron, that I should try to kill myself three times, that I should be in this horrible accident?"

THE NEGATIVE TRANSFERENCE

In the subsequent session, Mrs. Feinstein continued on the same theme. She was troubled by it and feeling under the weather. I noticed that she seemed cold and shriveled under the blanket. The next day, she abandoned her philosophical discussion about the spiritual conflict and spoke more directly of her inner experience of her inconsistent mother and her steady religious grandmother. She began by commenting on the present. Her reaction spoke to me of a negative transference to me and the internal maternal object who was connected with intense anal and genital sexual wishes.

"Your coffee smells stronger than I'm used to," she complained. "The smell reminds me of the kitchen when I was growing up. Mom always had a cup of coffee in her hand. I like the aroma but I've never liked drinking coffee. I've had it three times only. My husband says I've never given coffee a chance. I say I take my caffeine in a different form, as Coca Cola, and at a different temperature. Mom always used to take a cup of hot coffee and a cigarette into the bathroom when she was going to have a bowel movement. Disgusting!"

THE POSITIVE TRANSFERENCE

Mrs. Feinstein then switched over to the positive transference through which she got in touch with herself as a child that she could love.

"But I really like the smell of coffee. My grandma always had it around. But nowadays even when we go out to dinner, and the waiter asks if we want some coffee, I don't want anything. Lately, I've started to say I'll have a cup of tea. My husband teases me, 'Wow, soon you'll be up to coffee.' Like some day I'd be a real grown-up. Which brings me back to that little girl inside me. Remember when I went to that survivors' retreat, how I saw myself as a little girl, running through a meadow? And remember yesterday I was telling you how I felt poised outside my body, ready to join Daddy that day he came to me in a pool of light in the hospital? That's the little girl again. I take his hand and, running, pull him along. She seems so free and happy."

THE EMERGENCE OF THE INNER CHILD SELVES

After describing an incident in which she almost hurt her daughter Liz, Mrs. Feinstein went on to explore various aspects of her child self and became anxious that she was going crazy.

"Last night I was playing cards with Liz at the table near the window where the dog sits and supposedly guards our house. Liz's teasing the dog and I hate that. The dog ran away and I twisted Liz's arm behind her back and said, 'Don't do that.' She's laughing and teasing the dog and me. She thinks I'm teasing her, but I was that close to hurting her for real. I stopped and turned away. She pleaded with me to play some more. But I couldn't.

"There was that girl again. She was so happy, skipping through that field of open flowers. What's going on here, Dr. Scharff? I'm losing it.

"What if we all had been killed, or Liz and I? Who would have told my husband? How do you tell someone that? As I thought about how awful that would be, this little girl inside me came and put her arms around me. Then I looked over at Liz, and I realized I felt so jealous of her."

Switching to thinking of her son, Mrs. Feinstein continued, "I had to take Sam to my dentist for a filling. The dentist is a friend of mine and he suggested I come in with Sam. He doesn't want me to come in at the doctor's office so I was surprised. But he did want me, maybe because at the dentist's he didn't have to take off his clothes. The dentist came in and started working, and he and I started bantering. Sam couldn't hear us because of the suction machine."

Returning to her daughter, Mrs. Feinstein went on, "When I was with Liz, I wanted to be her, for me to *be* her. And I can't. I'm her mother."

I was struck by Mrs. Feinstein's move from herself in little girl shape to herself as mother of a boy at the dentist's, and back to herself as Liz.

I began to comment, "You are talking about Liz, a lucky little girl, and in the middle you switched away to yourself as Sam's mother. . . ."

"Doesn't make much sense, does it?" she concurred.

"But that's not my point," I corrected her impression. "You're thinking of yourself as the mother chitchatting with her friend while something is being done to her child, just like your mother and her neighbor used to laugh together while you had to suffer the enemas, because . . . "

"You think I was as bad as my mother," she interrupted again, sensitive to any hint of fault. "I shouldn't have done that."

"Wait," I said. "Here's what I mean. You were getting in touch with your little girl self with a mother both like and unlike your own mother. Then you had to show how really you are a mother, like and unlike your own mother. That's how it makes sense to me. It's hard to keep in touch with the little girl. You long to be the little girl with a good mother, but I think you also want to be all the little girls inside you — the angry one we've seen since the accident, and the one who was here earlier in this session, experiencing me like your disgusting, addictive mother. You shut that off very fast and moved on to a much less painful image of me as your grandmother with nice coffee, because you don't trust me with that little girl way of seeing me as a scary kind of mother."

"Do you think I don't trust you?" she asked incredulously. "I trust you," she said reassuringly and sincerely.

"I know you trust me a great deal," I responded. "But not enough to *dis*trust me, to feel about me as you did your mother."

"That's a conflict within me," she replied. "I don't want to face things, yet I expect you to make me face it so I can get better.

"There's also a little girl who's hidden away in a dark corner, crying all the time. I was told I have the saddest eyes and those are the eyes of that little girl. The happy little girl in the field is new since the incest survivor group.

"Are people who had experiences like me crazy? Like Daddy coming to the hospital — that was so real. If I'd just gotten up and walked away with him, I would've died that day. There would've been a little girl running free around heaven with him, something I didn't get to do when I was alive.

"Sam has a weird memory of the accident, which is of all the glass shattering in slow motion and then he realizes 'my mother is dead.' Witnesses said that he got out of the station wagon swearing at the other driver. It's strange, but I *need* to hear what happened. I have not one shred of knowledge about the accident except for what they give me. It's like it never happened. But it must have. And why?

"The dentist was saying 'It's so good to see you walking around, now. You looked terrible in the hospital.' Of course at the time in the hospital, they all said I looked wonderful! I'm upset I can't do what I did before. But the volunteers I work with are glad to have me anyway. They say I'm such an inspiration because I smile and act like there's nothing going on. They say they know inside I'm hurting."

I had been floating along as I often did, listening to a story of playing with the children, going to the dentist, and enjoying her impact on the other volunteers. Sooner or later she would mention something that drew me in to a deeper level. I had learned not to search or hope for these moments. Instead I tried not to want too much. I had to accept being a bit excluded, like a neighbor who can be there, but is not allowed to hold the baby. I had learned that if I could join in her going-on-being without invading her rhythm to bring myself to life, Mrs. Feinstein felt safer and would eventually reach into the areas of vulnerability for herself.

She returned to the inner child selves saying, "Ron and others sense this little girl who's happy and carefree, but inside she's hiding in the corner or so mad she wants to break something. It's so scary to talk with these three or four little girls inside me, who was never allowed to find out who I was, to do and say things I wanted to do. I was so restricted growing up."

Now I was drawn in to the material. It was always a relief to find the connection.

I brought her concerns together in the transference, saying, "You're still wondering if it'll be safe to express all of these little girls here with me because they weren't safe before."

Crying freely now, Mrs. Feinstein acknowledged her fears. "Intellectually I know it is, but emotionally it's still scary. I wasn't allowed to cry. I was stopped. I was called names. I was told in such a nasty voice: 'Big baby! I'll give you something to cry about.' I remember lying in my bed, no one home, curled up in a ball. I wanted to run away so badly, and I had nowhere to go. In my defiant mode, I'd say, 'I'll run away, I'll show you!' and Mom'd say, 'Oh, yeah, you think you're too goddamn good for the rest of the world. Who'd take in the likes of you?' She'd push me out the door and lock it. I'd go to my hiding place behind the school. I hate her so much! Then I'd think 'What am I gonna do now?' I'd go home and she'd say, 'Welcome back, your Highness' or if she was drunk, 'Your High Ass!' Other times she was so nice, 'Oh honey. I'm sorry I upset you.' If you met her now, you'd think she was so nice. Like when she calls, it's "Hi honey. How are you? Give my love to the children?' Oh, Oh. . . ." she trailed off crying softly.

This is what often happened. When she dipped into her memories, she became sad and lonely as she must have felt so often as a child. It helped me understand why she kept us both floating along on the surface, not just to postpone the pain of reflection but also to establish an easy place to come back to. Right now I felt deeply affected by her distress.

"You might be wondering what you're gonna do right now," I suggested. "You're upset. It's the end of the hour. I close the door. What then?"

"I'm all alone then," she sobbed. "When I was a kid, I couldn't cry 'til I got to my hiding place. I'll leave here. I'll ride around 'til I can fake it again. I hate when it's so open and so rotten. I feel like there's an elephant sitting on my chest. I just wanna be a normal okay human being."

THE REAPPEARANCE OF THE INNER CHILD SELVES

Some months later, I presented this material in a workshop on the adult survivor of childhood sexual abuse to Dr. Joyce McDougall, who predicted that more work would be needed with the little children that would emerge in the course of the analysis. I had not emphasized this language since Mrs. Feinstein first used it one time after she attended a survivors' retreat the previous year, nor had she used it since that session months before. During the afternoon when I had been presenting these vignettes of my work with her to Dr. McDougall, Mrs. Feinstein had been watching television, concluding with the Oprah Winfrey show. She told me about it the next day.

"I saw Bill Cosby on Oprah," she said. "He was brilliant and funny, of course, but of course he has an Ed. D., you know. He talked about the inner child and I felt I was back here! So I say to the TV: 'OK, Dr. Cosby, tell me, tell me! Dr. Scharff can't tell me, You tell me!' He says, 'Let the happy child out.' I have so many children inside, I don't know what to do."

I was quite amazed. I had not said a word about the inner children since the session some months previously nor since hearing Dr. McDougall use that language to speak of her understanding of Mrs. Feinstein's material. Was this coincidence? I kept thinking it over. Was Dr. McDougall simply applying the inner child formula, or was she exquisitely sensitive to what was about to emerge? Was the patient sensitive to a shift in my thinking that I had not yet verbalized? I responded and listened expectantly.

"You long for a doctor to tell you what to do with the children," I suggested.

"That'd be nice," she agreed. "Ron says, 'What does Dr. Scharff say?' I've told him it has to come from me. There are already lots of how-to books. He says, 'She should be saying, "Do this!"' I know it's gotta come from me but a little bit of me says, '*You* tell me!' Yet you did tell me it would be best to admit to my children when I don't feel all right instead of covering it up and getting mad at them for asking, and it works and I thank you for that. They ask, I admit it. I tell them I'm gonna be okay, and they go on and the tension's gone.

"But yet I had to clean out my closet. Cleaning usually means something's up. And right now it's really hard for me to do because of my back. So is that cleaning thing happening 'cause I formally brought up the inner child, so I talked about my self-pity?"

I said, "By cleaning despite your injured back, you made yourself take on a hard job as you expect me to force you to do here. If we're going to face the pain and the mess of inner children here, perhaps you wanted the pleasure of order somewhere, in your closet."

Ruefully she demurred, "The clean closet and drawers didn't give me as much pleasure as they used to 'cause now I know there's something else there."

Changing the subject, she went on, "A woman was vying with me for a handicapped place and yelled at me for taking it: 'You should be ashamed of yourself,' she screamed. I pulled out my permit and thought, 'You should be ashamed of judging me without knowing the facts.' Yet I myself yelled at the next person whose permit wasn't visible. I was as bad as she was. I beat up on myself for that all the way home. But I didn't take it out on the kids."

I said, "You're claiming your right to a handicapped place here, a place to express all the little girl feelings that you wish you didn't have to do because you are afraid the child in you will turn me into a bad mommy."

She dismissed my idea. "That's ridiculous," she said. After a moment, she worked with it. "Sound's like you're saying I'm scared of you, that I'm scared you'll get angry with me, condemn me, or send me to a psychiatric hospital or something. I don't think that's true, though. What I'm scared of is, it won't stay here. It'll overtake my dealing with everyone else. I'm also scared you'll say, 'OK, there it is. That's fine. Now on your way.' Plus, as you said, it's frightening. I don't know what's going on. *This* little girl is hiding, crying. *This* little girl is jumping up and down and breaking things. And here's *this* new little girl in the meadow. It's funny. I can picture the happy child going to the one that's crying easier than to the one that's screaming. Yet, it's easier for the scary one to stop screaming than for the crying one to stop crying and come forward. That's crazy, isn't it? The pain is so deep. You say I have trouble admitting to needing here for my handicap. In a perfect world, none of this should have happened.

"I sound like 'Sybil' with different people in my head struggling to come forward. *Three Faces of Eve* type stuff. It's crazy. Disjointed. Not real, not normal. Yet I also feel a physical feeling of I-don't-know-what when I see the little girl go through the fields and I know it's me as I was a little girl. I can play it forward and become a little girl again and take Daddy's hand and pull him along. That's really freaky. I honestly don't remember being that way when I was little, except when we'd go to his parents' house. I hated it there. They were so strict and regimented. You sat on the sofa, and you played with a doll. They had separate bedrooms, three bedrooms for two of them. We had a two-bedroom house for five of us. I was never comfortable there, and they didn't like me at all.

"I really wish I could go back like Thornton Wilder did in *Our Town* and live a day and find out who I was. It couldn't have been as bad as I remember. It couldn't have been. There had to be a lot of goodness there. But I don't remember it.

"The kids were talking about how they used to fight over who would sit on the bed next to me in the hospital. I asked them what I did about their fighting. They said, 'You just closed your eyes and went to sleep.' See, I don't remember the bad times in the hospital. I was so euphoric there. But of my childhood, I don't remember good times.

"My hospital roommate called. When she doesn't feel well, she remembers how much worse off I was. It's as though this happy little girl is the one that was in the hospital. I felt slapped when Daddy said, 'It's not your time yet.' I thought my children were already dead and I thought, 'Who's gonna take care of my children? I have to take care of them, but I have to die because I have to come with you.' And he said, 'It's not your time.' Daddy's been dead almost thirty years. What's going on? But in my heart I know he *did* come into my room. It wasn't threatening or menacing, it was just disappointing. Yet once I found out the kids were all right, it was bingo, take the respirator out! They had tried to take it out before, and it didn't work.

"It's strange to think of this child in the corner. I've talked so much about her and why she's crying. Isn't that enough to integrate her into me? And all the other jargon that's supposed to happen?"

"But you weren't just talking about her, you were being her in here," I said to clarify the authenticity of the work that I thought she was doing.

"And that's what I'm supposed to do?" she asked, always wanting me to tell her the right thing to do. "I wish there was a button to push to say to each inner child, 'It's your turn now, you're on.'"

Hearing this, I wondered if some therapists would say that Mrs. Feinstein needed and wanted a hypnotic technique to summon the alternate personalities. Because she maintained an integrated view of her different child selves, I chose not to abandon my analytic stance, and I decided to work on her experiences of inner children as parts of herself. I wonder if I would have found these parts of the patient accessible to this analytic technique if the degree of dissociation in her personality functioning were more extreme, as it is in multiple personality disorder. Recent reports (Olsen 1993, Silvio 1993) suggest that analytic technique may be modified to include hypnotic trance negotiation with the separate selves to achieve communication with the alters and their re-integration in cases of multiple personality. However, in Mrs. Feinstein's case, I believe that such a technique could have had an iatrogenically induced, disintegrating effect that could have pushed her to view herself as a multiple personality, instead of as someone suffering from less severe splits in the self when she was not switching between personalities, as far as I could tell. The following account of dealing with the inner children illustrates the object relational approach that offers an integrative way of dealing with the minor degree of dissociative process in Mrs. Feinstein's personality.

DISPLACEMENT OF THE TRANSFERENCE

In a session the next week, Mrs. Feinstein told of another moment of partial enactment of her mother's seductiveness and abuse with her daughter Liz. Again, she was able to interrupt the possibility of repetition of abuse.

"I'm really worried about me the last few days," she said. "I was in a position of tickling Liz or being close to hurting her. She was very disappointed because Ron wasn't there at the beginning of her performance at school. Ron left before the end, and Liz had to come home with me. She starts torturing the dog. I said, 'Stop it!' and sat on her. The next minute I was tickling her and she's laughing. Then she said, 'Stop!' So I stopped. She said, 'No, I was only kidding. Go on.' I said, 'No, I shouldn't have started in the first place.' I really wanna bash her. She goes on and on. She wants to cook. She wants to play. She won't leave us alone. Always wants to ask one more thing, wants to have one more party. I'm so fed up with her and her defiance every time I say 'No'. Inside of me, I see this little kid just like her, screaming and tickling to get revenge for all the times I was tickled and hurt."

"You were tickled too?" I asked, aware that tickling was often found in the histories of the survivors of sexual abuse and surprised at hearing this for the first time, four years into the analysis.

"Everybody tickled me," she began, and went on to elaborate. "Bottom of the feet, thighs, stomach, neck, ears, chin. I'd get tickled 'til I'd cry and flail. Everyone would laugh. My mother is like Ron, not ticklish anywhere. Uncle Bert would tickle me. All of them tickled. Makes my private area tense up to think about it. I used to tickle my brothers and my cousins, Sally and Linda. Cousin Renee used to tickle me. Oh, God, I hated it. She'd tickle me so much you'd wet the bed sometimes. I think it was very common in the fifties. My friends, all of us, would tickle each other."

Mrs. Feinstein paused, then said, "That little kid inside of me folded my arms stubbornly and said, 'Stop.' I don't know if that means they should stop tickling me, or I should shut up about them tickling me."

DEVELOPMENT OF SAFETY IN THE TRANSFERENCE

I felt glad that the little girl called a halt. I was listening, but everything seemed far away. All the excitement and drama had occurred back then. It seemed like an alternative to a transference experience. But before I had time to think, the story went on as before.

Mrs. Feinstein continued, "The man next door used to tickle me. It stopped in seventh grade except in the family, but until then everybody tickled. It was pleasurable at first, an acknowledged way of showing affection. But it was done by my older brother Tom to be mean. But when I was mad or in a bad mood and Mom was drinking or in a good mood, Mom would sit on me, like I did on Liz, and tickle me. She'd laugh and giggle and the anger would be gone, or else she'd continue 'til I cried and dampened my pants and then that would get her upset.

"Which reminds me, and maybe it has some bearing, Saturday Liz told me she was getting cramps. Could she be about to menstruate? Wait, she's only 12. Maybe that's why I'm tickling her to make her stay a little girl a little longer."

Finally I understood. "I can see that," I said, but I was thinking also of a transference explanation. I went on, "There's another way of looking at it. You had been talking about whether you could risk experiencing yourself as a parent and yourself as a child in relation to me. I think that you found that experience at home with Liz instead of in the relationship with me."

"That's what scares me, that I don't leave it here. The patient before me left crying and that's what I don't want. I feel like the defiant little one right now."

"You don't wanna play this game with me?" I noted.

"There aren't any rules," she complained. "I like boundaries. And it's not a game. It's my life and it hurts. The little girl runs down the hallway and all the doors are locked. She cries. I run over and shrink into the crying girl in the corner. Am I crazy? Is this the way it's supposed to be?

"There's another quiet, curious little girl. Who is that? She has sweaty palms. There's no safe place to go. Is this anywhere near normal? It feels so crazy to say the things in my head. Does everyone do this? It's like this little child has the key, will know which door to go into. Then I'll be a different person. I've seen enough skeletons in my past. I don't wanna look anywhere.

"Then, anyone just opened the door where that angry face was and punched it. It's crazy, these things just don't happen."

Mrs. Feinstein was quiet for a moment. I had a chance to reflect during her silence. "Inner child" language often sounds fake, trivial, and concrete to me. Mrs. Feinstein's inner child language felt quite foreign to me, and yet I felt more at home with her than I often did. I felt that she was letting me be with her as she skipped from one part of herself to another. Why was this happening? Perhaps she felt safer because her four analytic sessions a week were back in place. A bird sang outside the window.

"That bird singing makes me think of spring where I grew up. You'd smell grass being cut, that watermelony smell, everything crisp and fresh. You'd wake up, and it'd be the same old dirty, cramped room. You'd go in and turn on cartoons, get some Rice Krispies and a banana, and hope you didn't wake Mom or she'd come in and yell at you. I always dreamt of a house big enough that when you got out of bed you didn't bump into the wall or the dresser. And our town house will be big enough, as soon as the renovation is complete and I have my study.

"That little girl is not in the corner but she's sitting in the hallway crying, not sobbing, crying. Like I feel like doing now, but I won't."

"You are telling me of sadness that you don't want to show me, partly because it's Thursday," I said.

"Makes a long weekend," she concurred. "I wish I could see you every day, all day, for 6 weeks. Maybe then, I could be done with this."

My sense of closeness to Mrs. Feinstein was shared. When she brought the craziness of the little girls to me, we both felt more in touch and more confident of completing the work.

THE EMERGENCE OF A CURIOUS CHILD SELF

The next weekend, Mrs. Feinstein had been watching a movie.

"I watched *Stranger in the Family,*" she told me. "A movie of a family coping with an accident victim who had total amnesia. The victim's sister took him to the bumper cars for fun (like I and my Dad used to love to do), but it made the boy remember his accident. Then I (empathizing or imagining) felt myself thrown about in the car and felt the tremor of it, and I cried out loud, wishing to be held. Ron said, 'Turn that movie off.' Not one iota of sympathy there. So I did and began watching the World Series.

"My back hurts today. Maybe it's going to rain or be very cold. When I got dressed and put on my new necklace, I felt like a little girl dressing up—but I'm a grown-up! It's as though I'm finally aware of these different aspects of my childhood in the form of little kids battling for control of me. The little girl crying in the corner becomes me or I become her. When Ron thought my crying was silly, that little girl went back deeper into a huddle. I felt like Ron did, saying, 'Be quiet,' but inside I was screaming, 'It hurt and I want to know what happened.'"

Mrs. Feinstein shivered and pulled the blanket from the back of the couch to cover herself. "I thought I could do it without the blanket today, but I can't," she said.

I watched her snuggle appreciatively into the coziness of the blanket as she usually did, unlike the patient before her who hates to need anything of mine.

She continued, "One of the things I miss about my body since the accident is, I can no longer curl up in the fetal position. I just wanna roll up and cry and I can't physically do it. What does it mean, Dr. Scharff, with these little characters in my head? What is happening? I'm scared. I want an answer."

I answered, "I think that now that you have four sessions a week, you are, as you say, more willing to explore parts of yourself."

"Multiple personalities, like *Three Faces of Eve*," she said. "Really crazy."

"No," I said, aware of a wish to deglamorize the issue. "Not personality multiples, just parts of yourself."

Without direct comment about what I had said about her, she continued to talk about her actual children, not her inner children. "Sam was remembering cosy times we had together and times when I was yelling at Liz. I became that angry child. I lash out and Liz is the recipient."

"Liz, why?" I prompted, wanting to understand Mrs. Feinstein's projective identification of her daughter.

"I'm jealous of her," she replied. "She reminds me of my mother: she's arrogant, adorable, precocious, demanding, strong-willed. She gets her way. I wish I'd been like her, and the abuse wouldn't have happened to me. She had the nerve to say to me, 'I want this' and I said, 'I'll have to discuss it with Dad.' Why couldn't my Mom ever say that? And why could I never ask? I was such a wimp.

"There's this new vision that's emerged: this inquisitive kid looking around, dresses smartly. There's also another one: 'a prankster.' So when the prankster knocks, the curious one turns around, and there's no one there!

"Liz kept leaning on my shoulder and making my back hurt. I kept thinking I really almost died. I don't think I'll ever get over that. There's Daddy saying, 'It's not your time yet,'" and there's this little girl who feels like she just got whacked up the side of the head. 'Now what?' I thought, lying in that hospital bed. I was really bewildered. Ron doesn't believe that people can come back like Daddy did. He thinks it's just that my mind made him come back because I wanted him there. I said, 'You're plain wrong.' He said, 'That's the first time you've ever debated me. Good for you.' I said, 'He came. I nearly died.' He said, 'I know. I just can't deal with that.' I've also been going up to him and saying, 'I need a hug now!' and he'll say, 'Okay, I'd much rather give you a hug than have you yell at me for nothing.' I'm worried I'll always forgive him for every time he's late and not allow myself to be angry."

DREAMING OF THE ABUSIVE OBJECT IN THE TRANSFERENCE

Before resuming her analysis four months earlier, Mrs. Feinstein had allowed the videotaping of an interview of her talking with me about her experiences of childhood sexual abuse, survival, and psychoanalytic treatment; it was made for presentation to a scientific meeting at the local psychoanalytic institute on a certain date and at other teaching events that might require its use. She had given me permission to present the tape at the scientific analytic meeting, provided that only qualified professionals were present, because she wanted to contribute to discussion of therapy for incest survivors and she was also interested in raising the level of professional awareness of the problem. However, she realized that she would not be comfortable with her material being presented if interested untrained spouses or friends of the therapists attended the meeting. I was impressed by her foresight and her capacity to protect herself from abuse.

Mrs. Feinstein remembered that, because it was Halloween already, the date of my presentation at the winter scientific meeting must be due. Indeed, it was in two days time. She described the limited Halloween candy and minimal attempts to celebrate the holiday that she remembered from her childhood. She went on to describe the elaborate preparations she makes now for her children's amusement: she decorates the garden with gravestones, spooky music floats from the rafters, and she dresses as a witch with a gnarled false hand to open the door. She was really into it, but I was not included. There had been no worthwhile analysis of her material. I felt like a child full of awe at her door.

In her next session, which was the day before my presentation, she reported a physical reaction and a dream.

"I'm not feeling well today," she said. "I awakened from an awful dream. Then my bowels just erupted. I've been feeling squeamish and shaky ever since. Then I couldn't find my car keys; so my kids had to walk to school. I watched them leave in the cold and felt sorry.

"In the dream, I was there with someone else, it could have been a boy or a girl. I was the older of the two. Then there was a man like Bigfoot, huge and with lots of hair; yet, he had a full, angry hairless face. Whenever the two of us did anything, he'd hit us. Two police officers came out with a gun and he cowed them too. Then he fell asleep. The two police officers and the two of us determined we'd have to kill him and run away. The police officer with the gun was prepared to kill him. There were all these doors. We'd open a door and go in another room to get away, but he'd always pursue us. We were about to get him when this ambulance came over the hill, veered in, and hit a jeep parked outside the building, and went on its way. My brother arrived—I'm not sure which one it was—arrived and said, 'What do we do now?' The monster was hitting me and pushing me, and the police officer was firing bullets at it, and—nothing! And that's it.

"All through the dream, myself—my heart was pounding—but I was in control. The inquisitive girl was saying, 'Take control. It'll be all right.' This male figure didn't look like my father 'cause he had tons of black hair, whereas Daddy had short red hair and Daddy never hurt us. Yet he allowed all that—and more—to happen. I don't know, Dr. Scharff, what do you make of it?"

"I don't make anything of it yet," I replied. "I'm listening as you work on it. I don't want to interfere."

"It'd make sense to me if it was my mother threatening and pursuing, and if it had no doors," Mrs. Feinstein thought. "But in the dream it was a man, and in our house there were no doors. The dream, it's like in therapy, endless space with all these doors. In the dream, there was a front porch, which there isn't here."

I was interested in her move from the concrete to the symbolic, evidence of a maturing capacity to create a transitional space for creative thinking.

I said, "You're saying that the dream is not an exact replica of your history or of the actual office here, but that it seems to be a symbol of your experience here with me."

"Are you the monster, or the person beside me?" she asked.

"Does it have to be one or the other?" I countered.

"Or the police officer shooting holes in it, but it doesn't go away," she continued. "So you think you're not in the dream?"

"I didn't say that," I retorted, feeling misunderstood and momentarily off balance.

"You said you had to be one or the other, didn't you?" she challenged me, returning to the literal and getting my meaning backward.

"And you said 'or the police officer,'" I rejoined, reminding her of her newly enlarged tolerance for seeing multiple symbolic meaning in the dream condensation. "I think the dream shows your experience of me as the monster shaking you about and making you do difficult things, and also as the person beside you—in this with you—and also as the police officer shooting at the beast."

"But it's all to no avail," she said, sounding more annoyed than hopeless.

I said, "Maybe you're angry at me for not getting rid of the monster but also for making you come close to the monster and thereby frightening you. It was the inquisitive girl who felt in control in the dream."

In a surprisingly noncompliant moment that I welcomed, Mrs. Feinstein separated herself from me and asserted, "I don't like your interpretation of the dream. Why can't it be a simple memory? Why does it have to be about here? Why does it have to affect my bowels? Maybe it's about my trauma surgeon saying I have to be tested for AIDS. There were lots of doors along his corridor of the medical building—all of them closed, with the exception of the pharmacy."

Mrs. Feinstein elaborated, moving away from the personal to the societal dimension. "It just occurred to me the dream may be representing my fear that police can see evil and wrong intent, but fail to stop it. We were at a party and a doctor friend of mine who sings was talking about a bunch of records. This doctor said, 'I've never been able to listen to Beethoven's Ninth since *Clockwork Orange*.' I said, 'Me too!' Now I think—since the accident—of the Clockwork Orange, and what we are becoming, kids being bored and shooting one another. Random violence. I'm scared for my kids and I long to return to the 50s. It seemed so simple then. Even though what was going on in my own house was so awful then.

"Having to go through all the stuff in my attic to clear it for the renovation made me feel close to my past, and the little inquisitive girl comes to the fore. Ron and the kids think I'm sappy. Did doing the attic press me to a deeper level here, or vice versa? Or is it just necessity to get rid of stuff in order to build a study for me? Wait a minute—there's something wrong with this picture!" she exclaimed.

I was interested that the concrete, logical explanation suddenly did not make any more sense to her than the more ambiguous, symbolic approach. I wondered what was happening. Had I become the child who could not get it right and she was the inconsistent mother who kept changing her premises? If so, why? Perhaps she had become frightened of me as an abusive object and was trying to defend herself by reversal.

"I made lasagna yesterday," she said, making a connection between food and love, and reverting to the familiar and the domestic. "Everybody was so happy. First time in seven months I've felt physically able to handle the large pan and do all the preparation."

Remaining with a concrete view of solutions, she continued, "I found the keys I lost, by the way, in my purse in the zippered pocket. I wish I found the key that would unlock my head and let me figure out the buttons to push and the engine to start. I wish those things were easy. I wish you'd hook me up to an EEG and a screen so you could figure out everything and I didn't have to talk."

I said, "That way I could do everything for you, take care of you and make it all better without even asking, like a wonderful Mommy that you didn't have."

Mrs. Feinstein suddenly got in touch with her anger. She said, "I remember my mother sitting nice as could be in the hospital, perfect little grandmother, putting on her act. I feel like taking a knife and slashing her to pieces. I'm angry at mother today. I'm angry at all she did. I don't wanna remember it, but I do. With the accident I wanna remember and I can't."

Mrs. Feinstein had been ready to kill me, but she did not quite make the jump into the transference. I told myself that I must continue to be very patient and move slowly toward the transference, but I was beginning to see the way ahead. Then Mrs. Feinstein's first session after my Institute presentation seemed mundane again. It was disappointing to me, but not surprising. There would be no fancy analytic footwork here. In this case, analysis had to do with tolerating the splits and learning to communicate in language more concrete than I was used to. I had to let the symbolic links lie like sleeping dogs that would be upset if rudely wakened. I was learning how much must not be put into words, because words can push away and close off the ongoing experience that is fundamental to building sufficient safety for the traumatized patient to express the transference fully.

Mrs. Feinstein's comments were again in a domestic vein. She had been getting her house in order and throwing out more stuff from the attic. She felt great about it. She and her husband considered the bids, met with the architect, selected a builder, and signed the contract for building a study for her. She had felt abused by a disappointed contractor whose bid was not accepted, but she had stood up for herself and felt great about that. She was preparing to go to school again.

THE DISAPPEARANCE OF THE INNER CHILDREN

The next day, Mrs. Feinstein continued to discuss cleaning and sorting things out, but this time she moved into a more analytic stance, without any prompting from me. She realized that since she put her house in order, the little girls inside her had gone. Without them, she felt empty. She went on, "If talking about the little girl is the next thing to do to finish my therapy," she said, "I want to get on with it. So why has it all stopped? Maybe it has to do with cleaning out the house."

"Perhaps they calmed down because you got scared of how crazy you felt acknowledging them and because of how they change your feelings for me," I suggested.

"How's that?" she asked.

"As an adult, you tell me that you trust me. But as a little girl you feel about me whatever the little girl feels, depending on whether she is angry or sad," I replied.

"I had some of that with Liz," she responded. "She and her little friend were playing with their hair. Her friend wound Liz's very long hair around a comb and got it stuck. I had to get this huge snarl out of her hair. My mother would have got her scissors and cut the hair off at the scalp. I surprised myself. I stayed quite calm. It took half an hour, and it didn't cost her any hair."

Now that I know that the little girl selves did not reappear later, I think that my interpretation about their hiding from me in fear was wrong. I think that the little girls did not abandon Mrs. Feinstein, but were absorbed into her central self. The amount of aggression that Mrs. Feinstein experienced toward me in the Bigfoot dream had an integrating effect on her self. Analysis seems to consist of making hypotheses and then revising them. Mrs. Feinstein's image of patiently working to untangle the snarl and preserve the length and fullness of the hair fit with my vision of the analytic work: no sharp interpretations, just slow steady work, unleashing the various strands of experience and fantasy from the web of domesticity. So the work went on.

Later that same week, Mrs. Feinstein talked about the plans for her study and its decoration, the party where she was feted, and the continuing stress of getting through each day. Suddenly, near the end of Wednesday's session, Mrs. Feinstein surprised me when she told me that she had almost called me on Saturday (the day after my presentation) to tell me of a dream:

"You were in the dream, I was on the couch and you were in your chair. In an instant we were in a huge old Victorian building. You introduced me to an associate, Mr. Jones, and he brought in three clients. I started talking and the people interrupted, 'That's not true, that's not the way it was,' they said. I started to cry and you said to them, 'You'll have to leave,' and we were back here. You said to me, 'This is obscene. You can handle this without crying.' Instantly, we were back in the other building and the other people were there again. Mr. Jones thanked me and said that I had helped his clients very much, thank you.

"Woa, where did this dream come from? It's totally out of the ball park. I wonder if it has to do with your speech and the fact that my actual words were on the tape. A new member was introduced at our country club. He's a psychiatrist with the American Psychiatric Association. He doesn't know me from Adam but I thought, 'He'll see my tape!' So what does all this mean, Dr. Scharff?"

"You've figured it out all by yourself," I said. Then I asked, "How did you feel regarding me in the dream?"

"At first I felt safe," she said. "Then I felt abandoned 'cause I was all alone and people were attacking me, and then you chastised me and it was total abandonment. This would never happen, so why would I dream such a thing? It's the first time I remember where you've been in the dream as yourself, not hidden in my mother or grandmother."

"The dream speaks of feelings regarding me that you're usually not aware of," I said. "I mean feelings of being abused by my not preserving the usual boundaries and the usual attitude to you."

Mrs. Feinstein seemed to change the subject.

"I get a headache when I come here," she said. "It doesn't last, but it's like there's too much weight in the head, and the brain is pushing down against the cranium. It hurts. Like the memory storage part of the brain is collapsed down on itself. Or maybe I've talked it all out and it's just empty and there's nothing there."

"I've always been curious how psychiatrists can work with people every hour. When people came to confide in me when I volunteered at the synagogue, a lotta times I couldn't get it out of my mind: the childhood sexual abuse, the husband who was drinking, whatever. I would never repeat it, but I'd be thinking of that instead of what the next person was saying. I don't know how you keep it in when the next person walks in. I admire that. It's impressive."

I interpreted her praise of me and her focusing on her own headache as ways of undoing the dream's view of me as untrustworthy.

"But I don't think that," she objected. "It's just a dream."

Not to be fobbed off by a concretization of her valuable symbolic dream offer, I responded, "We can shove those ideas back into the dream, or turn away from them by pushing them down so your head feels heavy or turning them from distrust to admiration, or we can hold onto them and explore them. I know that your real relationship with me is trusted and safe, but the dream speaks of an inside relationship to me that includes these other concerns and gives us an opportunity to explore these other feelings."

My experience of presenting to my colleagues provided the context in which I heard Mrs. Feinstein's dream. I had experienced tremendous guardedness in making my presentation. I was aware of holding a great deal of anxiety about my presentation, with videotape being viewed as abusive by colleagues, and so I was well placed to detect the transference to me as an abusive object. I also think that Mrs. Feinstein's cooperation in the presentation opened her to presenting her experience of me as abusive more clearly than I had heard from her before. The fact that I was sharing my work with analytic colleagues seemed to have encouraged her to communicate in the symbolic form of the dream traditionally used by analysts. Perhaps she felt reassured that I was ready to deal with her transference.

DREAM EVIDENCE OF PROGRESS IN INTERNALIZING THE INTEGRATIVE ANALYTIC FUNCTION

Mrs. Feinstein had progressed to the point where she could both recall memories of abuse and experience those feelings with me. She still showed the object-coercive doubting (Kramer 1985) in which she tried to get me to decide that she had indeed been abused while she preferred to believe that she had imagined it. She no longer had epilepsy, had not made a serious suicide attempt since starting therapy, and was not at risk for hurting her children. Like many another abused patient whose parent has entered her psychic skin and obliterated the transitional space (Winer 1989) and the dream space of her night's rest (Bollas 1989), Mrs. Feinstein had few dreams, and her body functioning was still vulnerable to disruption by somatic memories. Aspects of her inner world were still somewhat frozen to devitalize the trauma, but the dream activity was a sign of the thaw. She was about to move from concretization to metaphor (Grubrich-Simitis 1984).

I was interested that her dreaming increased when she knew that I was presenting my work with her to my analytic colleagues. Anxious about presenting work of this type to an audience unaccustomed to using videotape, I experienced myself in their eyes as an abusing, exploitative object; the dream content suggests that the patient felt in touch with the abusive object in the transference too. Yet, her improved ability to dream most likely stemmed from her feeling that I had validated her experience in the forum of my respected colleagues and that I had risked abuse myself, thereby sharing the consequences of her abuse, and had survived.

Where the boundaries between self and other have been so invaded, the surviving adult often retains an uncanny sensitivity to the feelings and wishes of the other person. When I was to present this material to another workshop just before a two-week vacation, Mrs. Feinstein produced another dream, as if responding to the intrusion of my heightened alertness or ambition prior to my presentation, the date of which she did not know. Earlier in the week of my departure, she had been reconsidering the question of whether to confront her aging mother with her outrage about the physical and sexual abuse. The decision had some urgency because her mother had found out suddenly that she was terminally ill. On the last day of the week, Mrs. Feinstein reported her dream, which this time indicated her internalization of the analytic function.

"I had the all-time strangest dream last night, and it lasted all night. I was just exhausted.

"In the dream, Ron and I must have been on vacation because we were in a much smaller house. The kids and I were in a refrigerator. I turned round to get them out and they were dead. Ron and I were distraught, and we kept asking each other, 'How do we tell our mothers?' I looked around and there was my mother, looking like death. I whispered to Ron, 'She's about to die. How do I tell her?' He said, 'I don't like her anyway after what she did to you. Tell her, don't tell her, I don't care.' Then he's on the phone trying to get his mother. I said, 'How do you tell her a thing like this?' He said, 'I've been here before, remember. I had to call her to tell her you might be going to die. I'll just tell her.' But he couldn't reach her. I couldn't *tell* my mother and he couldn't *reach* his.

"I said again, 'The kids are dead. Ron, my babies are dead.' Before he could answer, I said to him, 'No, the kids aren't dead. This is me, my past, and the question of whether I should tell Mom what I feel about it.' Then he said 'Oh shit. Then let me outta here!' And that's not him. He doesn't speak like that.

"Next thing, I'm here asking you, 'Should I tell Mom?' And you're saying, 'It's up to you. Tell her if you want to, but it's not going to serve much purpose for her.'

"Then I'm back in the house I grew up in with Mom. Suddenly she says, 'I'm sorry if I hurt you.'

"Then I'm back here with you, telling you about it. I said to you, 'She admitted it, and I can't forgive her.'

"Then I'm saying, 'Dr. Scharff, my babies are in the box! I have to get them out of there.' You said, 'Let's analyze what was really in the box. Was it really the children?' I said, 'No, it's all my personalities.' You said, 'Well there you are, you got it! You don't need me anymore. Your mother's dead. Goodbye.'

"I woke up from the dream exhausted, but I didn't feel terrible, not like I usually would feel after a dream with my mother in it. It's as though I had the dream, came here, analyzed it, and then wanted to go back to sleep. I fixed breakfast, then I got Ron to take the kids to school for me. I got my pillow, went up for a nap—set my alarm so I wouldn't be late for here—and got here on time. And I feel fine!

"So! What do you think it means?" she asked me.

"I think you've got a lot of the work done on it already, and you're finding that that feels neat," I said.

"It does," she agreed. "I feel fine!"

She then went on to describe how much she had learned about her mother's condition from studying medical textbooks in preparation for making plans for her care.

"Ron can't understand why I would care about what happens to her. What she did was wrong, and unforgivable, but I'm a compassionate person, and she is my mother."

This dream showed me the presence of a self-analytic function, characterized by a rather concrete way of representing conflict and relationships. Was this evidence of autonomy or of a defensive declaration of not needing me at this time of major stress right before a vacation? I expected to find out when I returned.

After the vacation, I was stunned to learn that Mrs. Feinstein's mother had died, only 16 days after diagnosis. Mrs. Feinstein had had to deal with this situation without me. She had found my absence regrettable, but not devastating. She was able to respond to emergency calls, tolerate the pain of watching her mother cough up blood, confront her physician's denial of adequate pain relief for her mother, and remain attentive and kind to her during those last days. She told me that she was struck by the contrast between her sympathetic response to the dying woman in the hospital bed and her fury at the horrible things her mother had done to her. On the couch, she was bombarded with images of her mother as a hateful person who should not have lived. In the hospital she recovered some good memories and sympathy for her mother as a pathetic creature. Mrs. Feinstein discovered such compassion for her old, ill mother that she actually provided physical nursing care for her at the request of the nursing staff. Because of her need for closure after her mother's speedy demise, Mrs. Feinstein insisted on a funeral against her mother's wishes and made the arrangements efficiently with little help. Afterward, she felt depressed and took to her bed for a few days, but she recovered without help.

I saw that Mrs. Feinstein had internalized the analytic function and had access to it, even under extreme stress. I expected that she might now begin to consider terminating. Yet, I was not prepared for what followed.

REPETITION OF TRAUMA AT TERMINATION

Six weeks later, Mrs. Feinstein told me that she was ready to finish analysis. I felt stunned. Before her mother's illness, she had been feeling ready to manage on her own and had been aiming at stopping therapy as soon as she was re-established in her college course work. However, that would not occur for another 6 months. Her pre-vacation dream returned to my mind in which she had me saying, "You've got it. Your mother's dead. You don't need me." The dream had prepared me for her leaving in the not-too-distant future, but her sudden certainty about this being the time to go still seemed to be precipitous. She sensed my disagreement and tried to convince me.

"Yesterday was the six-week anniversary of Mom's death," she said. "And it suddenly struck me that I didn't even think of her all day. And I'm an anniversary person! I think I'm finished here, unless I'm denying something, but I don't think so. I'm wondering if you and I are stretching things out. I've been mourning, yes, but I've been going through the grief for years. Yes, I worried about whether to confront her. It never happened and now it never will. And that's a relief. It's also a loss, because I wanted to say to her, 'You're a creep,' but my last impression of her was of her as a pathetic person. My tears are already spent. I went through the grief before. So, that's why I want to finish, soon, before the end of next month. So, what do you think?"

I said, "We're agreed that you will be finishing this year. I hear that you are afraid that we will stretch this out indefinitely and to counter that you are thinking of leaving abruptly, rather than working out what's best for you. There's a date in between that would let you get finished and still have enough time to experience the feelings of ending our relationship after all these years of working together."

Mrs. Feinstein reminded me of a conversation that had confirmed her sense of readiness. Her neighbor had said, "You've changed so much in the last ten years, and it isn't because of the accident. I saw it before then. When you first moved in here, you didn't have enough self-confidence to fill a thimble. Now you've got lots."

Mrs. Feinstein had replied, "Well, I've been in therapy for years."

"That's it, then," her neighbor concluded. "It's some difference. You're a completely different person."

Mrs. Feinstein told me about her capacity to enjoy being on a boat and watch the water flow underneath her without feeling like she would drown, something that she could not have done before. She wanted to enjoy the summer with her family, and she wanted time to pursue her work. She demonstrated her capacity to face her mother's death and to face me down about who determined the end date. I agreed that she must decide when to leave me based on her own needs, not mine, but inwardly I did not want to be left so suddenly. When she next spoke directly to me, it was to ask my medical opinion for a friend about whose condition I would not speculate. I now felt that the steady, analytic relationship I had offered was being abused for the first time, and I felt an unfamiliar degree of longing and attachment to the patient that was uncomfortable.

The next day Mrs. Feinstein arrived on time for her appointment as usual, but I did not show up. A scheduling confusion hardly accounted for this lapse on my part, which I saw as a countertransference enactment of my response to her threat of sudden departure. Mrs. Feinstein tried to excuse me, but she remained puzzled and could not explain it away. Soon she discovered that she was not just puzzled by my inconsistent behavior, but angry. She was angry because she had better things to do and I was keeping her waiting. She asked me to account for why I had done this. She was already angry about my refusal to give her medical information and about my being away whenever I decided to go, even at a major time in her life.

"It really bothered me," she said. "To leave me just sitting here like some kid that doesn't know better! It made me mad. It seems as though you have all the cards. You make all the decisions. So my wanting to be finished might be seen as just retaliation, or me cutting myself off again, but I don't think so. It's not bad of me to be angry at you. It's not bad of you to forget one session in 6 years. It's not a big deal. I'm ready to leave and now I don't have to stay. I'm deciding when to stop. And I'm not waiting until you say when, I'm not waiting even to the end of the month, to please you. You say it's too short, but it feels right from my point of view. It's time to stop looking back and start looking forward. I want to take control. The last day of the week is to be my last day."

I felt that Mrs. Feinstein was determined to shortchange herself. At last there was a welcome turbulence in our relationship that I thought represented her being able to experience me as an inconsistent, selfish, and abusive object. Working this through from confrontation to reconciliation in the transference would complete the work and make for a neat termination. Yet, she would have none of it. She wanted to excuse me and leave me to avoid the conflict and the rage that she felt over losing her mother and losing me at that time. I had let her down fundamentally by being away at the time of the death. I remembered another patient who left me a few months after her relentlessly seductive, tormenting mother committed suicide during my vacation. Once the actual bad object is gone, it seems as if there is less need to work on it and more fear that it will be found in the transference. Nothing that I said made a difference to Mrs. Feinstein's decision.

I had to work hard to catch up to her idea of the ending date and get myself ready to be left. I had to get over my regret about my absence at the crucial time of her mother's demise and my hurt at meaning less to her than she did to me. I still felt abused by her withdrawing her anger before it was really worked through. And I felt robbed of a nice ending to the case. It felt abrupt to me. It seemed to freeze the therapeutic relationship in a traumatic constellation inside me. Even though she felt ready and had demonstrated the self-analytic function in her dream analysis, I did not feel good about this termination.

Then I realized that the whole analysis had been preparing for this, the first moment when she would repeat the trauma (Van der Kolk 1989). She could reverse her abuse and project into me the child's longing to possess the object while she identified with the abandoning object father and mother, and for the next moment when she could forgive me, but leave me anyway, because she was ready to be in control of her life. Like many other molested or medically traumatized patients, Mrs. Feinstein left me in a way that was traumatic to me. Now I knew what it was like to have lost the security of "going-on-being." Bearing this hurt was my last piece of work with her. It was vitally important to understand that she had to separate on her own terms.

Reviewing her experience on the last day, she said, "I've got a lot accomplished in this time frame, and for that I thank you and pat myself on the back. I really do want to thank you for all the time we've had. It hasn't been easy. At times it's been horribly boring, but it's really helped."

Bollas (1989) comments that the molested patient is unable to transform experience into reflectiveness and therefore cannot learn well from analytic experience, which will be experienced as a repetition of the original seduction. As soon as the analyst has been libidinally cathected, he or she will be experienced as ready and eager to intrude beyond the patient's psychic and somatic boundaries, and to dismantle an already impoverished psychic structure. When a victimized analysand tells of her abuse, Bollas (1989) writes, the analyst "may feel that he has lost the right to analyse just as the patient has lost the right to dream, to play, and to desire" (p. 178). In his own countertransference, Bollas finds himself angry and despairing, because, as he puts it, "I am out of work. Redundant. Relegated to the dole of psychotherapy. . . . I must stick to the fact: the actual event. It is to dominate, control, and centre the analysis" (p. 180).

Incest certainly was the central theme of Mrs. Feinstein's analysis. It dominated her analysis as it did her life. Over and over again, she construed her reality in terms of her experience of sexual and physical abuse perpetrated by a deranged mother, unrestrained by an unprotective father, and somewhat mitigated by a loving grandmother. Incest also dominated the free space for thinking, imagining, and playing. Fantasies of her own special gifts were not developed. Mrs. Feinstein's material was rarely enlivened with dreams and fantasy elaborations until late in the analysis. I was often working in a concrete realm, rather than playing with symbols and representations. Sometimes it was, as Mrs. Feinstein said, "horribly boring." I rarely had the narcissistic pleasure of wonderfully rich sessions in which to celebrate my worth as an analyst. The sessions presented here in this chapter describe the relentless ordinariness of the material in contrast to the poignancy of which she was capable when her work could reach a deeper level of understanding of the transference. Mrs. Feinstein's treatment illustrates the technical problems arising in the analysis of a patient who is not classically neurotic, but whose symptoms result from severe trauma to her personhood.

Trauma had fixed Mrs. Feinstein's identity. Claiming her identity as a survivor of incest was an act of courage. Exploring it in analysis was painful. Revealing it to others was a way of finding herself. Confronting her childish desire for incestuous contact was terrifying. Sharing her experience in a survivors' retreat was empowering. Analysis helped her explore her identity as a sexually abused person and finally to see beyond it.

As Mrs. Feinstein said near the end of her analysis, "So what if my mother was an alcoholic, so what if she buried her husband and her youngest son and lost her brother before that? Life has to go on. So what if she abused me? There is more to me than being an abused child. I just have to find out what it is that I can be."

12

Primal Scene Inclusion and

Father–Daughter Incest

For the first few years that I (DES) worked with Freda, she was completely clear that penetration by her father during childhood had never occurred. She had not even been harmed physically. Sure, she had been emotionally abused and neglected by him and her mother, both alcoholic, narcissistic people. Given my experience and training at the time, I saw no reason to disbelieve Freda or to suspect otherwise. In the next couple of years, she became more able to remember her father's sexual curiosity, his intrusiveness, and ultimately his masturbating her and requesting fellatio. Yet, she said he stopped short of vaginal intromission. Unlike some other patients who suffer from chronic pelvic pain, I believed hers was not related to a history of father–daughter intercourse. I wrote about her from this point of view in an earlier book, *The Sexual Relationship* (1982).

At the time of that publication, I had been seeing Freda for more than five years. She was a small, thin, intelligent, energetic person at her job and in her family. Talkative at home, she was desperately quiet in her therapy sessions. From the beginning, she found therapy difficult—even dreadful. She froze while trying to tell me about her internal experience. Each session comprised a few sentences spoken across a zone of agonized tension. She was dedicated to her work with me, and she trusted me, but she could not bring herself to say much to me. This echoed her paralyzed fear when she attempted intercourse with her husband. In the countertransference, I could feel the agony of being with her in each session, which I dreaded in a palpable way although I also liked her. When I presented aspects of her case to British colleagues Arthur Hyatt Williams and the late Shiona Williams, they suggested that I was feeling in the session what she had felt at her father's approach to her bed, as she lay in agonized dread. Now, she conveyed this to me in our encounters through projective identification of that aspect of herself, while she thus embodied the persecuting object of her father. I found their comments enormously useful in tolerating the ensuing experiences with her and with this help began to understand Freda in a new way.

Having thought more about the survivor of trauma in intensive psychotherapy, we now understand that the way Freda presented in her sessions and the form my countertransference took are typical in patients who have been sexually abused, but I was unaware of that then. Now, I would be more conscious of the likelihood of a more pervasive history of abuse. Yet, my suspicions could have been abusive if thrust upon the patient. I had to work at the patient's pace and from her level of recall. I needed to create a transitional space equidistant between not knowing and knowing, into which the patient could enter to discover and reconstruct her life narrative. To demonstrate the gradual rebuilding of a personal history, I want to give a detailed story of Freda's work with me, beginning with the description of it published originally. That her complete story evolved only over the course of many years is not atypical of this situation, although the tortuously slow pace is at the extreme.

PERSPECTIVES IN THE OPENING PHASE OF THERAPY

My report was written for a chapter linking the relationship of sexual functioning to the care and failures of parents (D. Scharff 1982, reprinted here with minor changes).

Freda's pelvic pain was part of a complex gynecological picture over several years. The initial focus of therapy was on how to live with exacerbations of the chronic pain, which were thought to derive from the adhesions of pelvic surgery for an ectopic pregnancy and perhaps also from complications of an IUD. Her dedication to her gynecologist, whom she trusted as an excellent physician, alternated with fears that no doctor would really play it straight with her, and with an unwillingness to talk about herself which even she did not understand, and from which she had every conscious wish to free herself. Try as she would, she usually could not talk to me, except about the trivia of everyday life. (This remained true throughout the years of psychotherapy after this description. Eventually I came to see that these topics remained an avenue of particular and paradoxical connection between us.) Sometimes something would "give" and she could begin.

After some months, the story began to change. Freda began to feel that the pain was not necessarily physical, and was related to a secret dread of sex, one which she related to the need to be constantly on guard against sexual intrusions from her father. It was her father who told her about sex and boys, who showed her how to use tampons, and who would on occasions ask her about her sex life or walk in while she was undressing. On the other hand, the mother had an extremely negligent attitude— "let matters take care of themselves as they will" —and she was unapproachable by Freda on these or other matters. Instead, mother criticized Freda as someone who could not take care of herself and would have accidents—mother predicted frequent automobile accidents when Freda got her driver's license at 16, for instance. On one occasion, cursing Freda's carelessness for falling ill prior to mother's departure on vacation, mother left anyway despite Freda's temperature of 104 degrees. In addition, the parents traveled for her father's business, and a series of maids looked after Freda and her brother. Freda was convinced that her parents did not care much about what happened to her, and then on the other hand, that they, and especially her father, wanted to pry into the core of her experience, especially her body and sexual growth. These issues came to a head at 14 when she and her family were on an evening cruise in the Caribbean. When one of the ship's crew tried to rape her, she was unable to tell her parents the full extent of the assault, fearing their curiosity as much as the likelihood they would not care anyhow and their neglect would be confirmed. She did tell her parents that a sailor had approached her, and found that just as she had feared, they reprimanded her for disturbing their bridge game and never investigated the matter of the crew member. In fact, during the next week a raucous male friend of the family was installed in the other bed in Freda's room for several months.

In therapy, the picture now emerged that the dyspareunia (pain on intercourse) was not just due to the adhesions. It reminded her of the diffuse "pain in her stomach" of her early school-phobic responses. When she was supposed to leave for school in first and second grades, she would have a feeling of nausea mixed with pain. The pain she experienced during intercourse now recalled a longing for care by her mother and anger at its being denied. It also filled her with the fear of sexual intrusion by her husband, which was transferred from the guardedness against seductive invasion by her father, to whom she wished to turn for substitute caring. Her wish to turn to her father made her own contribution to the fear of "penetration" by him all the greater. The surgery and problems in her body had reawakened this conflict about the care of her body by her parents. Sexual caring was now so threatening as not to be permitted.

In the treatment transference the same conflict about parenting was re-enacted—a longing to be understood by her libidinally exciting father alternating with mute retreat lest the therapist invade her for his own purposes. The same conflict kept her in turmoil about her husband who was, she rationally felt, really a loyal, kind, lovable man. The concreteness of the bodily fear was also linked to guilt over her childhood masturbation, remembered from age 4, which she consciously thought occurred as an attempt to replace her parents by her own pleasure and which was heightened in frequency and fervor when she missed them most intensely. Masturbation now made her feel guilty and lonely. Talking about it in treatment, she came close to tears, but she could not then trust herself enough to cry in her husband's presence or in therapy. Her parents had forbidden crying.

After two years of therapy, Freda wanted to attempt specific sex therapy. She now admitted that she had always feared sex, which she only performed for her husband's sake. Despite her husband's unthreatening and cooperative demeanor, she was frequently fearful and essentially phobic of the exercises. When he was to touch her breasts, she was initially reminded of the times her father held them, ostensibly to express concern over their assymetry during her adolescent development.

When the exercises reached the stage of genital involvement, she felt she had hit a brick wall. She became phobic, unable to touch her husband's penis. Then the rest of the story tumbled out. On top of all she had said before, her father had actually come to her room every few weeks from the time she was 8 years old for several years. He would be naked and drunk. She would be stiffly frightened while he manipulated her clitoris. He would urge her to manipulate his penis to ejaculation—a memory which was repressed until she began pleasuring her husband's penis in sex therapy. He never attempted intercourse with her, but holding his penis, she would feel a combination of nausea and abdominal pain. The nausea turned out to be a reaction to the memory of father thrusting his penis into her mouth and ejaculating, giving her also the feeling she would choke. She now recalled that her 3-year-old daughter had once told her that "women get pregnant by swallowing daddy's seed." She now said she must have thought she would be impregnated orally by her father. The memories of abdominal pain also led her to remember masturbating after father had finally left the room. Masturbation had then, at least consciously, been an attempt to get rid of a tortured sense of abdominal fullness which remained after her father left her humiliated but aroused. These episodes finally stopped during early adolescence when she felt her father's erection while dancing with him, screamed and ran from the room. When father followed her, she told him if he ever entered her room again she would tell her mother. Although a doctor was called who gave her an injection which put her to sleep for three days, father never again approached her sexually. [pp. 12–13, 79–82]

The literature published in the years since this report makes it clear that Freda's story as I knew it then was still crucially incomplete. The persistent pelvic pain, the dread of intercourse as she tried to work in psychotherapy, the frozen and almost dissociated states during her psychotherapy sessions, and the gradual but relentless emergence from repression of the story of abuse would today alert me to expect that intercourse had been an integral part of the early trauma. Greater awareness may be more sustaining to the therapist, but does not necessarily accelerate the patient's recovery of memory. This recovery has to proceed at its own pace.

MEMORIES RECOVERED DURING SEX THERAPY

Freda began to recognize that the prolonged incestuous contact with her father had been responsible for her fear of sex now as an adult, and for the panic attacks and depression that became more frequent as she proceeded. Sex therapy with her husband and 3 subsequent years of individual psychotherapy gave her some ability to respond to her husband Ed, but it also precipitated a flood of specific memories about her father that continued for years. In addition, whenever her father visited her—something she avoided whenever possible—he was still explicitly sexually provocative, stirring up her fear and panic each time. During sex therapy, she took my suggestion that she write down her responses, since it was easier for her than telling me in the sessions, which she often felt unable to do directly—a derivative of the fear she felt with the object that was supposed to promote safety. Then, slowly, she began to find the words to say these things directly to me after having first written them. The process was tortuously slow.

She said, "After I left you last time, I was thinking that it's not necessarily the weekend contact with my father that has me down. It's more that seeing him has aggravated accepting the fact that he did arouse me when I was younger. I'm having trouble knowing for sure that I was aroused even though you've been suggesting the possibility for some time. I'm finally putting two and two together and it's really getting to me. When I'm doing my own masturbation assignments and when I'm doing assignments with Ed, it seems safer not to touch him or to be touched. So then when I remember, it doesn't hurt as much. But I want to know why I keep asking Ed not to hurt me. I wish I knew what I mean when I do that.

" . . . I think that Ed might hurt me by putting something in my vagina—although I should know—I have two kids you know—that penises do fit sometimes. So why do I worry it'll hurt? It's sort of like I can remember where it hurts but forget what makes me hurt. I can remember my father putting his fingers in my vagina to show me where the blood came from. That hurt a lot—but I don't remember being aroused at all when he did it. I just know that something happened.

Here she picked up a piece of paper and wrote:

an erect penis = pain will come
stimulation = pain will come
arousal = pain

She continued, "I know I could enjoy Ed's massaging me. But then I began to feel aroused by it."

As the exercises proceeded, she needed to cover her genitals, then her whole body during the massage, and found herself saying to Ed, "Please don't hurt me!"

"I know he wouldn't," she said, "but I felt like I would be hurt." She discovered the lifelong confusion between arousal and the painful feelings of fright, pain, and nausea. At times, she asked Ed to hold her safely in his arms without doing anything sexual, and he always obliged. She felt safe as long as nothing happened sexually. At other times of greater security, she could proceed with the exercises and allow increments of progress. Once she told Ed and me that she often felt safer if her eyes were shut. "I guess I play a little of the game, 'if my eyes are shut and I can't see him then he can't see me.'"

In one exercise, she had been weepy, and Ed had held her soothingly. When he got an erection while holding her, she offered to have intercourse, in gratitude for his being so patient with her, but not really wanting to. The two of them agreed that they should not, both because of her fear and because it was not prescribed in the exercises. That night she dreamt:

I dreamed that I had been shot—I was with Ed and the kids in the car, and we needed to stop to deliver some letters somewhere. It looked familiar, but I can't place the house. Ed waited at the corner of the street while I took the letters in to the mailbox at the door. A car was parked in the driveway with a man with a gun in it. I saw only the gun, which was the size of a handgun but the front looked more like a cannon. I felt something hit and knock me down. I hurt vaguely on my right side lying on the sidewalk. Ed didn't get out of the car to help, but the man who shot me got out of his car and said he'd shoot me again if I left, but he also just stared at me. I tried to tell him to let me go, but he stayed with the gun in his hand. Then a younger man was there, and I told him I wanted to go, but they both said they weren't finished with me yet. I suggested they either kill me or go away. I looked for Ed, but the car seemed too far away. I wondered whether I was too hurt to get up and run for it and get help later, or whether he really would shoot me again so I wouldn't be able to get up. I couldn't make up my mind, and then I woke up.

The house was not identifiable, although it looked like an area where she had spent part of her youth, but the man who shot her looked like her father: "His face was the right shape only the wrong size; the man was shortish and pudgy, but a creepy resemblance was there," she added.

The dream contains the elements of threat in a familiar yet unknown place, a place from which her husband is too distant to protect her. The gunman is her father in a creepy form, and he has an assistant, whose age indicated to me that it might be a transference version of me, in a threatening partnership with her father for introducing and sponsoring the sexual threat in the form of the therapy that kept exposing her to her father.

She continued,

I finally went back to sleep only to have another weird dream. I was in a small sportscar with no top with another woman who looked like Mrs. H. (the woman who ran a women's group for exploring sexual issues that Freda was also in at this time). We were having a friendly conversation when we stopped at a construction site where children were playing. One little boy fell off a wall, and I jumped out of the car and ran down a hill barefoot in the snow to help him. When I got to the bottom there were lots of children lying wrapped in blankets in the snow. I found the boy who fell. He was already wrapped in a blanket because he was hurt. I asked him where his mother was so that I could call her. He said not to call because she wouldn't come. None of the children lying in the snow had mothers who would help them. I told him somebody had to care, but he said, "Nobody has to do anything." Then I woke up. Maybe I'll give up sleep!

The two dreams captured both the transference of danger Freda felt toward me as the sex therapist and toward Mrs. H. whom she felt to be the negligent mother, further exposing her to risk and failing to come to her rescue when she was in danger. Freda had already told me of numerous times when her mother failed to protect her, scolded her for being hurt, and failed to come after her even when she was lost in foreign cities. On the few occasions when Freda had cried as a child, her mother had exploded at her for crying, so that she learned to stifle the tears and try to dissociate herself from pain.

About a year before sex therapy had begun, her mother had been diagnosed as having terminal leukemia, and Freda had taken her into her house to die. She did so under pressure from her father and brothers, because she felt too guilty to refuse. Her mother was, for the first time in Freda's life, grateful and responsive, so that she felt she had the only good time with her mother she had ever had. However, her father, when he was not brooding and smoking by her mother's bed, roused himself from the sick room to make sexually provocative comments. He seemed not to have changed much in the 30 years since Freda's childhood. She remembered how he had used her instead of having a sexual relationship with her mother. When her brother told her father he was leaving his wife because he was impotent with her, her father said to him, "So what? I was impotent with your mother and I didn't leave her. Find someone else for the sex, anyone inside or outside your family, but don't hurt your family by breaking it up just because of the sex."

Slowly Freda began to remember more: a memory of her father dressing in her mother's clothes, stuffing the bra with socks to give himself breasts; a memory of sleeping on her stomach to avoid her father touching her breasts as he lay with an erection on her buttocks; fears of rectal penetration and fantasies of dogs locked together to make babies. Freda still did not believe that babies could come out of their mothers. Her own two had been born by Cesarean section. In her fantasy, the penis she remembered got bigger and bigger until it became a baby. She was gagging because of having to take it in her mouth. Then the penis became a baby that got into her through her mouth, making her gag and leave the room to vomit. Freda was fearful of every orifice—the vagina, the rectum, the throat. Each invitation to intercourse with Ed threatened her with the return of these memories, which grew increasingly vivid.

In between these memories, sex was becoming more comfortable, at least some of the time. She could relax and enjoy Ed. She could feel trust, comfort, and gentle arousal, sometimes even longing for an orgasm that might come without danger.

Nevertheless, sex therapy ground to a halt. Freda was able to tolerate more closeness to Ed than formerly, but was only occasionally able to face arousal without having to fend off panic. Since he was so patient with her, she could coax herself to stand sexual encounters with him periodically, but they were not reliable. Freda could not bear to continue, because she was aware of being much nearer to internal sexual material that threatened her more than ever before.

COUNTERTRANSFERENCE DISSOCIATION
PRECEDING REVELATION

We shifted from sex therapy to resume twice-weekly individual psychotherapy with occasional couple's sessions, and more material began to emerge slowly. I felt that I was supporting her survival, rather than exploring new territory and analyzing conflict, especially as she became more depressed over time. Freda sat staring at me, wondering if she could dare trust me enough to tell me. I felt a dread at her arrival for each session, even though I was fond of her and admired her for carrying on so well despite the trauma she had endured. Her sessions were characterized by long periods of quiet during which she would seem to be intensely preoccupied with material that was about to emerge but against which she was struggling. She seemed to become dissociated, at which time I would sink into a corresponding reverie. Yet, at the same time we were intensely aware of each other's presence. Her recurrent, prolonged silences were relieved only by humorous stories about the trivia of her everyday life, of her caring for her children, her community activities, and job—at all of which she seemed to be skilled. If she began to talk about something more substantial, she was apt to interrupt and say she had to go to the bathroom.

The sessions with her filled me with a crushing sense of boredom. I kept feeling that I was coasting. I felt guilty that I was not pushing more aggressively to get her and me to do what I thought of as the "real work" of uncovering the trauma. I began to wonder if analytic psychotherapy were justified. Freda grew more and more depressed, and I had to refer her to a colleague for antidepressant medication, which she continued to need as an adjunct to her psychoanalytic psychotherapy.

In retrospect, this feeling of depression and our surviving it were the nub of the therapy. She needed me to help her go on being. Her using me to listen to and reflect upon daily trivia, which I looked forward to hearing and often invited, was the evidence of her wish for an ordinary, unthreatening relationship that she could count on. In between sessions, I experienced her as though I were her and she were her father stalking me with the deadly evil eye that she felt he focused on her. I responded with boredom, a feeling that I recognized as a countertransference response of dissociation, of not being all there, resulting from my identification with her as she faced his approach and held her tongue lest he do something worse to her than he was already doing. My capacity to stand her transference in which she was invoking in me both a frightened child and a frightening father let her gradually tolerate more. Identified with her, I shared her dread of my invasive therapeutic curiosity. I was afraid that my wanting to know more, like her father's reaching into her vagina and his holding her breasts in curiosity about her development, was more destructive than helpful. I think that this inhibition of my analytic curiosity was crucial in facilitating the retrieval that followed.

RECOVERING MEMORIES OF INTERCOURSE WITH FATHER

As I tolerated these hours and contained the feelings that character-ized them, new memories gradually emerged, each coming at an agonizingly slow rate. Freda knew that her father had forced fellatio on her, had mounted her from behind and pressed his erection into her back, and had reached into her vagina supposedly to help her when she began to menstruate. Now she told me that she was convinced that he had had frequent intercourse with her from almost as far back as she could remember. Her mother must have known about it and not cared. No one cared. She had a dream in the seventh year of treatment: "My tongue was coming out of a mouth and became a snake coming out. I cut it, and it blew up like a balloon."

Freda's associations took her to her memories of the snakes in Africa where her family lived when she was a child. Once their gardener cut off his leg when decapitating a snake crawling up his leg. Her father's penis inside her felt like it was coming into a big empty space like that in a doll and then coming up and right out her mouth. She wanted to cut it, but it got bigger without stopping and she felt helpless. As she told me this, she felt an enormous emptiness and an arousal that she had to disown and fight off. She drew a picture of a vague face with a protruding object that seemed to be an enormous penis-tongue that could also have been a fecal mass (Figure 12–1).

The material was certainly no longer boring. It was now agonizingly graphic, riveting, and more perverse than anything I had imagined.

It was in the session after she told me the dream about the snake-tongue that she told me how she had arrived at the conclusion that her father had had intercourse with her—from a dream.

She said, "Can I tell you another dream? It was the one which made me realize that I had to tell you about having intercourse with my father. I've known now for a while that it did happen. But I have to ask: 'Will you ever tell me I can't come back? Is there anything I can't say? Will the headaches and the having to go to the bathroom that I feel now and everytime I'm here, does that ever go away?'

"I dreamt I was having a bowel movement from my vagina, which went down and around my legs and between them and came up on my stomach. Then the head of it was the head of a penis, uncircumcised like my father's, instead of Ed's circumcised one.

"I felt the disgust when I woke up and found that I felt aroused by it. Is it bad? I feel I'm bad!"

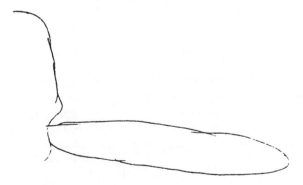

Figure 12–1. Vague-face and penis-tongue.

I asked if it felt like her father's hands on her legs, and she agreed. She went on to say that she had begun to feel a more palpable fear every time she had her period, unable to tell anyone—even me— because that was when her father would press intercourse on her. Then she remembered her father against her back pressing his penis between her legs as if he were going to enter her rectum—and it hurt.

Then she said, "I don't have to go to the bathroom now."

This material seemed to express the depth of her despair. It was connected to a sense of deep personal shame, to a feeling that she wanted to cry but that once she began she would go on forever. Periods of the old agonized silence now alternated with immersion in the experiences with her father, which would then recede while she gained a measure of equilibrium. She wondered if she would ever be normal, not depressed, and able to feel good about herself. She knew that she felt at bottom that she had been bad, had brought this abuse on herself. She remembered fleeing from home after she got her father to stop having intercourse with her. She returned to boarding school a week later and, crying and crying, told the only teacher whom she felt she could trust. This comforting woman put Freda to sleep in her own bed, but when Freda awoke some hours later, the woman was in bed with her, now drunk and fondling Freda's breasts and vulva. Freda had never again told anyone what had happened with her father.

I have come across this situation in other cases. The abused person confides in someone who proves untrustworthy and becomes a perpetrator. It must be that the abused person chooses as confidant someone whose qualities of being sympathetic and nonjudgmental turn out to derive not from maturity but from the kind of poorly integrated ego that is more familiar to her.

RECOVERING EARLIEST MEMORIES

Therapy continued, but Freda once again became more blocked and cried through many of her hours. I suggested once again, as I had several years earlier during sex therapy, that she write down her thoughts and mail them to me or bring them to the sessions. I also accepted her suggestion that she bring in old pictures. She reminded me, "I told you that if I started to cry, I wouldn't be able to stop, and that I'd need to do that to get to these things."

Then she came to a session with a strange look, staring at me in a paralyzed but wild way. She seemed more dissociated and distressed than usual. Finally she spoke.

"I tried writing, but after four or five pages, I ran into the sadness, the pictures without words. I looked at the old family pictures. Whenever I was with my parents, I was pouting, but I was smiling when I was alone."

She sat silently for a while staring at me. Then she blurted out, "Can dogs get stuck together when they have sex?"

"What are you asking?" I countered, caught off guard, shaken from the sadness I had felt as she spoke.

"Just what I said: can dogs get stuck together?"

"I don't quite know what you're driving at," I said.

Slowly she said, "The writing took me back to age 2 or 3. I think I saw my parents having sex doggie-style. My father had me touch his penis. It was hard, but it was wet and yucky. I didn't have any clothes on. They touched me down there, and had me touch them. My mother's breasts hung down like a cow. I think I hurt because I didn't know where the penis was going. It seemed to go inside her and it hurt.

"And then there is something else without words: a huge hand across me, I'm trying to get away from it. It hurts me, down there." She was quiet a long time. "I think my father had sex with me when I was very little. When I was 8 for sure, because I remember the places and the dresses, but I think maybe when I was really little.

"How do you put words on this when it was so young? I was so young! I don't even know what I felt—fear. I was afraid, hurt. I was excited too.

"Can I come back next time? Will you be mad if I cry? Can I come back? Can I trust you?"

"Yes," I said. "You can come back." I felt like I was talking to a 2-year-old.

There was a hiatus in her material during which she seemed blocked again. Three weeks later, she was able to resume. She had been writing and, after writing a great deal, was able to begin to talk to me again about the experiences.

"I'll try to talk to you again. I'll probably be embarassed. Sometimes, though, I feel like the only way I'll talk to you is with some sort of invisible barrier between us and the only thing that varies is the thickness—but it is always there. That's why it's easier to write sometimes.

"Perhaps you should have been a surgeon who could give me a strong anesthetic and then look inside and reconnect the torn wires. Other times I'd prefer to be here too to make sure you know which ones are broken. My thoughts and feelings don't come to me organized 1–10. For example, very often I intend to say that Ed and I had sex last night, which is true. It was OK for a while and then it wasn't.

"OK, I should be able to say that first we snuggled and he started to rub my arm and worked toward my breast and that felt good. Then what happened? I don't know."

She looked speechless, and then took up the pad on the table and wrote for a minute, and handed me a diagram (Figure 12-2) without saying anything.

After a few minutes, she could speak again. "Only all that happens fast and I lose track. I can't answer all at once or even as fast as it all happens. Sometimes nothing happens, except that I feel aroused and I just enjoy it and feel good about feeling a part of Ed. But sometimes I just gag as Ed starts to ejaculate.

In another session she said, "Sex isn't supposed to equal love.

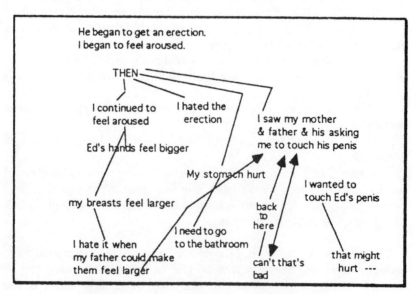

Figure 12-2. Freda's diagram of sexual abuse.

Sex is supposed to be an extension of love. I think I see it backward. I let my father do whatever he wanted; then he'd say he loved me. I could then masturbate and feel the same way and then feel loved. I don't like that.

"It feels like I draw a blank or close off the idea that I want or need to feel loved. If I don't admit that I want to feel loved then I'm a victim instead of a participant.

"I'm not sure why I have the view that a 3-year-old can really make a decision to participate in a sexual relationship with parents. But I can't think of any reason why I feel guilty and bad about watching their intercourse and touching my mother's breasts and my father's penis. They wanted me to, and said they loved me when I did. I don't remember being told that they didn't love me if I didn't do it, only that they would if I did what they said.

"But I do feel bad. Like I did something bad. I also feel dirty— but I didn't when it was happening. Only afterward. Maybe not even until I started to masturbate to feel loved."

And on another occasion she said, "Sometimes it seems like I can freely admit to masturbating, and at other times I blank it all out. It's like I didn't think I thought of it as having anything to do with sex until you sent me to the women's group. It was more of a very bad thing I did to feel the same as I did when Daddy told me he loved me.

"Sometimes I'm trying to tell you something you can't hear and I can't focus on. It's like chipping away at an egg shell, and neither of us knows what monster will be hatched. You chip on the outside while I push on the inside. But when the shell starts to crack, I panic until the crack heals."

She drew another picture (Figure 12–3) and handed it to me, this time with less hesitation.

She continued, "Sometimes I get curious as to what is there. Other times I feel frightened and don't want to know. Who knows, maybe there is nothing there at all. Maybe what is there is a grown-up child with no way to grow up or shrink backward. I keep getting stuck!"

Another session revolved around the repeated experience of watching her parents have intercourse at about the age of 3: "What I couldn't say in the last session was that I must have known that it was

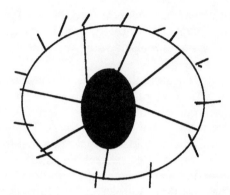

Figure 12-3.   Freda's monster in the egg.

possible for my father to put his penis inside me because when I sat and watched, I would suck my thumb and hold myself—one thumb in my mouth and one hand covering my genitals. But I think I would feel that I was holding back the need to urinate. Maybe that's why I have to go to the bathroom so often here.

"Also, sometimes when I would be in bed with just my father his hands would cover my genitals and my stomach, and it would feel like he was holding a flood of urine—I would probably use the word 'pee' instead. But it also feels like he was pushing to get inside me like when I was 8 and my period started, and he did push inside with his fingers. The same pressure kind of feeling.

"The pain that you can see didn't happen until he really did push inside and I was torn. There was blood and lots and lots of burning—like scrapes and cuts. It hurt and burned to go to the bathroom for a long time. And when I took a bath it hurt a lot."

Telling me of these memories, her voice and intonation changed to that of a young girl. Freda identified the voice as different from her usual voice and told me that she felt as if a small child in her were talking. I did not get the impression that this child part of her was unconnected to her central self.

On another occasion, Freda brought photographs from before and after her earliest memories of abuse to show me its effects on her. Showing me the pictures, she said, "I guess I was an average baby—no hair, no teeth, big mouth. But, when I sat up, I looked like a baby.

I ran, loved my blankie and I could swing on a trapeze. But what spooks me are the eyes. They change and become sad. These pictures where I'm about 3 are where they change. This is the time when I used to crawl in bed with my parents and watch them have intercourse."

She found it difficult to talk again, and slowly, looking away, continued in a staccato rhythm. "I sucked my thumb. My stomach hurt. My blanket was with me. I was afraid of dogs. I can see snatches of my mother on her hands and knees, with my father behind her. I see my mother's breasts hanging and I think, 'Cow!' And when Daddy puts something very BIG inside—I think it is inside because it disappears—but it's there because I've seen it and touched it. It is hard, long, squishy, wet, slippery, red, ugly and can disappear. My stomach hurts to write, I can feel the push between my legs. His hands are too big, and I don't want to sit next to him.

"In this picture, we were at our country house. Now my period has started and I'm afraid of the blood. But we've been over this. This is when he hurt me. I know it is about this time because I remember the dress. It was green and white. I loved it until it got bloody. Then I hated it and never wore it.

"I want to leave the pictures here for now for us to talk about, but please don't lose them. Some day they may not make me sad, and in any case the children may want to know where they came from. They won't make them sad unless I tell them they should."

RECONSTRUCTING THE NARRATIVE OF ABUSE

Finally, we had the story of Freda's childhood, much of which had remained repressed for the first 9 years of therapy despite the trust she felt with me. We now understood that Freda must have been subjected to continual sexual abuse, taken into her parents' bed on repeated occasions, perhaps while her mother was pregnant with the next child, and encouraged to participate by touching her parents genitally while being touched genitally by them. Her mother seemed to have been a full participant.

While all this was going on, Freda was being cared for by a variety of nannies, as the family moved a great deal. Her mother was rejecting in times of need, screaming at her if she hurt herself or cried. No one came to find her one time when she was lost in a strange city at the age of 5. She was returned by the police after several hours. On the other hand, she felt the nannies were loving to her. In retrospect, it may have been far better that she and her brother were left to their care. She was never sure if intercourse with father occurred through the years before she was 8, but she was certain he fondled and stimulated her, coming to her bedroom at night, demanding that she stimulate him and, most dreaded, that she perform fellatio, which made her gag.

When her period began at the age of 8, he put his fingers inside her vagina to demonstrate where the blood came from. It was this episode that hurt her the most and that stayed frozen in her memory. He followed then or soon after with penile penetration. Thereafter he would inquire frequently about her periods and would seek her out for intercourse, especially when she was menstruating. She lay frozen, feigning sleep in her bed, dreading his drunken visits, then trying to dissociate herself from the episodes that followed. As she put it, "If I wasn't there, it didn't hurt." What alarmed her the most as she recalled these episodes in therapy finally was that she had been aroused and used to masturbate after her father left, trying both to regain the feeling and to rid herself of it, and most of all to feel loved.

Later she was sent to boarding school, but the intercourse continued whenever she was at home until the episode at age 14. Exactly what happened is less clear to me now than I thought it was when I first wrote about it before the de-repression of so much material. She was home from school for the first time in many months—so she was older and more aware than the previous time it had happened. Her father was drunk at a party at their house. Freda was menstruating and left the party after having a couple of drinks herself. He followed her to her bedroom, put her face down, lay on her back, pinning her arms under her, and tried to enter her from behind. She felt he was trying to turn her into the picture of her mother, doggie-style. She screamed, and threw up, and then threatened to kill herself. She threw such a fit that her father left her, and she was given the injection of a sedative by a physician friend who was at the party.

This was not the last material to emerge. A year after we learned of this episode she was still working on difficult material. She remembered having her fist around father's penis while keeping a hand over herself. Or she would try to keep a thumb in her mouth too, to keep father from doing to her what he did to mother. She imagined having a penis because her mother seemed to have one when father had been putting his into her. As Freda said, "My father was trying to turn me into a cow, to make me like my mother with breasts hanging down and penises growing out of me. I had to go along with having his penis in my mouth, or he'd push it into me and I'd bleed to death."

Then there was the picture of her father's penis with her menstrual blood on it. After her first menses came, the school called him to pick her up. "When I came home," Freda said, "he took me in a room and said to kiss his penis, and then he put his fingers in me, and it hurt. I could tell it hurt because of the blood." She covered herself with a blanket as she described the picture and then wondered once again if I would ever let her come back.

RECOVERING PREADOLESCENT MEMORIES DURING WORKING THROUGH

When we had been working for more than 10 years, I moved most of my practice to an office that happened to have a fireplace. In our first meeting there, Freda was vividly reminded of the bedroom of the house her family had lived in when she was 11 and 12. She was panicked about meeting me in my new office, and we moved back to the old office she preferred, although I could only see her there at times that were inconvenient for her. The experience of fearful recall begun in the new office continued to precipitate new memories of what had happened in her bedroom in this house.

It was a room particularly isolated from the family, so her father could accost her at will. She spent many weeks telling me how she had used a collection of dolls he had brought her from all over the world (Figure 12–4). She would undress them and then stimulate the breasts and genitals of the dolls. She cut the heads off some dolls of the kind that wet so that she could fill them with ketchup so they would appear to menstruate. She took a knife to the other dolls in the collection, cut them between the legs, and smeared their genitals with ketchup. She slept on the floor of her closet with a doll, hoping her father would not be able to find her. And she tried to commit suicide by lying in a patch of poison ivy behind the house, which did not kill her but gave her a raging case of total body itching and oozing.

She felt despairing and intermittently suicidal when she talked about this material, as she remembered feeling at the time. The

Figure 12–4.   Freda's doll.

antidepressant medication helped, but she still felt that the situation was haunting her as though it were recurring now. She wrote me a letter after one of our sessions:

> I didn't like it when my father:
> came in and woke me up by crawling in bed and stroked my breasts and made me feel like I had to go to the bathroom
> or He would lay next to me and I could feel his penis in the small of my back
> or he would put his hands between my legs and a finger in my vagina.
> or when he would ask me to kiss his penis
> or when he would ejaculate & I thought he was urinating on me or in my mouth.
> I did like it when I saw him & my mother having intercourse. I thought he would hurt me & I couldn't not watch & then he would ask me to touch him when they were together.

I thought that Freda meant to write that she did not like this either, and that her slip indicated that, in part, she did like it—a slip consistent with the arousal she experienced.
The note continued:

I didn't like it when I couldn't make my stomach stop hurting without masturbating.

I got scared when I discovered that I could make myself feel the same way that he made me feel.

I didn't like it when he would come in the bathroom when I was in the shower to see how my breasts were growing—Would they ever be the same size? I thought that there was something very wrong with me. I'd feel sick when I saw the dolls with no clothes on & would try to get rid of their genitals & breasts by cutting them or writing all over them.

I didn't like it when he asked me how it felt to wear a tampon—was it like walking around with a penis inside? Or was it very arousing? All sorts of questions like that.

I don't like it when I do get my period now—I feel if anybody knows then I'll get hurt. I don't like remembering how I tried to hide it.

I didn't like being in school & not being able to tell why I always had to go to the bathroom. I couldn't not remember his hands all over me.

I didn't like the way he smelled.

I didn't like it when I always felt dirty when I thought about what he did—

I didn't like it when I thought that getting aroused was going to kill me because there never seemed to be any relief from the tension.

I don't like feeling like he owns me & I have to do what he wants.

I didn't like it when my mother hit me when I cried & I couldn't tell her why I was crying.

I didn't like it when I got aroused when I thought about what he did. I want to kill myself when this happened.

Again I thought I detected a slip. Freda's change in tenses to "I want to kill myself" suggested to me that she does now still feel like killing herself. The suicidal feeling must still haunt her when she remembers these events.

I didn't like it when he said that I should like how he made me feel— I would learn to like kissing his penis. I thought he would like me if I did & if he liked me then he wouldn't ask me to do it again.

I didn't like it when he drank. I slept on the floor of the closet with a pillow & a doll. But he would tell me to get in bed. Nobody asked why I slept in the closet . . .

The work with Freda was only periodically as intense as the excerpts I have given, but the feeling could become intense in any session, which was then apt to threaten both of us with the strain of the pull toward dissociation, depression, and impasse. The punctuation of these periods with periods of narrative about her children, family, and community events continued throughout the years of work, the repeated reiteration of the trivia of "going-on-being" that let us both re-establish a baseline of interest, trust, and of being there together. It was not until late in our work together that I came to understand just how important these apparently superficial phases of the work were in supporting the painful moments of remembering and working through.

TRANSMISSION OF TRAUMA TO THE NEXT GENERATION

Throughout the years of working with Freda, I felt tortured by her turmoil, but I continually admired the way she struggled to remember and overcome the effects of her history. Not the least of the causes for my admiration was her dedication to her family. Her children, like her husband Ed, experienced the spillover of her depression and periodic self-absorption, but she remained a dedicated, funny, and flexible mother. Most of the stories that filled so much of our time together were about the children, Thomas and Junie, and their friends, so I felt I got to know them well. I had also met with the children in a few family sessions over the years for fleeting developmental concerns, but mainly they did well. Freda and Ed handled an incident so well in which Junie, aged 8 or 9, was accosted by a flasher that Junie was not traumatized by it. Then during the children's adolescence, a crisis was to develop that called for a more concerted family intervention. During this time of brief family therapy, we could see the currents of Freda's struggle intersect with her children's development, despite her lifelong efforts to protect her children from her history.

In nonabused children of parents who were physically and sexually abused, the parent's object relations internalized from the abusive relationship with the previous generation are taken into the psychic structure of these children, despite the admirable behavior of their parents. We had the opportunity to understand both parent and child in enough detail to follow this influence in Freda's case and in the cases of Tony and Theresa's child, Tony, Jr., in Chapter 9 and Lars and Velia's family reported briefly in Chapter 1 and in detail elsewhere (D. Scharff 1989, Scharff and Scharff 1992). Like the effects of the Holocaust on the children of its victims, the legacy of trauma and violence does not disappear in a single generation.

Freda and Ed had bent over backward to do better with their

children and extended themselves as well to other neighborhood children in need of care and protection. Through the years, Freda had always taken in stray children whose parents seemed neglectful or abusive. She had done this in her position as a den mother for the Cub Scouts and in various roles in the children's schools and in the citizens' association. This became a model for their son, Thomas, who found a needy girlfriend, Cindy, a fun-loving histrionic girl whose parents seemed unconcerned that she drank heavily. Thomas and his sister, Junie, had joined forces to get Freda and Ed to take this girl into the family's extended care system. During Thomas' senior year, Cindy became pregnant, presumably by Thomas, although she also had other sexual contacts. It was Freda who helped arrange the abortion and who accompanied the teenagers to the clinic, while the girl's mother refused to participate and dismissed Cindy as lazy and reckless. This girl continued to be an informal part of the family during the rest of the school year, until Thomas finally broke up with her when he was leaving for college on the West Coast.

In December later that year, Freda asked for help with Junie, now a high-school senior. She was depressed and seemed to be pining for Thomas since he had left for college. Formerly an A student, Junie had stopped doing homework so that her grades had fallen to C's and D's for the first time ever. This was happening during the time when Freda was working on the depth of her feelings about some of the remaining aspects to be revealed of the incest. I had been asking whether her children would be better off knowing about her experience and the causes of her profound depression that they had experienced periodically all their lives. She had resisted. It was all she could do to deal with it with me, much less with the children.

However, now I began to feel that the assumption that sex is destructive had begun to surface in the children's generation through Thomas' dedication to the waif, who was alcoholic and promiscuous and who may have been abused herself, and through Junie's adolescent depression. We agreed that I would see Junie, who responded well to the idea. When I did, she put the burden of her scholastic slide on missing her brother and on feeling that Thomas and his former girlfriend no longer cared about her, and had used her only as a conduit between them to re-establish and promote their continued contact. She felt bereft without them. She sometimes wished she could die. She agreed to family sessions that would include Thomas, who was shortly to return from his freshman year at college for the long winter break.

FAMILY THERAPY FOR THE FAMILY'S REENACTMENT OF TRAUMA

The family sessions turned out to be critical. The family discussed the parents' fear that Junie was out of control and drinking. In view of Thomas' drinking in high school (and presumably in college) and Freda's experience with alcoholic parents, it was understandable that Freda and Ed might be worried about alcohol abuse. However, with no evidence of this in Junie's case, they all agreed that it was an odd assumption to make. I thought that their focus on alcohol was a cover for their concern about sex. Junie had recently begun going steady with a new boyfriend, and her parents might be worried about the potential of sex to disrupt her life, in the wake of the trauma of Cindy's pregnancy the previous year, after which this troubled girl and her promiscuity had dominated the family's life. Junie said that the family did not seem to trust her. Her family had accused her of lying and staying out late when they had always trusted her before, and Thomas burst into tears as he learned of his sister's suffering.

I said that as a group they were trying to take care of their own suffering by helping the girlfriend-waif while each of them felt uncared for in important ways. The children agreed and elaborated: Junie felt the family cared far more for Thomas' girlfriend than for her, and Thomas felt they dismissed his concern about Cindy, to whom he was again committed.

I had been talking again with Freda about telling the children about the contribution that incest made to her depression and compulsive need to take care of waifs. She felt that she still could not discuss this with them, even though she could see that Thomas' adolescent sexuality and Junie's depression expressed a fantasy of being responsible for damage suffered by others. Junie and Thomas felt bad unless they could make reparation. Freda also related Junie's low self-esteem and both children's conviction that they were at fault for other's unhappiness as deriving from her own feeling, rooted in the dreadful experiences with her parents, of being bad and damaging.

"How can I tell the children that I am bad?" Freda asked me in her next individual session. "They are just going to think I'm bad. No, it isn't that they'll think I'm bad—or even that they'll think badly of me—it's that they'll *know* I'm bad. I am. I'm rotten. My mother told me

I was rotten all the time. Don't you think I must have done something bad? Why else would my father have done that to me?"

I showed Freda how she had made her children—compassionate and understanding children—into her neglectful and critical parents. She might find that they could be as understanding and helpful to her as they were to their friends if she could tell them what had happened to her. She left her session before my vacation saying that if this had to be done, she should just kill herself now, but quickly reminded me that she often says she cannot do something and then will do the contrary.

We were in the middle of the series of family sessions when I left for a 10-day trip, with Jill Scharff covering my practice. The crucial family sessions occurred while I was away.

The Emergency Phone-Call

Ed called me (JSS) to say that his wife had become very upset. Her individual therapist (DES) who had also been seeing the family was out of town, and the family was too worried about her to wait for his return. Freda was having stomach heaves. She had been crying for two days without respite. All this began after her son Thomas yelled abuse at her when he was confronted with his parents' anger at his staying out all night and coming home late without calling. Ed thought that her reaction was out of proportion to the events, and he had the idea that it must be related to her childhood history of physical and sexual abuse. She kept saying to him that she was on the edge of something, that she was at a place she had never been at before, and that she was terrified. The family was meeting for a series of family therapy sessions with Dr. David Scharff because of the daughter Junie's failing school performance and wish to die. Ed readily agreed to an emergency family meeting as the best way to deal with the problem of his wife's distress and his family's concern.

Emergency Family Therapy: First Session

I was surprised that Ed and Freda arrived for their session without their symptomatic 15-year-old daughter, Junie, who was left home in bed, because they thought that she was not involved in the upsetting incident. They were accompanied only by their 18-year-old son

Thomas, a strikingly attractive young man. Freda, who seemed mainly withdrawn and depressed, lolled back on the couch in a way that also reminded me of a child who is feeling regressed and seductive toward grown-ups. At times she became hysterical and rolled her eyes in an alarming way.

Ed, who sat forward so that his chair seemed too small for such a tall man, began to give a circumstantial account of the events. Thomas was not home at 7:00 A.M. when he was supposed to run an errand. Anxiously trying to find him, his parents asked his sister for help. Knowing that he might be with his old girlfriend, she lied to protect him, and said that he was at his friend Chris' house. Ed and Freda called Chris' father who did not know that Thomas was there, and so the parents were home all morning thinking that Thomas had been pushed off the road. When Thomas arrived home after noon, Freda had said, "Where the hell do you think you have been?"

Thomas had said, "At Chris's." He felt entitled to spend the night at his friend Chris' house, but he realized that he had come home later than expected. He had already thought to himself, "You're late. You're dead." Thomas said that he could have accepted their anger about that. Yet, he did feel entitled to be believed about where he had been. When his mother would not believe his story, wrongfully accused him of lying about his whereabouts, and started to scream at him, he became furious. He yelled, "Fuck you, fuck you!" at his mother, hit the post of the doorway that she was blocking, pushed past her, and walked out. Freda, distraught, screamed after him, shrank against the doorpost like a shivering child, and could not be comforted for days.

"It was like something else was happening to her," Ed concluded. He quickly diverted my attention to the details of how he yelled at Thomas, tried to restrain him from storming out, and then had followed him outside to talk. "I wanted him to understand how he had screwed up by being late," Ed added.

I said, "I think that 'You're late, you're dead' is a family-wide substitute for 'You're sexual, you've left the family.' Thomas swore — as he might have done with his friends at college, but when he said 'Fuck you' to his mother, Dad felt that he really screwed up because that's not an appropriate way to talk to a mother." Directing myself to Thomas, I said, "But with *your* mother, Thomas, it had a catastrophic effect, because it cut through to a vulnerable part of her and made her act as if something else was happening." Turning to Freda, I asked, "Could you say something about that?"

"I won't discuss it," she said hysterically.

"Do you know what it is?" I asked.

"Yes," she said tersely.

"Okay," I said. "You decide about your privacy, but the cost is that Thomas can't understand what he triggered."

Thomas nodded thoughtfully. No one spoke.

I went on, speaking from my countertransference position of feeling stuck. "I'm in an awkward spot here," I said. "From how you felt, Freda, I can see that Thomas' saying 'Fuck you' cut through to an earlier area of experience, and from what Ed told me on the phone, I know the general area of that experience. But without your sharing it, the family and I are stuck. I can't help you to understand something that was serious enough to cause a blow-up that can't be understood. But maybe I can help you to think about why you'd rather not know."

I do not believe that the sharing of history that has been secret is in itself curative. However, I do believe that without that sharing no work can be done. So I waited. I could feel the tension in the impasse.

Groaning and seeming to faint on the couch, Freda said, "I just want my stomach to feel better. I feel I'll throw up."

I said, "Your stomach is saying that you are ready to get rid of something that the rest of you is fighting to hold back."

Freda began to speak. "Well, maybe it's that I felt punished by Thomas for something I hadn't done. I couldn't've been that bad."

She would have continued, but there was a flurry of words from the rest of the family. They talked about Junie and the amount of fighting in the family since Thomas left for college. The parents' relationship was secure, but the family seemed to be falling apart. Everyone was wondering why Freda was always acting out of proportion and why Junie was suddenly getting such poor grades.

Drowning in the details of Junie's grades, I decided to interrupt. I said, "You are all willing to be distracted by talk about Junie who isn't even here to help, rather than address the main point, which is the point at which the family got stuck. How much support is there in the family for Freda to share the information that you need to work on things?"

Thomas said that he wanted to know. Ed wanted to know what she meant about being punished by something so trivial, but he then went on to give more details in defense of his decision to let Junie stay home.

I said, "The main point is that you, Freda, reacted in a way that you all agree was out of proportion to the annoying external situation with Thomas. But I suggest that it may not be out of proportion to whatever internal situation his angry words and violence triggered. If Thomas can see that he is not responsible for that, maybe he'll find it easier to take responsibility for what he did say and do, instead of blowing it off, because, although it was totally unacceptable, it wasn't as bad as you made it seem."

Thomas agreed, but then talked about how unfair it was.

Freda sat forward in the couch. Leaning toward him angrily, her body braced as if for action, she screamed at him, "Don't talk to me like that. You can't do this to me."

Ed intervened. "Don't scream any more," he said. "Why do that here?"

I said, "I'm glad you've let me in touch with the anger. I think that a whole lot more screaming will have to be done before you can understand the history that you are unknowingly trying to cope with here."

The time was up. They said that it had been helpful to meet and that they would be alright now until Dr. David Scharff got back, when they would talk more at the next scheduled family meeting. As they left, Freda said to me coquettishly, "I think I thank you."

The Phone Call from Freda

A few days later, Freda telephoned me. "I'm feeling better since the last meeting. You're good. You were well-primed. As you know, Dr. David Scharff's been at me to tell them because he thinks it's linked to Junie's falling grades."

"Not so," I said. "It was your husband who told me about your childhood physical and sexual abuse, and it fit so clearly with what happened, it was obvious to me."

"Well," she said, "What I'm saying is, we'd like another meeting with you. It's not an emergency except that Thomas has to go back to school before Dr. David Scharff gets back. May I ask you a tacky question? Will your husband mind?"

I wondered why the question should be viewed as tacky. I guessed that she was afraid of some sort of parental collusion or reprisal, but all I said was, "No. He'll be glad that you are going on with the work, and he'll pick up with you when he gets back."

Emergency Family Therapy: Second Session

Ed and Freda, Thomas and Junie were there. Freda looked much more competent, as she began the meeting in a matter-of fact tone.

"I asked for this meeting," Freda began, "because I wanted to explain what was getting triggered. When Thomas and his father were yelling and tussling, it recreated the scene of my parents fighting. They were both alcoholic, as you know, and had terrible tempers, and they both abused me badly, as you know. I always felt 'What did I do that was so bad that they'd beat the shit out of me?' So it wasn't bad to be mad at Thomas, was it?"

It was so confusing. I knew that the children could not yet understand. Freda seemed to be asking us if she had been as bad to him as her parents were to her, and excusing her anger on the grounds that unlike her, a good child, he had really done something bad to earn his parents' anger. At first, it seemed that the family understood, but the more they talked, the clearer it became that they hadn't got it. Junie said that her Mom had meant that it wasn't bad of Thomas to stay out all night, which wasn't fair because she gets hell for being 5 minutes late. Freda said that Junie had misunderstood. What she had meant was that she wondered if it was bad to be angry at Thomas, or indeed if it's all right to be angry at anything or anybody.

When Junie and Ed both said that there was something they weren't quite getting, I said that what Freda had said was clear as far as it went and that their "not getting it" was due to Freda not giving them the specifics that had triggered her reaction to Thomas's words.

"I don't know if I want to tell them," she said. "It won't help me. I have to work it out in therapy. The only bad thing I did was to let it out at home instead of in therapy."

My heart sank. We were not going to get anywhere.

However, to my surprise, she went on, without missing a beat, to ask, "Do you know what incest is?"

"Yeah," said Thomas, laughing. "Sex in the family."

"Well that happened in my family," said Freda bravely and calmly. She looked for their reaction. Thomas was laughing anxiously. Junie was shaking her head. There was a stunned silence.

I said, "It's shocking for you to hear this, because it's so different from what happens in your family. Do you feel ready to deal with it?"

Thomas said, "I don't believe it!"

Junie said, "Yeah, I do. Her brother is weird. I don't go near him. Was it him?"

Freda said, "No, it was my father. He forced me to have intercourse with him. I was only 8 years old. I'm telling you because I want Thomas to know why I couldn't deal with him getting that 15-year-old girl pregnant last year. Fifteen-year-olds aren't supposed to be sexually active, but her mother didn't care just like my mother didn't care and didn't ever do anything about it. Plus she drank, her parents are both alcoholic and neglectful. And I can't stand for Thomas to be around anyone who's drinking and who gets so changed by it as she did."

Thomas now looked grave. He made no more attempt to laugh things off. Junie wanted to know if it happened more than once.

"Oh yes," said Freda. "From when I was 8 years old to 14 years old, but I was away in boarding school that last year so it wasn't often then."

"Oh my God," said Junie. "When I was 8, I was in second grade. It's scary."

Thomas was now able to speak. He said, "I'm so glad you told us. I never imagined this, but now I know why you were so upset."

"Yes," Junie agreed. "You were like a child up against that door."

"I know," said Freda. "That's what was so bad. Even now I was so stupid, getting myself in a corner up against the door, so scared. And, of course, against the door I couldn't let myself out."

"She wasn't herself at all," Junie volunteered.

"So that's why you've seen Dr. Scharff all these years," Thomas said, comprehending the severity of her condition. "Time to let it out now, Mom," he added firmly and kindly.

"I figured that when your Mom was dying and you were so crazy, it was because you had your parents living with us and one of them was dying," said Junie. "That was enough to make anyone depressed, but there was a lot more to it than that." Like Thomas, she gave advice and encouragement and concluded, "You mustn't swallow it any more."

Ed spoke. "Now I see why it was so awful having them there. I knew about the abuse, but not all I heard today. It helps me make sense of how depressed you feel."

Freda protested, "I don't have a right to act like that. I don't want to."

"Of course not every day," Junie agreed.

"But if a picture comes in your mind," said Thomas, "you have to. Don't push it down."

"*You* do. You bottle everything up that you felt about Cindy and the abortion," Freda reminded him. "I've taught you well."

"No," said Ed. "You can't teach someone what he doesn't know you're doing."

"Oh yes you can!" Freda disagreed ruefully.

Freda was now well aware of how her attempts to hide her history had failed to protect her children from its consequences to her and now to them, even though they had not been abused. They had learnt a depressed and secretive way of dealing with pain. Not knowing had led Junie to not know her school subjects well. Losing her brother and his friends when he left for college had thrown her back on her parents, and especially on her depressed mother. Not knowing had led Thomas into a situation of early unprotected sex with a child of uncaring alcoholic parents, a girl with whose life of neglect Freda identified. As Thomas and Cindy each confided in her, Junie then felt caught between them and their sexual turmoil, just as the young Freda had been in the middle of her parents' strange relationship.

I said, "A child is scared and has no one to tell. What happened to stop it when you were 14? Did you find someone to tell then?"

"No," Freda replied. "I tried to kill myself and my father left me alone after that."

Together Junie and Thomas protested, "You never told us that either, Mom!" Thomas went on to say, "Don't ever let him trick you into believing it was your fault. That was his problem."

"Did you ever have problems with your grandparents?" Ed asked the children.

"No," they said. "Not that kind." Turning to me, Junie explained, "We didn't like them much. They were mean and selfish. Our grandfather still is. He's a lech."

Ed said, "Well if that's all, that's alright. A child can be so intimidated by parents, I guess that's why she didn't tell."

Freda said, "Who could I tell? My mother wouldn't listen, or she'd be so drunk that she'd give ten different answers and forget them all."

Thomas pursued the issue. "What did she say when you told her?"

Freda replied, "I didn't tell her. She knew."

"How?'" Junie asked.

"She was there," Freda said sorrowfully.

"Oh my God," said Junie. "You mean she watched?" She covered her head in her hands.

"Don't bug me with questions," said Freda.

"That's how I feel when you bug me about my grades," Junie shot back.

I commented that Junie had connected her need to know her mother's secret with her wish for privacy about her slipping grades. The family went off on a sprightly discussion about grades and how Thomas got great grades even though he never studied.

I said, "This reminds me that all this came to a head when Thomas was home from college. I wonder if it has anything to do with feelings about his leaving the family?"

Immediately Junie admitted, "I miss him. I lost him and all his friends that I hung out with when he left. I lost Cindy too. After they broke up, she didn't want to be my friend any more."

"I miss Thomas too," Freda said. "He's fun."

"Thanks, Mom," said Junie. "That makes me feel peachy."

"No, you're fun too," Freda clarified. "I don't know how to say this without hurting your feelings, but Thomas always got good grades. Junie's bright too, and she studies all the time, but somehow she's not getting the grades, and if she doesn't she won't get into a good college. Then she can just stay home another year."

The revelation was made, and the family work continued with Dr. David Scharff. In her individual therapy Freda struggled with feeling that she was bad. In family sessions, the family worked on their difficulties in dealing with anxiety about alcohol and sex. When they felt afraid of his growing up, they saw Thomas, their energetic and only mildly acting out boy, as a rapacious, potentially alcoholic sexual male for whom sexual knowledge had already proved destructive. As Junie grew up and no longer looked like the little sister that Thomas had always protected, the family was fearing for her victimization as a sexual young woman. She must be protected from a fate similar to what had happened to Thomas and Cindy and at a deeper level must not be exposed to sexuality at all because it had hurt her mother so much as a child. Adolescent sexuality was now at the leading edge of development, threatening the family's defenses and challenging all their resources.

In her individual work, Freda remained puzzled about whether her father was bad, still tending to prefer the idea that she was bad and that that was why the abuse occurred. Fairbairn (1952) noted this preference as a universal one among abused children, a technique for preservation of the self that he called the moral defense. If the self is bad, at least the object can be preserved as good. However, if the object is bad, the self has nothing and cannot imagine being valued at all. It is the difference, Fairbairn said, between being a sinner in a world ruled by God and a lost soul in a world ruled by Satan.

When Freda later received a hospital report that her niece had been sexually abused by her brother, she knew it must be true because she was completely clear that her brother would do such a thing. When her father called to talk to her about it, he asked her to reassure her brother that what he did was not a big deal. "I told him," Freda exclaimed, "'Well it was a big deal when you did it to me. It was traumatic.' And do you know what he said to me? He said, 'No it wasn't. I don't think so at all.'"

Freda got angrier and angrier at him. Her father slammed down the phone. Emboldened by her outrage against her brother, Freda was able to confront her father finally. He freely acknowledged what had happened, but she could not get him to admit that it was abuse. She could not understand why he had no conscience. She was determined that she would not let him off the hook. However, a moment later, she was again wondering if he had done something bad to her or if she was really bad. Her guilt led her to worry about damaging her children.

In subsequent family meetings, Freda became extremely fragile, self-blaming, and suicidal. However, with her family's support, she also joined in mourning the loss of Thomas' adolescent relationship with Cindy and discussing Junie's sexuality, even championing her need for birth control against Ed's objections. She modified her fears of alcoholism as a genetically transmitted disease that would be handed down to the children from their grandparents. Junie's grades recovered. Thomas got over his relationship with Cindy. Ed became more insightful and was able to tolerate feeling the full extent of his unhappiness over the loss of their apparently well-functioning latency-age family.

THE END PHASE OF TREATMENT

Family therapy ended, and Freda continued for another four years, in individual therapy that became more supportive and less investigative during this period. Both children had difficult and under-achieving freshman years in college, but pulled together for strong finishes with Freda and Ed's help. Freda was able to support Ed through a time of economic instability and job loss during the recession of the early 1990s. She continued to become sturdier as the therapy became less intensive and more supportive during an atten-uated termination. And then the death of her father from a heart attack removed a remaining threat and reminder of her pain.

Freda had protected herself by almost never seeing her father in the years after her mother died, but she continued to make occasional telephone calls and to see him on family occasions. When she talked to him, she felt herself to be uncomfortable, but hid this from him. Except for these times, she was considerably less in turmoil in the relationship with her father. She had successfully distanced herself from him emotionally by the time of his death. The circulation of fabulous eulogies about the accomplishments of his interesting career and his good deeds in community service released a tremendous invective against his hypocrisy. She had come to understand how destructive and perverse her parents had been, hated them fully for involving her in their perversion, and yet developed some empathy for them as adults who had themselves grown up in traumatic and neglectful circumstances and had not survived as well as she had. She also realized that her brother had become just like her parents in neglecting and molesting his own children and in leading a life of rampant and destructive sexuality. She was proud that she had not. Although she had to bear more depression than he seemed to, she had not been compelled to act as he did. She began to feel a considerable sense of accomplishment in the family she had held together with Ed and in the successful growth of her children. She could not become fully comfortable in receiving sexual pleasure from Ed, but she was able to maintain a sexual relationship with him and to enjoy a loving marriage overall.

Freda could at last consider terminating. Showing insight about her needs, and afraid of managing on her own, she requested a gradual weaning. We decreased the frequency of sessions to every other week for several months and then to once every six weeks. When she had to cancel what would be her final session because of snow, Freda felt confident in her independence from therapy and did not reschedule. However, she did delay making her final payment to me, as if to keep a hold on me. Because I did not doubt that she would pay me when she was ready, I did not keep her in mind in an anxious way, but I did recognize this unusual behavior on her part as a minor way of passing on the trauma. Eight months after her father's death, Freda stopped altogether with the knowledge that she could come back if ever she was in need.

Through the fifteen years in which we worked together, Freda struggled with the issues of the incest, her parents' alcoholism and negligence, and her own depression. Although there were periods in which she was freer to talk and felt inwardly better for having done so, there was never a time when it was easy for her, or when I could speak as freely as with some other patients. The recurrent experience of being haunted by the sexualized and negligent relationship with her parents persisted to the end of the therapy. Through it all, I wondered if I was doing her much good. Was she any better after almost fifteen years of work together? She still felt depressed much of the time and had to struggle to continue a sexual relationship with Ed. Although these doubts are part and parcel of a therapist's work, they resonate more with some patients than others. For me, they were more persistent with Freda than with anyone with whom I have worked. And yet, I believe that she felt our work was life-saving. It was certainly far more than supportive therapy. At times the uncovering of material was dramatic. However, neither of us ever had the sustained satisfaction of feeling that the work went well nor the confidence that healing could occur. Freda doubted that she could ever heal, and I finally do not believe she can ever heal completely, although I am inclined to see her recovery as a journey that will continue beyond therapy.

Those around her get some sense of what Freda deals with, but have no idea of how much she is able to keep inside herself without going crazy. I often wished that I could have had the satisfaction of seeing Freda's depression lift more reliably. I ask myself if de-repressing the memories brought her less suffering or more. I often wonder if the most I did for her was to help her contain her pain and go on living. It is only in reviewing the course of our work for this book that I can see the enormous distance she covered, the slow unfolding of deep understanding and reparation to her guilty child-hood self, the detoxification of the abusive transference, and the value of the fabric of a psychotherapy that was life-saving and life-giving.

The sheer unremorseful quality of the abusive parenting that Freda suffered from both parents was more extreme than that of anyone else I have treated. I learned more from Freda because she was dedicated to moving beyond the experience despite the pain in doing so. In staying the course, she taught me in depth about the cost of repeatedly dissociating her experience of the sexual assaults, the agony of trusting when no one can be trusted, and the strain of trying to construct an adult sexual relationship when her body had been so violated. She also showed me the joy of doing better for her husband and children than had been done for her. She taught me how a traumatized person survives to create a meaningful marriage and a loving family, even where there are few ideal moments and love is not easy.

13

Recall of Childhood

Sexual Trauma and

Object Relations Technique

Memories of abuse return in a variety of ways. They may occur as fantasies, flashbacks, associations to a transference experience, or reconstructions arrived at after an affective exchange with a spouse, child, or therapist. They may come crashing into focus, but more commonly they gradually appear out of the mists as the work of therapy peels away the layers of the fog of repression. They may take years to recover. In the following cases, a general memory becomes sexually explicit through the analysis of a dream, an inarticulate wife finds her voice when she resonates with the female therapist's experience of being inhibited by the husband's take-over style, and a woman's reaction to her child's diagnosis encourages her to tell her former therapist of adolescent sexual abuse of which she was always conscious, but which she had been too embarrassed to reveal to him when she was a young girl in treatment.

Yet the process of refinding a voice does not inevitably result in uncovering bonafide memories of actual abuse or incest. In the final example in this chapter, we detail the treatment process in a woman who had a similar evolution of memory recall in treatment, up to the point where the evidence of the treatment process pointed strongly to the fantasy nature of her trauma, set in place not by physical or sexual abuse, but by the traumatic loss to her family when her half-brother was killed during her childhood. The point we wish to make by juxtaposing these cases is that the treatment process, if not imposed upon from a prejudged position by the therapist, allows room for the unfolding of either picture and for their subsequent working through. In these days of debate about the frequency of child sexual abuse, on the one hand, and of the false recovery of memories of such events, on the other, it is important to remember that treatment is fundamentally about the discovery of truth in each patient's unique personal situation, and that we must allow time and space for this discovery to occur, with confidence that a nonjudgmental approach will, in most cases, get us where the patient needs to go.

IN INDIVIDUAL THERAPY, STAGES IN RECALLING THE MEMORY OF ABUSE

In the following case, a memory of abuse was couched in a more general memory of being held. It was expressed as a fantasy of anal penetration that was not, however, an actual memory, but a distortion of the actual memory. For some time it seemed as if the fantasy was a wish to eroticize the comfort offered by an uncle as a substitute for the longed-for father. The fantasy was experienced as shameful and sometimes led to phobic avoidance of sexual relatedness. Experiencing the fantasy in the transference was an important part of the work and led to a greater capacity for autonomy, but it did not lead directly to uncovering sexual abuse. That was arrived at after the analysis of physical symptoms and psychic silence led to a revealing dream.

Mrs. Brown, a married woman who works as a biology teacher, was left at home to care for the children when her husband was sent to Africa on another three-month field study in connection with his job at the World Bank. Now in the fourth year of analysis, she was more in touch with her feelings and found that she missed him much more intensely than before. She had analyzed her use of anal erotism to hold on to abandoning objects and had fully experienced this in the transference. She had been reliving her loneliness at the time her previously devoted father abandoned the family and disappeared when she was 10. Her mother was too shocked and deeply depressed to encourage her children to express their grief. The family got support from neighbors and the extended family, including Mrs. Brown's uncle, her mother's alcoholic brother. Mrs. Brown had remembered earlier her uncle comforting her in her bed and giving her money secretly, as if there was a deal between them about which she felt guilty. Since being without her husband, she relived her grief at losing her father and her fearful excitement about her uncle. She remembered her uncle lying behind her in her bed, just one time or possibly twice, holding her tightly, ostensibly to comfort her, breathing heavily, and pressing his body against her back. So far, she was sure of her memory. She also imagined him pressing his erect penis against her bottom, but she could not be sure that this actually happened. This image dominated her masturbation and haunted her sexual relationship with her husband, but she had not experienced that feeling of her uncle being near her in analysis and she still could not tell if she was dealing with a fantasy or a memory. Either way, the event with her uncle in childhood had left her with excited and guilty fantasies of anal penetration that she enacted in masturbation and avoided in sexual intercourse. She also thought that the event might be connected to her difficulties with asthma.

After four years of analysis, and separated geographically from her husband, Mrs. Brown had entered a resistant phase. She lapsed into silence and then missed some sessions because of asthma. She was worried that her chest infection was spreading. I said that I thought that she was afraid to continue to explore the subject of the childhood, that her silence was suggesting to me that she was afraid to tell, and that her body was giving me the idea that, if it was a memory, it might have spread to another time or place. I wondered if she was afraid to recognize the possibility that her memory of just once or twice might be encapsulating a longer-term involvement with her uncle. Mrs. Brown's voice was reduced to a mumble that I could hardly understand. Near the end of the session, I focused on her resistance as a defense against painful discovery. That night Mrs. Brown dreamed that she recovered an image along with a feeling so vivid that she was led to a sense of certainty that this was a memory.

Mrs. Brown began the next session in a more confident tone. "In the dream, my uncle was towering above me, kicking me in the back all over, acting crazy, like he used to act in rages when I was younger.

I thought he was going to kill me. Someone seemed to say, 'Well, you kicked him first.' It is so vivid. He's kicking me in the lower back with his foot with a hard shoe on. I'm thinking of my picture of him masturbating against my back. You know the fantasy."

Mrs. Brown fell silent, but was clearly working inside herself. She went on, as if with no break, to show that the dream was recreating the experience. "Actually it was a memory. I feel the jarring of it, jabbing into me."

I said, "The dream seems to say that you experienced an event with your uncle not as a sexual situation that arose to comfort you, but as a terrifyingly abusive, near-murderous attack."

Mrs. Brown burst into tears and cried for some minutes. When she was able to speak again, she told me that she was remembering her uncle hitting his wife, his daughter, and maybe herself. Her uncle was in such a rage, she feared for her safety and called her mother to come and pick her up.

She continued, "I'm so glad I'm away from him. I'm not thinking of being with him. I'm thinking about what I'd like to do to him. I just feel really angry. I'd like to have him in a vulnerable position and kick him like in my dream. I'd like to kill him. Part of me would. I'm ashamed of the relief I had with him—of taking money from him.

"The feeling in the dream is the feeling I have now—that I'm still vulnerable to that kind of attack. My husband's gone and I can't decide anything about the important things that happen. I do feel very protected around him."

I realized that she was afraid of being seduced by some stranger, but I thought that she was more afraid of being left alone with me. I said, "You're afraid that, without him to protect you, you'll experience me as a neglectful mother or an abusive uncle."

After this interpretation, Mrs. Brown retrieved more memory of the event with her uncle. She was talking about preferring to masturbate her anus because it was a much less anxiety-provoking space than her vagina, which seemed unending. One day she experienced much anxiety of a diffuse sort, accompanied by a vague memory or fantasy of a finger in her vagina. The anxiety became terrible, but she tried to keep talking.

I had a fantasy of my own: her words seemed to be disappearing on strands of smoke.

As she told me about the terrible anxiety, her language became diffuse as if trauma was spreading and invading her mind. She agreed with me that her thoughts were disintegrating and explained that the underlying anxiety was intense, because it seemed to her as if a finger was in her vagina right now and she was afraid that, because of that, I would not want to see her.

I said, "I think that you are afraid that the vividness of your experience will overwhelm me and excite me so that I will be associated with the finger and so become the same as the abuser."

She seemed relieved to hear me say this and cried quietly until the end of the session.

The next day, she returned to the topic. "The way I'm remembering now is not just remembering the things that happened, but the feeling too. I'm comforted by this. The two times this happened were both in bed. I might've been upset about what was happening. The first time was close to when my Dad left—that's what I think—in my room at night when I was crying. Yesterday in the night I was crying about my husband being gone and wishing I were being held. I started to remember what my uncle was doing to me while he was holding me. At least what he was doing behind me, pushing his penis against my bottom.

"But now I remember he was all around me, and I can feel it. There's nowhere he wasn't in or around. I feel yuk about that. It's a claustrophic feeling I can't shake off. That's how I feel when I can't breathe well. It's not something I notice until I'm winded and the breath won't come back. That's when I notice what's going on.

"Talking to you about it yesterday has made that part worse. I feel dirty and soiled. Like there is no part of me that's clean. The image of my uncle is his hands and where they were. It's extremely stimulating to me. I can almost . . . It's as if his hand is on me right now. I can't deny that I'd like that. It's very pleasurable. I am thinking about my husband: when any touching like that comes up between him and me, I don't like it. It's not associated with pleasure for me, because I start seeing him in a different way. Most of the time I see him as caring and supportive and not at all pushy. Sometimes when we are making love, I get really frightened—like when he starts talking to me about what he wants me to do or what he's feeling, or whatever, when he is aroused. It's the intensity of his arousal that frightens me because I feel he's going to take over. I've been masturbating constantly since the other night. When I have orgasm it's pleasurable because of the degree of my arousal due to some fantasy or memory—I don't know what. It doesn't matter what it is.

I feel really ashamed. But I feel less alone with this now than I've been feeling.

"I need to talk about something else. I don't understand what he was doing with me or why. I don't think my uncle did this to his daughter. I asked my cousin and my Mom too, and they both said 'No.' I think these events contributed to me feeling a certain way about myself, my body, my femininity, and certainly my sexuality. I've been going over and over the first time I had sex, which was the most humiliating experience and captures everything. It was awful. I had the feeling I was just no good, but I had felt that all through grade school. It didn't come from the episode with my uncle, but that intensified it.

"I'm talking now about masturbating all the time, but–I know for a fact that, as a child, I didn't. I completely cut off anything. I don't remember masturbating until after I began analysis. I just couldn't because I was afraid of all the fantasies–and I still am.

"I keep thinking, in that time, 'Where is my Mom?' I think my uncle was in bed with me in a house full of people. But maybe we were alone when my Mom was doing all the stuff with the agencies that tried to track him.

"That other time–my cousins shared a room but my aunt had them in bed with her and so I was in their room alone and so there was another bed vacant in that room. My uncle came home, but he got into bed with me. I remember him having his hands all over me.

Quietly and surely she continued, "And I remember now he put a finger in my vagina. I felt something like I never felt before. I think I had never done that to myself. I remember it hurting a little and being very big. And I don't understand why I let him do that. I feel both anxious and ashamed, and I don't know what you're going to think about me letting him do that to me. I don't think he would've forced me to. It's awful. I've buried a lot of the feelings, but the one feeling I can't block out is the physical feeling of arousal. Masturbating lets me get rid of that and maybe that lets me keep all the other feelings buried away. But I must've been so desperate. It's been two years since I've seen my uncle and I wish he would die. He goes over to my grandmother's all the time. She has a way of attracting troubled men, I guess.

"In a way I'm glad my husband and I are apart right now because I really don't want to be touched. But that's not true. I wanna be involved with you that way. With him it would be actual. With you it's not, yet I feel enveloped in all this. There's nowhere to go. It's all around and in me. It's very similar to the breathing thing. Sort of has a mind of its own. When I leave here, I'll need to masturbate, and after I've been masturbating, I'll be crying. I don't feel anywhere near that at the moment."

I said, "There's a split between how you feel today and how you felt yesterday. You also feel split between thinking about the pain so as to master it versus feeling the pain because you are worried about my reactions to your having the fantasy about me while I'm here."

"Yes, I feel so split," she replied. "I had the feeling even before I remembered the picture this time. That's how I knew it was a memory. I just knew. I have to get it out and feel it here with you when I am talking about it, so I can master it."

Mrs. Brown's work in therapy shows the slow, progressive uncovering of a traumatic memory, at first as a recollection of being comforted that was eroticized and distorted by her longing for her abandoning father, and persist as an incestuous, perverted fantasy. Defense analysis led to the de-repression of unconscious material in a dream that revealed the aggressive aspects of the fantasy that had been defended against by erotic aspects. Finally, interpretation of the fantasy operating in the transference led to the de-repression of the memory of childhood sexual abuse. By the time this happened, Mrs. Brown was able to tolerate admitting to her compliance with the abuse without turning the aggression against her observing self that could tell what was going on. It took longer until she was able to stop turning the aggression against her sexual self. After further working through, she remained sure of the memory, decided not to confront her uncle, stopped having the fantasy during sex, and was able to re-establish a satisfying sexual relationship with her husband shortly after his return.

REFINDING THE VOICE OF THE ABUSED
IN FAMILY THERAPY

In the next case, childhood sexual abuse had left its mark in the form of symptoms of poor self-esteem, illiteracy, depression, panic attacks, and wordlessness. Despite—or rather because of—the mother's great care to safeguard her daughters against repetition of abuse by a perpetrator, the next generation of girls showed sexual symptomatology in adolescence. The eldest daughter precociously sought a sexual relationship that unfortunately led to pregnancy and the physical and psychological trauma of a late miscarriage, after which the young girl felt too ashamed to attend school. The middle daughter was sexually, socially, and academically phobic. Only the youngest daughter, who was still in latency, was free of symptoms.

Wendy Sheldon and her 40-year-old husband Will (also described more fully in J. Scharff 1992) were about to retire from the military after 20 years of service and had hoped to realize a lifelong dream by spending a year sailing with their family round the coast of the United States to celebrate their retirement and the twentieth anniversary of their marriage. Their 8-year-old daughter Sandra was functioning well, and their 19-year-old daughter Bobbie was newly happily married. However, the Sheldons were concerned about their 14-year-old daughter Wilma's school and social phobia and about Mrs. Sheldon's low self-esteem, depression, and fears about the future in view of Mr. Sheldon's medical condition. Two years earlier, Will Sheldon had been diagnosed as suffering from scleroderma, a chronic connective tissue disease that had already compromised his muscle strength, even to the extent of compromising his ability to breathe deeply. The worst thing to bear was that the prognosis was uncertain. The disease might stabilize, go into remission, proceed slowly, or accelerate rapidly to cause his death within five years.

The Sheldons' marriage had been founded on a projective identificatory system in which Will took care of everything while Wendy was an adoring, grateful, helpless partner. He supported the family financially, fixed things around the house, dealt with the children's emotions, arranged the family's camping vacations, and dealt with all the paperwork and any communications with the outside world. In his own words, he was the "commander of the family unit." Wendy, for her part, stayed home, managed the household, cleaned and cooked, pursued her hobby of painting seascapes from memories of their boating trips, fixed Will's lunch and ate it with him, and was always there to take care of him and their three girls. Many military families might have made a similar division of duties between the military male and the military-dependent wife. Yet, as each girl approached sexual and cognitive maturation in adolescence, their problems raised further doubts about their mother's competence. Bobbie, the eldest, as a 16-year old had catapulted herself into premature sexual activity that led to enormous distress when she hid her resulting pregnancy until it was lost in a massive vaginal hemorrhage due to an ovarian cyst, at which point her boyfriend abandoned her. The whole family had been traumatized by her sexual irresponsibility, her secrecy about her pregnancy, and her loss, but they thought that they had put that behind them and were pleased about her new marriage. The middle daughter Wilma could not maintain her strength in school functioning, the area of her mother's weakness, and had become aversive to sexual and social interaction in anticipation of teenage sexual activity. Only the latency-age child was doing fine, probably because she was not yet required to face sexual issues at her age.

The family symptomatology suggested an unresolved conflict in the couple's view of sexuality, having to do with an assumption that sexual knowledge should be avoided or would be traumatic. Because the Sheldons presented as a couple with a satisfying intimate life, the source of the family difficulty with sexual issues was puzzling. All that I could be sure of was that the marital projective identificatory system had been challenged by the onset of serious illness in Mr. Sheldon, the overfunctioning partner, and that the family system had broken down under the strain of the couple's inability to reach a new adaptation to his illness, presumably because of unresolved issues that had attracted them to each other in their adolescence. As therapy progressed, I would learn how these issues that each spouse brought to the marriage had been accommodated by the couple's original projective identificatory system.

In the opening phase of family therapy, Will did all the talking, as he did in life generally. I could only surmise what Mrs. Sheldon was going through from her silent nods, slight sighs, and misted eyes.

In my countertransference to the couple, I felt compassionate toward Mr. Sheldon, a competent, physical man robbed of his powers and still under strain. At the same time I felt totally squashed by his manic and counterphobic defenses. How would I ever express my own competence to help him and his family? From Mrs. Sheldon I felt an unspoken appeal across a helpless, wordless void in relation to him. I tried to relate to her wordlessness silently so as to make space for her thoughts in my mind and in the flow of the conversation in the session.

I found that Mrs. Sheldon could signal her upset to me, but then had to suppress it before her tears actually came. She could hardly find the words to tell me about herself. I learned gradually that she felt helpless, frightened, and unable to cope in the face of Mr. Sheldon's illness. She was miserable that his hands, once so competent and so sure in their intimate life, were now like stones. She had been overeating because of her anxiety and despair, and felt even worse now that she had become shapeless and ugly. By the fifth session, Will trusted me sufficiently to follow my lead in waiting for Wendy to find her voice.

The family came to the fifth session with the two older girls, Wilma and Bobbie, but without the 8-year-old Sandra, who had been allowed to attend her school balloon launch. With a small intervention from me, Will kept quiet for the first time. Wendy began tentatively, "I'll talk about Will and I'll start crying, but basically I don't know what I'm thinking. Just the word 'Will' sets off something. It's got to be deep! I don't know what I'm thinking and what's upsetting me. I guess it's just everything. When you say his name, it triggers everything you ever think about and worry about."

Wendy went on to explain that she did not expect Will to die, but that she was worried about his becoming unable to do what he had done before. "He might get pretty dependent on us," she continued. "But that's not how we've seen him. We've always seen him as taking care of us. And it scares us to think that we might have to take care of him. We already have to do a lot that he used to do."

The most important thing that Will used to do was to think for the others in his family. It was painfully obvious that, when Will was kept quiet, they found it unfamiliar and hard to find words for themselves. Their inhibition was pleading for Will to rescue them.

Bobbie and Wilma were anxious, but listening quietly. I could feel Will next to me itching to protest, to speak for Wendy, to make everything alright. I was determined to protect the space so that Wendy could find her voice. I did not want to be foiled by Will. How was I going to deal with his anxiety and still keep him quiet?

Responding to my own feelings and observations, I said, "You are struggling to find your own words because you are people for whom Will has usually spoken—and he's ready to start any minute now. If I don't keep talking he'll be in there!"

"He's ready to burst," Wendy agreed. Responding to my countertransference comment, she found her voice and continued, "I go to do something, and you can feel him ready to take over. I think a lot about things that have happened and why. Maybe if Will had married someone different than I, he might not be so dominant. But he's got a big responsibility with me because—. I wanted to say this, but I've been putting it off. I don't think I can say it," she sobbed.

"We'll wait 'til you are ready," I said, mainly to keep Will from filling in the space. He was able to follow my cue.

After minutes of tense, pregnant silence, Wendy pushed herself forward through her tears, gaining in confidence as she continued, "I think a lot of the problems I've had with Will being sick stem from my past. I don't feel special. Oh, Will has made me feel special, but . . ." Suddenly she blurted it out, "I was sexually abused by my grandfather for two years when I was about 8 years old. I was in second grade and I had emotional problems. I didn't learn well. So when I met Will, I had never told anyone. I told him two days before the wedding, and I really thought he wouldn't want to marry me. But he did. So, after that, he just basically ran things, and I let him, because he'd make everything better and I felt safe. Because of that, I don't feel I'm good enough so I let him have everything his way to make up. Now that he's sick, I have to change things."

As the family talked with Wendy about their history, 19-year-old Bobbie described how cunningly the whole family worked together to prevent outsiders from knowing that their mother could not read. Wendy admitted her shame that she had never learned to read or write. She was proud that all of her children were competent in school work and was upset that her brightest child was now school phobic.

Will brought the conversation back to the subject of abuse. He said that Wendy had just found out that her grandfather had tried the same thing with her sister.

"Yes," Wendy confirmed. "But she told Mom, and then we moved anyway. But I didn't tell anyone. For years, I've wondered why I didn't. It would kill me if Mom ever found out. Still I want her to know. I'd want her to give me all the love and comfort she never gave me."

Wendy's revelation provided information necessary for understanding her contribution to the couple's system of projective and introjective identifications and the resulting family dynamics. In her man, she looked for and admired academic success since this was a part of herself that was lacking. He gave her structure that she had not had from her parents. She was wonderfully protected, cared for, and loved as someone special in a way that she had not known as a child. At the same time, she remained in a helpless state in which a powerful man had control over her life and inhibited her achievements by his existence. Now that Will had a disease that diminished his capacity to protect her, Wendy's anxieties had resurfaced.

Wendy had taken the opportunity of Sandra's absence to make

her revelation, because she thought that the information could harm her, if she heard it. She had told the older girls already, but there had been no discussion of what actually happened, and they assumed that it was not much.

In the next session, Sandra said that she did not have to know what had been said when she was away. "It's okay," she kept reassuring them. "I don't have to know." With further work, when the Sheldons were gradually able to understand that keeping secrets inhibited learning and personal growth for all of them, they dared to tell Sandra and talk more openly. Wendy and the girls began to look and sound more competent, and Will was able to be less controlling.

Months later, Wendy was able to talk about the incest experience with her grandfather with all the children present. It had gone on when she stayed over at her grandparents' house during the weekends and summers.

"Was it like he was just touching you?" Wilma ventured to ask. "Or did he, did he, you know . . . ," she trailed off.

"No," said Will clearly. "He raped her and she was only Sandra's age."

With the usual downplaying of abuse that falls short of penetration, Wendy said, "Usually it was just him making me sit on his lap and him touching me. He didn't do anything, except twice, and he did that when we were leaving. That really hurt. He closed the door and came over to my bed. It was frightening. That's why if we are going to have sex or something, and Will goes to close the door, I can't let him do it. Because that's what my grandfather did. He closed the door and came over and forced himself on me. And that's where I get my phobias of not being able to breathe from. So now when I look over at Will and see him struggling to breathe because of his disease, I see him getting old and I see him trapped the same way I used to feel. And it just keeps it going."

In adulthood, Wendy's development was compromised by the residuals of her incest history. Her sexual relationship with her husband was restricted by lack of privacy because she could not tolerate a closed bedroom door. Her self-esteem was so poor, she could not admit to her illiteracy and learn to read as an adult. She believed that she was unemployable. She could not earn money from her remaining talent, because she could not believe that her admiring friends and neighbors really wanted to buy her paintings, no matter how often they admired them. She remained dependent on her husband, who for his own reasons enjoyed total control until his illness forced him to experience the dreaded helplessness that he had been projecting into her. Wendy was able to avoid a repetition of the abuse cycle by marrying a well-functioning man with good values and by restricting his contact with his daughters so that he was never left alone with them. Her need to control their environment constrained her husband's adult development as a father who might well have been trusted to contain his feelings for his daughters. He, for his part, must have been sufficiently afraid of his own sexual impulses that he agreed to this level of restraint. Constantly on the lookout, unlike her own mother and grandmother, Wendy ensured that her daughters did not suffer as she had. Nevertheless, in her efforts to avoid repetition of abuse, Wendy conveyed her fear of strangers, of men, and of sexuality to her daughters: Wilma reacted phobically in identification with Wendy, Bobbi counterphobically in identification with Will, whereas Sandra in seeking not to know of matters beyond her years was identified unconsciously with her mother.

Mrs. Sheldon would never have considered individual psychotherapy or psychoanalysis as a treatment method. She felt too insecure to seek couple therapy or group therapy with other incest survivors. She could tolerate treatment only in the supportive atmosphere of family therapy. Psychoanalytic concepts regarding the defensive aspects of the couple's projective identificatory system and the expression of trauma in the next generation were, however, helpful when presented in an interactive family group format. After twenty family therapy sessions, the family retired from the military, ended therapy, and moved away. Two years later, I heard that Mrs. Sheldon had been able to enter group therapy and that she and her husband had opened a business to sell her artwork. In other words, sharing the trauma and working on it in the family group led Mrs. Sheldon to an improved ability to differentiate herself from her husband and children, to recognize her needs and meet them, to accept support outside the family, and to feel a measure of self-esteem.

REVELATION OF CHILDHOOD SEXUAL ABUSE IN A 25-YEAR FOLLOW-UP INTERVIEW

Judy Green, a borderline adolescent, was the first patient assigned to me (DES) as a psychiatric resident in the 1960s. Her family was

among the first I saw in family therapy, and she was the subject of my
first publication (D. Scharff 1969) and of several subsequent writings
on family therapy and dreams (D. Scharff 1982, 1992, Scharff and
Scharff 1987). I am still learning from her.

In 1993, twenty-six years later, she called me to say that I was
the only therapist whom she trusted, and therefore she wanted my
opinion about what therapy she should undertake for a new problem
that had arisen. She now had a 7-year-old son who had developed
symptoms that had required psychiatric evaluation and warranted a
diagnosis that she found upsetting. Guiltily searching for causes for
his condition, she began to have recurring visions of her own
childhood, in particular of sexual incidents that occurred when she
was about his age. She wanted to know if she had told me about all
of them. Indeed, she had not. What she eventually told me altered
my previously published understanding of her in a way that is
pertinent to this book on trauma.

Judy was 14 when she was transferred to the teaching hospital
where I was in training. Her initial, emergency hospitalization two
months earlier followed the ingestion of 100 aspirin. The story she
and her family told then was of her being wildly out of control. She
had had incest with her brother on several occasions and had sex with
several boys in the period preceding her suicide attempt. I thought I
had heard everything about her sexual history. In the hospital, she
acted out provocatively and hallucinated in a manner that caused the
staff to doubt its authenticity. When I asked the hospital superinten-
dent's opinion about giving her electroconvulsive therapy (ECT), this
well-known psychiatrist replied that it would only make sense if the
electrodes were applied to her rear end. Everyone was angry at her.
After about 4 months, she got herself thrown out of the hospital for
provocative behavior—despite my wish to keep her there. She was
transferred to a large state hospital that offered mostly custodial care.
Being in that environment was quite a confrontation to Judy. She
promptly pulled herself together, returned to therapy with me, and
went back to school. During my third year of residency, I also saw her
family, after her younger brother was referred for depression and
failing school performance. The individual and family therapies both
ended when I left the following year. Judy was almost 18.

I heard from Judy again sixteen years later, when she was 34.
She had had a rough young adulthood. She had graduated from a

first-rate women's college, but then foundered academically and ended up in an alternative religious community under the domination of a charismatic, abusive cult leader, an experience not uncommon in the 1970s. With great difficulty, she had wrested herself from his domination and reported him to the larger community, as a result of which he had been investigated and censured. She had then met and married a rather straight and unassuming man and gone into business with him. Their business was a modest success, but she felt she had to keep propping him up. In this way he was too like her own unsuccessful stepfather. She still went by the religious community name she had adopted, had no children, and was not sure that she would ever have any. She did not want anything particular from me, just to let me know she was alive and doing fairly well. She also gave me follow-up information on her family members, knowing that I would be interested to hear about them. Her mother, who was depressed then, had not been able to make much of her life, but had carried on without collapse in a survivable but not good marriage. Her older brother was doing well in business, her younger brothers and sister had done quite well as professionals, and all of them had married. The youngest boy who had drawn particularly interesting pictures in the family therapy had gone into a field of applied art.

What Judy told me seemed to confirm what I had understood about her and her family while I had known them. The children had considerably more positive energy than the parents, and although Judy had done well to stay alive and be in a relationship, I was not surprised to conclude that she would have done better with more therapy than I was able to offer.

Then in 1993, Judy had something different to tell me. She was calling because, after her 7-year-old son was diagnosed as having attention deficit disorder, she was overcome with the feeling that she had damaged him and that the damage came from not being able to protect him from the effects of what had happened to her at the same age. Judy suspected that she had not told me everything, and she needed to complete the picture of her that I held before now going on to work on herself in therapy.

"Did I ever tell you," she asked on the telephone, "about what my older brother made me do sexually with his friends? It seems to me that I've never told anyone, but I just wanted to check with you to see if I told you at the time or whether I kept it from you too."

"I knew you slept with your brother when you were about 9 or

10, and that you had intercourse with several boys shortly before you were hospitalized," I said. "That's all I know, and we never did talk much about that. It seemed too close in for you to discuss."

"That's not really it," she said. "There was something else that I felt much worse about, and no one knows about it except my older brother. I wouldn't even be surprised if he's shut it out of his memory. That's all I can say, now. I want to talk to you in person."

She said that she would like to travel from where she now lived to see me at my office, because talking seemed safer out of town and with someone who had known her as an adolescent. We arranged to meet to review her situation and think together about what would make sense for her at this point in her life. When she met me at my office, Judy, now a mature woman and mother, could speak quite openly about this troublesome aspect of her sexual history.

"When I was little—7, 8, 9—he taught me to perform sexually for his friends, the boys who lived in a new neighborhood we moved to. All sorts of things short of intercourse. He would say to me that it would help him have friends, and I did it for him willingly. It would make me feel nauseated, but I wanted to do it for him. He was the only person I really felt cared for me. In a way, I still think it's true—that he was the only one who cared, even though what he did was awful. Our parents really did neglect us—all of us."

Additional things she told me that day changed my view of her early history and consequently of the burden she and her family had carried when I had known them. Judy now told me for the first time that her stepfather, whom her mother had married after Judy's father died when she was 5, had been physically abusive to her mother early in the marriage, and occasionally afterward. Although he had generally stopped beating his wife by the time Judy was in treatment with me, on one occasion during that time, he had slapped her so hard that she had bruises that no one mentioned to me. I knew that the parents had been generally depressed and neglectful, but now I learned from Judy that the two of them had been so thoroughly depressed and preoccupied that their general neglect of the children—which had fostered Judy and her brother's sexual behavior—had been far more profound and especially longer lasting than we in the treatment team had understood at the time.

Judy told me that she and her younger siblings had continued to do fairly well. They all received some therapy for the effects of the experiences they had shared. However, her older brother, she told me, had failed in business and in his marriage. Judy described how alcohol had destroyed some of his memory, and she guessed that he had psychologically blotted out the rest of it because he too could not stand to think about what had happened with Judy when he was a child. Her stepfather had a career only modestly successful at best, but he managed to botch it in later years, and his stubborn wasting behavior meant that he came to retirement without a pension. Her mother stayed depressed during most of her adulthood, and maintained a shifting interest in several fields without success in any of them.

Based on the original individual and family therapies and on Judy's follow-up phone call in 1982, I had written about a dream introduced by Judy's mother into a family therapy session in 1970, the dream of "Andy, the purple lion" (D. Scharff 1987, 1992). Mrs. Green dreamt that a purple lion seemed to threaten her middle son who was an infant in the dream, and that she was in a dilemma about whether the lion was friendly or dangerous. The family then worked on the dream, realizing that the lion represented the stepfather within the family, and me in the transference.

What I did not appreciate, until I heard what Judy had to tell me twenty-three years later, was the dream's encapsulation of the actual threat of violence still occurring within the family. Surely, I would have understood this aspect of the dream and would have worked differently if I had understood the extent of the violence current at that time.

In a similar way, I could neither understand nor work with Judy's shame and degradation concerning the sexual acts that were the source of her deepest humiliation, because I did not have access to the full extent of her brother's abusive practices and her parents' neglect. Her willing acquiescence shows the depth of her gratitude for the awful attention shown by her brother, and attests to the strength of her attachment to the bad object for psychic survival. A bad object is generally preferable to no object at all. I did not know enough then to ask extensively about histories of sexual abuse, nor to suspect it on the basis of the borderline and dissociative behavior Judy displayed. She showed mildly dissociative behavior, disorders of memory, and a sexualization of her development with incestuous and peer acting out. It was not until Judy specifically told me about her childhood sexual favors that I saw her symptoms as clues to earlier trauma history. Even though we were already studying and writing about the trauma of sexual abuse, and even though I have often thought back over my work with Judy, it had not occurred to me to rethink Judy's case as one of childhood trauma.

Judy and I agreed that her own potential had not been fully tapped and that she had managed to be self-defeating in subtle but sure ways. For instance, the blind obedience to her brother in childhood had been followed by the blind obedience to her religious master who did not encourage her growth. Fortunately, she had chosen a nonabusive husband, although she thought he was not often fully effective. For instance, like her stepfather, he had never earned a very adequate living, although unlike the stepfather, he loved what he did professionally. I was glad that Judy's ambition and grit had remained and had driven her impressively toward a vision of what she could be. I thought that she was ready to maximize her growth and I recommended for her a low-fee analysis, because she was capable of making and benefiting from such a commitment to intensive long-term work and because psychoanalysis as a field is more ready now to deal with the sequelae of actual childhood sexual abuse.

WHEN ONE ACTUAL TRAUMA REAPPEARS AS A FANTASY OF SEXUAL ABUSE AND FURTHER WORK DOES NOT UNCOVER A MEMORY

Mrs. A., an overweight, divorced woman in her forties, was unable to stay married, to love intimately, or to work independently. She tried to eat diet food at carefully scheduled, social mealtimes, but frequent grazing when alone made weight control impossible. Overweight and breathless, she did not have the energy to do her work as a retail manager, to keep her house, or to bother with having sex. Her marriage ended. Mrs. A. noted the extreme discomfort she felt if anyone saw her eating, especially chewing and biting. These eating problems dated from the shock that she suffered at age 5 when her young adult half-brother from her mother's first marriage was unexpectedly shot to death in a drug-related killing. After this, her mother and stepfather were preoccupied with his memory and too depressed to pay attention to her. She turned to food for comfort. Unconsciously she was driven by the fantasy of eating her brother to keep him alive and to replace him in her parents' love so that they would stop grieving for him.

Mrs. A. had been spinning her wheels in analysis. In one session, she reprimanded herself for wasting her time and having nothing worth saying. Ten minutes from the end of that session, she launched into telling me a long and involved dream.

"I've been delaying mentioning this dream because it was confusing. In this dream, I'm watching a mini-series on TV. Then I sort of transport myself into it, so I'm not watching it, I'm living it. Only I don't have a specific part. The movie is about a family—a father and mother and three sisters and two brothers.

"It was very confusing, because, from time to time, I'd become one of the other sisters—the second or the third one. The mother was not in it much, and the father was a background figure. The movie was about a woman. A strange, attractive, dangerous man came into the household in the guise of being friendly and useful, like a workman, a lawnman, or a brother's friend. It's unclear which he was. He terrorized them, scared them, threatened them. It was not clear what he wanted from all of them, but he definitely wanted intercourse with the oldest girl. The oldest girl always said 'No.' He tried to pressure her, and she left the household thinking he would leave, but he didn't. She was not yet free, but would come back. I didn't understand that.

"Then there was the younger girl he did sleep with. She was 13 or 14, developed but young. Then there was me, the middle sister, and I was not attractive to him. The younger sister wanted to possess his attention and got jealous if he gave it to others. She didn't know sex with him was not a good idea. The father would protest a little but did nothing. The mother was scared that the man would kill one of her boys, but she backed away from her daughter because the man was sleeping with her. The parents weren't in it much at all. Why didn't the father call the police? Why did the situation stay as it was for some time? And he was handsome and very sexual.

"He had managed to dig a hole below the house. It was to be a containment room that was sealed off. Everyone was afraid to say anything because they'd be put down there. Then two things happened:

"Number 1). The older brother came home. He was physical and powerful. All of them were looking forward to him saving them, but he was just another bully. He didn't want to hear anything about the sex or the threats. He was just one more person to be afraid of.

"Number 2). The eldest daughter came back home. She was very pretty. She'd been chosen as a spokesmodel and she was famous now. Nothing was gonna stop this guy from forcing her to have sex with him. I just floated around having interactions. I was attracted to the man but he wasn't to me 'cause I'm too fat. But I wanted to save the family. So I thought, 'If I create a big scene I'll be able to stop this from happening. I thought if I incited his rage, he'd hurt me and that'd draw his rage away from her.'"

I noted that Mrs. A. had waited until near the end of the session before dealing with her dream. Now that the time was up, we could not do justice to the complexity of the dream in this session. Without knowing her associations, I could not know what it meant, but I noted that it seemed to refer to sibling incest and parental neglect. On the other hand, the dream was also fanciful and elaborate, suggesting an oedipal fantasy, rather than an actual memory, which would probably not reveal itself in such a complete and transparent way.

The next day she started in on the dream immediately. "You should know the ending. I was the middle sister, and I had to stop that guy from forcing sex on the older sister. I didn't know how I'd do it, but I had to get attention somehow. I knew if I teased the brother, he'd become violent. I poked him in the ribs and he hit me and threw me across and up onto the roof of a car. I fell off onto the ground and my arms broke. This is all very painful and scary. He comes over and he asks if I'm all right, but he's still menacing. I say, 'You've gotta listen to me. The guy in the house is bad. He's having sex with the younger sister and going to get the older sister.' The odd thing is he was on my chest and I couldn't breathe. So I couldn't get enough breath to tell him. When he finally heard me, he increased his weight so I couldn't say it, 'cause he didn't wanna hear it. Without a word, he seemed to be saying, 'This is a family secret we don't want anyone else to know, and he's OK.' With his weight on me, I passed out and woke up in a hospital.

"Then it moved to when I came back home. The little sister looked at me with contempt and said, 'Do you really think your doing that would stop anything?'

"You probably wanna hear what I think. I don't like this at all, but there are actually—I know you're gonna say this is it—some resemblances to my family. The two brothers are my brother, in his friendly mood and in his brutal mood. So that'd mean that the strange guy was Ronald, my dead half-brother.

"Now the sisters are all me. The older girl leaves home, does well, and refuses to have sex like I did in my marriage. There's the pouty young one who really wants to have sex and just does it with him because he's the only one paying attention to her. She feels important because she's his mistress. I'm also the middle sister who sometimes exists and sometimes doesn't. One has sex with him and is controlled by him. The other wants to leave. The father is ineffectual. The mother is worried but ineffectual.

"The part beneath the house is a tomb. If I fail to win this fight with myself, all the girls in me will go to that tomb to die. Now, why would I go to Carl to get beaten up? So the older girl can escape. As for the rest of it. . . . There's a definite pull toward the man who stands for my dead brother. I know it's wrong to be sick and live under the control of my need to be him. Yet, there's an attraction about it. As a younger child, I'm under his sway. Now as an older child, I try to deny it and defuse it.

"At first, when I woke up, I thought this dream doesn't make any sense at all, but after a bit things are coalescing."

I commented, "Until now it has seemed that the beating your body takes from your difficulties with overeating happens to prevent you being successful. Here it's to free the older girl and let her be successful." By the word 'here' I had meant 'here in the dream' but Mrs. A. thought that I was referring to 'here in the analysis.'

She corrected me, "But in the dream the reason was to get the attention to tell the secret story of the male living in my house. The Ronald figure would be inside me, threatening me—sexually, too, which I don't understand. Intercourse is a pain, so I don't do it. That's how I've always thought about it. I'm loathe to connect it to a dead brother. So I'd rather think that was just another issue in the dream and not connected with Ronald because I don't understand that."

I asked myself, What was the dream communicating? Had there been sexual abuse by the late brother, or was this dream a 6-year-old's version of sex encapsulated and frozen by the impact of the trauma of Ronald's death by violence? Mrs. A. had no memory of sexual abuse or even of sexual fantasies about him, although she did remember sexual curiosity about her brother Carl. She thought that Ronald had been too much older and too far away in college for her to have had much to do with him. On balance, I thought that she was defending against connecting her fear of sexual rejection to her attraction to her late brother, probably as an object onto whom to displace oedipal feelings for her father who was a retiring, undemonstrative man.

It is important to keep in mind the possibility of sexual abuse without introducing it as a premature explanation that limits exploration. Such an explanation can close the transitional space of the therapy as surely as actual incest closes the potential space for the developing personality. On the other hand, the therapist should not deny the possibility of actual memory rather than fantasy, but should hold it in the mind until the patient expresses it in the transference and arrives at conviction or acceptance of uncertainty.

In her next session Mrs. A. brought a transference dream that had upset her terribly.

"In my dream, you were enjoying a social hour with another patient during my time. I knew it wasn't right and I was angry. You said that I could come for a social hour too. I said, 'You shouldn't be asking me to do this.' And you said, 'I know it's inconvenient to have to wait for your session, so you can stay at my house.' (like that made it better). I said, 'No, no!' and you said, 'But you can have the room right below mine' (as if that made it more attractive an offer). I woke up like I'd been in a horror movie. Nothing physical and horrible happened, but it was a nightmare."

Here the abuse was being experienced in the transference with me as an inappropriate, unremorseful seductress. Then she linked the theme of exclusion from the pair to her oedipal conflict.

"I dressed up last night to join Mom and Dad at the club they stay at when they are in town. Mom went to the ladies' room, and Dad complimented me about the way I looked. I liked it, but I felt uncomfortable and worried that Mom would be mad at me.

"And I'm much more easily startled these days. I'm more aware of tiny stimuli. Anything that drops, or a door shutting, or—like today—the person coming out of the room startles me more than it used to."

Still wondering about sexual trauma, I asked, "Are you on the lookout for something that will follow a noise, because in the past something that frightened you did follow the noise of something dropping?"

"Oh, yes," she concurred. "A perfect example. Remember the night I kept hearing noises under my bed? I got so tense I started hearing them all the time. But the thought of a memory and a noise doesn't trigger anything for me. It's just that I'm edgy."

What Mrs. A. was edgy about was her fantasy about her parents' intimate relationship and her wish to join them or split them up.

This session rounds out a sequence of recall that, in other patients, might have seemed to confirm an experience of actual sexual abuse. Unlike the unfolding memories of actual abuse in the cases of Mrs. Brown and Wendy Sheldon in this chapter, or of Freda in Chapter 12, Mrs. A.'s dream "memory" of an incestuous event does not lead to the uncovering of an actual memory of such events, even though it seems to be about to. Instead it leads to an elaboration of the incestuous fantasies in her memory of childhood, in her current life more than thirty years after the developmental period of traumatic loss when freezing of the internal situation occurred, and in the here-and-now of the transference.

It is these oedipal losses that the 5- and 6-year-old Mrs. A. was suffering from in a current of family-wide depression when her young adult brother was killed. We later came to see how that loss cemented her guilt about wishing for him as an incestuous object as a substitute for her distant, unavailable, and depressed father. The reaction formation to her guilt had kept her frozen in a position of denying her sexual wishes beginning in her adolescence, when obesity first compromised her attractiveness and mobility, and lasting through the twenty-five years since adolescence, essentially unchanged. Despite the passage of so much time, her inner world had remained unchanged because it was frozen in the closed inner system of the traumatic constellation.

The central point to make in the context of this chapter is that Mrs. A.'s experience was *not* that of actual incest or sexual trauma. Rather, it was one of internal developmental loss made traumatic by family depression and her early experience of the death of a young adult sibling. And for her that reality, partly internal and partly external, was as traumatic as the actual traumas were for other patients. Analytic work led to a gradual exposure of the internal situation with its ramifications in the transference and within both patient and analyst, all without imposing a preformed judgment about whether sexual abuse or incest had occurred. Her narrative had a naturally unfolding contour that looked initially similar to those of actual abuse, but was ultimately quite different, had a different "feel," and received a different kind of corroboration in the current external world.

When patients who come to believe that there was no actual incest or abuse look at their extended family, they can usually see patterns of relatedness that reflect depression and impoverishment, but no signs of currently abusive relationships. Unlike Mrs. A., when such patients as Judy Green, Mrs. Brown, and Wendy Sheldon in this chapter, or Freda in Chapter 12, look at their families, providing their parents or siblings are still alive, they usually see behavior currently that, at a common-sense level, fits with the memories they have recovered. They may find continuing or at least acknowledged alcoholism, rampant sexual invasiveness of the kind Freda's father showed until his death, disavowal of responsibility and lack of remorse, or sometimes, acknowledgement and requests for forgiveness.

  Sometimes the picture is not clear for a long time. In some cases, it never becomes clear. However, in the majority of cases, the therapist's open-minded, supportive attitude during extended inquiry will allow patients to find their own way toward understanding the loss and trauma that have marked their development without imposing a pre-existing theory or judgment on either side of the question: "Was there actual abuse, or was it fantasy elaboration of inner pain?"

14

Trauma in Termination

Treating the traumatized patient can be quite a challenge to the narcissism of the analytic therapist. It requires us to adapt our analytic ways that were tried and tested with neurotic patients so that we have a methodology with which to respond therapeutically to the process that is unique to the trauma situation. Once we are willing to do that, we can learn the importance of going-on-being. We can find gratification in our ability to follow and to be there without turning every experience into words. We can learn to titrate our interpretive interventions to suit the patient's ego state or states.

Sometimes we do not get it right. If we do not have a theory to understand the therapist's experience of the trauma, we may feel traumatized by the patient, we may be traumatized by colleagues who do not understand either, or we may pass the trauma back to the patient. Lack of understanding of trauma leads to a less-than-optimal outcome for the patient and for the therapist.

PASSING THE TRAUMA BACK TO THE PATIENT

Fifteen years ago, before we were studying trauma, a young man, Herb, sought individual therapy for depression and difficulty maintaining intimate relationships. Herb was an artist, the son of two survivors of the Holocaust who had created a financially secure middle-class life in the United States. He had not been traumatized, but he was preoccupied with his parents' trauma. He recalled feeling consciously constrained by his parents' fears for their future, and burdened by their pinning their anxious hopes on him, their only child. As a successful middle-class adult, he painted pictures of children of the inner city, with haunted, empty, hungry faces, and old men and women emptied of experience—apotheoses of starvation and loss. The trauma of his parents seemed to live on in his art.

Soon after telling me (DES) about his need to succeed in order to reassure his parents that they had avoided continuing the trauma, he told me about his adolescent perversion. He would go to the basement of their New York apartment building, take off all his clothes, and masturbate, hoping a girl would come by and see him. No one ever did, but he remembered these secret episodes with a mixture of glee and guilt. The exhibitionistic masturbation seemed unconsciously designed to free himself from the clutches of his parents and their trauma.

Despite my interest in his case and in the connection between his perverse fantasy, his art, and his being the vehicle for defending against the transgenerational transmission of trauma, I found that I dreaded working with Herb. I saw him in the early afternoon, when I was normally quite alert, but with him I found myself excruciatingly tired. Herb spoke, but nothing seemed real or immediate. I had nothing to work with. It was as if he was not really there with me. I felt dead. I told myself that, because of the vacuous quality to the work, the patient was not suitable for individual therapy. Without ever discussing my experience with him, I decided to end the therapy by recommending that we not continue to work together because it was not beneficial to him. In other words, I got rid of him. It was the boring, painful deadness in his personality and its resonance in mine that I wanted rid of, and it was not difficult to accomplish.

This therapy ended because of my intolerance for his schizoid deadness, the burden of his parents' trauma that he carried. Not knowing why he was so deadened, I was unable to help. I blamed him for the missing parts of our experience, and put my feeling of having to do without him back into him so that he was the one who had to do without me. Instead of understanding my countertransference as an identification with dead objects that haunted him and his parents, I wanted to get away from them. Instead of realizing that in making me do without him in the sessions, he was usefully reversing the trauma of his parents' need for him, I felt anxious and uncertain of the future, like his parents, and, like them, I wanted too much from him. After our last session, he sent me a postcard print of one of his paintings: two raggedy, unhappy children separated by a long stretch of sand.

TRAUMA AT TERMINATION

Even when the work with trauma has gone well, we face the trauma of the termination. A final vignette of a man, who recovered two traumatic memories and who was resonating unconsciously with his mother's unspoken trauma, brings us face-to-face with the inevitability of our sharing our patients' dilemmas; for in some ways we are as dependent on them as they are on us. We are always vulnerable to experiencing the abandoning object in the patient who wants to flee treatment because the work hurts, even when massive trauma is not the issue. Just as there is no such thing as an infant without a mother there is no therapist without a patient to treat. In this example, the interdependence was heightened in the late phase of treatment because this patient's therapist (JSS), as an advanced candidate in psychoanalytic training at the time, needed one of her cases to satisfy the criteria for satisfactory termination held by the American Psychoanalytic Association. Her progress depended on his.

Mr. Hendry, a handsome man in his late twenties, complained of painful bloody diarrhea and a compulsive attitude that compromised his cognitive functioning so that he could not tell the forest from the trees, and that kept him so preoccupied with work that he had no time or inclination to date. In the course of analysis, he had a memory of being humiliated by a seductive college baseball coach who spanked him once when drunk. Mr. Hendry had fled from the party and would not play for that coach again. After recovering this memory, his diarrhea cleared up. Much later, after having an intense reaction to a program on sexual abuse, he remembered an earlier incident similar to this one in which, as a 6-year-old boy, he was hurt when struggling free from a male babysitter who had exposed himself and tried to involve Mr. Hendry in his masturbation fantasy. Mr. Hendry had not been able to tell his parents what had happened because he was sure that the knowledge would have upset his fragile mother. Then he had forgotten the incident until he had analyzed his transference to me as a woman who, like his mother, would feel too much if told of his pain, and, simultaneously, the trigger of seeing a program on abuse brought it back to mind.

Mr. Hendry compulsively tried to analyze his difficulties in rather abstruse, intellectual language that was hard for me to follow. By experiencing in the transference his need to be at one with me as his mother in order to preempt feelings of unspoken grief that he sensed below her surface, he became able to be more separate from her and to appreciate me as separate from him. He decided to visit his parents and confront his fantasies about his mother's pain. He dared to ask his mother about the details of the source of her misery and learned of her experience of having witnessed torture and discrimination and of losing family members. When he pushed his mother a little too far to answer some of his questions, his father intervened to protect her, punched Mr. Hendry, and knocked him to the ground, an attack that surprised and hurt him but against which he did not retaliate, even though he was much stronger than his father.

In his next session Mr. Hendry announced that he was ending analysis that day. I felt quite hit. I felt powerless to detect in the transference a reason that he would suddenly reject me. I said that I thought that he had to hit me because his father had hit him when he wanted to know things about his parents, and that he wanted me to know how deeply it hurt, even though he was acting on the surface as if such a sudden departure would not matter to me.

He surprised me by returning for another session during which he remembered several similar occasions of violence by his father toward him in adolescence, all of which he had totally forgotten. Things settled down again, and he completed the work of extricating himself from his obsession with his mother's feeling states. He became capable of well-organized intellectual work, and he began a loving relationship with a woman. However, a year later, after three years of analysis, Mr. Hendry peremptorily decided to terminate, because he had finished all that he was willing to do. This time he resisted all my efforts to understand why he felt that he had to leave suddenly. Within a month of telling me that he meant to stop, he was gone.

Was Mr. Hendry ready to go? Had he resolved the transference? Or had he displaced it successfully in order to have a reason to leave me prematurely? I had to agree with his view that he had analyzed his projective identification of his mother. He had recovered his memories of the threat of childhood and young adult sexual abuse and of the actual teenage physical abuse from his father. He had moved beyond his fixation with his mother to become able to be sexual with a nonincestuous object. His body was healthy, and his intellect operated freely. He had a termination dream, the last in a sequence of only three dreams that he reported in a three-year analysis—again, a common finding in the traumatized patient. It seemed to me to be a reasonable time for a young adult to take a break from analysis. Yet, he had to do it his way.

TRAUMA FROM COLLEAGUES' RESPONSES

This takes us to the trauma of the therapist. Although I agreed that Mr. Hendry had now achieved goals that were reasonable for his life-phase, I would have felt better about a termination that was planned with me and that occupied three or four months of work on the loss of the analysis itself and its resonance with early losses. This way, the loss that it resonated with was mine.

Even though my supervisor agreed with me that Mr. Hendry's was a complete analysis with an unusually short termination phase, the committee at the analytic institute could not allow it as a "completed case," because the termination period was not long enough, the decision to terminate had been impulsive, and the date had been set unilaterally. I had to accept their decision, just as I had to accept Mr. Hendry's. I had to bear the loss and live with the pain of my future being dependent on his way of negotiating the relationship at the stage of separating from me. How like his mother I was with her secret grief. How like the child whose development depended on the mother's way of managing her pain. How traumatized I felt by my colleagues. Like the patient, I had to deal with it by studying more and working harder.

Even when we get it right, not uncommonly the relationship that has meant so much for years suddenly appears to mean nothing to our patient. We feel hurt, betrayed, discarded, used, and thrown away. Sometimes it is only in the termination, when the patient's guard is finally down, that she conveys the full impact of the trauma to us. We remind ourselves that there is frequently a traumatic ending, and that it is a necessary component of the treatment experience, a final, painful gift in which our patients, like Mr. Hendry or Mrs. Feinstein in parting, are free to convey in the transference some of the hurt they have carried for so long.

This brings us to the central point about working with such traumatized patients. Classical analytic theory has long failed to take account of and interpret the traumatized patient's need to enact the trauma during the treatment. We are now learning about the special needs and experiences of patients like Herb, Mr. Hendry, or Mrs. Feinstein, and the many others whom we have been treating without distinguishing the form of their treatment process from that of the classically neurotic. We now know to value a traumatic ending as an expectable, even welcome, development, a final statement of outrage, a declaration of independence from the newly autonomous self.

15

Putting It Together: Theory and Technique in Trauma

In Section I, we reviewed aspects of theory that are helpful in conceptualizing the impact of physical and sexual trauma on the developing personality (Table 15-1). From object relations theory, amplified by various elements from trauma theory, multiple personality studies, studies of hysteria, memory research, infant research, feminism, family therapy, and psychoanalysis, we have put together an object relations therapy approach that meets the needs of the patient who has been physically or sexually traumatized. In Section II, we illustrated the functioning of the adult traumatized personality in family life and in various treatment modalities, such as couple and family therapy, individual psycho-therapy and psychoanalysis, in which we demonstrated the object relations therapy approach following trauma. Here, we want to draw together these studies of the literature and clinical experience in a summary of the theory and technique of the object relations therapy of physical and sexual trauma.

Table 15-1. Effects of Physical and Sexual Trauma on Personality Development

Encapsulation of traumatic nuclei
Dissociation and gaps in the psyche
Splits in the self with awareness
Splits into multiple selves with separate memory banks and noncommunicating consciousness
Impaired capacity for fantasy elaboration and symbolization
Thinking that is literal, concrete, and sometimes non-verbal
Defensive preoccupation with the mundane
Preoccupation with bodily symptoms
Implicit memory behaviors that repeat the trauma

SPLITTING AND REPRESSION IN NORMAL PERSONALITY DEVELOPMENT

Object relations theory holds that an individual's psychic structure is built—through processes of introjective and projective identification, repression, primal repression, and dissociation—from the internalization of usual and unusual experience with the significant figures in the child's life. Experience is roughly sorted into categories of good and bad. The good, shorn from the bad, is taken in and welcomed. It suffuses the personality and enhances life-affirming, generative responses that tend to secure further good experience. The bad, split off from the good, is taken in and dealt with in ways that attempt to control it and separate it from the good experience to keep the good experience good. Bad experience is further sorted into categories of badly need-rejecting and badly need-exciting, bad and excessively bad, unpleasant or overwhelming. After sorting and splitting, bad experience gives rise to an internal object that is then bound by split-off parts of the ego. Parts of ego and parts of object associated with unpleasant experience are subject to horizontal repression at different levels of the personality by the central ego. All these mechanisms are part and parcel of normal personality formation.

PRIMAL REPRESSION AND DISSOCIATION: ENCAPSULATION AND MULTIPLICITY AFTER CUMULATIVE TRAUMA

When sexuality and aggression are hopelessly commingled as they are in childhood sexual abuse and the usual mechanism of multilayered horizontal repression fails to deal with the impact, the experience is downright overwhelming. This experience is traumatic. The self feels helpless and desperate. Primal repression and dissociative mechanisms take over. The child does not feel conflicted; the child feels overwhelmed, or the child does not feel at all. Repression proper fails under the impact or has not been well enough established to withstand the assault. Compromise formation and symbolic equivalence are impossible, and the self resorts to the primary process route of primal repression. In dissociation, the child enters a trance-like state through autohypnosis in which relaxation and numbness replace terrifying fear and helplessness. A passive adaptation with resignation to the trauma secures survival, but it reduces the sense of the active, competent, valuable self. Defensive encapsulations—due to primal repression—coexist with their opposite, gaps in the psyche—due to dissociation—where no structure was built in response to experience. A static, constricted set of internal objects and egos in a state of terror and dread is created around gaps in the psyche where nothing is felt, thought, remembered, or anticipated. This frozen tableau puts a hold on the dreaded potential for the recurrence of trauma. Splintered traumatic subselves are not properly repressed and remain out of contact with other parts of the self. Any one of them may take over as if it were the central, managing self, but it cannot do an effective job because of lack of access to all parts of the system. Vertical splits in the self occur. Proscribed views of the self as victim or survivor of trauma limit the personal idiom, the sense of destiny, and the capacity to build generative relationships.

When a child is traumatized under the age of 8 years, there is a greater likelihood that dissociative mechanisms may result in the full-blown psychic organization of multiplicity, especially in a child who is constitutionally disposed to dissociate. Under the impact of trauma, the self enters a default position of active dissociation and alternative association resulting in a state of relative non-integration. The degree of non-integration depends on the previous level of personality development, the capacity and opportunity for narrativization, and the meaning ascribed to the trauma. Traumatic encapsulations and dissociations coexist to preserve a relatively conflict-free area of going-on-being.

THERAPEUTIC FUNCTIONS

These are summarized in Table 15–2.

Table 15–2. Technique of Object Relations Therapy for Trauma

Welcome going-on-being
Relate to splits
Recreate the transitional zone of fantasy
Monitor the holding environment
Move between context and focus
Translate body communications
Hold a neutral position equidistant between trauma and going-on-being
Recover images in the transference–countertransference
Put images into narrative form
Refind the self as its own object
Be there as both object and absence
Transmute trauma to genera

Welcoming "Going-on-Being"

In the object relations approach to the traumatized individual or family, the fundamental principle is to respect this area of going-on-being. We must appreciate and experience our response to this going-on-being in the countertransference, whether it makes us feel sleepy, bored, restless, or hyperactive. We understand it not only as a defense for survival but as a vital communication of early life experience in relation to important objects. We expect to experience dissociative states in the countertransference, concordant with this aspect of the patient's self. Therapists find these dissociative states harder to recognize and value than more dramatic examples of being perceived as traumatized like the patient's self or traumatizing like the perpetrating parental object or intrusive physician. We use these countertransference responses of emptiness, nothingness, and vacuousness to understand the patient's experience.

Relating to Splits

We do not confront the denial and the splits in the personality abruptly. We relate to each of them respectfully, always keeping in mind those that are absent. We remain alert to the emergence of more subselves during therapy as a defense against the threat of repetition of trauma to the single self as therapy intensifies. We interpret dissociation as a defense at times, but we more commonly welcome it not as a resistance but as a sharing of the dissociative experience in the transference–countertransference. We use the transference–countertransference dialectic in object relations therapy to breach the closed system of parts, to gain access to missing parts of the self, and to allow for integration as the patient identifies with the containing, integrating function of the therapist.

Recreating the Transitional Zone for Fantasy

The betrayal of family trust and the collapse of the zone for transitional relatedness in family life where play and fantasy can be enjoyed lead to an internal constriction in ability to experience pleasure, hatred, sexual desire, or to discriminate between fantasy and reality. In contrast to this area of reduced functioning in the personality, hypertrophy of the stimulus barrier, which occurs to protect against the impingement of stimuli that might rekindle the trauma, results in an imperviousness to fantasy and unconscious communication that makes the patient seem resistant to psychoanalysis, when in fact the patient is simply exercising necessary survival mechanisms.

Monitoring the Holding Environment

With this in mind, we are careful to analyze the nature of the therapeutic alliance, to create a good holding environment for self-discovery, and to secure it from threatening stimuli and traumatic enactments before we become available for use as objects for "I-I" relating. We create a safe psychological space with due attention to boundary-keeping functions. This prepares the way for the gradual construction of a transitional space between patient and therapist in which reality can be examined, fantasy can be explored, play can be enjoyed, work can get done, and growth will occur. Playing within the analytic relationship, patient and therapist create healing nuclei of relatedness. The patient takes in this generative quality of non-traumatizing relatedness that seemed nonexistent before, and from this experience builds up generative nuclei that counteract the traumatic nuclei and fill in the gaps in the personality.

Moving between Context and Focus

We learn to move between the parts of the personality, from the relatively secure space of going-on-being to the traumatic constellation and the holes in the psyche. From this base, we may interpret conflict or resistance as we would do more freely with the neurotically impaired patient, but we do so only when we have gained confidence that repressive mechanisms have come into use, rather than dissociative adaptations to the trauma. We make ourselves available to be related to as contextual figures and as objects both somewhat like and crucially different than the internal ones.

Translating Body Communications

Hysterical symptoms no longer appear as dramatic paralysis, aphonia, and seizures of the kind that Freud and Charcot frequently saw in earlier times. Now they more often take the form of anorexia, physical distress, and disorders of sexual desire. In classical Freudian terms, in hysteria a bodily symptom substitutes for a feeling in connection with an idea or a wish that has occurred in response to a trauma. In object relations terms, the bodily symptom represents an identification with a part-object or part-ego projected into the body or a primary identification by a part of the self with a whole object that has not been distinguished as "other." The trauma has been overwhelming, or it happened in circumstances that precluded adequate verbal outrage.

Remaining Equidistant between Trauma and Going-on-Being

In object relations therapy, we offer a safe holding environment. We listen and follow the affect without talking too much, but we do not use silence to create ambiguity, because this is too much like the secrecy surrounding the original trauma. We listen without interruption or interpretation of resistance when the patient's material seems to be getting nowhere, because we know that being nowhere is where the patient is. We follow as the patient makes a graded series of approaches to the traumatic material, interspersed with periods of relatively affectless going-on-being. In these discrete exposures to trauma, like crashing waves disappearing in a calm sea, the patient gradually experiences the intense affect associated with the trauma in the transference, and always has a relatively low-affect place to return to. The therapist finds a reflection of the trauma in the countertransference and works to contain it there and understand it from inside the experience. The therapist remains neutral but not withholding or intrusive, because the therapist does not want to identify with the trauma-inducing and trauma-maintaining function of the internal object.

Recovering Images in the Transference–Countertransference and Putting Them into Narrative Form

The traumatic experience is encoded in an implicit/iconic/sensorimotor/ visuospatial memory system where it is stored as a sense image or a behavior and is not processed in an explicit/symbolic/linguistic/ narrative form, partly because the overwhelming nature of the traumatic stimuli leads to a regression in thinking and memory storage to the implicit level, and partly because the trauma is not talked about in the family enough to reach the explicit level, because it causes grief, guilt, and anxiety. This lack of narrativization is particularly true in cases of childhood sexual abuse that have remained secret under threat, but we also find it in those where there has been denial of body deficit or damage from physical trauma. Traumatic experience is then carried as behavior rather than memory. In the patient's history we see the tendency to repeat the trauma instead of remember it.

This finding that implicit memory predominates in those who have been traumatized has implications for therapy where memories can be inferred from behavior in the transference rather than recovered in a narrative form. The process of therapy has to do with developing the inferences and creating a narrativization, always with care to avoid injunctive statements that preclude the slow process of discovery within the therapeutic relationship. The capacity for explicit memory then develops from the translation of implicit memory behaviors without falsification.

Refinding the Self as Its Own Object

We put the patients at the center of the therapeutic effort. We mold our own aims to the level of their ambition for their growth. While we may care more for the patients' core selves at times in the therapy than they do, we cannot care more about their recovery than they do, or their progress would be a false activity to appease us, instead of an act of courage and autonomy. In the therapeutic relationship, patients find that their selves can be recognized instead of being subordinated as narcissistically desired, external objects for the significant others. We encourage the expression of ambivalence and rage against us by interpreting how these feelings were denied to maintain a semblance of having a good object for whom to be a good object, and so feel like a good self, however falsely. We put words to the communication of bodily symptomatology. We relate to the patient as a body-self that is unsure of its shape and needs to redefine its edges in relation to us as a noninvasive object. We are aware of ourselves as objects for the patient, and we speak to the patient about how we are being experienced. We experience and then interpret the various parts of ego and object—abusive, bystanding, loving, hating, rejecting, seductive, disgusting—with which patients identify us at different times.

Being There as Both Object and Absence

We do not want to become encapsulated as admired and idealized objects under the force of having to oppose patients' disintegration or identify with the traumatic encapsulation of the nuclei of their selves. One way of freeing ourselves of this liability is to interpet patients' envy of the freely active nuclei of our selves and our wholeness so as to free them from destructive attacks against their therapy and their selves. Another support against becoming encapsulated is to be aware of ourselves being used as the space between the capsules and to be sensitive to our own disappearance. So, we attend to and analyze our countertransference feelings of fear, boredom, and frozen helplessness so that we understand from inside our own experience the meaning of the patients' unconscious communication of their affect states. Ultimately, we are experienced as the void—the nonresponsive mother who could not prevent or absorb the trauma.

Transmuting Trauma to Genera

During the process of therapy, iconic memories are recovered by association and given a narrative form, so that different systems of memory can reconnect in an adult form and the disparate parts of the self can be reintegrated. Good empathic therapy offers a holding context and a focused relating that facilitate the emergence of genera—free-form nuclei of the self built out of the relationship with the therapist. These new and renewed elements of the self are not repressed, but diffuse through the personality. Attracting further good experience, they offer an alternative to the accretions of badness in the dissociated traumatic nuclei. Disseminating goodness, they ease the sense of overwhelming badness that led to the need for splits. This fosters healing of the splits and progressive personality integration. Patients who have derived their identities with reference to their victimized and surviving aspects of the self gradually feel safe enough to enter a transitional space for play, work, and growth. Instead of seeing themselves as the guilty or ashamed objects of their parents' desires or their physicians' therapeutic ambition, traumatized patients become able to find and care for their selves. Gradually the self comes to be defined in terms of its potential, its capacity for growth and change, and its individuality expressed in current work and pleasure choices, and in intimate relationships with spouse and children.

One hundred years ago, patients whose impairment was due to sexual trauma were the inspiration for Freud's invention of psychoanalysis. His interest moved from actual trauma, dissociated states, hysterical double consciousness, and adolescent sexuality to infantile sexuality, oedipal fantasy, loss, repression, and neurosis. With a few exceptions like Ferenczi, Freud's colleagues followed his lead. As a field, psychoanalysis and psychoanalytic psychotherapy moved away from trauma to neurosis, from dissociation to repression. As a result, we have not had as thorough an understanding of the effects of trauma and their treatment as we have for conceptualizing and treating neurotic difficulties. In this long interval, we did not advance our knowledge about actually traumatized patients and consequently had less to offer them than we might have had. But, as we have discovered in reviewing our own clinical experience—and as we believe most clinicians would similarly find—they have been with us all along, lifting their silent voices to us, hoping we would hear, accept, validate, and understand, as they simultaneously concealed and conveyed their experience. As we read the emerging literature, reviewed our clinical experience, and wrote about our work with traumatized patients, we have come to understand them better. We hope this volume will propel us along the shared journey, as we and our patients together continue to develop and refine object relations therapy for survivors of physical trauma and childhood sexual abuse.

References

Anzieu, D. (1989). *The Skin Ego*, trans. C. Turner. New Haven: Yale University Press.

Apprey, M. (1991). Psychical transformations by a child of incest. In *The Trauma of Transgression: Psychotherapy of Incest Victims*, ed. S. Kramer and S. Akhtar, pp. 115–147. Northvale, NJ: Jason Aronson.

Aronson, E. (1969). The theory of cognitive dissonance: a current perspective. In *Advances in Experimental Social Psychology*, vol. 4, ed. L. Berkowitz, pp. 1–34. New York: Academic Press.

Barnhouse, R. T. (1978). Sex between patient and therapist. *Journal of the American Academy of Psychoanalysis* 6:533–546.

Berman, E. (1981). Multiple personality: psychoanalytic perspective. *International Journal of Psycho-Analysis* 62:288–300.

Bernstein, A. E. (1990). The impact of incest trauma on ego development. In *Adult Analysis and Childhood Sexual Abuse*, ed. H. B. Levine, pp. 65–92. Hillsdale, NJ: Analytic Press.

Bick, E. (1968). The experience of the skin in early object relations. *International Journal of Psycho-Analysis* 49:484–486.

―――― (1986). Further considerations on the function of the skin in early object relations. *British Journal of Psychotherapy* 2:292–299.

Bigras, J. (with Biggs, K. H.). (1990). Psychoanalysis as incestuous repetition:

some technical considerations. In *Adult Analysis and Childhood Sexual Abuse*, ed. H. B. Levine, pp. 173–196. Hillsdale, NJ: Analytic Press.

Bikel, O. (1993). "Innocence Lost: The Verdict." Public Broadcast Television, July 5–6.

Bion, W. (1967). *Second Thoughts*. London: Heineman.

——— (1970). *Attention and Interpretation*. London: Tavistock.

Bleuler, E. (1950). *Dementia Praecox or The Group of Schizophrenias*, trans. J. Zinkin. New York: International Universities Press.

Bollas, C. (1987). *The Shadow of the Object*. London: Free Association Press.

——— (1989). *Forces of Destiny*. London: Free Association Books.

——— (1992). *Being a Character*. New York: Hill and Wang.

Boszormenyi-Nagy, I., and Spark, G. (1973). *Invisible Loyalties: Reciprocity in Intergenerational Family Therapy*. New York: Harper and Row.

Bowlby, J. (1969). Anxious attachment and some conditions that promote it. In *Attachment and Loss. Vol. 1: Attachment*, pp. 245–274. London: Penguin.

——— (1980). The trauma of loss. In *Attachment and Loss. Vol. 3: Loss: Sadness and Depression*, pp. 7–22. New York: Basic Books.

Braun, B. G. (1984). Towards a theory of multiple personality and other dissociative phenomena. *Psychiatric Clinics of North America* 7(1): 171–193.

——— (1985). The transgenerational incidence of dissociation and multiple personality disorder: a preliminary report. In *Childhood Antecedents of Multiple Personality*, ed. R. P. Kluft, pp. 127–150. Washington, DC: American Psychiatric Press.

Braun, B. G., and Sachs, R. (1985). The development of multiple personality disorder: predisposing, precipitating and perpetuating factors. In *Childhood Antecedents of Multiple Personality*, ed. R. P. Kluft, pp. 37–64. Washington, DC: American Psychiatric Press.

Breuer, J., and Freud, S. (1893). On the psychical mechanism of hysterical phenomena: preliminary communication. *Standard Edition* 2:3–17.

——— (1893–95). Studies on hysteria. *Standard Edition* 2:1–335.

Briere, J. N. (1992a). *Child Abuse Trauma: Theory and Treatment of the Lasting Effects*. Newbury Park: Sage.

——— (1992b). Studying delayed memories of childhood sexual abuse. In special issue on child and adult memory, *The Advisor, Journal of the American Professional Society on the Abuse of Children* 5(3):17–18. Reprinted with permission in *Childhood Memory*, ed. D. J. Siegel. Proceedings of Institute IV, American Academy of Child and Adolescent Psychiatry, San Antonio, October 29.

Briere, J. N., and Runtz, M. (1990). Differential adult symptomatology associated with three types of child abuse histories. *Child Abuse and Neglect* 14:357–364.

Briquet, P. (1859). *Traite Clinique et Therapeutique de l'Hysterie*. Paris: Balliere.

Burland, J. A., and Raskin, R. (1990). The psychoanalysis of adults who were sexually abused in childhood: a preliminary report from the discussion group of the American Psychoanalytic Association. In *Adult Analysis and Childhood Sexual Abuse*, ed. H. B. Levine, pp. 35–41. Hillsdale, NJ: Analytic Press.

Casement, P. (1985). *On Learning from the Patient*. London: Tavistock.

Christianson, S. (1992). *Handbook of Emotion and Memory*. Hillsdale, NJ: Erlbaum Associates.

Clyman, R. B. (1993). Implicit memory and child psychiatry. In *Childhood Memory*, ed. D. J. Siegel, pp. 1–13. Proceedings of Institute IV, American Academy of Child and Adolescent Psychiatry, San Antonio, October 29.

Cohen, J. (1984). Structural consequences of psychic trauma: a new look at *Beyond the Pleasure Principle*. *International Journal of Psycho-Analysis* 61:421–432.

———— (1985). Trauma and repression. *Psychoanalytic Inquiry* 5(1):163–189.

Cohen, J., and Kinston, W. (1984). Repression theory: a new look at the corner-stone. *International Journal of Psycho-Analysis* 65:411–422.

Cohen, N. J., and Squire, L. R. (1980). Preserved learning and retention of pattern-analyzing skills in amnesia: dissociation of knowing how and knowing that. *Science* 221:207–210.

Courtois, C. (1988). *Healing the Incest Wound*. New York: Norton.

Crews, F. (1993). The unknown Freud. *The New York Review of Books* November 18, pp. 55–66.

Davies, J. M., and Frawley, M. G. (1992). Dissociative processes and transference-countertransference paradigms in the psychoanalytically oriented treatment of adult survivors of childhood sexual abuse. *Psychoanalytic Dialogues* 2(1):5–36.

———— (1994). *Treating the Adult Survivor of Childhood Sexual Abuse. A Psychoanalytic Perspective*. New York: Basic Books.

Deutsch, F. (1957). A footnote to Freud's "Fragment of an analysis of a case of hysteria." *Psychoanalytic Quarterly* 26:159–167.

Dewald, P. A. (1989). Effects on adults of incest in childhood: a case report. *Journal of the American Psychoanalytic Association* 37:997–1014.

De Young, M. (1983). Case reports: the sexual exploitation of victims by helping professionals. *Victimology* 6:92–98.

Diagnostic and Statistical Manual of Mental Disorders-IV (1994). Washington, DC: American Psychiatric Association.

Dickes, R. (1965). The defensive function of an altered state of consciousness: a hypnoid state. *Journal of the American Psychoanalytic Association* 13:336–403.

Donaldson, M. A., and Gardner, R. (1982). Stress response in women after childhood incest. Paper presented at the Annual Meeting of the American Psychiatric Association, Toronto, May 15–21.

_____ (1985). Traumatic stress among women after childhood incest. In *Trauma and Its Wake: The Study and Treatment of Post-Traumatic Stress Disorder*, ed. C. R. Figley, pp. 356–357. New York: Brunner/Mazel.

Emde, R. N., Biringen, Z., Clyman, R. B., and Oppenheim, D. (1991). The moral self of infancy: affective core and procedural knowledge. *Developmental Review* 11:251–270.

Erdelyi, M. H. (1990.) Repression, reconstruction and defense: history and integration of the psychoanalytic and experimental frameworks. In *Repression and Dissociation: Implications for Personality, Psychopathology and Health*, pp. 1–31. Chicago: University of Chicago Press.

_____ (1992). Psychodynamics and the unconscious. *American Psychologist* 47(6):784–787.

Erikson, E. H. (1962). Reality and actuality. *Journal of the American Psychoanalytic Association* 10:454–461.

Esterson, A. (1993). *Seductive Mirage: An Exploration of the Work of Sigmund Freud*. Chicago: Open Court.

Etezady, M. H. (1991). Victims of incest. In *The Trauma of Transgression: Psychotherapy of Incest Victims*, ed. S. Kramer and S. Akhtar, pp. 149–166. Northvale, NJ: Jason Aronson.

Fairbairn, W. R. D. (1927). Notes on the religious phantasies of a female patient. In *Psychoanalytic Studies of the Personality*, pp. 183–196. London: Routledge & Kegan Paul, 1952.

_____ (1929a). Is the superego repressed? In *From Instinct to Self: Selected Papers of W. R. D. Fairbairn*, vol. I, ed. D. E. Scharff and E. F. Birtles, pp. 101–114. Northvale, NJ: Jason Aronson, 1994.

_____ (1929b). Repression and dissociation. Thesis for doctorate of medicine at the University of Edinburgh. In *From Instinct to Self, Selected Papers of W. R. D. Fairbairn*, vol. II, ed. E. F. Birtles and D. E. Scharff. Northvale, NJ: Jason Aronson, 1994.

_____ (1935) Medico-psychological aspects of the problem of child assault. *Mental Hygiene* (April) 13:1–16. Reprinted in *From Instinct to Self: Selected Papers of W. R. D. Fairbairn*, vol. II, ed. E. F. Birtles and D. E. Scharff. Northvale, NJ: Jason Aronson, 1994.

_____ (1943a). Phantasy and internal objects [originally untitled]. Paper read by Dr. Glover in W. R. D. Fairbairn's absence, February 17, 1943 at the British Psychoanalytical Society, London. In *The Freud–Klein Controversies 1941–1945*, ed. R. Steiner, R. King, and P. King, pp. 358–360. London: Routledge, Chapman, Hall and the Institute of Psychoanalysis, 1991.

_____ (1943b). The repression and return of bad objects (with special reference to the "war neuroses"). In *Psychoanalytic Studies of the Personality*, pp. 59–81. London: Tavistock, 1952.

_____ (1944). Endopsychic structure considered in terms of object relationships. In *Psychoanalytic Studies of the Personality*, pp. 82–136. London: Routledge and Kegan Paul, 1952.

_____ (1952). *Psychoanalytic Studies of the Personality*. London: Routledge and Kegan Paul.

_____ (1954). Observations on the nature of hysterical states. *British Journal of Medical Psychology* 27:105-125.

_____ (1958). On the nature and aims of psycho-analytical treatment. *International Journal of Psycho-Analysis* 39:374-385.

Faller, K. C. (1992). Can therapy induce false accusations of sexual abuse? In Special issue on child and adult memory. *The Advisor, Journal of the American Professional Society on the Abuse of Children* 5(3):3-6. Reprinted with permission in *Childhood Memory*, ed. D. J. Siegel. Proceedings of Institute IV, American Academy of Child and Adolescent Psychiatry, San Antonio, October 29.

Ferenczi, S. (1929a). Letter dated 25 December 1929 in The Freud-Ferenczi correspondence. In *The Clinical Diary of Sandor Ferenczi*, ed. J. Dupont, trans. M. H. Balint and N. Z. Jackson, p. xii. Cambridge, MA: Harvard University Press.

_____ (1929b). The principle of relaxation and neo-catharsis. In *Final Contributions to the Problems and Methods of Psychoanalysis*, pp. 108-125. New York: Brunner/Mazel.

_____ (1933a). Confusion of tongues between the adult and the child. In *Final Contributions to the Problems and Methods of Psychoanalysis*, pp. 156-167. London: Hogarth Press, 1955.

_____ (1933b). *The Clinical Diary of Sandor Ferenczi*, ed. J. Dupont, trans. M. H. Balint and N. Z. Jackson. Cambridge MA: Harvard University Press.

Figley, C. R. (1985). *Trauma and its Wake. The Study and Treatment of Post-Traumatic Stress Disorder*. New York: Brunner/Mazel.

Finkelhor, D. (1980). Sex among siblings: a survey on prevalence, variety and effects. *Archives of Sexual Behavior* 9:171-194.

Finkelhor, D., and Browne, A. (1985). The traumatic impact of child sexual abuse: a conceptualization. *American Journal of Orthopsychiatry* 55:530-541.

Fisher, R. M. S. (1991). The unresolved rapprochement crisis: an important constituent of incest experience. In *The Trauma of Transgression: Psychotherapy of Incest Victims*, ed. S. Kramer and S. Akhtar, pp. 39-56. Northvale, NJ: Jason Aronson.

Fivush, R. (1993a). Developmental perspectives on autobiographical recall. In *Child Victims, Child Witnesses: Understanding and Improving Testimony*, ed. G. S. Goodman and B. L. Bottoms, pp. 1-24. New York: Guilford.

_____ (1993b). Theoretical and methodological issues in memory development research. In *Childhood Memory*, ed. D. J. Siegel, pp. 1-26. Proceedings of Institute IV, American Academy of Child and Adolescent Psychiatry, San Antonio, October 29.

Fleiss, R. (1953). The hypnotic evasion: a clinical observation. *Psychoanalytic Quarterly* 22:497-511.

Frank, A. (1969). The unrememberable and the unforgettable: passive primal repression. *Psychoanalytic Study of the Child* 24:48–77. New York: International Universities Press.

Franz, S. I. (1933). *Persons, One and Three: A Study in Multiple Personalities.* New York and London: McGraw-Hill, Whittesley House.

Freud, A. (1936). *The Ego and the Mechanisms of Defence.* New York: International Universities Press.

––––– (1967). Comments on trauma. In *Psychic Trauma*, ed. S. Furst, pp. 235–245. New York: Basic Books.

––––– (1981). A psychoanalyst's view of sexual abuse by parents. In *Sexually Abused Children and their Families*, ed. P. B. Mrazek and C. H. Kempe, pp. 33–34. New York: Pergamon Press.

Freud, S. (1892–1899). Extracts from the Fliess papers. *Standard Edition* 1:177–280.

––––– (1893a). Case histories: Fraulein Elisabeth von R. *Standard Edition* 2:135–181.

––––– (1893b). Case histories: Katharina. *Standard Edition* 2:125–134.

––––– (1893c). On the psychical mechanism of hysterical phenomena. *Standard Edition* 3:27–39.

––––– (1893d). The psychotherapy of hysteria. *Standard Edition* 2:253–305.

––––– (1894). The neuropsychoses of defence. *Standard Edition* 3:41–68.

––––– (1895). Draft H–paranoia. *Standard Edition* 1:206–212.

––––– (1896a). Extracts from the Fliess papers: letter 52. *Standard Edition* 1:233–240.

––––– (1896b). The aetiology of hysteria. *Standard Edition* 3:191–221.

––––– (1897). Extracts from the Fliess papers: letters 60–71. *Standard Edition* 1:259–266.

––––– (1900). The interpretation of dreams. *Standard Edition* 4/5:1–626.

––––– (1905a). Fragment of an analysis of a case of hysteria. *Standard Edition* 7:3–122.

––––– (1905b). Three essays on the theory of sexuality. *Standard Edition* 7:123–243.

––––– (1906). My views on the part played by sexuality in the aetiology of the neuroses. *Standard Edition* 7:271–279.

––––– (1914a) On narcissism. An introduction. *Standard Edition* 14:67–104.

––––– (1914b). Remembering, repeating and working through. *Standard Edition* 12:147–156.

––––– (1915a). Repression. *Standard Edition* 14:146–158.

––––– (1915b). The unconscious. *Standard Edition* 16:166–204.

––––– (1917a). General theory of the neuroses. The paths to the formation of symptoms. *Standard Edition* 16:358–377.

––––– (1917b). Resistance and repression. *Standard Edition* 16:286–302.

––––– (1918). From the history of an infantile neurosis. *Standard Edition* 17:7–122.

––––– (1919). Introduction to psycho-analysis and the war neuroses. *Standard Edition* 17:205–210.

_____ (1920). Beyond the pleasure principle. *Standard Edition* 18:7–64.

_____ (1923). The ego and the id. *Standard Edition* 19:12–66.

_____ (1925). An autobiographical study. *Standard Edition* 20:1–71.

Freyd, P. (1993). Executive Director's letter. *FMS Foundation Newsletter* 2(1):1, Jan 1994. 2(1):1.

Frischolz, E. J. (1985). The relationship among dissociation, hypnosis and child abuse in the development of multiple personality disorder. In *Childhood Antecedents of Multiple Personality*, ed. R. P. Kluft, pp. 99–126. Washington, DC: American Psychiatric Press.

Furman, E. (1974). *A Child's Parent Dies*. New Haven: Yale University Press.

Furst, S., ed. (1967). *Psychic Trauma*. New York: Basic Books.

Gabbard, G. O., ed. (1989). *Sexual Exploitation in Professional Relationships*. Washington, DC: American Psychiatric Press.

_____ (1992). Commentary on "Dissociative processes and countertransference paradigms . . ." by J. M. Davies and M. G. Frawley. *Psychoanalytic Dialogues* 2(1):37–47.

Gabbard, G. O., and Temlow, S. W. (1994). Mother–son incest in the pathogenesis of narcissistic personality disorder. *Journal of the American Psychoanalytic Association* 42(1):171–189.

Gardner, M. (1993). The false memory syndrome. *Skeptical Inquirer* 17:370–375.

Gardner, R. (1992). *True and False Accusations of Child Sex Abuse*. Cresskill, NJ: Creative Therapies.

Gelinas, D. J. (1983). The persisting negative effects of incest. *Psychiatry* 46:312–332.

Glover, E. (1943). The concept of dissociation. *International Journal of Psycho-Analysis* 24:7–13.

Good, M. I. (1994). The reconstruction of early childhood trauma: fantasy, reality and verification. *Journal of the American Psychoanalytic Association* 42(1):79–101.

Goodwin, J. (1985). Post-traumatic symptoms in incest victims. In *Post Traumatic Stress Disorders in Children*, ed. S. Eth and R. S. Pynoos, pp. 155–168. Washington DC: American Psychiatric Press.

_____ , (ed.) (1989). *Sexual Abuse: Incest Victims and Their Families*, 2nd ed. Chicago: Year Book Medical.

_____ (1990). Applying to adult incest victims what we have learned from victimized children. In *Incest Related Syndromes of Adult Psychopathology*, ed. R. P. Kluft, pp. 55–74. Washington, DC: American Psychiatric Press.

Goodwin, J., Simms M., and Bergman, R. (1979). Hysterical seizures: a sequal to incest. *American Journal of Orthopsychiatry* 49:704–708.

Gray, P. (1993). The assault on Freud. *Time*, November 29, pp. 47–51.

Greenacre, P. (1971). *Emotional Growth*, vol. 1. New York: International Universities Press.

Greenberg, M. S., and Van der Kolk, B. A. (1987). Retrieval and integration of traumatic memories with the painting cure. In *Psychological Trauma*, ed. B. A. Van der Kolk, pp. 191–215. Washington, DC: American Psychiatric Press.

Greer, J. M. G. (1992). "Return of the repressed" in the analysis of an adult incest survivor: a case study and some tentative generalizations. Paper presented at the meeting of the American Psychoanalytic Association, New York, December.

Grosskurth, P. (1991). *The Secret Ring*. Reading, MA: Addison-Wesley.

Grotstein, J. (1981). *Splitting and Projective Identification*. New York: Jason Aronson.

_____ (1992). Commentary on "Dissociative processes and countertransference paradigms . . ." by Jody Messler Davies and Mary Gail Frawley. *Psychoanalytic Dialogues* 2(1):61–76.

Grubrich-Simitis, I. (1984). From concretization to metaphor. *Psychoanalytic Study of the Child* 39:301–319. New York: International Universities Press.

_____ (1988). Trauma or drive—drive and trauma: a reading of Sigmund Freud's phylogenetic fantasy of 1915. *Psychoanalytic Study of the Child* 43:3–32. New York: International Universities Press.

Herman, J. L. (1981). *Father–Daughter Incest*. Cambridge, MA: Harvard University Press.

_____ (1992). *Trauma and Recovery*. New York: Basic Books.

Herman, J. L., Russell, D., and Tracki, K. (1986). Long-term effects of incestuous abuse in childhood. *American Journal of Psychiatry* 143:1293–1296.

Herman, J. L., and Schatzow, E. (1987). Recovery and verification of memories of childhood sexual trauma. *Psychoanalytic Psychology* 4:1–14.

Hilgard, E. R. (1976). Neodissociation theory of multiple cognitive control systems. In *Consciousness and Self Regulation: Advances in Research*, vol. 1, ed. D. E. Shapiro and G. E. Schwartz, pp. 138–157. New York: Plenum.

_____ (1977). *Divided Consciousness: Multiple Controls in Human Thought and Action*. New York: Wiley.

_____ (1984). The hidden observer and multiple personality. *International Journal of Clinical and Experimental Hypnosis* 32:248–253.

_____ (1986). *Divided Consciousness: Multiple Controls in Human Thought and Action*, expanded edition. New York: Wiley.

Hocking, S. J. and Company. (1992). *Living with Your Selves. A Survival Manual for People with Multiple Personalities*. Rockville, MD: Launch.

Holmes, D. (1990). The evidence for repression. In *Repression and Dissociation*, ed. J. Singer, pp. 85–102. Chicago: University of Chicago Press.

Hopper, E. (1991). Encapsulation as a defense against the fear of annihilation. *International Journal of Psycho-Analysis* 72(4):607–624.

Horowitz, M. J. (1986). *Stress Response Syndromes*. 2nd ed. Northvale, NJ: Jason Aronson.

Huizinga, J. N. (1990). Incest as trauma: a psychoanalytic case. In *Adult*

Analysis and Childhood Sexual Abuse, ed. H. B. Levine, pp. 117–135. Hillsdale, NJ: Analytic Press.

Jaffe, A. (1965). *Jung's Memories, Dreams, Reflections.* New York: Vintage Books.

Janet, P. (1889). *L'Automatisme Psychologique.* Paris: Ballière.

Jaroff, L. (1993). Lies of the mind. *Time,* November 29, pp. 52–59.

Johnson, A. M. (1953). Factors in the aetiology and fixation of symptom choice. *Psychoanalytic Quarterly* 22:475–496.

Johnson, M. K., and Hirst, W. (1992). Processing subsystems of memory. In *Perspectives in Cognitive Neuroscience,* ed. R. G. Lister and H. J. Weingartner, pp. 197–219. New York: Oxford University Press.

Kardiner, A. (1941). *The Traumatic Neuroses of War.* New York: Hoeber.

Kaufman, I., Peck A., and Tagiuri, C. (1954). The family constellation and overt incestuous relations between father and daughter. *American Journal of Orthopsychiatry* 24:266–277.

Kempe, C. H., and Helfer, R. H. (1968). *The Battered Child.* Chicago: University of Chicago Press.

Kernberg, O. (1975). *Borderline Conditions and Pathological Narcissism.* New York: Jason Aronson.

Kerr, J. (1993). *A Most Dangerous Method: The Story of Jung, Freud and Sabina Spielrein.* New York: Knopf.

Khan, M. M. R. (1963). The concept of cumulative trauma. *Psychoanalytic Study of the Child* 18:286–306. New York: International Universities Press.

―――― (1964). Ego distortion, cumulative trauma, and the role of reconstruction in the analytic situation. *International Journal of Psycho-Analysis* 45: 272–279.

Kihlstrom, J. F. (1994). *The False Memory Syndrome.* Philadelphia: Foundation.

King, P., and Steiner, R., eds. (1991). *The Freud–Klein Controversy 1941–1945.* London: Routledge.

Klein, M. (1946). Notes on some schizoid mechanisms. In *Envy and Gratitude and Other Works 1946–1963,* pp. 1–24. New York: Delacourt, 1975.

Kline, M. V. (1958). *Freud and Hypnosis.* New York: Julian Press and the Institute for Research in Hypnosis Publication Society.

Kluft, R. P. (1984a). Multiple personality in childhood. In *Psychiatric Clinics of North America* 7:121–134.

―――― (1984b). Treatment of multiple personality disorder. *Psychiatric Clinics of North America* 7:9–30.

―――― (1986). Preliminary observations on age regression in multiple personality patients before and after integration. *American Journal of Clinical Hypnosis* 28:147–156.

―――― ed. (1985). *Childhood Antecedents of Multiple Personality.* Washington, DC: American Psychiatric Press.

―――― ed. (1990a). *Incest Related Syndromes of Adult Psychopathology.* Washington, DC: American Psychiatric Press.

_____ (1990b). On the apparent invisibility of incest. In *Incest Related Syndromes of Adult Psychopathology*, pp. 11–34. Washington, DC: American Psychiatric Press.

Kluft, R. P., Braun, B. G., and Sachs, R. (1984). Multiple personality, intrafamilial abuse and family psychiatry. *International Journal of Family Psychiatry* 5:283–301.

Kolb, L. (1987). A neuropsychological hypothesis explaining post-traumatic stress disorders. *American Journal of Psychiatry* 144:989–995.

_____ (1993). Trauma revisited. *Academy Forum* 37(4):4–7.

Kramer, S. (1983). Object-coercive doubting: a pathological defense response to maternal incest. In *Defense and Resistance*, ed. H. Blum, pp. 325–351. New York: International Universities Press.

_____ (1990). Residues of incest. In *Adult Analysis and Childhood Sexual Abuse*, ed. H. B. Levine. Hillsdale, NJ: Analytic Press.

_____ (1991). The technical handling of incest-related material. In *The Trauma of Transgression: Psychotherapy of Incest Victims*, ed. S. Kramer and S. Akhtar, pp. 167–180. Northvale, NJ: Jason Aronson.

Kramer, S., and Akhtar, S., eds. (1991). *The Trauma of Transgression: Psychotherapy of Incest Victims*. Northvale, NJ: Jason Aronson.

Krener, P. K. (1993). Assessment of memory in children. In *Childhood Memory*, ed. D. J. Siegel. Proceedings of Institute IV, American Academy of Child and Adolescent Psychiatry, San Antonio, TX, October 29.

_____ (in press). Acquired disorders of memory in childhood. In *Language, Learning and Behavioral Disorders*, ed. J. H. Bietchman, N. Cohen, R. Tannock, and M. Konstantareas. New York: Cambridge University Press.

Krystal, H., ed. (1968a). *Massive Psychic Trauma*. New York: International Universities Press.

_____ (1968b). Patterns of psychological damage. In *Massive Psychic Trauma*, ed. H. Krystal, pp. 1–7. New York: International Universities Press.

_____ (1985). Trauma and the stimulus barrier. *Psychoanalytic Inquiry* 5(1):131–161.

Krystal, H., and Neiderland, W. G. (1968). Clinical observations of the survivor syndrome. In *Massive Psychic Trauma*, ed. H. Krystal, pp. 327–348. New York: International Universities Press.

Lakoff, R. T., and Coyne, J. C. (1993). *Father Knows Best: The Use and Abuse of Power in Freud's Case of Dora*. New York: Teachers College Press.

Lasky, R. (1978). The psychoanalytic treatment of a case of multiple personality. *Psychoanalytic Review* 65:353–380.

Laub, D., and Auerhan, N. C., eds. (1985). Knowing and not knowing the Holocaust. *Psychoanalytic Inquriy* 5(1):1–193.

Levine, H. B. (1990a). Clinical issues in the analysis of adults who were sexually abused as children. In *Adult Analysis and Childhood Sexual Abuse*, ed. H. B. Levine, pp. 197–218. Hillsdale, NJ: Analytic Press.

_____ (1990b). Introduction. In *Adult Analysis and Childhood Sexual Abuse,* ed. H. B. Levine, pp. 3–19. Hillsdale, NJ: Analytic Press.

_____ (ed.). (1990c). *Adult Analysis and Childhood Sexual Abuse.* Hillsdale, NJ: Analytic Press.

Levine, M. D. (1992). Neurodevelopmental variation and dysfunction among school-aged children. In *Developmental Behavioral Paediatrics,* 2nd ed., ed. M. D. Levine, W. B. Carey, and A. C. Crocker, pp. 477–490. Philadelphia: Saunders.

Lew, M. (1990). *Victims No Longer: Men Recovering from Incest and Other Sexual Child Abuse.* New York: Harper/Collins.

Lifton, R. J. (1967). *Death in Life: Survivors of Hiroshima.* New York: Random House.

Lisman-Pieczanski, N. (1990). Countertransference in the analysis of an adult who was sexually abused as a child. In *Adult Analysis and Childhood Sexual Abuse,* ed. H. B. Levine, pp. 137–147. Hillsdale, NJ: Analytic Press.

Loewenstein, R. J. (1990). Somatoform disorders in victims of incest and adult abuse. In *Incest Related Syndromes of Adult Psychopathology,* ed. R. P. Kluft, pp. 75–111. Washington, DC: American Psychiatric Press.

Loftus, E. F. (1975). Leading questions and the eye witness report. *Cognitive Psychology* 7:560–572.

_____ (1992). The malleability of memory. In Special issue on child and adult memory. *The Advisor, Journal of the American Professional Society on the Abuse of Children* 5(3):7–9. Reprinted with permission in *Childhood Memory,* ed. D. J. Siegel. Proceedings of Institute IV, American Academy of Child and Adolescent Psychiatry, San Antonio, October 29.

Loftus, E. F., Donder, D., Hoffman, H. G., and Schooler, J. W. (1989). Creating new memories that are quickly accessed and confidently held. *Memory and Cognition* 17:607–616.

Lorand, S., and Schneer, H. I. (1967). Sexual deviations, III. Fetishism, transvestism, masochism, sadism, exhibitionism, voyeurism, incest, pedophilia, and bestiality. In *Comprehensive Textbook of Psychiatry,* ed. A. M. Freedman and H. I. Kaplan, pp. 977–988. Baltimore: Williams and Wilkins.

Margolis, M. (1977). A preliminary study of a case of consummated mother-child incest. *Annual of Psychoanalysis* 5:267–293. New York: International Universities Press.

_____ (1984). A case of mother-child incest. *Psychoanalytic Quarterly* 53:355–385.

_____ (1991). Parent–child incest: analytic treatment experiences with follow-up data. In *The Trauma of Transgression: Psychotherapy of Incest Victims,* ed. S. Kramer and S. Akhtar, pp. 57–91. Northvale NJ: Jason Aronson.

Masson, J. M. (1984). *The Assault on Truth.* New York: Farrar, Strauss, Giroux.

McClelland, J. L., and Rummelhart, D. E. (1985). Distributed memory and the representation of general and specific information. *Journal of Experimental Psychology* 114:159–188.

McDougall, J. (1989). *Theaters of the Body*. New York: Norton.

McDougall, W. (1938). The relation between dissociation and repression. *British Journal of Medical Psychology* 17(2):141–157.

McGuire, W., ed. (1974). *The Freud/Jung Letters*. Princeton, NJ: Princeton University Press.

Meiselman, K. (1978). *Incest: A Psychological Study of Causes and Effects with Treatment Recommendations*. San Francisco: Jossey-Bass.

Mitchell, J. (1984). *Women: The Longest Revolution*. New York: Pantheon.

———— (1994). Hysteria, dissociative and related phenomena and gender. Paper presented at a weekend conference of the Object Relations Theory and Therapy Training Program, Washington School of Psychiatry, Washington, D.C., January.

Mrazek, P., and Kempe, C. H. (1981). *Sexually Abused Children and Their Families*. New York: Pergamon Press.

Murray, J. M. (1955). *Keats*. New York: Noonday Press.

Nelson, K. (1993a). The psychological and social origins of biographical memory. *Psychological Science* 4(1):7–14.

———— (1993b). Narrative and memory in early childhood. In *Childhood Memory*, ed. D. J. Siegel. Proceedings of Institute IV, American Academy of Child and Adolescent Psychiatry, San Antonio, October 29.

Ofshe, R., and Watters, E. (1993). Making monsters. *Society* 30(3): 4–16.

Ogden, T. (1986). *The Matrix of the Mind*. Northvale, NJ: Jason Aronson.

———— (1989). *The Primitive Edge of Experience*. Northvale, NJ: Jason Aronson.

Olsen, C. (1993). Multiple personality disorder, neither rare nor neat: a cautionary tale. 37th Annual Meeting, American Academy of Psychoanalysis, San Francisco, May 20–23.

Palombo, S. (1978). *Dreaming and Memory*. New York: Basic Books.

Perry, N. W. (1992). How children remember and why they forget. In Special issue on child and adult memory, *The Advisor, Journal of the American Professional Society on the Abuse of Children* 5(3): 1–2, 13–16. Reprinted with permission in *Childhood Memory*, ed. D. J. Siegel. Proceedings of Institute IV, American Academy of Child and Adolescent Psychiatry, San Antonio October 29.

Peterson, M. R. (1992). *At Personal Risk*. New York: London.

Piaget, J. (1936). *The Origins of Intelligence in Children*. 2nd ed. New York: International Universities Press, 1952.

Pickle, B. (1994). Reflections on dissociation and repression in Fairbairn's M. D. thesis. Paper presented at the Washington School of Psychiatry Conference on Hysteria, Dissociative Phenomena and Gender, Washington, DC, January.

Pillemer, D. B., and White, S. H. (1989). Childhood events recalled by children and adults. In *Advances in Child Development and Behavior*, ed. H. W. Reese, pp. 297–340. New York: Academic Press.

Pines, D. (1993). *A Woman's Unconscious Use of her Body*. London: Virago Press.

Pope, K. S. (1989). Teacher–student sexual intimacy. In *Sexual Exploitation in Professional Relationships*, ed. G. Gabbard, pp. 163–176. Washington, DC: American Psychiatric Press.

Prager, S. (1993). The false memory syndrome furor. *Psychiatric Times* 10(11): 11, Nov.

Prince, M. (1906). *The Dissociation of a Personality*. New York: Longmans.

_____ (1919). The psychogenesis of multiple personality. *Journal of Abnormal Psychology* 14:225–280.

Putnam, F. W. (1989). *Diagnosis and Treatment of Multiple Personality Disorder*. New York: Guilford.

_____ (1990). Disturbances of self in victims of childhood sexual abuse. In *Incest Related Syndromes of Adult Psychopathology*, ed. R. P. Kluft, pp. 113–131. Washington, DC: American Psychiatric Press.

_____ (1991). Dissociative disorders in children and adolescents. *Psychiatric Clinics of North America* 14(3):519–531.

_____ (1993). Memory and dissociation. In *Childhood Memory*, ed. D. J. Siegel. Proceedings of Institute IV, American Academy of Child and Adolescent Psychiatry, San Antonio, October 29.

_____ (1994). Multiple personality, dissociative phenomena and gender. Paper presented at the Object Relations Theory and Therapy Training Program Conference on Hysteria, Dissociative Phenomena and Gender. Washington School of Psychiatry Audiotape Collection, Washington, D.C, January.

Putnam, F. W., and Cole, P. (1992). Effect of incest on self and social functioning. *Journal of Consulting and Clinical Psychology* 60(2):174–184.

Putnam, F. W., Guroff, J., Silberman, E., et al. (1986). Clinical phenomenology of multiple personality disorder. *Journal of Clinical Psychiatry* 47:285–293.

Raphling, D. L. (1990). Technical issues of the opening phase. In *Adult Analysis and Childhood Sexual Abuse*, ed. H. B. Levine, pp. 45–64. Hillsdale, NJ: Analytic Press.

_____ (1994). A patient who was not sexually abused. *Journal of the American Psychoanalytic Association* 42:65–78.

Rascovsky, M., and Rascovsky, A. (1950). On consummated incest. *International Journal of Psycho-Analysis* 31:32–47.

Reich, J. C. (1993). *Tarnished Silver*. Minneapolis MN: RCR Enterprises.

Reich, W. (1994). The monster in the mists. *New York Times Book Review*, pp.1, 33, 35, 37, 38. May 15.

Rinsley, D. B. (1979). Fairbairn's object relations theory: a reconsideration in terms of newer knowledge. *Bulletin of the Menninger Clinic* 43:489–514.

Rosenfeld, A. (1979). Incidence of a history of incest among 18 female psychiatric patients. *American Journal of Psychiatry* 136:791–795.

Rummelhart, D. E., and McClelland, J. L., (eds.). (1986). *Parallel Distributed Processing. Explorations in the Microstructure of Cognition. Vol. 1, Foundations.* Cambridge, MA: MIT Press.

Rutter, P. (1989). *Sex in the Forbidden Zone.* Los Angeles: Jeremy P. Tarcher.

Sandler, J., et al. (1991). An approach to conceptual research in psychoanalysis illustrated by a consideration of psychic trauma. Unpublished paper.

Schachtel, E. (1947). On memory and childhood amnesia. *Psychiatry* 10:1–26.

Schacter, D. L. (1989). On the relation between memory and consciousness: dissociable interactions and conscious experience. In *Varieties of Memory and Consciousness: Essays in Honor of Endel Tulving,* ed. H. L. Roediger and F. I. M. Craik pp. 355–390. Hillsdale, NJ: Lawrence Erlbaum.

Scharff, D. E. (1969). The inpatient treatment of a borderline personality disorder. *Psychiatric Opinion* 6:37–43.

—— (1982). *The Sexual Relationship: An Object Relations View of Sex and the Family.* London: Routledge & Kegan Paul.

—— (1989). Transference, countertransference and technique in object relations family therapy. In *Foundations of Object Relations Family Therapy,* ed. J. Scharff, pp. 421–445. Northvale, NJ: Jason Aronson.

—— (1992). *Refinding the Object and Reclaiming the Self.* Northvale, NJ: Jason Aronson.

Scharff, D. E., and Birtles, E. F. (1994a). *From Instinct to Self: Selected Papers of W. R. D. Fairbairn,* vol. I: *Clinical and Theoretical Contributions.* Northvale, NJ: Jason Aronson.

—— (1994b). *From Instinct to Self: Selected Papers of W. R. D. Fairbairn,* vol. II: *Applications and Early Contributions.* Northvale, NJ: Jason Aronson.

Scharff, D. E., and Scharff, J. S. (1987). *Object Relations Family Therapy.* Northvale, NJ: Jason Aronson.

—— (1991). *Object Relations Couple Therapy.* Northvale, NJ: Jason Aronson.

Scharff, J. S. (1992). *Projective and Introjective Identification and the Use of the Therapist's Self.* Northvale, NJ: Jason Aronson.

Scharff, J. S., and Scharff, D. E. (1992). *Scharff Notes: A Primer of Object Relations Therapy.* Northvale, NJ: Jason Aronson.

Schetky, D. H. (1990). A review of the literature on the long term effects of childhood sexual abuse. In *Incest Related Syndromes of Adult Psychopathology,* ed. R. P. Kluft, pp. 35–54. Washington, DC: American Psychiatric Press.

—— (1993). Clinical applications of memory: assessing memory in legal contexts. In *Childhood Memory,* ed. D. J. Siegel. Proceedings of Institute IV, American Academy of Child and Adolescent Psychiatry, San Antonio, October 29.

Shengold, L. (1963). The parent as sphinx. *Journal of the American Psychoanalytic Association* 11:725–751.

_____ (1967). The effects of overstimulation: rat people. *International Journal of Psycho-Analysis* 48:403–415.

_____ (1974). The metaphor of the mirror. *Journal of the American Psychoanalytic Association* 22:97–115.

_____ (1980). Some reflections on a case of mother-son incest. *International Journal of Psycho-Analysis.* 61:461–475.

_____ (1989). *Soul Murder.* New Haven, CT: Yale University Press.

Sherkow, A. E. (1990). Consequences of childhood sexual abuse on the development of ego structure: a comparison of child and adult cases. In *Adult Analysis and Childhood Sexual Abuse,* ed. H. B. Levine, pp. 93–115. Hillsdale, NJ: Analytic Press.

Siegel, B. (1992). Personal communication.

Siegel, D. J., ed. (1993). *Childhood Memory.* Proceedings of Institute IV, American Academy of Child and Adolescent Psychiatry, San Antonio, October 29.

Silber, A. (1979). Childhood seduction, parental pathology and hysterical symptomatology: the genesis of an altered state of consciousness. *International Journal of Psycho-Analysis* 60: 109–116.

Silvio, J. (1993). An analyst's first encounter with M. P. D: struggling with dissociation and multiplicity in theoretical and technical orientation. 37th Annual Meeting of American Academy of Psychoanalysis, San Francisco, May 20–23, 1993.

Simon, B. (1992). "Incest—see under Oedipus complex": the history of an error in psychoanalysis. *Journal of the American Psychoanalytic Association* 40(4):955–988.

Singer, J., Ed. (1990). *Repression and Dissociation.* Chicago: University of Chicago Press.

Sonnenberg, S. M., Blank, A. S., and Talbott, J. A. (1985). *The Trauma of War: Stress and Recovery in Vietnam Veterans.* Washington, DC: American Psychiatric Press.

Spencer, J. (1978). Father-daughter incest. *Child Welfare* 57: 581–590.

Spiegel, D. (1984). Multiple personality as a post-traumatic stress disorder. *Psychiatric Clinics of North America* 7(1):101–110.

_____ (1990). Hypnosis, dissociation and trauma. In *Repression and Dissociation,* ed. J. Singer, pp. 121–142. Chicago: University of Chicago Press.

Spiegel, H. (1963). The dissociation-association continuum. *Science and Psychoanalysis* 6:152–159.

_____ (1980). Hypnosis and evidence: help or hindrance? *Annals of the New York Academy of Science* 347:73–85.

Spitz, R. (1945). Hospitalism: an inquiry into the genesis of psychiatric conditions in early childhood. *Psychoanalytic Study of the Child* 1:53–74. New York: International Universities Press.

_____ (1946). Hospitalism: a follow-up report. *Psychoanalytic Study of the Child* 2:113–117. New York: International Universities Press.

Squire, L. R. (1986). Mechanisms of memory. *Science* 232:1612–1619.

———— (1987). *Memory and Brain*. New York: Oxford University Press.

———— (1992). Declarative and non-declarative memory: multiple brain systems supporting learning and memory. *Journal of Cognitive Neuroscience* 4(3): 232–243.

Steele, B. (1970). Parental abuse in infants and small children. In *Parenthood*, ed. T. Benedek, pp. 449–457. Boston: Little Brown.

———— (1980). Psychodynamic factors in child abuse. In *The Battered Child*, ed. C. H. Kempe and R. Helfer, 3rd ed., pp. 49–85. Chicago: University of Chicago Press.

———— (1981). Long-term effects of sexual abuse in childhood. In *Sexually Abused Children and their Families*, ed. P. Mrazek and C. H. Kempe, pp. 223–234. New York: Pergamon Press.

———— (1990). Some sequelae of the sexual maltreatment of children. In *Adult Analysis and Childhood Sexual Abuse*, ed. H. B. Levine, pp. 21–34. Hillsdale, NJ: Analytic Press.

Stekel, W. (1895). Ueber coitus im Kindesalter, *Wiener Medizinische Blatter* 18(16):247–249.

Steward, M. S. (1992). Preliminary findings from the University of California, Davis, Child Memory Study: development and testing of interview protocols for young children. In Special issue on child and adult memory, *The Advisor, Journal of the American Professional Society on the Abuse of Children* 5(3):11–13. Reprinted with permission in *Childhood Memory*, ed. D. J. Siegel. Proceedings of Institute IV, American Academy of Child and Adolescent Psychiatry, San Antonio, October 29.

———— (1993). Understanding children's memories of medical procedures: "He didn't touch me and it didn't hurt!" In *Memory and Affect in Development: The Minnesota Symposium on Child Psychology*, vol. 26, pp. 171–225. Hillsdale NJ: Lawrence Erlbaum.

Summit, R. C. (1992). Misplaced attention to delayed memory. In Special issue on child and adult memory, *The Advisor, Journal of the American Professional Society on the Abuse of Children* 5(3):21–25. Reprinted with permission in *Childhood Memory*, ed. D. J. Siegel. Proceedings of Institute IV, American Academy of Child and Adolescent Psychiatry, San Antonio, October 29.

Symington, N. (1993). *Narcissism: A New Theory*. London: Karnac.

Terr, L. (1983). Chowchilla revisited: the effects of psychic trauma four years after a school bus kidnapping. *American Journal of Psychiatry* 140:1543–1550.

———— (1988). What happens to early memory of trauma? *Journal of the American Academy of Child and Adolescent Psychiatry* 27:96–104.

———— (1991). Childhood traumas: an outline and overview. *American Journal of Psychiatry* 148:10–20.

———— (1993). Psychological defenses and memories of childhood trauma. In *Childhood Memory*, ed. D. J. Siegel. Proceedings of Institute IV, American Academy of Child and Adolescent Psychiatry, San Antonio, October 29.

_____ (1994). *Unchained Memories.* New York: Basic Books.

Thigpen, C. H., and Cleckley, H. (1957). *The Three Faces of Eve.* New York: McGraw Hill.

Tulving, E. (1972). Episodic and semantic memory. In *Organization of Memory,* ed. E. Tulving and W. Donaldson, pp. 381–403. New York: Academic Press.

Tustin, F. (1984). Autistic shapes. *International Review of Psycho-Analysis* 11:279–290.

_____ (1986). *Autistic Barriers in Neurotic Patients.* New Haven: Yale University Press.

Vaillant, G. (1990). Repression in college men followed for half a century. In *Repression and Dissociation,* ed. J. L. Singer, pp. 259–273. Chicago: University of Chicago Press.

Van der Kolk, B. (1987). *Psychological Trauma.* Washington, DC: American Psychiatric Press.

_____ (1989). The compulsion to repeat the trauma. *Psychiatric Clinics of North America* 12:389–411.

Wallerstein, J. S., and Kelly, J. (1980). *Surviving the Breakup.* New York: Basic Books.

Watkins J. G., and Watkins, H. H. (1982). Ego state therapy. In *The Newer Therapies: A Source Book,* ed. L. E. Abt and I. R. Stuart, pp. 127–155. New York: Van Nostrand Holt.

_____ (1984). Hazards to the therapist in the treatment of multiple personalities. In *Psychiatric Clinics of North America* 7(4):111–119.

Westerlund, E. (1992). *Women's Sexuality After Childhood Incest.* New York: Norton.

White, S., and Quinn, K. (1988). Investigatory independence in child sexual abuse evaluations: conceptual considerations. *Bulletin of the American Academy of Psychiatry and Law* 16(3):269–278.

Wilbur, C. B. (1984). Multiple personality and child abuse. *Psychiatric Clinics of North America* 7:3–7.

Williams, L. M. (1992). Adult memories of childhood sexual abuse: preliminary findings from a longitudinal study. In Special issue on child and adult memory, *The Advisor, Journal of the American Professional Society on the Abuse of Children* 5(3):19–20. Reprinted with permission in *Childhood Memory,* ed. D. J. Siegel. Proceedings of Institute IV, American Academy of Child and Adolescent Psychiatry, San Antonio, October 29.

Winer, R. (1989). The role of transitional experience in healthy and incestuous families. In *Foundations of Object Relations Family Therapy,* ed. J. S. Scharff, pp. 357–384. Northvale, NJ: Jason Aronson.

_____ (1993). *Ethics Curriculum.* Washington, DC: Washington Psychoanalytic Institute.

Winnicott, D. W. (1945). Primitive emotional development. *International Journal of Psycho-Analysis* 26(3 and 4):137–143.

—— (1951a). Transitional objects and transitional phenomena. In *Collected Papers: Through Paediatrics to Psycho-Analysis*, pp. 229–242. London: Tavistock.

—— (1956). Primary maternal preoccupation. In *Collected Papers: Through Paediatrics to Psycho-Analysis*, pp. 145–156. London: Tavistock, 1958.

—— (1958). Collected Papers: *Through Paediatrics to Psycho-Analysis*. London: Tavistock.

—— (1960a). The theory of the parent–infant relationship. In *The Maturational Processes and the Facilitating Environment*, pp. 37–55. London: Hogarth, 1975.

—— (1960b). Ego distortion in terms of true and false self. In *The Maturational Processes and the Facilitating Environment*, pp. 140–152. London: Hogarth, 1975.

—— (1963a) The development of the capacity for concern. In *The Maturational Processes and the Facilitating Environment*, pp. 56–63. London: Hogarth, 1975.

—— (1963b). Communicating and not communicating leading to a study of certain opposites. In *The Maturational Processes and the Facilitating Environment*, pp. 179–192. London: Hogarth, 1975.

—— (1971). *Therapeutic Consultations in Child Psychiatry*. London: Hogarth.

Yapko, M. D. (1993). Memories of the future: regression and suggestions of abuse. In *Ericksonian Methods*, ed. J. Zeig, pp. 225–230. New York: Brunner/Mazel.

—— (1994). *Suggestions of Abuse: True and False Memories of Childhood Sexual Trauma*. New York: Simon & Schuster.

Credits

The authors gratefully acknowledge permission to reprint material from the following sources:

Excerpts from *The Collected Papers, volume 3* by Sigmund Freud. Authorized translation under the supervision of Alix and James Strachey. Excerpts from *The Standard Edition of the Complete Psychological Works of Sigmund Freud*. Translated from the German by James Strachey. Published by Basic Books, Inc. by arrangement with Hogarth Press, Ltd. and the Institute of Psycho-Analysis, London. Reprinted by permission of BasicBooks, a division of HarperCollins Publishers, Inc.

Excerpts from "Memories of the Future: Regression and Suggestions of Abuse," by Michael Yapko, in *Ericksonian Methods*, ed. J. Zeig. Copyright © 1993 by Brunner/Mazel and used by permission of the author and the publisher.

Excerpts from *The Sexual Relationship: An Object Relations View of Sex and the Family* by David E. Scharff, pp. 12–13, 79–82. Copyright © 1982 by Routledge & Kegan Paul and used by permission.

Tables 5–1 through 5–4 are based on material in *True and False Accusations of Child Sex Abuse* by Richard Gardner. The information is used with the kind permission of the author.

Index